Commonsense Anticommunism

Commonsense
Anticommunism

Labor and Civil Liberties between the World Wars

JENNIFER LUFF

The University of North Carolina Press
Chapel Hill

© 2012 The University of North Carolina Press
All rights reserved
Set in Minion by Tseng Information Systems, Inc.
Manufactured in the United States of America

⊗ The paper in this book meets the guidelines for permanence
and durability of the Committee on Production Guidelines
for Book Longevity of the Council on Library Resources.

The University of North Carolina Press has been a member
of the Green Press Initiative since 2003.

Library of Congress Cataloging-in-Publication Data
Luff, Jennifer.
Commonsense anticommunism : labor and civil
liberties between the world wars / Jennifer Luff. — 1st ed.
p. cm.
Includes bibliographical references and index.
ISBN 978-0-8078-3541-8 (cloth : alk. paper)
1. Communism—United States. 2. United States—Politics
and government—1901–1953. 3. Anti-communist movements—
United States. 4. McCarthy, Joseph, 1908–1957. 5. American
Federation of Labor. I. Title.
HX89.L84 2012
335.430973′09041—dc23

2011044464

16 15 14 13 12   5 4 3 2 1

Contents

Illustrations

Acknowledgments

Roy Rosenzweig convinced me to write this book. As a new Ph.D., I taught a survey class as an adjunct at George Mason University, and met Roy in early 2006. He asked me to visit one of his graduate courses to talk about dissertation writing, and his unaffected kindness immediately put me at ease. Roy insisted on driving me home, a long drive from Fairfax, Virginia, to Washington, D.C., and his warmth loosened my tongue. In class he had already heard about my dissertation on labor spies. Now he listened intently as I told him about the fascinating clues I had found about labor anticommunism. I confessed that I wanted to put aside my dissertation and work on this new project instead. "Go ahead!" he said. "It's a great project!" I had not realized that Roy was a member of the editorial board of the journal *American Communist History*, and he knew a lot about Communism and anticommunism. The car periodically drifted across the freeway lanes as we gossiped about labor conservatives and Communists. "Send me your research," he urged as he dropped me off, and I promised to do so, suddenly resolved to start the book. Roy Rosenzweig died the following year. As one of untold scholars who benefited from his encouragement, I want to say thanks to Roy Rosenzweig.

Generous funding made my research possible. A postdoctoral fellowship from the Center for the United States and the Cold War at New York University's Tamiment Library gave me a glorious year in the archives and access to the remarkable librarians and holdings of the Tamiment. Thanks especially to Michael Nash and Peter Filardo for their support and advice. A second postdoctoral fellowship year at UCLA's Institute for Research on Labor and Employment (IRLE) allowed me to draft the manuscript in a stimulating and nurturing environment. At the IRLE, Ruth Milkman created an extraordinarily warm scholarly climate and helped me test and develop my ideas. A short-term fellowship at the Newberry Library introduced me to its friendly community of scholars and especially James Grossman, who is a model of collegiality.

Many librarians and archivists tracked down documents and helped me interpret my findings. I am especially grateful to Peter Filardo at the Tamiment Library; Jim Quigel at Penn State's Historical Collections and Labor Archives; Sarah Springer and Robert Reynolds at the George Meany Archives; Patrizia Sione and Barb Morley at Cornell's Kheel Center; and Traci Drummond of Special Collections and Archives, Georgia State University. Darlene Mott at the Sam Houston Regional Library and Research Center and Aaron Lisec at the Southern Illinois University's Special Collections found important materials for me. Rod Ross at the National Archive's Center for Legislative Archives spent time helping me navigate the papers of congressional committees. John Earl Haynes graciously helped me with the John Frey papers at the Library of Congress, and a visit to San Francisco State University's Labor Archives and Research Center was productive and fun thanks to Catherine Powell. A special thanks to Peter Drinkwater at Footnote.com, the digital repository of several collections of the National Archives. When I complained about difficulty navigating the huge Franz von Rintelen file in the Department of Justice papers, Peter burned a CD of the entire file for me. The interlibrary loan service at Georgetown University's Lauinger Library supplied me with obscure materials quickly and efficiently.

It has been wonderful to work with the staff at the University of North Carolina Press. Chuck Grench supported this project in its earliest stages, and his encouragement sustained my resolve through the long writing process. The good cheer of Beth Lassiter, Rachel Berry Surles, and Katy O'Brien made the editorial process fun. Paul Betz and Liz Gray's painstaking work on the manuscript enabled me to produce a much better book.

Many people read and critiqued chapters of the manuscript in seminars and colloquia. Writing groups in New York and Los Angeles helped me puzzle through the earliest drafts. In New York, Jonathan Soffer, Nancy Kwak, Sarah Phillips, Anne Kornhauser, Richard Greenwald, and Neil Rosendorf gave me invaluable comments and advice, along with plenty of good cheese from Murray's. In Los Angeles, the long-running Los Angeles Social History Study Group welcomed me to their convivial dinners and rigorous discussions; thanks to John Laslett, Becky Nicolaides, Steve Ross, Frank Stricker, Allison Varzally, Toby Higbie, Hal Barron, Nancy Fitch, Leila Zenderland, and Craig Loftin. Beverly Gage and Donna Haverty-Stacke generously read and critiqued chapters, and I am indebted to them for their insightful comments and suggestions.

Discussions and debates with other scholars and friends helped me sharpen my ideas. Gabe Kramer's comments on an early draft of the book proposal have shaped my thinking throughout the entire process of research and writing. Thanks especially to Toby Higbie, Anthony Destefanis, David Chu, Rich Yeselson, Patrick Iber, Christine Walker, Robin Veder, Katie Corrigan, Sandy Jacoby, Nancy Maclean, Ruth Milkman, Leon Fink, Seth Newton Patel, Donna Haverty-Stacke, and Kim Phillips-Fein. Ruth Price shared her vast knowledge of American radicalism and antiradicalism, and sent me the announcement for the Tamiment fellowship, right after my inspirational conversation with Roy Rosenzweig. I am grateful to readers at the Newberry Seminar in Labor History, the Tamiment Library, the U.S. History Colloquium at UCLA, and the Pennsylvania Labor History Workshop, especially Rosemary Feurer, Colleen Doody, Ellen Carol DuBois, Will Jones, David Montgomery, and David Witwer. Conference audiences and commentators provided helpful comments at the American Studies Association, the American Historical Association, the North American Labor History Conference, the Policy History Conference, and the University of Arizona's "Decentering Cold War History" conference. A visiting teaching post in the Student Recommended Faculty Program at the University of California, Irvine, allowed me to try out some of my research in the classroom. Thanks to my students at Irvine and colleagues in the history department there; thanks also to my students at Georgetown University, who discussed some of these ideas as well.

Friends and family gave me places to stay on research trips, shared dinners and drinks, and lent a friendly ear. Thanks to Ed Keyser, Janet Mitchell, Sam Luebke, Traci Zambotti, Philip Giordano, Robin Veder, Vanessa White, Katerina Semyonova, Emily Mieras, Scott Zdrazil, David Miller, Rebecca Hanson, Cathy Feingold, Susan Dundon, Eric Perkins, George Boas, Shari Nutter, Kim Armbrecht, Chris Bohner, and Pilar Weiss. It is a pleasure and honor to work with my colleagues at Georgetown's Kalmanovitz Initiative for Labor and the Working Poor: Joe McCartin, Katie Corrigan, Seth Newton Patel, Sarah David Heydemann, and John Tremblay. My parents, Diane Luff and Dick Luff, taught me to love books and learning. Christine Walker, my sister, moved me in and out of various apartments, talked through my research, and gave me refresher history lessons along the way. My brother, Thomas Luff, inspired me with his wisdom and grace and gave me hope. Thanks also to my extended family of in-laws, cousins, and aunts and uncles who cheered me on and buoyed my spirits.

Over the years, my graduate advisers have begun to feel like family members. (They remember my youthful follies but tactfully never bring them up.) Bob Gross taught me a lot, but one of his best lessons was in the art of historical empathy. I often heard his voice in my head as I struggled to understand historical actors who were very different from me. Scott Nelson relishes the practice of history and takes joy in digging up obscure data and unlikely evidence. He reminds me that it's worth writing history just for the hell of it. Cindy Hahamovitch has been an adviser, colleague, and friend, and you could not wish for a better one. In word and deed she exemplifies labor's best visions of solidarity, generosity, and hope. Although their professional duties to me were long ago fulfilled, they all helped me with this study and I am grateful for their advice. Several people read the entire manuscript. Eric Arnesen and Ellen Schrecker gave me the gift of very thorough readings, which were invaluable. They helped me rethink and sharpen the argument and showed me where to push my thinking further. Joe McCartin, an insightful historian, also read the manuscript with a discerning eye and helped me work through some knotty ideas. Cindy Hahamovitch did a painstaking reading on very short notice. They saved me from error and excess and showed me fresh ways to look at my work.

Finally, thanks to the workers, organizers, staffers, and leaders I have met over the years in the labor movement. Talking to workers, union and non-union, about labor, organizing, and politics taught me to avoid making assumptions about the views of people whose voices are often lost to historians. The dedication and commitment of labor staffers and leaders, often in the face of bruising defeats, reminds me that it is easy to find fault with historical actors, but hard to figure out what to do in the present day. Here's to the steadfastness of heart that allows them to keep boring such hard boards.

Commonsense Anticommunism

Introduction

Between the world wars, the conservative leaders of the American Federation of Labor (AFL) played a paradoxical role in American politics. They were leading proponents of popular anticommunism, and steadfast opponents of statutory restrictions on Communist organizing. In contrast to other anti-radicals, AFL leaders advocated a commonsense approach to Communism. Doubting the capacity of the law to distinguish between legitimate militancy and subversive radicalism, labor conservatives disapproved of legislation outlawing sedition. Instead they pursued a voluntarist program of evangelizing about the evils of Communism and excluding Communists from AFL unions. In the aftermath of the first Red Scare, labor conservatives formed a crucial backstop against reaction.

In the late 1930s, the situation changed. Alienated from the New Deal order and at odds with liberal union leaders in the competing Committee for Industrial Organization (CIO), labor conservatives abandoned commonsense anticommunism for calculated red-baiting. AFL leaders backed new antisubversive laws such as the Smith Act and the Hatch Act and strategically smeared federal labor officials and CIO competitors as Communists.

The history of labor anticommunism recasts our understanding of the origins of popular anticommunism and McCarthyism. Historians often treat anticommunism as a conspiracy of capitalists and conservatives who whipped the nation into a red-baiting hysteria after World War II in order to reverse the New Deal order. After enduring a merciless onslaught intended to roll back labor's recent gains, labor unions yielded to pressure and drove Communists and leftists out of their ranks. In these accounts, unions appear as the victims of anticommunism rather than as critical organizers and sustainers of the movement.[1] On the other hand, many historical studies of labor and anticommunism examine internecine wars among workers and union officials from the late 1930s through the McCarthy era. This literature often emphasizes how purging union radicals leached vitality from the labor movement, casting labor anticommunism as a "conflict that shaped American unions."[2]

There is much to learn from this scholarship, but there is also more to the story, because the fight over Communism reverberated far beyond the house of labor. Labor anticommunism was a conflict that shaped the American state. Labor leaders did more than decide on union policy toward Communism. From the outbreak of World War I to the attack on Pearl Harbor, unions played a critical role in shaping federal legislation and policy on policing political radicals. Unionists had a unique perspective on Communism before the Cold War. The Communist Party (CP) was tiny and marginal in the interwar years, and few Americans encountered actual Communists. The party devoted most of its energy to recruiting workers, and especially members of AFL unions (even though the AFL was relatively small as well, representing less than one in ten workers before the Wagner Act). Thus in 1935 the AFL justly declared itself America's "first line of defense" against Communism.[3]

During much of this period, the legal status of unionism itself was also dubious. In this context, AFL leaders thought seriously about the proper posture of the state toward domestic subversion, debating whether a policy could be contrived that distinguished between seditious conspiracy and militant but loyal labor protest. In the process, they crafted a distinctly laborist politics of civil liberties that rejected statutory limits on speech and assembly and opposed the expansion of federal political policing but acquiesced in ad hoc state repression of radicals. Thus AFL president William Green could simultaneously testify publicly against empowering the Department of Justice (DOJ) to pursue Communists—and privately request assistance from the Bureau of Investigation (BI) in identifying Communist unionists, as he did in 1930. It was a highly nuanced approach.

This nuance challenges historians to make sense of seeming contradictions in the federation's stance. Different strands of historical scholarship contain pieces of the story. Traditional accounts of the history of civil liberties discuss the role of radical unions in free-speech fights but omit evidence of labor's collaboration in antiradical repression. Historians of radical labor movements such as the Industrial Workers of the World (IWW) identify some of these instances of collaboration but overlook the AFL's reluctant defense of the rights of Communists and Wobblies to speak and organize. Meanwhile, although its anticommunist rhetoric was unvaryingly antagonistic, the federation's position on anticommunist repression changed over time. The consistency of the AFL's polemics obscures alterations in its policy.[4]

This book untangles the complicated story of labor anticommunism in the interwar years, showing how labor conservatives became reluctant civil libertarians in the 1920s, and proto-McCarthyists in the late 1930s. It charts the turning points when AFL policy and practice changed on a timeline that begins before World War I with the birth of the modern civil liberties movement and follows the American Civil Liberties Union (ACLU) along with the AFL through the first Red Scare and the New Deal years. Although the ACLU and the AFL diverged ideologically, as the ACLU became more radical and the AFL more conservative, they often converged politically on civil liberties questions, arriving at common ground from different directions. In the late 1930s, both organizations shifted right, as the federation embraced Red Scare politics and the ACLU adopted the AFL's voluntarist approach to civil liberties, exposing and expelling Communist ACLU members but opposing statutory limits on their civil liberties.

The clarity of this account of national politics comes at the expense of local variations. This is the story of the actions of a small number of men who led the national AFL, which was itself a federation of unions. For much of its existence, the American Federation of Labor infuriated its opponents and confounded its allies. Historians often experience the same effect, finding the federation's expansive rhetoric of social justice to be at odds with its exclusive membership and moderation in bargaining and politics. From the beginning, the AFL was a political project, not an expression of the popular views of the working class. AFL leaders ruled the federation with a firm hand, engineering convention votes and adopting policy positions with little consultation from union leaders, let alone rank-and-file union members. At the same time, state and local branches of the federation exercised considerable autonomy and often pursued policies directly at odds with the AFL's national agenda. Affiliated national and local unions displayed even more heterodoxy. The actions of the national AFL cannot be taken to represent the desires of individual union members or workers more generally.

In fact, the AFL is interesting because it was not representative at all. Having mastered the art of federal lobbying, AFL leaders could exert influence far disproportionate to its membership, and often counter to their wishes. Building on the work of historian Julie Greene and political scientists Elizabeth Sanders and Elisabeth Clemens, this book explains how the AFL developed its distinctive political repertoire. By the Progressive Era, federation leaders turned to the new techniques of lobbying, forgoing formal party alliances and machine politics and instead dispensing political chits to supporters of narrowly defined nonpartisan demands. Despite fluctuations in its membership and the shifting fortunes of the Democratic Party (an ally more often than the Republicans), the AFL remained a powerful force in national politics. The emergence of the CIO in 1935 undercut this influence, driving federation leaders to seek strategic alliances even with reactionary politicians, and demonstrating how instrumental a lobby the AFL had become. This instrumentalism made the AFL a formidable advocate.[5]

When the AFL spoke up about civil liberties, people listened. Numerous studies have shown how union organizing and worker militancy challenged prevailing orthodoxy on the freedom of speech and assembly. The IWW's free-speech fights feature prominently in this literature, as does the AFL's fight against the labor injunction. "Labor's constitution of freedom" insisted on the right to boycott, picket, and protest, and the long campaign for labor rights formed an additional, often-forgotten front in the broader struggle for civil liberties. By demanding industrial democracy, unionists expanded the meaning of political democracy. Yet these accounts of alternative labor visions rarely mention labor lobbying on traditional civil liberties issues: the rights of citizens to speak against the government and assemble in parties, and the proper role of the state in policing political activity. The AFL's influence in these debates far outweighed the importance of the IWW or other radical unionists, in part because its reliable antiradicalism gave the federation political credibility.[6]

Antiradicalism was bred in the bones of the AFL, and anticommunism grew organically out of AFL leaders' ideological opposition to socialism and syndicalism. From the earliest days of the Bolshevik Revolution, the federation pronounced its implacable antagonism to the Soviet experiment, and that antagonism never abated. In contrast to antiradicals who saw Communism as a cultural tendency or a symptom of social disorder, labor anticommunists understood Communism as a discrete political movement with a defined political program. Anticommunism was an ecumenical sentiment among AFL members; liberal and socialist unionists disapproved of the Communist Party's aims and methods as often as did conservative union leaders. Yet liberal union leaders generally saw Communists as annoying but bona fide radicals and confined themselves to denunciations of Communist treachery. Conservative unionists led the federation's fight against Communists in union halls and on Capitol Hill, and they helped define Communism as an alien doctrine propagated by agents of a foreign dictatorship. In the end, conservative labor anticommunists prevailed.

Since the fall of the Berlin Wall, history has seemed to vindicate AFL anticommunists. From the 1960s through the end of the Cold War, historians rehabilitated the reputation of American Communists, documenting the party's advocacy of civil rights for African Americans and creative labor organizing in CIO unions and investigating the excesses of McCarthyist suspicions of Communist espionage and sabotage. In the process, some historians sanitized the CP, downplaying its revolutionary ambitions and discounting evidence that Soviet officials directed American Communist strategy. In these accounts, American Communism looked like a vibrant leftist social movement with internationalist affinities. Revelations from Soviet and American archives decisively altered this portrait. When researchers got their first glimpse of the records, they swiftly found confirmation of Soviet control of the American Communist Party and, to everyone's surprise, evidence that the party conducted significant espionage operations to collect U.S. military and diplomatic intelligence.[7]

What we now know about CPUSA clandestine operations, though, was largely invisible at the time. Labor conservatives' implications of Communist treason were based on rank speculation, and there is little evidence that they knew any more than contemporaries about the party's espionage operations. Labor conservatives who charged a vast Communist conspiracy were opportunistic, not omniscient, and subsequent archival confirmation of some of their wildest claims does not vindicate their case. Nevertheless, the end of the Cold War permits researchers to stand down from scholarly combat and dispassionately reconsider the origins of McCarthyism and the Cold War. In retrospect, it seems clear that the debates about Moscow's control over the American party grew out of then-current political concerns. Party activists and allies tried to shield themselves from opprobrium and suppression by insisting on their American roots and local allegiances. But the obvious appeal of the Bolshevik Revolution to American Communists was exactly the opposite. After 1917, Communism presented a global, disciplined force of revolutionaries capable of defeating tsarism and governing a major country. Its American adherents joined the party, and some members worked as American spies, to advance its revolutionary program.[8]

I rely on this post-1989 historiography on the Communist Party, and particularly research on its labor organizing; I contribute no new findings to scholarship on American Communism. I do contribute to the growing scholarship that reinterprets American anticommunism as a frequently rational response to the political blunders of American Communists and revulsion from the dictatorial tendencies of Soviet Communism. While labor conservatives knew little of espionage, they knew a lot about the Soviet Union, and they were among its earliest critics. Acknowledging the rational aspects of anticommunism does not confer absolution for the red-baiting abuses described in this book. Anticommunism often provided a specious rationale for political chicanery. But unscrupulous manipulations of anticommunist sentiment do not invalidate the origins of the sentiment itself.[9]

Shared anticommunist attitudes helped build links between labor conservatives and the broader conservative movement. Anticommunism was a common thread that knitted together capitalists, farmers, and workers into a loosely organized conservative coalition. Studies of the origins of the modern American Right have found its organizers among Orange County housewives and City College intellectuals. I believe we can find their working-class counterparts in craft union halls.[10] The AFL's antistatist philosophy of "union preeminence" led its leaders to consistently favor privately negotiated union benefits over broad social programs.[11] Simultaneously, anticommunism drove AFL leaders to support robust political policing at home and interventionist Cold War policies abroad. The combination of these tendencies produced a distinctively laborist conservatism that abided for decades after World War II.

J. Edgar Hoover's FBI plays an unexpected role in this account. After taking over the bureau in 1924, Hoover insisted on statutory authority to police radicals and refused to abet AFL red-baiting. In the 1930s, Hoover's rectitude helped protect radical workers from AFL-instigated repression, earning the approbation of the ACLU. My study offers only a partial glimpse of the workings of the FBI, but it points to the need for a more thorough reconsideration of Hoover's role in the second Red Scare. Scholarship on state repression often treats people such as J. Edgar Hoover as power-mad and autonomous autocrats, but Hoover and other officials frequently resisted pressure to police radicals. As Hoover put it to a closed-door congressional session in 1930, "No one wants any legislation that abridges the freedom of the press or the freedom of speech, or the right to strike, or any inalienable right."[12]

Hoover's statement may seem incredible to anyone familiar with his villainous behavior at the bureau in 1919, when he orchestrated illegal dragnets to capture foreign-born radicals, or in 1962, when the FBI wiretapped Rev. Martin Luther King Jr. Hoover's words remind us that history matters, and anticommunism and McCarthyism were contingent, not inevitable. The FBI's actions in 1930 cannot be inferred by what the bureau did in 1919 or 1962. Likewise, the motives and deeds of labor anticommunists are not easy to predict. Here is their surprising story.

PART I

The AFL and the Origins of Modern Civil Liberties

CHAPTER ONE

Labor and Liberties

The American Federation of Labor, 1886–1915

In 1908, Samuel Gompers, president of the American Federation of Labor, became a civil libertarian. He and other officers of the federation had been charged with contempt of court for publishing a notice to boycott Buck's Stove, a nonunion iron-stove manufacturer. In their defense, the AFL leaders invoked a right to free speech and freedom of the press. "In all the history of the American Federation of Labor," Gompers wrote, "no greater struggle has taken place than that for the preservation and the maintenance of the right of free press and free speech." This defense was an unorthodox argument in an era when the notion of a categorical right to free speech was novel. Gompers explained that the AFL pursued this fight for First Amendment protection on behalf of all Americans, "because this attack upon free press and free speech among the workers is only the insidious beginning of the entire withdrawal of those rights from the whole people."[1]

In the Progressive Era, the AFL was struggling for respectability. Strikes, boycotts, and the notion of unionism itself were of dubious legality and seemed to reflect workers' unseemly pursuit of self-interest. For years, Gompers had tried to find ways to cast the federation as a champion of the common good. The language of civil liberties let him make that case in a fresh, universalist way.

Gompers was unpleasantly surprised when Theodore Schroeder, the crusader who helped develop the new theory of free speech, questioned his sincerity. Schroeder, a lawyer and pamphleteer, took an absolutist approach to defending the right of free speech. Schroeder disliked "partisan defenders" of civil liberties who, when "called upon to defend against some particular abridgment of freedom, have been so overwhelmed by its importance that they have failed to define or defend freedom in general." Gompers was a prime offender, as he "wants only freedom to advocate the boycott," not a "general 'freedom of speech.'"[2]

Schroeder was right. Gompers was indifferent to violations of the civil liberties of others and hostile to the free-speech campaign being waged by radicals in the Industrial Workers of the World. From street-corner soapboxes across the West, IWW organizers bellowed abuse of capitalists, preachers, and Gompers himself. Schroeder and other civil liberties advocates backed these free-speech fights as important test cases. But Gompers and the AFL leadership saw this defiance as insolence, and the Wobbly free-speech fights as damaging to the cause of labor rights, and the federation consistently refused to support the IWW campaign. The AFL leaders were like other advocates who "desire unlimited liberty for themselves" but "suppress the opinions of which they disapprove," said Schroeder. Civil liberties were a tactic, not a commitment.[3]

Since the founding of the federation in 1886, repeated political defeats had taught AFL leaders that tactical alliances were safer than ideological commitments. They learned to distrust the state—judiciary, executive, and legislative branches alike. They grew skeptical of the potential of political parties to represent unionists' interests fairly. They doubted the intentions of reformers who sought to improve working conditions with social policy. And they viewed leftists—socialists, anarchists, syndicalists—as hopeless dreamers who diluted labor's strength by dividing it. Workers could not rely on anyone else to defend their interests, AFL leaders believed. Trade unions were the only hope for workers to build and sustain enough power to make material improvements in the things that mattered: wages, hours, and working conditions.

This notion put the AFL out of step with potential allies in the Progressive Era. At a time when reformers lobbied to expand the state's role in regulating relations between workers and employers, Gompers argued to keep the "juggernaut of government" out of the workplace. As activists organized new political parties to press for social change, the AFL insisted on nonpartisanship. Rather, federation leaders sought political power through lobbying, claiming to speak on behalf of all American workers, although its member unions represented only a small share of the workforce and many nonmembers saw their interests differently.

When AFL officials spoke, they were making arguments, not registering consensus views. Increasingly, those arguments were characterized as "conservative," by AFL leaders and observers alike. By the outbreak of the Great

War, the AFL had become the chief proponent and organizing force of a distinctly laborist conservatism that valorized collective bargaining over state
intervention as the best tool for social redistribution. In an era of creative
experimentation with new forms of state action and social engineering, this
political vision sometimes marginalized the AFL. But Gompers and his colleagues had mastered the new technique of lobbying, and they displayed
remarkable political agility, exercising influence far beyond their apparent
reach. Even as the federation lost popular support, it gained political influence.

On the issue of civil liberties, though, the AFL found common ground with
many progressives. In the early twentieth century, the rights of freedom of
speech and of the press were far from settled law in U.S. courts. Individuals
were regularly and successfully prosecuted for defamation, explicit materials
from medical guides to pornography could not circulate in the federal mail,
and police arrested public speakers who professed syndicalism and other subversive ideas. As historian David M. Rabban shows, "free speech in its forgotten years" had few defenders. In the years before World War I, Gompers
and the AFL became vocal proponents of the notion that Americans enjoyed
a broad right to "freely speak and print for the wrongs that need resistance
and cause that needs assistance." Should those causes include syndicalism or
socialism? Over the next thirty years, the federation would grapple with that
question.[4]

Founding the Federation

In his long career, Samuel Gompers accumulated an impressive array of de-
tractors. He was a man "between the two millstones," according to a sympathetic magazine profile in 1910. "The upper stone is capitalism. The lower is
international Socialism." Oddly, capitalists and socialists used similar terms
to describe Gompers and the American Federation of Labor. The AFL was
selfish, grasping for advantage at the expense of nonmembers. The *Los Angeles Times*, whose printing plant had been bombed during a citywide union
drive, derided Gompers as "a special pleader" who served only those "who
drop their tribute into the coffers of the American Federation of Labor."[5]
Likewise, Socialist Eugene V. Debs deplored "the crime of craft unionism,"
whose adherents "do not care what becomes of the rest, if only they can get
what they are after for themselves."[6]

Having survived decades of violent strikes and virulent quarrels among
unionists, Gompers was unmoved. "We welcome any attack or abuse," he

told his critics. The AFL was hardly self-serving, he argued; rather, the federation sought to "promote, advance, and protect the rights and interests of the working people," regardless of their occupation, and to "make for the greatest sum total of human happiness." In Gompers's mind, the vision behind the AFL was no less utopian than the socialist dream. Attaining this vision, however, required tough-minded realism.[7]

Short, squat, and pugnacious, Gompers had learned the arts of disputation in the New York cigar-making shops where he began working at the age of thirteen. Gompers migrated to the United States from England with his family in 1850, entering a vibrant milieu of artisans forming organizations of all sorts. In the early 1870s, Gompers fell in with socialists in the International Workingmen's Association, a disorderly congress of unions and radical parties that Communists later termed the First International. Gompers taught himself German so he could read Marx's treatises and join the debate.[8] Artisans in New York, like their counterparts in Geneva and London, were arguing about the proper balance between political and workplace mobilization. Should workers dedicate their energies to confronting capitalism by striking and seizing industrial control, or were they more likely to transform the workplace by building political power and seizing control of the state?

In Europe, where few workers had the franchise in the 1870s, the debate resonated differently. In the United States, universal white male suffrage gave workers a far greater range of political options. In the postbellum American party realignment, the Republican and Democratic parties divvied up the labor vote. Native-born northeastern artisans mostly went to the Republicans, the growing immigrant factory workforce tended toward the Democrats, western miners and timber workers switched between the two parties, and black workers everywhere preferred the party of Lincoln, although encroaching Jim Crow laws suppressed the southern black vote. Women workers, of course, could not vote at all except in a few sparsely populated western states. Urban machine politics helped the parties hold their constituents regardless of platform. This diffusion of labor's political power limited the rallying potential of a national labor movement.[9]

Efforts to unite the producing classes—farmers and laborers—in repeated failed third-party drives fell apart as the Democrats and Republicans strategically picked off supporters. Gompers saw this dynamic play out firsthand, from Henry George's New York mayoral campaign in 1886 to the electoral campaigns of the Populists in the 1890s and the Socialists and Progressives in 1908 and 1912. From these defeats, Gompers took a lesson: third parties offered little hope, and neither major party functioned as a labor party. Nonpartisanship was the safest policy for building unity among American workers. This was not a foregone conclusion. In Australia, as historian Robin Archer has shown, universal white manhood suffrage did not preempt the formation of a labor party in the same years. Moreover, AFL unions could have attempted to vote as a bloc within one of the major parties, concentrating their strength, a strategy that unions would embrace in later years. But in the early years of the federation, Gompers insisted that partisan loyalties threatened solidarity. As much as anyone, Gompers helped dig the city trenches that came to divide workplace from community in American politics.[10]

Union, not party, promised the most immediate advantage in Gompers's mind, but here again diversity jeopardized unity. Gompers had learned this from watching the rise and fall of the Knights of Labor. Founded in 1869, the Knights had drawn on the ideological heritage of republicanism to call all producers together into local assemblies of a national organization. Anyone who worked—farmer, factory laborer, artisan, housewife—could join the Knights (lawyers, liquor dealers, and bankers could not). A fusion of union, party, and revival movement, the Knights of Labor adopted a broad populist program. They marched for the eight-hour day, demanded government ownership of the railroads, and ran candidates for election in numerous cities. Knights assemblies also enrolled workers in industries ranging from railroading to cigar making, making no distinction by skill. This heterogeneity helped the Knights grow rapidly. After winning concessions from Jay Gould's railroads in the early 1880s, the Knights mushroomed to 750,000 members.[11]

But to skilled workers such as Gompers, mixing up membership impaired militancy. In New York, the Knights of Labor assembly urged workers to conciliate their demands and pushed to settle conflicts with arbitration rather than strikes. Since the early 1870s, Gompers had been building up the Cigar Makers' International Union (CMIU) on an entirely different basis. Open to cigar makers anywhere in the city, the CMIU charged high dues to fund generous strike and unemployment benefits for members. Union officers monitored all the cigar-making shops in the city, setting work rates for members and subduing recalcitrant employers with strikes and boycotts. Soon CMIU members could enforce real wage and working-hour demands. When the Knights tried to enlist New York cigar makers to join the city assembly, Gompers balked. Dispersed in a large organization with multiple demands, how could the cigar makers maintain the internal structure and unity that allowed them to sustain their hard-won standards?[12]

By 1886, disaffected Knights—ironworkers, carpenters, miners, and cigar makers—had reached the same conclusion. They joined Gompers to form the American Federation of Labor, an organization dedicated to the idea that workers should unionize along occupational and industrial lines. At their founding meeting in Columbus, Ohio, unionists designed the AFL as a sort of coordinating committee to promote this style of organizing. The federation was constituted as a weak central governing body, charged with mediating conflicts among unions about jurisdictional rights (in an industrializing economy, it could be hard to tell whether a metalworker belonged in the Steel Workers, Iron Molders, Machinists, or some other organization). Its founders agreed that the federation should focus on organizing unions, not pursuing broad social reforms. Once enough workers built sufficiently powerful unions, they would have the economic and political wherewithal to actually achieve reform. The delegates in Columbus named Gompers president of the new federation.[13]

From its founding, then, the AFL was making an argument about the best way for workers collectively to transform their material conditions. In Gompers's many speeches advocating trade unionism, he painted a vision that rivaled any radical's: "I believe that the trade unions will bring about both the improvement of conditions and the ultimate emancipation of workers," he said in 1890.[14] Indeed, Gompers believed his approach best reflected Marx's analysis of how working-class political consciousness developed through direct collective action, once going so far as to write to Engels for support.[15]

But almost from the beginning, the AFL was characterized as a "practical and conservative" force.[16] For one thing, the federation's emphasis on skills as the basis for solidarity necessarily excluded the great mass of unskilled workers—common laborers, factory operatives, domestic workers—who were migrating to the United States in huge numbers. Native-born and northern European men dominated the skilled trades. It seemed as though the AFL was rallying members who were already the most powerful in self-defense rather than sharing their strength for the advantage of everyone. And the market logic underlying the AFL's approach rankled. Rather than challenge existing divisions of skill and rank among workers, the federation worked within them, attempting to amplify labor scarcity and corner labor-market niches. To Daniel DeLeon, leader of the Socialist Labor Party, AFL unions "organize themselves in such a way as to leave their fellow wage-slaves out in the cold."[17] The logic of Gompers's style of trade unionism led inexorably, in radicals' eyes, to collusion with the wage-labor system.

But radicals seemed to be losing the argument. In 1886, just as the federation launched, the Knights of Labor began to disintegrate. After the May 4 Haymarket riots in Chicago incited widespread recriminations against the

Knights, who had led the charge for the eight-hour day, the organization lost a third of its membership in one year. By 1890, the Knights' power had collapsed. AFL unions picked up the remnants, doubling the federation's ranks by 1890. With 780,000 workers enrolled in AFL unions by 1900, the AFL had surpassed the Knights' high-water mark. Gompers's claims for the virtues of coalition were vindicated by successful joint actions. With sympathy strikes and boycotts, affiliated unions provided mutual aid, and workers from typographers to teamsters won real ground in their negotiations with employers.

Gompers could take much of the credit. He was a tireless organizer and the driving force behind the AFL. He led the federation until his death in 1924, losing the presidency only once, in 1894. Gompers built a corps of staffers who traveled the country to proselytize for the virtues of trade unionism and keep a finger in the political winds within the organization. He kept up a heavy schedule of public lecturing, letter writing, and editorializing in the federation's chief publication, the *American Federationist*. To a large extent, the actions of the national federation reflected his personal views and predilections. He governed the AFL through a layered and complex structure of city and state federations, an annual national convention, and a permanent executive board of leaders from affiliated unions. A delegate-based system of voting that advantaged affiliated unions over city and state federations meant that it was hard for any challenger to build up enough support to unseat him.[18]

Yet challengers came close, and they usually came from labor's left wing. In 1894, when the country was mired in the second year of a profound depression, socialists forced a floor debate at the AFL's convention in Denver. They proposed to bind the federation to an openly socialist platform, calling for collective ownership of "all the means of production and distribution," public ownership of utilities and railroads, and the eight-hour day. Over a week of impassioned floor speeches and intense hotel-room meetings, delegates reconsidered all the premises on which the federation was founded. Did labor need a party? Should unions pursue social reform along with shop-floor bargaining? It looked like the AFL would change course, as a majority of delegates arrived in Denver with a charge to support the platform.[19]

But Gompers and his allies prevailed on the vote by a wide margin. Gompers convinced delegates that party loyalties would only dilute labor's strength and no third party had much chance of success. Better to bet on what they could win at the bargaining table. Gompers's claims resonated in the midst of the Populist Party's short-lived bid for power, which fractured some unions and disrupted settled political arrangements in the South and West. Although his ideas prevailed, his opponents managed to oust Gompers from the president's chair that year. He won the office back in 1895, and thereafter he showed less patience for socialist heterodoxy in the federation's ranks.[20]

Still, a vibrant left thrived in most AFL unions. Among miners, garment workers, and machinists, socialism of all sorts persisted. A Debsian populism swept railroad workers and hard-rock miners, while German brewery workers pursued a Marxist socialism and Irish shoe workers embraced Daniel DeLeon's Socialist Labor Party. In New York's Lower East Side, a unique leftist subculture grew among Jewish migrants from eastern Europe. German socialists worked with Russian intellectuals to organize Jewish workers into a distinctively Jewish labor movement with its own large organizational infrastructure, including the Bund, the Arbeter Ring, and unions such as the Ladies' Garment Workers.[21] Gompers tolerated what he could not change. The AFL granted affiliated unions wide autonomy, and as long as socialists did not try to take over the AFL's leadership, they were free to organize within its constituent unions.[22]

The AFL and the State

Paradoxically, the AFL was both more and less than the sum of its parts. At its peak in the prewar years, the AFL claimed only about 9 percent of the nonagricultural workforce as members. Yet in the absence of a competing national organization, AFL national leaders claimed to speak for American workers as a bloc, arrogating a representational role not warranted by its actual membership or reflective of all workers' interests. In truth, the federation could hardly be said to speak for members of its constituent unions, let alone all workers. The attenuated relationship between the federation's national leaders and rank-and-file unionists meant that AFL officers frequently acted autonomously without consulting or even notifying members. The federation's political decisions cannot be assumed to reflect the will of union members, let alone nonunion workers. The AFL, then, was less than the representative of labor.

At the same time, Gompers and other AFL officials parlayed their positions as union leaders into outsized political influence. During the Progressive Era, AFL leaders learned how to lobby. Alongside farmers, suffragists, and capitalists, Gompers and his staff developed new tactics to influence legislation and policymaking in Washington. Over time, the AFL lobby's increasing sophistication produced victories that were inordinate to the federation's capacity to mobilize union voters. Necessity had bred invention. Like other constituencies who struggled to be heard by the major political parties, the AFL looked for ways to influence legislation and policy outside of the party structure. During the Progressive Era, in statehouses around the country, organized farmers, unionists, and women developed tactics such as publishing legislators' voting records on issues of interest to labor and maintaining a permanent corps of staffers to track legislative and policy debates. As Elisabeth S. Clemens has shown, the rise of organized "interests" was controversial, evidence of self-interest trumping the common good. But the entrenchment of a two-party system grounded in machine politics and resistant to controversies that challenged fragile party coalitions left reform-minded groups few alternatives to such pressure tactics.[23]

Gompers's renunciation of "party slavery" held little sway with local unionists, who built party coalitions (and sometimes independent labor parties, as in Washington state) opportunistically. In state and local labor federations, unionists had more luck winning political victories such as the eight-hour day, workmen's compensation, and protective laws for women and child workers. But state and local victories secured on the picket line and in the statehouse rarely survived judicial review. The federal judiciary increasingly forced workers to focus on Washington.

At the turn of the century, the success of tactics such as the boycott and the closed shop, in which unionists demanded that employers hire only union labor, were critical reasons for union growth. Irate employers turned to the courts for help. Under the 1890 Sherman Antitrust Act, courts enjoined strikers for restraining trade, subjecting strikers and union leaders to criminal prosecution if they violated the injunction. Thousands of injunctions were issued to strikers who posted boycott notices or struck in sympathy with other workers.[24] In states from Illinois to California, unionists won state laws exempting labor from the Sherman Act, but none of these statutes survived judicial review. Federal judges quashed labor's state victories.

By 1906, Gompers had had enough. He called for a "strike at the ballot box," marshaling AFL members to measure congressional candidates in the midterm elections against labor's "Bill of Grievances." At the top of the list: exempting labor from federal antitrust law. Gompers and the AFL leadership carefully avoided endorsing any candidate or party, instead insisting that unionists should "reward their friends and punish their enemies." Gompers had abjured party slavery, but he had not given up on electoral politics.[25]

Gompers threw himself into the 1906 campaign, barnstorming around the country, deploying organizers to turn out voters, and personally visiting members of Congress. In November, he had little to show for it. As Julie Greene has shown, none of the congressional enemies targeted by Gompers had lost his seat. Unionists succeeded in electing four union members to Congress, but the national federation played minor roles in these campaigns. The pattern was repeated in the 1908 presidential election. Democratic candidate William Jennings Bryan enthusiastically signed on to the Bill of Grievances, and Gompers ran an even bigger operation to turn out the labor vote for Bryan. The result was even more disappointing. In northeastern urban districts where the labor vote was concentrated, Republican William Taft dominated the returns.[26]

Although in principle, the AFL's support was nonpartisan, in practice most of the candidates who signed onto its principles were Democrats. Yet Gompers's years of proselytizing against party entanglements had produced an organization uncomfortable with formal party endorsements. The 1906 and 1908 campaigns helped cement a de facto alliance between the AFL and the Democratic Party. But the campaigns also showed everyone, inside the federation and outside, that the AFL could not reliably deliver its members' votes. Thereafter, Gompers and his staff gave up on attempts to mobilize union voters. They honed their skills as Washington lobbyists, tracking legislation, testifying on legislation, and contending with the growing ranks of Washington lobbyists from other interest groups, such as temperance advocates and the National Association of Manufacturers. "To an extent out of all proportion to its real strength," the AFL "succeeded in terrorizing members of Congress," said one observer in 1906.[27]

The AFL's Washington influence was magnified by the successful electoral campaigns waged by local unionists. Rather than direct electoral strategy, AFL staffers helped support local efforts. In heavily unionized districts, union activists ran for congressional seats, and by 1910, thirteen "union-card" representatives sat in the House. Most were Democrats, riding the party's growing popularity. With a stronger base in Congress and a tighter connection to the Democratic Party, which retook the House in the 1912 elections, Gompers enjoyed a new prominence in Washington.

Increasingly, Gompers used that influence to advocate a politics of labor laissez-faire: minimize governmental oversight in any realm that might undermine collective-bargaining victories. As Gompers told the Commission on Industrial Relations, "the American Federation of Labor has some apprehension of placing additional powers in the hands of the government which may work to the detriment of working people, and particularly when the things can be done by the workmen themselves."[28] Over time, Gompers's vision of workingmen's self-help increasingly rested on a skepticism of the state. Years of bitter experience had annealed his early idealism. Gompers

"Here Puss, Puss!" Cover of Puck magazine, August 5, 1908. Library of Congress, Prints and Photographs Division.

and fellow unionists had poured enormous energy into winning protective labor legislation, only to see virtually every law overturned by state and federal judges. "Judicial supremacy" taught them that the only solid ground workers could stand on was the territory seized in industrial battles. Agreements struck with employers and underwritten by labor solidarity were more reliable than any laws. This "minimalist path," as William Forbath calls it, was a fallback strategy, not a starting point.[29]

Problems with Progressives

Over time, though, this strategy hardened into an ideology. The AFL's stance on eight-hour laws was a case in point. Although Gompers had long argued that collective bargaining was the best way to secure the eight-hour day, the federation did not formally oppose eight-hour laws when local unionists sought them. By the Progressive Era, the AFL took a tougher line. In 1914, Gompers led the federation's convention to pass a motion holding that "the regulation of wages and the hours of labor should be undertaken through trade union activity, and not made subjects of laws," except in regard to women workers.[30]

But the world was changing around Gompers. By 1914, Gompers was sixty-four years old, and progressives were on the march in America. Years of organizing to fight corporate trusts, urban blight, and machine politics created a chorus of demands for political change. At the top of progressives' to-do list: the "labor problem." Violent strikes in East Coast factories and western mines created a sense of crisis. Even President Woodrow Wilson asked in 1913, "Don't you know that there are mills in which men are made to work seven days in the week for twelve hours a day, and in the three hundred sixty five weary days of the year can't make enough to pay their bills?"[31] Reformers buzzed with ideas for new laws and public commissions to regulate working conditions.[32]

Gompers detected a strong whiff of condescension from progressive reformers, as have historians who show that many progressives saw labor conflict as a plague rather than a symptom of a deeper social disorder. Moreover, progressives perceived unions as both problem and solution. Many, such as Ray Stannard Baker, saw unions as a "labor trust" that helped artificially inflate wages and consumer prices. Violent urban strikes and corrupt "walking-delegates" dismayed supporters such as Jane Addams and John Commons. To Gompers, these reformers were meddling busybodies. "Workers are not bugs to be examined under the lenses of a microscope by 'intellectuals' on a sociological slumming tour," he said.[33] Traditional trade unionism, as represented by the AFL, was the proper vehicle for workers' advancement. If laws protected workers' rights, what incentive would they have to join unions?

But the progressives had a point. The AFL promoted a particular form of organization, the craft union, which represented primarily skilled workers rather than the swelling ranks of laborers filling unskilled jobs on factory floors. Most of the AFL's unions barred African Americans from membership. Gompers's AFL represented a largely white, native-born, well-paid, male subset of the workforce. And by the federation's own standards, AFL unions would never represent most of the unorganized workforce, since their low-skilled jobs made them too easily replaceable to exert power on the shop floor. By opposing the eight-hour day and other protective legislation for all male workers, the AFL sometimes obstructed the interests of the many millions of workers excluded from its ranks. This miserly solidarity elbowed most American workers back as the AFL pushed forward. When people such as Eugene Debs called the federation "selfish," this is what they meant.[34]

A number of new labor lobbies popped up during the Progressive Era to fill in the gap. The American Association for Labor Legislation attracted reformers such as John Commons and Florence Kelley to push for policies including compulsory unemployment insurance and health insurance. The National Consumers' League called on women to use their purchasing power to boycott sweatshop-produced goods and pressed for laws setting maximum hours for women workers.[35] Gompers generally regarded these organizations with suspicion. Meanwhile, he had cultivated his own progressive organization. The National Civic Federation was a reliable mouthpiece and useful intermediary for Gompers and conservative union leaders in national policy debates.

Ralph Easley, a newspaper editor and Republican Party activist, launched the Civic Federation in Chicago in 1893 as a tripartite organization of labor, capital, and progressive citizens dedicated to devising cooperative solutions to knotty social conflicts. When the Pullman Palace Car Company locked out its workers in 1894, the Civic Federation waded into the debate and established a characteristic approach to the labor question. Easley convened a "National Conference on Industrial Conciliation and Arbitration," featuring the U.S. commissioner of labor, the head of the National Association of Builders, and Samuel Gompers, and achieved general agreement on one point: the government should stay out of strikes. Attendees roundly condemned a pending bill in the Illinois legislature that would create a state labor-arbitration board. The conference did more to scuttle the arbitration bill than to settle the

strike. In this and future labor conflicts, the Civic Federation proved ineffectual at reconciling unionists and capitalists on any matter except one: hostility
toward state oversight of labor-capital relations.[36]

In 1900, the NCF moved its headquarters to New York and restyled itself as
a national organization. Easley's gift for public relations and self-promotion
helped him build the National Civic Federation's advisory council into a
254-member roster of academics, reformers, union officers, and clergymen,
by 1908. The more important executive council, however, was filled with industrialists and bankers who pledged cash to finance the NCF and exercised
close control over its activities. Andrew Carnegie, Vincent Astor, and Samuel
Insull all served terms on the NCF executive board in its early years. So did
Samuel Gompers, an NCF vice president from its founding. Gregarious and
voluble, Easley courted new contacts with a mix of flattery and frequent references to his prominent connections. Easley used his bulging masthead of big
names to promote the NCF, although most members of the advisory board
performed no service to the organization. The NCF's promise to open doors
to powerful figures appealed to union leaders such as Gompers, who would
customarily never glimpse such people, let alone serve alongside them on a
distinguished board.

Thus Gompers and other union leaders such as John Mitchell of the Mine
Workers and P. J. McGuire of the Carpenters stayed loyal to the NCF even
after its notorious failures at conciliation. The Murray Hill agreement of 1902,
a national contract brokered by the NCF between the Machinists and metal
manufacturers, was supposed to be the NCF's model settlement. But Murray
Hill exposed the limits of national industrial coordination in the Progressive
Era. Local Machinists lodges resented its wage caps and metal manufacturers
flatly refused to recognize the union in their shops, and within a few months
the agreement had collapsed. The NCF had even less success mediating between the Mine Workers and coal operators that year. NCF's launch as a national labor conciliator fizzled immediately.[37]

As a lobby, though, the NCF shone. The NCF advocated a brand of reformist, antistatist progressivism that relied on enlightened businessmen, responsible unionists, and intelligent experts to come up with private-sector
solutions to public problems. Labor conciliation shrank in the NCF's port-
folio, while Easley organized conferences and studies of the big issues of the
day. The NCF was quite conservative from its founding, opposing women's
suffrage, public ownership of utilities, and socialism. But its endorsement of
trade unionism and support for welfare capitalism made the NCF progressive

in the eyes of many businessmen. Through the early 1920s, its roster of union leaders included the presidents of most AFL unions.

Unionists of all political stripes questioned their leaders' association with the NCF. Consorting with company executives—many of whom declined to bargain with their employees—struck many union members as unseemly. As the NCF drifted further right over the years, criticism from the membership mounted. In 1908, United Mine Workers (UMW) president John Mitchell retired from his union office and took a well-paid job with the NCF, while retaining his membership in the UMW. At the UMW's 1911 convention, socialist miners reacted by barring any union member from also holding membership in the NCF, and a number of other local unions followed suit.[38] But Gompers remained on the NCF board. In 1914, socialist Morris Hillquit asked Gompers to justify his ties to the NCF. Gompers retorted, "I will appeal to the devil and his mother-in-law to help labor if labor can be aided in that way."[39]

Socialists and Wobblies

Gompers's sharp words reflected his frustration with adversaries who attacked from all sides. In the early twentieth century, two major rivals emerged: the Socialist Party challenged the AFL's political program, and the Industrial Workers of the World its union model. Socialists argued that labor laissez-faire was hardly the best hope of the American working class and pointed to their electoral victories in mayoral and congressional races to counter the AFL's pessimism about third-party politics. The Socialist Party made big inroads into AFL unions in the Progressive Era, with Socialists winning union office in the Machinists, the Mine Workers, and the Boot and Shoe Workers, among others.[40]

The IWW, meanwhile, ridiculed the AFL's suggestion that only well-paid white artisans could muster the militancy to win strikes. From its founding at a Socialist Party convention in 1905, the IWW set out to train miners and loggers to turn their fitful rebellions into a sustained movement. Despite its tendency to sectarianism, the IWW hung together and launched an East Coast factory-organizing drive in 1912, startling authorities and the AFL alike when thousands of striking workers poured out of textile mills in Paterson and Passaic. The party had claimed a prominent AFL scalp when a Socialist defeated a stalwart conservative for the presidency of the Machinists union in 1911, and a year later, the Socialists polled nearly 1 million votes for Debs in the presidential race.[41]

The AFL's hold on its constituency was tenuous. The AFL, after all, was a federation of national unions that were themselves made up of local unions, all structured as autonomous entities. Fractious debates over socialism and industrial unionism swirled through AFL unions, and groups of workers regularly departed the AFL. The Structural Iron Workers disaffiliated in 1901 and reaffiliated in 1903; the militantly socialist, German-dominated Brewery Workers union stayed in the AFL until 1907, when Gompers kicked them out in a dispute over union jurisdiction. Likewise, a moderate socialist leadership in the Ladies' Garment Workers kept the union in the AFL, but the AFL expelled the equally moderate socialist leaders who aimed to unite skilled and less-skilled textile workers in the Amalgamated Clothing Workers.[42]

To many radicals, this tumult suggested opportunity. The masses of workers in AFL unions could be convinced of the virtues of socialism and industrial unionism and their unions converted into armies of revolution. This idea took hold in Europe, where syndicalists argued that mass unionism could build a militant working class, while the moderation of elected Socialists showed the bankruptcy of electoral politics. Better for socialists to "bore from within," or organize among existing unions and workers' movements, they believed. Boring from within required radicals to join unions and stay there, painstakingly cultivating recruits with speeches, pamphlets, and industrial actions. In the United States the chief proponent of this idea was William Z. Foster.

Foster grew up selling newspapers and laboring in a foundry in Philadelphia in the 1890s. While still a teenager, he was electrified by a soapbox lecture on the science of socialism. Foster struck out on the road, working on railroads in Florida and Chicago, sailing on a British ship that docked in Australia and South Africa, and clearing lumber in Oregon. He had a talent for organizing and developed a good sense for gauging when a little prodding could turn aggrieved workers into strikers. Foster fell in with the Wobblies in the Northwest around 1910, joining the free-speech fights, and he admired their militancy and inclusive unionism. But Foster was never convinced that the IWW should segregate itself from already-established unions. Foster believed that a latent revolutionary momentum underlay all union struggles; as workers won more they wanted more, until only sweeping social transformation could satisfy their escalating demands.[43]

Having seen militant strikers on Philadelphia streetcars and New York garment work floors, Foster thought that the mainstream labor movement had plenty of radical potential but not enough radical leadership. By attracting the best radical organizers and leaders into a separate organization, the Wobblies robbed AFL unions of the "militant minority," leaving the unions in the hands of cautious conservatives, and the Wobblies on the sidelines trying vainly to catch the attention of the usually indifferent mass working class. Rather than banding together in the IWW, Foster argued, radicals should spread out into the AFL.[44]

Having failed to sell this idea to the IWW, Foster set out to test it himself. In 1915, he settled in Chicago and got himself elected to the leadership of the Chicago Federation of Labor (CFL). Progressive leaders had built the CFL into a hive of organizing, pushing unions to reach out to women and immigrant workers, backing local reform initiatives, and nurturing independent working-class political movements. John Fitzpatrick, president and patriarch of the CFL, welcomed Foster's organizing talents and soon put him in charge of a campaign to unionize the city's vast meatpacking industry—an effort that had languished in the past, in part because thirteen craft unions claimed jurisdiction over parts of the packinghouse work. Adroitly mediating between these territorial leaders, Foster and Fitzpatrick formed a Stockyards Council to coordinate the drive in 1917. Their success in recruiting black workers along with native-born and immigrant workers spurred the federal government to step in and order mediation. When in March 1918 the mediator awarded packinghouse workers the eight-hour day, a big wage increase, and a pledge of pay equity for women and black workers, Foster was vindicated.[45]

Gompers, of course, had no truck with radical "boring." Foster had openly attacked both Gompers and the NCF in the past, most recently at an international conference of trade unionists in 1911, where he insisted that as a Wobbly he deserved to be seated instead of AFL delegate James Duncan, whose NCF membership should automatically disqualify him.[46] But Gompers appreciated Foster's changing politics. "Your past experiences," Gompers wrote him in 1916, "together with your mental development should surely prove an advantageous lesson to those who have not yet seen the true light of all that true trade unionism portends." Gompers encouraged Foster to write up his conversion for the AFL's magazine.[47]

Free Speech

The AFL badly needed good publicity. In 1910, in the midst of a citywide union organizing drive, bombs had ripped apart the *Los Angeles Times* building, killing twenty workers. As an employer and a publication, the *Times* had vehemently opposed unionization. The city called in William J. Burns, a former U.S. Treasury agent who ran a private detective agency, to investigate. Burns's detectives had a long history of battling unions as "labor spies" who infiltrated unions to report on their activities to employers, and also as armed guards hired to break strikes.[48] In April 1911, when Burns arrested John and James McNamara, two top officers of the Ironworkers union, for the crime, Gompers's AFL jumped in to help. Gompers toured the country raising money to defend the McNamaras. The AFL issued special commemorative coins and held rallies denouncing the McNamaras' arrest as an outrage against labor. In December 1911, however, the McNamaras abruptly confessed, leaving Clarence Darrow, their attorney, to defend himself against charges of suborning perjury. It was a disaster for the AFL, and a personal humiliation for Gompers, who reportedly broke into sobs upon learning of the confession.

At the time of the confession, Gompers himself was out on bail. In 1908, he and two other AFL officers had been found guilty of contempt of court for violating a labor injunction. Metal polishers who worked for Buck's Stove and Range Company, a large St. Louis stove factory, had walked out on strike in 1906 to win a nine-hour workday. When the company refused, the Metal Polishers asked the AFL to add Buck's Stove to the "We Don't Patronize" list published in the AFL's newspaper. Buck's Stove's sales nosedived, and in late 1907 the company sought and won an injunction against the boycott. Gompers published the list anyway. The federation was in the middle of its big lobbying push to outlaw the labor injunction, and Gompers believed it was time to test the law. The AFL executive council levied a special fee on members to fund its legal expenses, and Gompers defied the boycott with a novel argument: the First Amendment protected the publication.

The federation borrowed the idea from Theodore Schroeder, who had elaborated a comprehensive theory of "free speech." Schroeder helped create the Free Speech League in response to the anti-anarchist backlash that erupted in 1901 after the assassination of President William M. McKinley. The Free Speech League took an absolutist view of the right to free speech. Schroeder sued on behalf of anarchists, pornographers, and Mormons, and league members lobbied for free speech in legislatures and lecture halls. The league believed, Lincoln Steffens said, that it should be legal "for anybody to say anything anywhere."[49]

This notion appealed to Gompers and other trade unionists, who were regularly prosecuted for promoting boycotts. It also appealed to the Industrial Workers of the World, who used town-square tirades as an organizing tactic. A soapbox set up near a saloon was the best way to reach the mostly itinerant timber workers, miners, and ranch hands that labored on dispersed tracts of western land. And the very act of public speaking was a form of direct action that attracted workers. Around the same time that the AFL added Buck's Stove to its boycott list, the IWW started inciting "free speech fights" in cities across the West. In Spokane, San Diego, and other cities, Wobblies stepped onto soapboxes and called on fellow workers to pay attention. As police plucked one Wobbly off the makeshift podium for violating any number of city ordinances, another took his place, and soon the city jails filled up with IWW members. The Wobblies lost every court case that relied on the right to free speech as a defense. But their campaign stirred debate across the country about the limits and responsibilities of free speech.[50]

Schroeder and the Free Speech League supported the IWW with legal aid and money, seeing the free-speech fights as exemplary test cases. Gompers and the AFL's lawyers likewise bet on free speech in the Buck's Stove boycott. A federal constitutional right to free speech would invalidate the constraints of the Sherman Act and free labor from the injunction. But in December 1908, Gompers and the other federation leaders met the same fate as the Wobblies. A federal judge found them all in contempt and sentenced all three to prison terms.

As his lawyers litigated the appeal, Gompers took up the cause of civil liberties. He published and spoke frequently on the matter, echoing the absolutist arguments of Schroeder and the Free Speech League. "Free press and free speech were guaranteed that men might feel free to say things that displeased," Gompers said. The fight for free speech united labor's interest with the common welfare, bringing "to the attention of the people as a whole the noble aspirations and the splendid achievements of the labor movement in behalf of right, justice, and humanity."[51] Theodore Schroeder showed interest in the case, initially sending along some advice and asking to be kept apprised on developments.

Then Schroeder pilloried Gompers for using free speech as a "shibboleth" to protest labor injunctions while denying free-speech protection to others. Gompers "conceives himself to be making a great fight for freedom of speech," said Schroeder, "but he deplores the havoc which would come from a general 'Freedom of speech and the press.'" Schroeder included Gompers in a broader critique of people who draped their own causes in the mantle of civil liberties that they refused to extend to others.[52] Gompers immediately disputed the charge. Schroeder was "entirely mistaken," Gompers explained, insisting that he himself had "stood for the fullest freedom of speech and of the press" and was "unalterably opposed to any invasion" of those rights.[53] It was true. In public settings and speeches, Gompers declared an unqualified endorsement of the absolute right to free speech.

In practice, though, the AFL rarely defended other victims of civil liberties violations. The Wobblies were the most glaring example. As the Wobblies stewed in jail, Gompers made disparaging remarks about their unfamiliarity with American custom. The federation declined to speak out on their behalf or otherwise assist in the free-speech fights. As Schroeder pointed out, this behavior was hardly unusual. Few claimants to free-speech rights bestirred themselves on behalf of other interest groups or issues. Yet the IWW fights bore at least passing resemblance to the AFL's struggles. Both sought to invoke the right of free speech to protect the right to organize unions. As Schroeder pointedly wondered, why didn't the AFL see these causes as connected?

In truth, Gompers's approach reflected mainstream opinion. In the years before World War I, few people argued for an unrestricted right to freedom of speech, and even fewer saw civil liberties as a political program that obliged its advocates to defend the right to speak "the thought that we hate," in Oliver Wendell Holmes's famous phrase. In the early twentieth century, the civil liberties movement largely represented libertines, anarchists, and syndicalists who had been barred from lecture halls and banned from the mail. In 1902 Emma Goldman urged the American people to "awake from the pleasant dream into which they have been lulled by the strains of 'My Country 'tis of Thee'" to protest her ejection from Chicago's meeting halls. But few Americans took up the cause of people like Goldman. Neither did radicals speak up for the speech that they hated. Wobblies such as Big Bill Haywood did not defend Gompers in his fight against Buck's Stove, and Emma Goldman's *Mother Earth* magazine only mentioned the case to deride the AFL. During World War I, widespread federal crackdowns propelled many Americans toward a more libertarian approach to free speech. In the Buck's Stove era, simply claiming the right to free speech was uncommon.[54]

It took five years, but eventually Gompers and his codefendants beat their contempt case. Arcane procedural rulings rather than sweeping Constitutional arguments vindicated the AFL. The judge dismissed the contempt charges in May 1914. By then, the political climate had shifted. A restive spirit in the country was reflected in the 1912 election returns. Eugene Debs's Socialist ticket polled nearly a million votes, and the new Progressive Party took a quarter of the vote. Woodrow Wilson won the White House with a moderate reform platform and the support of the American Federation of Labor. With a Democratic majority in Congress and a friendly president, Gompers was elated.

The AFL needed support from above, because unrest was building within its ranks. Socialists held a quarter of all delegate seats at the AFL's 1912 convention, and they won a third of the convention's votes for their candidate for the federation's presidency. Rather than dying out, the radical insurgency seemed to be swelling. At the same time, the Industrial Workers of the World had migrated east. Unskilled steelworkers in McKees Rocks, Pennsylvania, struck under the IWW banner in 1909, and textile workers in Lawrence, Massachusetts, did the same in 1912, suggesting that for the first time in decades AFL unions faced a real rival.

Unionists everywhere received help from an unexpected quarter. In response to widespread public dismay about the McNamaras' confession, labor-friendly progressives called for a Congressional Commission on Industrial Relations (CIR) to investigate the underlying causes of labor violence. The commission held hearings from 1913 to 1915. Its chair, Kansas City lawyer Frank P. Walsh, showed a decided partiality for the railroad workers, millwrights, and telegraph operators who lined up to tell the commission about their grievances. Their constitutional rights to free speech had been violated, Theodore Schroeder told the CIR. To the delight of Gompers, the CIR indicted tyrannical employers as the culprits behind industrial unrest. The solution: "industrial democracy." Walsh helped popularize the idea that workers deserved a say in their workplace much as citizens had a vote in the polity. The commission's final report cited civil liberties as a necessary safeguard for democracy.[55] Given the recent experiences of the AFL and the IWW, though, civil liberties looked like a chimera.

Legislative Humbug

Gompers kept his distance from the CIR, wary of the meddling tendencies of outsiders. He kept his eye on the longstanding goal of wiping out the labor injunction. With a contingent of sixteen union-card congressmen now in the House and a Democratic president, the prospects brightened. In 1914, the House debated a controversial revision of the Sherman Antitrust Act. Securing the union-card representatives' votes required adding an antitrust exemption for unions.

Civil liberties claims had virtually no role in the arguments for and against the Clayton Act exemption. The debate played out in the terms of antitrust policy. Gompers and the AFL reasoned that a worker's labor power could not be alienated from his humanity and exchanged in the market, and thus labor was not a commodity. Since the Sherman Act forbade illegal combinations that restrained free trade of commodities, labor combinations should be exempt. Opponents such as former president William Howard Taft scoffed at this claim. Union actions such as strikes and boycotts, not abstract ideas about labor power, were the issue, and combinations of workmen manifestly interfered with interstate commerce. These arguments had been polished over the previous twenty years, and neither side convinced the other. It was a straightforward political battle. With the support of the farm lobby, the AFL had the votes and prevailed in the House.[56]

But a furious backlash from employers and Wilson's tepid support for the exemption caused the Senate to temper the language of the exemption. Only "lawful" union activity would receive the protection of the law. Whether boycotts and strikes qualified as lawful was a matter of debate. To the *New Republic*, this was a "pusillanimous" compromise intended to mollify the AFL; Oliver Wendell Holmes Jr. called the Clayton Act "a piece of legislative humbug—intended to sound promising and to do nothing."[57] Everyone knew that the Supreme Court would have the last word, and the watered-down language of the labor exemption only increased the likelihood of its invalidation. But it was a victory nonetheless. It would take time for a challenge to make it all the way to the Supreme Court, and in the meantime unions could take the fullest advantage of the law.

The newly organized U.S. Chamber of Commerce decried the law as "class legislation," and the *North American Review* called the law "a complete sop to unions."[58] Gompers was triumphant, and unrepentant. In his jubilance, he attenuated his customary rhetoric of universalism. "The labor sections of the Clayton Anti-Trust Act are a great victory for organized labor," he said. The law was "the Industrial Magna Charta upon which working people will rear their structure of industrial progress."[59] Years of appealing to the public interest had finally enabled Gompers to build up the power to win real advantage for his fellow workers.

In the middle of the congressional debate over the Clayton Act, Gavrilo Princip shot Archduke Franz Ferdinand on a Sarajevo street. Gompers led the AFL into a partnership with the American wartime state, and federation membership mushroomed under its protection. The war years deferred the Supreme Court test of the Clayton Act exemption. But the war also intensified the debate about civil liberties. The Constitution did not extend an absolute right to free speech, for strikers or anyone else, according to the Supreme

Court. For unions, it looked like the negative liberty of the antitrust exemption — the right to be left alone by the state — was a better bet than free-speech claims.

After the war, the situation changed. As expected, the Supreme Court threw out the labor provisions of the Clayton Act, subjecting unions to even more injunctions than before. In the end, the Clayton Act exemption turned out to be a chimera. Civil liberties, on the other hand, suddenly had a host of new champions. Could the First Amendment become labor's new Magna Carta?

CHAPTER TWO

Spycraft and Statecraft

Surveillance before the Great War

Had German spies infiltrated American unions? In the summer of 1915, Samuel Gompers worried. Nearly a year into the Great War, the European powers had spent materiel at an alarming rate. England and France relied increasingly on American munitions to resupply troops. American arms manufacturers ran their factories flat out, and East Coast ports swarmed with ships loading up rifles and cannon for the trenches in France. Then, in June, Frank Buchanan, a labor-card Democratic congressman from Illinois, called for nationalizing the American munitions industry. The "armor trust," charged Buchanan, would drag the United States into war unless the government checked the power of "these pirates." The government should take over all munitions factories, acquire the patents for all armaments, and stop selling weapons to belligerent nations.[1]

Gompers was startled. He had gone on record in opposition to the war from the beginning. But nationalizing industry sounded like a socialistic proposal. Where had Buchanan, a moderate former ironworker and reliable AFL spokesman, come up with this idea? And why had Buchanan suddenly thrown himself into antiwar agitation? Worse, Buchanan had somehow convened a group of union officials into a new lobby, Labor's National Peace Council (LNPC), to push for his demands. Something strange was going on, Gompers thought. Were German secret agents at work?

In fact, they were. Franz von Rintelen, a German Admiralty officer, had landed in New York in April with a $500,000 budget and orders to sabotage the American arms trade. Rintelen hoped to underwrite strikes in munitions factories and among longshoremen handling weapons shipments. Rintelen recruited the unwitting Buchanan to convene Labor's National Peace Council as the vehicle for labor sabotage.

Gompers and his old friend Ralph Easley helped crack the case. They had created their own "secret service bureau" and hired agents to investigate the LNPC. When the newspapers broke the story of Rintelen's arrest, the prosecuting U.S. attorney approvingly noted Gompers's quick detection of the scheme. This heady foray into international intrigue taught Gompers and the AFL leadership a valuable lesson. Several years later, radical organizers would resurface in AFL union shops urging militant strikes. This time, the AFL was ready. Hunting German saboteurs during World War I was a dress rehearsal for labor conservatives' campaign to identify and expel Communist organizers in the interwar years.

The Rintelen episode also established the AFL as the labor wing of the vigilant network mobilized on the U.S. home front before World War I. Lacking a strong federal police force, the American government relied on voluntary groups to patrol ports, factories, and public space. Ordinary citizens entered into public service when they monitored and reported on their neighbors and coworkers. Like the American Protective League and other vigilant groups, the leadership of the AFL developed a close working relationship with the nascent federal Bureau of Investigation. And like other vigilant leaders, Gompers learned how to wield his new authority against old enemies such as the IWW.

Pacifism and Belligerence

Labor's National Peace Council aroused the AFL's suspicion in part because the federation had already opposed U.S. entry to the war. In late 1914, the federation's executive council even offered "to initiate a movement for peace at the opportune time or to assist in any effort to bring this terrible war to a close."[2] The AFL was in line with progressive activists who organized a multitude of antiwar groups, from the Women's Peace Party to the American Union Against Militarism. The Socialist Party condemned the war, and so did the IWW at its 1916 convention. "The only ones who arc ready to see us involved," wrote Gompers to a friend in 1915, "are the captains of big business, financiers, dealers in bonds, and those who hope to reap a rich harvest by trading with the nations of Europe." On this matter, Gompers sounded as radical as any Wobbly.[3] At the outset of war, American popular opinion strongly favored neutrality, even as the United States reaped billions from sales of weapons, raw materials, and loans to Europe.[4]

By the spring of 1915, naval warfare between Germany and England had turned the Atlantic into a battleground, and domestic debate over U.S. neutrality was correspondingly volatile. While officially neutral, the Wilson administration defended the longstanding American position that the state would not restrict citizens' arms trafficking, and American manufacturers accordingly boosted weapons production and sales. British naval domination and close trade ties with the United States turned the munitions trade into a lopsided boon for the British. Germany complained bitterly that the munitions trade undermined U.S. claims to neutrality.[5]

Pacifists and proponents of neutrality also pointed to the "war traffickers" as a corrupting force pulling the United States into the war. A groundswell of popular outrage against the war united progressives, farmers, socialists, and isolationists. Irish Americans and German Americans joined the denunciations of American partiality toward Britain.[6] They seized on the arms trade as especially egregious, and began calling for an arms embargo in late 1914. Mass meetings and petition drives whipped up popular support and helped propel embargo legislation into Congress that winter. The German ambassador to the United States, Johann von Bernstorff, happily contributed $5,000 to this campaign.[7]

"From the very outset of the present war," Wilson later told Congress, Germany had "set criminal intrigues everywhere afoot against our national unity of counsel, our peace within and without, our industries and our commerce." History has borne out Wilson's complaint. From his Washington office, Bernstorff orchestrated a large and complex propaganda and espionage campaign in the United States, beginning immediately upon the European declarations of war. Working in German archives, historian Reinhard R. Doerries has confirmed the outlines and many details of American allegations of German propaganda and covert work in the United States. His findings, he argues, "correct the view that Washington, for the purposes of propaganda, grossly exaggerated the activities of the German intelligence services in America."[8]

During the first global war, Germany, England, and the other great powers created public-relations bureaus as agencies of combat. Britain's Wellington House and France's Maison Presse sought to influence public opinion among their subjects and enemies alike. Germany's efforts were similar. Bernstorff purchased a major newspaper, the *New York Evening Mail*, made contacts with Irish American leaders and supplied their newspapers with pro-German news releases, and supported German American political rallies. The German effort in the United States was largely eclipsed by Great Britain's propaganda campaign. British agents churned out reports of German atrocities in Belgium and blanketed the country with tracts depicting German soldiers as bloodthirsty monsters. Neither country sent their best agents to America, which was a very minor public theater.[9]

Stirring up trouble among an enemy's discontents was a popular tactic in the war. Most famously, Great Britain deployed T. E. Lawrence to organize rebellions among Arabs against the Ottoman Empire. As the largest empire, though, Britain itself was especially vulnerable to anti-imperial revolts. Germany backed rebellions in Ireland and India, and Bernstorff used the United States as the launching ground of these insurgencies. Bernstorff met with Roger Casement, the Irish revolutionary, in Washington and agreed to fund insurrection against British rule in Ireland. While Casement organized an Irish Brigade of captured Irish troops in Germany, Bernstorff collected funds from Irish American leaders for an armed uprising, which was scheduled in Dublin for Easter, 1916. The botched Easter Rising failed in part thanks to Bernstorff's poor planning.[10]

German-backed efforts at insurrection in India likewise collapsed. The Ghadr movement, made up of revolutionary Punjabi Indians and based in San Francisco, hoped to raise a military force to storm India and start a rebellion against British rule. Bernstorff reached out to the Ghadrites once the war started and followed the same script as he had with the Irish: he promised guns and military support. By December 1914, Bernstorff had acquired an arsenal of 250 Mauser pistols, 8,000 Springfield rifles, and 2,400 carbines for the Ghadrites. The problem was getting the weapons to India, given the blockades. A German shipping agent bungled the shipping arrangements, and the Americans and British seized the steamer and its cargo as it left the Mexican coast. American investigators discovered a sizeable contingent of Irish American radicals among the Ghadrites, in an early example of anti-imperial cooperation.[11] The polyglot population of the United States and the relative political freedom residents enjoyed made the U.S. an ideal training ground for rebellion.

In North America, the United States uneasily monitored rebellion on its own southern border. The chaos of the Mexican Revolution inflamed old resentments of the American annexation of Texas and seizure of Mexican territory in the nineteenth century, to the U.S. government's dismay. Since 1910, Mexico had been convulsed by coups and insurgencies, and American diplomats regularly intervened with military and financial support for their favored contestants. Victoriano Huerta seized power in 1913 with the assistance of the Americans, but Woodrow Wilson soured on Huerta's rule, in part due to Huerta's close relationship with Kaiser Wilhem. When Wilhelm

William A. Rogers, "Assorted Cargo for the Return Trip." Library of Congress, Prints and Photographs Division.

sent Huerta a large arms shipment in 1914, Wilson sent American troops to occupy Veracruz, driving Huerta from the presidential palace. Wilson's concerns about Mexican unrest were fueled by border skirmishes in Texas, where radical Tejanos and Mexicans aspired to retake the border states in a scheme called the Plan de San Diego. The outbreak of world war unsettled sovereign authority in the United States and European imperial powers alike.[12]

German operations on U.S. soil were generally more ambitious than effectual, Doerries emphasizes, and some were patently ludicrous. Fomenting strikes fell on the ludicrous end of the spectrum. Workers struck or not as they chose, and rarely in service of a goal concocted outside of their workplaces. While socialists, Communists, and other radicals dreamed of the strike as a great engine of revolution, they generally had to wait around for one to happen. German diplomats would prove no more successful than radicals at ordering up worker unrest.[13]

Labor's National Peace Council

Cutting off the American traffic of weapons to England was one of Bernstorff's highest priorities. Persuasion was useless, as Secretary of State William Jennings Bryan learned when he vainly protested against the arms trade to

Wilson. In April 1915, Franz von Rintelen arrived in the United States to help stop the arms trade by subterfuge. Rintelen was an aristocratic young officer in the German Admiralty with a background in banking; he had previously traveled to the United States to open a branch of the Deutsche Bank. Now assigned as an eager but inexperienced intelligence officer, Rintelen drew on his earlier contacts.[14]

He met with David Lamar, a Wall Street speculator with a long history of fantastic scheming. Lamar learned to manipulate financial transactions and political relationships as an aide to the head of a big New York street-car company. Later he grew wealthy speculating in steel and railroad stocks, often starting rumors of imminent trust-busting and trading on the resulting share-price dip. Lamar even started a front group, the Anti-Trust League, to lobby for antitrust legislation. In 1913, Lamar was caught posing as A. Mitchell Palmer, then a congressman from Pennsylvania, in one of these schemes, and he served a stint in the federal penitentiary. Shortly after Lamar's release, Rintelen contacted him. Lamar's experience with front groups may have led him to propose creating a new one that would attack arms manufacturers—the "munitions trust"—and coordinate munitions strikes. Rintelen could devote at least $200,000 of his budget to fund this effort.[15] Lamar quickly agreed to help.[16]

In early April, Lamar recruited Henry B. Martin, an old partner and the former secretary of the Anti-Trust League, who arranged a meeting with Illinois congressman Frank Buchanan and former Illinois congressman H. Robert Fowler. Both had been elected to Congress as Democrats in 1911, but Fowler lost in 1915 and resumed his law practice in southern Illinois. Buchanan had been president of the national Structural Ironworkers union before his election to Congress, and he still had close ties with the labor movement.[17] Much as Lamar had organized his Anti-Trust League, the men launched Labor's National Peace Council with a masthead and a big budget. It is not clear whether Martin knew who was funding the effort; likely Fowler and Buchanan had no idea but were attracted by generous stipends.[18]

They looked to the vigorous peace movement inside the AFL for members to fill out the LNPC's ranks. Although the 1914 AFL convention declined to formally oppose U.S. entry to the war, a number of the AFL's largest unions had been caucusing separately to plan neutrality campaigns, and New York City's Central Labor Union called a peace rally for late June with William Jennings Bryan as the headliner. (Bryan had recently quit his job as secretary of state in protest of war preparations.) Having announced the formation of the LNPC a few days earlier, Buchanan piggybacked on the peace rally and got a slot on the speaker's roster to sign up members. The LNPC program: nationalize the munitions industry, halt U.S. arms trafficking, and build an international labor peace movement. Buchanan and others had signed up seven union leaders to its executive council. Most were relative unknowns from unions with no involvement in war industries, such as the Meat Cutters, Leather Workers, and Commercial Portrait Artists. But Ernest Bohm, head of New York's Central Labor Union, stood out. Bohm was a well-known moderate and a powerful local leader, and his name gave the LNPC real credibility.[19]

Gompers snapped to attention. He had heard about the LNPC directly from Buchanan, who had paid Gompers a courtesy visit to describe the effort, and Easley had been sending along private letters sharing intelligence on Bohm's meetings with Buchanan.[20] While neutrality remained the AFL's official stance on the war, Gompers held no truck with the nationalization of any industry, and he was strongly disposed to dislike anyone organizing within the AFL. Meanwhile Gompers had also heard rumors that in Boston, a German agent had offered generous payments to Irish longshoremen for planting bombs among munitions cargo and refusing to load munitions on ships. The Longshoremen union's president, T. V. O'Connor, quickly squelched the rumored sabotage campaign and reported the offer to Secretary of Labor William Wilson, but Gompers was alarmed.[21]

Then in late June came news that Machinists at the Remington Arms plant in Bridgeport were preparing to walk out unless management conceded an eight-hour workday. Remington manufactured rifles, handguns, and ammunition, and by 1915 the plant produced two-thirds of the entire U.S. small-arms cargo for the Allies.[22] Gompers knew that the Machinists union had a strong tradition of socialist and radical leadership. Had they been drawn into some plot?

Gompers spent the July Fourth holiday at Ralph Easley's country house in New Canaan, Connecticut. Easley, head of the National Civic Federation, recently had been helping Gompers organize against socialist influences in the federation, and Easley helped convince Gompers that socialist-led peace movements aided the kaiser. Gompers and Easley had been friends for fifteen years, and both were seasoned strategists, having weathered strikes, electoral campaigns, and lawsuits together. They talked over the rumors of German industrial sabotage. Why not investigate the matter themselves? Easley suggested.[23]

A few days later, Easley wrote to the British ambassador to the United States. Gompers ("born in London," Easley noted) had intelligence that "pro-

German money" was being spent to "induce strikes in factories," "get seamen to strike," and stir up antiwar sentiment and "hocus-pocus" among working people. Gompers had "put his foot down emphatically against any strikes," Easley said. The ambassador replied immediately with warm thanks for the letter and for "the attitude of the gentleman you mention, which as a matter of fact has made a *vital difference* and averted a *great* danger." Indeed, the ambassador confirmed, German agents were scheming to organize munitions strikes and "intimidate by murder the men engaged in making or furnishing supplies. . . . No means will be regarded as too costly, or too atrocious, to be adopted."[24] His encouragement energized Gompers and Easley.

As preparations for a strike grew more serious, Gompers called the heads of the Machinists union to Washington for a meeting, and then personally traveled to Bridgeport to intervene. He "made no secret of his belief that emissaries of the Teutonic empires" were at work.[25]

The Bridgeport Machinists reacted to Gompers's accusations with astonishment. "Mr. Gompers has no jurisdiction over me," said John Keppler, the strike leader; and a Machinists official complained that until Gompers "tells the world that he doesn't know what he was talking about," the "strike will never be settled."[26] After a day in Bridgeport, Gompers backpedaled fast. He discovered that a dispute over which union should organize millwrights had sparked the strike. Keppler had reasoned, "If this jurisdictional dispute is going to cause trouble, I'm going to insist on the eight-hour day" and called his men out.[27] Bridgeport unions seized the chance to organize in a manufacturing boom—a strategy familiar to trade unionists everywhere. There is no evidence German influence was at play in their strike.[28]

Gompers hastily announced that he deemed the demands of the Remington strikers to be "reasonable and just and, therefore, indorsed" by the AFL, and Remington settled, agreeing to the eight-hour day.[29] Gracelessly, Gompers never conceded his error—instead, he insisted that he had been misquoted, claiming that he actually said that "agents of foreign governments" were exerting a "corrupting influence" among longshoremen.[30]

Although the LNPC had no part in the walkout, the coincidence of the munitions strike with the formation of the LNPC instantly inflated its apparent influence. Flush with Rintelen's cash, the fledgling group set up a two-day conference in Washington in early August, and LNPC's organizers recruited participants by promising to pay all their expenses. Two Detroit-area trade unionists accepted the invitation but, feeling uneasy about the generous subsidy, stopped by the AFL offices in Washington when they arrived for the LNPC conference to find out if the LNPC was "on the square." At AFL secretary Frank Morrison's urging, they attended the conference, where they found "less than a dozen" labor men, but plenty of delegates who were "all for Germany."[31]

The Detroit delegates took careful notes for Morrison and Gompers. Some of the other unionists grew more suspicious at the conference; executive board member William Kramer remembered that some delegates took credit for the munitions strikes. "We labor men have been made the goats in this thing," he later said.[32] Milton Snelling, a Washington, D.C., union leader, resigned from the LNPC shortly after the conference, and an alert Bureau of Investigation officer sought him out to ask why. Snelling met with the BI agent at the AFL's office in late August, and Gompers and Snelling shared all they knew. "There is no doubt but that German influences are behind this movement," Gompers assured the BI agent.[33]

Launching the Secret Service Bureau

As the Washington LNPC conference unfolded, Gompers and Easley prepared their investigation. They enlisted Herman Robinson, an old political operative, to find out how far the LNPC had penetrated into the AFL. Robinson was a Gompers loyalist who had worked as an AFL organizer in New York for several years before a Tammany mayor appointed him as New York City's license commissioner in 1910.[34] Having lost his post under a new mayor in 1914, Robinson was available and trustworthy. To investigate "those who were active in the so-called "'Peace Movement,'" Gompers and Easley sent Robinson off on a multicity tour beginning in mid-August. Over the next two months, Robinson traveled throughout New York State and to Pittsburgh, Cleveland, Detroit, Chicago, Bridgeport, New Haven, Providence, and Springfield, Massachusetts. He sent regular reports, marked "confidential," to Easley, who wrote to Gompers's home address when there was fresh news. This arrangement kept the investigation at arm's length from the AFL, and presumably secure from German saboteurs in the house of labor.[35]

Robinson questioned union leaders about their connection with the LNPC and other peace groups (such as Friends of Peace, led by William Jennings Bryan). When he found a unionist who had gotten involved with peace movements he explained "the methods that were being pursued" by German agents and often collected a copy of the unionist's resignation on the spot. He also got copies of telegrams and resolutions from the LNPC, all of which he forwarded on to Easley. Robinson heard tantalizing stories about a Machinists official making big bank deposits and an Ironworkers business agent who was "acting suspiciously," but he gathered nothing definitive. In Bridgeport, Robinson made a special effort to track down the source of rumors about that summer's munitions strikes. At the end of October, he finally found the man whom everyone named as their source. But the man said "he must have been misunderstood in this matter" and could produce only vague hearsay as evidence.[36] Robinson returned to New York the following day.

While the purview of their secret service bureau expanded, the grounds for its founding crumbled. Union leaders started defecting from the LNPC shortly after the Washington conference.[37] Gompers's office released a resignation letter from unionists on the LNPC board accusing the LNPC of seeking to "play into the hands" of Germany.[38] Buchanan himself resigned soon afterward. When the LNPC stopped paying its bills, its official printer tried to find the group's backer, and he ran into "some federal investigators who were also looking for the source of the organization's revenues."[39] The money had dried up once Rintelen was arrested. The Secret Service had been trailing Rintelen since early July. In late July, British naval intelligence officers sent him a message in German code ordering him to return to Berlin, and they arrested Rintelen at Dover a few weeks later.[40] As the cash spigot closed, the LNPC fell apart fast.

Gompers, the self-appointed investigator, appeared before the grand jury investigating the LNPC and "turned over two large portfolios filled with correspondence, circulars, proclamations, and other data" (collected by Herman Robinson). He condemned the "moral and industrial wrong against the United States" perpetrated by the LNPC.[41] His efforts won praise from the U.S. attorney, who emphasized Gompers's "energetic" opposition to the LNPC from the outset.[42] BI head Bruce Bielaski echoed the sentiment in 1919, saying that the LNPC's failure "was due in great measure to the wisdom and action" of Samuel Gompers.[43]

The U.S. attorney charged Rintelen, along with David Lamar and Henry Martin, with perjury and conspiracy to "restrain foreign commerce" and other offenses. They were tried in New York in May 1917. Buchanan and Fowler faced similar charges. In the end, none of the labor officials on the executive board were indicted as the grand jury apparently credited their claim of being unwitting "boobs." At the trial, the union men sometimes looked more like grafters than dupes, as when New York Central Labor Union head Ernest Bohm admitted that he had used free-flowing LNPC money to pay cash subventions to himself and friends and settle old debts. Of the eight men indicted, only Rintelen, Lamar, and Martin were convicted; Rintelen was sentenced to twenty months in federal prison, while Lamar and Martin received one-year sentences.[44] In the eyes of the law, the AFL unionists were the victims of the Labor's National Peace Council conspirators.

Gompers saw it the same way. The LNPC episode confirmed his tendency to see treachery when he was opposed, whether by an AFL member or an IWW radical. Moreover, in an era of international political movements, Gompers learned that "political organization, which had lagged so far behind industrial progress, would shortly involve the whole world in one struggling mass of contestants." Just as radicals looked to international struggles as symbol and inspiration for their own circumstance, Gompers and labor conservatives began to view domestic disputes as instances of global political conflicts. And their experience with German subterfuge taught them to look for hidden motives. Gompers later wrote that as "Americans were unaccustomed to the subtleties of international propaganda or secret service work," the AFL "had to learn much before we could protect ourselves from the penalties of ignorance."[45]

Working with the BI

Gompers was a quick study. As he learned the conventions of detective work, he immediately thought of ways to use them against old adversaries. While Robinson investigated AFL unions, Gompers and Easley also hired a detective to track Wobblies and anarchists. Beginning in August 1915, they received regular undercover reports from IWW organizing campaigns in Harrison, New York, and Paterson and Passaic, New Jersey. As Easley later recounted, "while we originally intended to get, for the benefit of Mr. Gompers, information as to what the Germans were doing in the plants, much material began coming in through the splendid efforts of our bureau which had nothing to do with that particular phase but which dealt with all kinds of German activities in other fields."[46]

Detectives continued to work among the Wobblies and anarchists through early 1917. NCF files contain hundreds of pages of anonymous reports describing IWW meetings, radical speeches, and, sometimes, fanciful Masonic conspiracies involving William Jennings Bryan or J. P. Morgan. Investigators sought links to connect radicals to German espionage, collecting rumors such as, "Four months ago the leaders of the IWW offered to engage with the German interests for a stipulated sum of money—by time or by the job—to destroy by fire, etc. American industry, call strikes, etc."[47] A detective trailed Italian anarchist and IWW organizer Carlo Tresca up and down New Jersey in 1917. In Passaic, as Tresca "spoke against President Wilson, by saying he would protect Capitalists, and run down the poor people," the detective noticed that "the hall was full with Germans and German Jews, and very few Italians." A few days later, in Clifton, New Jersey, the detective spotted a German giving Tresca a "big roll of bills," and later "saw two refined German gentlemen after Tresca's speech, take him over to the saloon and treat him to champagne and those two were well to do men, and I do believe that if they were not under the influence of liquor the revolution would have started Saturday night at twelve o'clock."[48] But the Wobblies were notoriously anti-imperial and anti-war. It was hard to believe that Wobblies would work on Germany's behalf.

Detectives recorded an IWW organizer explaining that in their campaign to "ruin the I.W.W.," the AFL had "unite[d] its strength, politically and other-wise, with the 'Hounds of the Law' and were 'sicking them on like dogs.'" In Paterson, Wobblies said that AFL leaders had "developed into stool pigeons for the police."[49] The IWW was right: just as they suspected, the American "Scaberation" of labor was following them, and reporting to the police. But the Wobblies were not cynical enough to suspect that the AFL accused them of being German agents. Notwithstanding their long mutual antagonism, this was a craven ploy by the AFL—especially considering the rising nativist, anti-German sentiment in the country.

Gompers and Easley made haste to use their information. In August 1915, Easley met with A. Bruce Bielaski, head of the federal Bureau of Investigation, and sought to meet with the U.S. attorney general to share information that had "come to me through my attempt to get data for Mr. Gompers, who is being attacked on all sides."[50] In contrast to their respectful acceptance of the LNPC intelligence, Justice Department officials treated the IWW infor-mation skeptically. Apparently Bielaski raised questions about the reliability of Easley's investigator. In response to charges that the investigator "may be crooked and not to be trusted," Easley confessed, "I am not unaware that it is easy for a layman to be very enthusiastic and more or less gullible" about "investigators, secret service men, etc," and he replaced the man shortly after-ward.[51] Likewise, the ostensible targets of IWW sabotage plots were uninter-ested in the NCF's intelligence. Easley wrote urgent letters warning the Du Ponts of IWW threats against their chemical factory in Harrison, New York. But the company head replied mildly that they considered the plot to be "comparatively little danger" and declined to meet with Easley.[52]

The Justice Department's relative lack of concern about the IWW contrasts sharply with the AFL's unease. In 1915, the IWW's reach was largely confined to the mines and lumber mills in the West and Southwest. Spectacular strikes in eastern textile cities in 1912 and 1913 had neither produced enduring IWW

locals nor sparked more organizing. Local officials and state militias, sometimes joined by crowds of citizens, attacked and imprisoned IWW organizers
and strikers. The federal government did not pursue Wobblies in any system-
atic manner. Indeed, the Justice Department made an effort to distinguish
syndicalism as a legally protected political belief from anarchism.[53] But the
AFL had been battling Wobblies wherever they organized—and increasingly
working with state officials. The previous year, in Butte, Montana, Gompers
helped the Western Federation of Miners (WFM) in their fight with the IWW
for miners' loyalty. Gompers and the WFM had gone so far as to support the
governor's enlistment of state police to drive the IWW out of town.[54] With
its secret service bureau reports of IWW collaboration with German agents,
the AFL tried to drag the Justice Department into the fight. Employers also
claimed that IWW agitation reflected collusion with Germany. By 1917, they
helped convince the Justice Department to take action.

The AFL and the BI

As Gompers and Easley launched their secret service bureau, the Bureau of
Investigation was looking for sources of intelligence. Founded in 1908, the BI
had only about one hundred agents in 1915, and little experience doing domestic policing. Compared to European countries with powerful state police
forces accustomed to domestic political surveillance, the United States had
a weak federal police force. As the rest of the federal government ballooned
during the war, so did its policing agencies. The BI grew to 300 agents by 1917,
while the army's Military Intelligence Division grew from 2 to 282 agents.[55]
    Many of these new agents came from private detective agencies. Hundreds
of private detective agencies operated around the country, another reflec-
tion of the relative weakness of state policing. Allan Pinkerton, the founder
of the American private detective industry, had started his agency with an
investigation into railroad worker graft, and labor investigations comprised
a large share of most detective agencies' business. Private detectives customarily tailed union organizers, posed as workers at strike meetings, and led
military-style ambushes of picket lines. The influx of private detectives into
the BI brought their labor expertise and industry contacts to the new force,
and the BI relied heavily on tips and intelligence volunteered by private detectives.[56]
    Still, the bureau had far too few agents on staff to police the entire nation.
In March 1917, a Chicago advertising executive proposed to rally a corps of
volunteer Bureau of Investigation agents to "secur[e] information of activi-

ties of agents of foreign governments or persons unfriendly to this Government." The bureau agreed, and the American Protective League (APL) swiftly enrolled 250,000 operatives carrying Justice Department badges and authorized to investigate disloyalty wherever they found it. Businessmen filled the ranks of the APL, and they focused most of their investigations on employee agitation in mills and mines—disloyalty to one's employer being equally unpatriotic as fealty to the Axis.[57]

The wartime BI, then, was less a trained force of civil servants than a loose confederation of vigilant citizens with government badges. Its porous walls made the BI especially susceptible to political pressure. It is not surprising that pursuing IWW and radical workers quickly jumped to the top of the BI's agenda. Before the war, the BI had ignored the IWW, considering labor disputes to be a matter for local authorities. By mid-1917, however, APL squadrons had attacked and arrested Wobblies throughout the West, putting pressure on BI leaders to act.[58] At the same time, information flowed freely from the BI. Officials readily shared reports and gossip with friendly inquisitors.[59]

Long before the American entry to the war, and long before the crackdown on domestic dissent that became known as the Red Scare, Gompers took on the role of policing labor's loyalty. His recent championship of free speech was challenged as the wartime state restricted the right of all citizens to speak freely. The new Bureau of Investigation took on the task of policing speech, investigating suspected disloyalty, and helping arrest, prosecute, and deport accused subversives. The AFL made the most of this new arrangement.

By helping to detect and prosecute German subterfuge, the AFL repaired some of the damage done to its reputation by the McNamara bombing scandal and strengthened its relationship to the Wilson administration. But the disadvantages of a growing federal police force soon became apparent. Once the war began, Gompers saw Bureau of Investigation agents—many of them private detectives wearing a federal badge—suppress steel workers striking under AFL banners. His loyalty could not protect AFL members from the predations of a new federal force. After World War I, the authority of the BI was implicated in any discussion of civil liberties. Seeing how the bureau's repressive forces could be strategically deployed gave Gompers a permanent respect, and distrust, for the BI.

CHAPTER THREE

Sedition and Civil Liberties
The AFL during World War I

By the fall of 1918, the Espionage Act had been in force for over a year, and American editors knew the rules: nothing that might "hamper" the war effort could be printed and mailed. Thus, when the postmaster general prohibited the *Nation* from mailing its issue dated September 14, 1918, editor Oswald Garrison Villard was "utterly dumbfounded." He and his staff combed over the issue looking for objectionable content but found nothing subversive. One editorial supported an inquiry into the Department of Justice's mass arrest of 75,000 suspected draft dodgers, but President Woodrow Wilson had ordered the inquiry, so surely that was not the problem. Another editorial criticized Wilson's dispatch of AFL president Samuel Gompers on a fact-finding trip to Europe. Gompers was a "sturdy partisan drummer," said the editorial, touring Europe like a traveling salesman selling the war, and he was unlikely to produce any usable intelligence. "Obviously that could not be the trouble," Villard reasoned.[1]

But it was. Villard caught the train from New York to Washington to find out the cause of the censorship. The solicitor for Postmaster Albert Burleson "came right out with the complaint. It was the Gompers article." He told Villard, "'Mr. Gompers has rendered inestimable services to this government during the war in holding union labor in line and while this war is on we are not going to allow any newspaper in the country to attack him.'" Villard was astonished: "It seemed incredible that we had come to such a pass that an American newspaper could not criticize Samuel Gompers." Villard protested directly to Wilson's personal secretary. The next day, Wilson overruled Burleson, and the offending issue of the *Nation* went into the mail. Just a few years earlier, Gompers had championed the freedom of the press to "say things that *displeased*." Now the press required presidential intervention to say something that might displease Gompers.[2] The war years led Gompers, along with the members and leaders of the American Federation of Labor, to rethink their civil liberties commitments.

Labor, State, and War

As the Great War dragged on, it was hard to gauge public sentiment inside or outside the labor movement. Observers trying to assess the balance of public opinion weighed mass peace rallies against the antipacifist mobs that attacked them. In factory districts, "there were many who denounced the imperialist war, but many more who bought Liberty Bonds," writes David Montgomery. "Someone singing 'The Yanks are Coming' could always be heard in the streets."[3] Progressives everywhere agonized over whether to mortgage their domestic agendas with support for Wilson's war plans. "To break with this man who has been the embodiment of so much hope is hard; yet to follow him in the new course he has laid out is harder," wrote one.[4]

Gompers was less ambivalent. Invited by Wilson to serve on the war-planning Council for National Defense in late 1916, Gompers had gradually embraced the cause of war. Since the outbreak of hostilities in 1914, Gompers had seen that "people responded to their colors, whether for Kaiser, Czar, president, or king," and a reflexive patriotism arose in him as well. And incidents such as the *Lusitania* bombing and the Rintelen affair convinced him that German belligerence demanded an American repulse. Numerous union leaders had experienced the same conversion. Gompers called a special meeting of the AFL's executive council in early March 1917 to consider the federation's war position. Two days later, the executive council announced a unanimous vote to endorse a declaration of war. But the federation hoped to parlay its support for a voice in the Wilson administration. "Organized labor should have representation on all agencies determining and administering policies of national defense," the AFL contended, and it demanded to be the "recognized defender of wage-earners" in war industries.[5]

For many in the labor movement, labor's cause was peace, not war. Just as the AFL's executive council was meeting, Russian revolutionaries were arguing over whether to withdraw Russia from the war. To the excitement of socialists and pacifists around the world, the Bolsheviks called for an immediate negotiated peace settlement among all belligerents. Exhilarated by the Russian Revolution, American socialists and radicals were not inclined to temper their militancy or antiwar sentiment. In May, American pacifists called an emergency meeting in New York to decide whether to promote the Bolshevik proposal or develop an explicitly American peace plan. The former argument prevailed. Socialists immediately began organizing a peace movement, modeled on Russian worker's councils. Their People's Council attracted leading socialists including Scott Nearing, Roger Baldwin, and Morris Hillquit, while many moderates such as Jane Addams and Senator Robert M. La Follette backed away. Few union leaders enlisted, but when 20,000 people flooded Madison Square Garden for the People's Council inaugural meeting in late May, it looked like workers would join.[6] The People's Council did especially well among Jewish workers in New York, where an energetic canvass signed up thousands. This was the turf of the radical garment workers, both the International Ladies' Garment Workers Union and the Amalgamated Clothing Workers of America (ACWA), who had quit the AFL in 1914 to form an industrial union of garment workers.[7]

Gompers fought back. Having just committed the AFL to support the war, he regarded the People's Council as a hostile incursion discredited by its socialist ties and Bolshevik rhetoric. For help, Gompers turned to the growing ranks of socialists who had left the party over its opposition to the war. Longstanding fissures in the Socialist Party began cracking wider in 1917. The war was stirring nationalist affinities among its largely European-descended membership, undercutting the party's internationalist aspirations and scrambling old moderate and radical alliances. The Russian Revolution had introduced a new axis of conflict, as a number of euphoric socialists recalibrated their political compasses toward St. Petersburg, while others insisted that the socialist program must derive from the special conditions of each country. After a national conference in early April 1917, at which the party had voted to formally oppose the war, a steady stream of defections began. Prowar socialists such as William English Walling and John Spargo migrated out of the party and into Gompers's orbit.[8]

Robert Maisel, editor of the socialist newspaper the *New York Call*, resigned the party in April but kept up ties with old friends. In June, Maisel approached Gompers with a provocative claim: he had been in a secret meeting with socialist leader Morris Hillquit and had learned that the People's Council planned to "take over" New York's unions and lead them into the peace movement. Given the strength of the People's Council and the ACWA in New York, this was a credible threat, and Gompers knew what to do. He asked Maisel to continue reporting to him regularly and called Ralph Easley. By the middle of July, Gompers had enlisted Ernest Bohm (fresh off the witness stand from the Rintelen trial) to help him launch the American Alliance for Labor and Democracy (AALD), a new prowar organization. Its aim was to "Americanize the labor movement in New York."[9] With Easley's help, Gompers got the government to pay for it. George Creel, the head of the newly created Committee for Public Information, provided the funding and substantial advisory support to the alliance.[10]

This embrace of a pro-American patriotism marked a change for the AFL. Since its founding, the federation had promoted unionism, not patriotism, and Gompers and other leaders often invoked the practices and policies of other European countries as examples for the United States to follow. With the advent of hyper-Americanism during World War I, the AFL draped itself in red, white, and blue bunting and became an agency of Americanization. During the war, labor Americanism meant loyalty to the government, support of the United States and the Allies in the war, and a definition of "democracy" that excluded socialism, syndicalism, and Bolshevism. In the decades after, this new definition of democracy abided as the creed of conservative unionists.[11]

Gompers and AFL leaders spent the war years promoting this vision. A first step was attacking the People's Council. When the People's Council scheduled a national convention in September in Minneapolis, the American Alliance for Labor and Democracy set up a competing meeting in Minneapolis on the same day. The AFL's opposition seemed to have its intended effect. The governor of Minnesota withdrew the People's Council invitation; the governor of North Dakota denied its members entry; and when they finally met in Chicago, the governor of Illinois sent the National Guard to evict them from the state. In contrast, the AALD used Creel's cash to arrange for "red, white, and blue special" trains to carry delegates from each coast to Minneapolis. Military bands played at the train station, and delegates received a laudatory telegram from President Wilson.[12]

In general, the AALD's war evangelizing was made easier by the fact that militant pacifism was centered not in AFL unions but in the socialist New York needle trades and among western miners and lumber workers.[13]

Once the United States joined the Allies in the spring of 1917, most workers and unions sought advantage by demanding recognition of their contribution to the war effort. In "trench warfare" on the factory floor, American workers pushed hard against employers' "Kaiserism" under the slogan "industrial democracy." Having been mustered into the war effort, industrial workers cast their bosses as autocrats and their strikes—strikes they were not supposed to be waging, according to Gompers—as crusades for liberation. This vision frequently invoked a liberal version of labor Americanism, entailing civil liberties, a decent standard of living, and cultural pluralism.[14]

To secure unions' allegiance to the war effort, the Wilson administration devised a new, provisional program of federal oversight of labor relations. This included a National War Labor Board, an independent panel of employer and union representatives empowered to arbitrate disputes in war industries. Frank Walsh, labor's champion from the Commission on Industrial Relations, was named to head the War Labor Board, and he vigorously promoted collective bargaining to boost war production. Gompers and AFL conservatives had a limited role in designing this corporatist scheme. Unsurprisingly, they opposed the expansion of state authority and the involvement of "experts" outside of AFL unions. But Wilson knew that the AFL spoke for a small minority of American workers, and that labor conservatives faced a substantial challenge from the Left. Felix Frankfurter reminded Wilson that the AFL had little influence with "non-English speaking workers," and Lincoln Steffens cautioned that "the Administration seems to think that Mr Gompers and the Central Organization of the A.F. of L. represent labor. They don't."[15] These crosscurrents in federal policy complicated the AFL's relationship to Wilson's government. Progressive activists clustered in agencies including the Labor Department and the War Labor Board found ways to empower more democratic and broad-based forms of workplace organization such as shop committees. When the state took an active role in managing labor policy, the AFL was obliged to share its seats at the bargaining table with reformers and radicals.

Nevertheless, Gompers and his fellow conservatives remained loyal to Wilson in gratitude for his pro-union policies. Gwendolyn Mink has characterized the AFL's politics as "a doctrine of union preeminence" that aimed at ensconcing unions as "the sole vehicle for pursuit of occupational and economic security." Progressives inside and outside the AFL who saw the state as a more equitable means of social redistribution nevertheless insisted on union presence in a democratic social order.[16] For the AFL, it was a win-win situation. Although the wartime labor regime bolstered progressive unionists and eroded the authority of labor conservatives, AFL union membership swelled by 50 percent, from 2 million members in 1916 to 3.2 million members in 1919.[17]

Civil Liberties and the War

With the nation so divided over the war, Wilson sought to shut down debate. In February 1917, even before the United States joined the Allies, his administration proposed the Espionage Act. Ostensibly, the Espionage Act targeted enemy spies and sympathizers who would sabotage the war effort. Franz von Rintelen, standing trial in New York City that spring, exemplified the threat. Yet Rintelen hardly featured in the debate over the Espionage Act, perhaps because his swift apprehension under existing law undermined the arguments for the bill. The Espionage Act's framers at the Department of Justice were more concerned with the conduct of Americans than Germans. The bill eviscerated the First Amendment by criminalizing speech intended to "interfere with" the recruitment or deployment of the armed forces and empowering the postmaster general to seize any publication or document advocating "treason" or "resistance to any law of the United States."[18]

The real intentions of the bill were immediately apparent. In the congressional hearings on the Espionage Act, proponents and opponents framed their arguments in terms of the rights of citizens under the First Amendment. The Free Speech League sent a witness to say that the Constitution contained "no suggestion that the press or speech is to be less free in war than in peace." Jane Addams insisted that the Women's Peace Party had "the right to agitate against existing law which we would consider to be against public policy."[19] In the protest against the Espionage Act, a powerful new civil liberties coalition began to form, and the AFL was a charter member. Arthur Holder, the federation's lobbyist, called the Espionage Act a "veritable Pandora's box," and he told Congress that "we do not propose to abdicate any of our liberties." The bill was likely to criminalize labor protest, and workers "have foes at home that are worse than any Prussians," he said.[20]

After Congress approved the war resolution in early April 1917, lawmakers took up the legislation again. Once again a coalition of civil libertarians formed to oppose the bill, but the AFL was already pulling back from the coalition. Holder testified again before Congress, but this time he modulated his objections. "We want—and I do not want to go so far as to say it, but probably you have it in your hearts, and know what I mean—we will eventually insist on our right to complain, and I want to know whether that is assured," he ventured. He was concerned with protecting unionists' rights to object to their working conditions and made little mention of broader free-speech principles. Holder promised that regardless of any law, "if we find that graft-

ers are trying to take advantage of the necessities of the people, or the patriotic sentiment of the people, by trying to squeeze out more profits," the AFL
would speak up. A puzzled congressman asked, "What do you think there is
in the bill that would prevent that?"[21] The bill passed into law without further
objection from the AFL.

Over the next year, Postmaster General Burleson energetically used his
censoring authority, and to no one's surprise, he seized socialist and radical
papers such as the *Masses*, the *Appeal to Reason*, and the *International Socialist Review*. When progressive lawyers Clarence Darrow, Frank Walsh, and
others protested, Wilson said, "I can only say that a line must be drawn, and
we are trying, it may be clumsily but genuinely, to draw it." Burleson's zeal
dismayed even the Justice Department, which periodically refused to defend
him in federal court. His censorship of the *Nation*'s editorial on Gompers was
an overreach, and even Wilson's boosters at the *New York World* called Burleson's decision "asinine." Wilson's reversal of the *Nation* decision was a rare
check on the postmaster's authority. For his part, Gompers made no public
comment on the *Nation* affair; he certainly did not disavow the notion that
criticizing him could be considered seditious.[22]

The government returned to Congress in early 1918 to expand the Espionage Act via a series of amendments known as the Sedition Act, which criminalized any "disloyal, profane, scurrilous, or abusive language" about the government, the military, or the flag. This time, the AFL spoke up. Before its
summer convention, while the legislation sat on the president's desk, the federation clarified its position on the law for its members. The AFL endorsed
the Sedition Act. "This country is engaged in a desperate conflict," said the
executive council, and "every fiber of the national being must be exercised."
Given the "polyglot character" of the "unassimilated" American citizenry,
and recalling "the insidious propaganda which emanated from the imperial
German government," strong state action was necessary. The Sedition Act
passed into law in May.[23]

Yet virtually all of the government's Espionage Act prosecutions involved
antiwar speech by Americans, not espionage by a foreign power. Eugene Debs
was the most famous victim of the crackdown, arrested in June 1918 for giving
an antiwar speech at a Socialist Party picnic. IWW members were particular
targets; nearly half of all Espionage Act prosecutions occurred in thirteen
federal districts concentrated in western states where the IWW organized.[24]
Before their eyes, old AFL enemies were silenced, arrested, and incarcerated.
Zechariah Chafee warned that "the use of the tremendous power of the state

on behalf of employers and the conservative unions" would likely confirm radicals' belief that "government is only the organ of capital."[25]

The new system of repressive laws extended to the states. Criminal syndicalism laws criminalized "crime, violence, sabotage, or other unlawful methods as a means of industrial or political reform," as Idaho's law phrased it. On their face, such laws implicated any union activity; violence erupted in many strikes, and all kinds of activity could be considered "unlawful." Between 1917 and 1920, twenty states and two territories enacted laws banning criminal syndicalism. But in most cases neither national nor local AFL affiliates raised a protest, because in each state, the law targeted IWW organizers, making it "criminal ipso facto to belong to organizations like the Industrial Workers of the World."[26] In some states, such as Michigan, lobbyists succeeded in getting farmers and AFL unions explicitly excluded from the law. In nine states, including Ohio, California, and Indiana, no union or AFL affiliate opposed the passage of criminal syndicalism laws; and in some states, including West Virginia and Alaska, union-card legislators endorsed the laws. The national AFL did nothing to block criminal syndicalism legislation. State prosecutions of IWW members under the criminal syndicalism statutes did more harm to the IWW than did federal action.[27] By the end of the war, the IWW was nearly wiped out.

All in all, the AFL had made a dramatic turnaround on the matter of civil liberties. Why? It was true that the federation's institutional interests, narrowly defined, were served by its new stance. But there was more to the story. Gompers and other leaders were recent converts to the civil liberties cause. As Theodore Schroeder had correctly assessed, their concern for their own liberty was stronger than their commitment to protecting others' freedoms. In this tendency, AFL leaders were not unique. Many radicals also declined to exert themselves on behalf of ideas they despised. Gompers's interest in civil liberties had flagged after his First Amendment defense failed in the 1908 *Buck's Stove* case. Promoting unionism, not free speech, was his main concern.

Censorship of antiwar speech was popular. Congress passed the Espionage and Sedition Acts by wide margins, and the "war hysteria" that troubled people such as Jane Addams gripped many Americans, who joined the American Protective League, the Boy Spies of America, and other vigilante groups. As historian Christopher Capozzola has shown, for many people, obligation accompanied civil liberties, and "responsible speech" balanced citizens' personal freedom with the collective interest of the nation.[28] During war, national unity trumped individual conviction. In 1917, Gompers explained this need to the New York State Federation of Labor with a homely analogy: "Supposing in any of our unions a question, a wage reduction or the demand for a wage increase came up and the question of striking was adopted by two-thirds of the men," he said. "Do you think for a moment that the one-third" who opposed the demand should "play the part of the scab and the strikebreaker? I hold that the same rule applies to the republic in which we live."[29]

Working with the Bureau of Investigation

Suppression of wartime dissent required a dramatic expansion of the state's policing power. In the new security state, the AFL had excellent contacts. From his work with Ralph Easley, Gompers had built credibility with the Justice Department. John Lord O'Brian, director of the department's War Emergency Division and deputy attorney general, had served as a federal special prosecutor on the Rintelen case. During the trial he and other prosecutors remarked on Gompers's important role in helping to check the Rintelen conspiracy. A. Bruce Bielaski, head of the BI, likewise praised "the wisdom and action" of Gompers in the Rintelen affair.[30]

One marker of the AFL's close relationship with the bureau was its assignment of an agent to guard Samuel Gompers during the war. Agent Irish traveled with Gompers and kept an eye out for "any cranks or radicals who might attempt to approach Mr. Gompers." This escort also gave the BI a vantage point to observe the AFL's doings, although there was little objectionable to report: Irish described the "most loyal nature" of the AFL's 1918 convention, with delegates shunning the "numerous socialists and other radicals [who] frequented the hall."[31] Periodically, Gompers passed along radical literature for the bureau to investigate, such as a circular denouncing war profiteers and Gompers both.[32]

The Justice Department grew to appreciate the AFL's conservatism. In 1918, an assistant attorney general explained the difference between the AFL and the IWW: "the I.W.W. is more opposed to and offensive to legitimate labor organizations than it is to anything else in the world." The IWW stood for "'slowdown,' sabotage, and destruction," while "legitimate labor organizations" stood for "a fair day's wage for a fair day's work delivered, the right to organize . . . the right to strike peacefully."[33]

In contrast to the jostling reformers in the labor agencies of the Wilson administration, the AFL had few competitors within the policing and enforcement arms of the state. At the Justice Department, the War Department, and the censoring Postal Department, AFL officials were the only legitimate representatives of labor. Through collaborating in the repression of labor radicals, AFL officials won the respect of federal law enforcement. Likewise, the state's foreign policy apparatus appreciated the federation's help in propagating a conservative labor program overseas. During the war years, the AFL often found its best friends among federal law enforcement agents and diplomats, not labor-policy officials.

Gompers did not hesitate to use his position strategically. He repeatedly contrasted the loyalty of AFL members to the disloyalty of the IWW, calling the IWW "pro-German" and emphasizing the heavy representation of Germans in the Socialist Party.[34] (Of course, there were many German members of AFL unions as well, but Gompers seemed to believe that the federation's jingoism protected all its members with a mantle of loyalty.) In public speeches, Gompers characterized the IWW and the Socialist Party as "seditious" and denounced the "traitors who talk peace and anti-Americanism and say they are talking for the American working man."[35] With the Espionage Act in force, these words had weight. Accusing anyone of sedition could trigger federal repression.

In 1918, Gompers's ally Ralph Easley made more concrete charges. The National Civic Federation published a pamphlet authored by dime novelist T. Everett Harré that purported to show that the IWW was an "auxiliary of the German espionage system." Harré claimed that "a comparison of the activities of German spies and those of the I.W.W. reveals startlingly identical methods and acts." In many cases, Germany was actually working through IWW organizers, "convenient instruments for the continuance of [Germany's] fell work." Mysterious deposits in the IWW treasury suggested payments by the kaiser. Easley concluded that "both the I.W.W. and German malefactors" opposed the U.S. government, and that "both must be detected and stamped out."[36]

Gompers and Easley had made this case before, of course, claiming in 1915 that their investigations had proved a German-IWW connection. Repeating it in 1918 was a different kind of aggression, however. Popular sentiment had turned sharply against the Wobblies. In 1916 a crowd of citizens had herded Wobblies onto a train in Bisbee, Arizona, and had them dumped unceremoniously in the desert. Later that year a mob of several hundred people fought back two shiploads of Wobblies trying to land in Everett, Washington.[37] By 1918 federal prosecutors considered "public sentiment to be so inflamed against radicals" that convictions could be achieved "as a matter of course."[38]

The AFL abetted the federal prosecutors. After the Justice Department executed a national raid on IWW offices in September 1917, Gompers personally met with Attorney General Thomas Gregory, ostensibly because he feared that loyal AFL members were falsely accused of Wobbly sympathies. Gregory assured Gompers that "great care would be exercised in differentiating the bona fide and normal activities of workers to organize," and added that the evidence proved the IWW to be "treasonable, treacherous to a very marked degree." Gregory supplied Gompers with Wobbly membership cards seized in the raid—useful information for the AFL, which forbade its members from joining the IWW.[39]

Using material seized from IWW offices, the BI coordinated a mass prosecution of IWW members and leaders for interfering with the war effort. The AFL offered its help as the Justice Department prepared its case. A Justice Department agent coordinating evidence for the case met with Easley in January 1918, and Gompers arranged for the president of the Cigar Makers' union to meet with the agent as well.[40] In a showpiece trial, held in Chicago in the summer of 1918, the Justice Department won convictions and long prison terms at Leavenworth for one hundred Wobblies.[41] In other federal districts, the prosecution had faltered. But several cases were still outstanding when the NCF publicized its new charges against the IWW.

Did Gompers or Easley actually believe that the IWW or the Socialist Party was in league with the kaiser, or did they engage in deliberate slander? There is little evidence to go on. In the case of the IWW, it is hard to imagine hardheaded Gompers crediting the wild claims of the NCF investigators. Certainly Gompers did consider slacking and striking as harmful to the U.S. war effort, but he knew it was not necessarily suborned by German agents. Given his familiarity with the exaggerations of private detectives, and his long experience with the IWW, Gompers likely saw imputations of German-IWW alliances as false but useful. Notably, Gompers did not reiterate these accusations in his 1,200-page, two-volume memoir, *Seventy Years of Life and Labor*, published in 1924.[42]

The Socialist Party, on the other hand, did have an organic connection to Germany, the birthplace of Marx and many American socialists. Gompers did not retreat from imputing German ties to the American Socialist Party, which he termed "the most important disrupting agency" among foreign-born American workers. "The Socialist Party largely emanated from Germany," he wrote in his memoirs, and "the sympathy of its devotees was with that country." Indeed, Gompers argued that German Chancellor Otto von Bismarck had schemed to export socialism as a powerful Trojan horse of subversion, "inculcating international Socialism among the citizens of all countries with which Germany might some day come in conflict," while promoting German nationalism at home.[43] As Gompers's own nationalism swelled, his dislike of both German autocracy and international social democracy likewise grew. The Bolshevik Revolution in Russia welded both tendencies into a reflexive anticommunism.

The Notion of Totalitarianism

Pleased with the AFL's war work at home, Wilson enlisted the federation into international diplomacy as well. As Gompers marshaled the AFL behind Wilson's war effort in the spring of 1917, the overthrow of the tsar threatened to pull Russia out of the war. Throughout the year, as Gompers barnstormed American factory districts to rally workers behind the war, he bombarded Russia's Provisional Government with cables urging the revolutionaries to reject Bolshevik calls for an immediate armistice. In January 1918, as the Bolsheviks concluded a separate treaty with Germany at Brest-Litovsk, Gompers sneered, "The Bolsheviki have caused Russia to crawl to the boots of the Kaiser to demand mercy from him."[44] Thereafter, Gompers denounced the new Russian regime as a tool of Germany, and he implored European and American socialists and radicals to close their ears to the Bolsheviks' siren call for peace. Mimicking the AFL's domestic prowar campaign, AFL delegations swept through Europe in 1918 to exhort unionists to boycott international peace conferences and support an Allied invasion of Russia to counteract "the sinister influences of the Central Powers upon the so-called Bolshevik Government, which has suppressed the utterances and the aspirations of the great majority of the Russian working classes."[45]

Consumed with the war, Gompers saw the Russian Revolution through an Allied lens. Brest-Litovsk created a lasting association between Germany and Russia as autocracies with a shared genotype. Gompers was among the various wartime observers who set forth the notion of totalitarianism as a modern form of tyranny rooted in the seizure of state power by an antidemocratic cadre who ruled by violence. These thinkers saw socialism and Communism as expressions of a "Germanic" political style. "Leninism does not differ from German imperialism. . . . Socialism has its headquarters in Germany," wrote William Howard Taft.[46] Adherents of this idea pointed to the fact that Germany gave Lenin safe passage back to Russia in the spring of 1917, and also to the "Sisson Documents," released by the deposed Mensheviks and purporting to show that the Bolsheviks worked hand in glove with Germany. The documents were later proved to be forgeries, but the link had been made. Unlike other antiradicals, Gompers did not credit the Sisson Documents, yet he repeatedly attacked American pacifists and radicals supporting the Bolshevik peace proposals as "the conscious or unconscious agents of the Kaiser in America."[47]

More than war fervor underlay this reflexive anti-Bolshevism. For some AFL leaders, ascension to state policymaking, both foreign and domestic, kindled a passionate commitment to Wilsonian internationalism and corporatist power sharing. In this new world, labor leaders would sit with capitalists and civil servants at the helm of the state, solving stubborn social problems in the spirit of cooperation. Gompers and his allies worked hard to entrench this "messianic vision" on the home front in industrial planning and oversight boards, and Gompers led an effort to enact it internationally as well by organizing the International Labor Organization, "an adjunct" to the League of Nations with a tripartite business/labor/state governance structure.[48] With the revolution, the Bolsheviks burst onto the scene with a dramatically different vision. By reconstituting the Socialist International and demonstrating that a militant and armed working class did not need alliances to seize state power, the Bolsheviks threatened to peel off European and American unionists from Gompers's coalition.

To contain the revolutionary contagion in Russia, Gompers insisted, the United States must not recognize the Bolshevik government. He was one of the first and most influential voices on the question. On the heels of Brest-Litovsk, in February 1918, Gompers sent Wilson a memo written by William English Walling, a onetime socialist turned reactionary, who argued that any "friendly steps" toward the Bolsheviks would only encourage revolutionary strikes and pacifist movements in Europe and, worse, "Chicago, New York, San Francisco, and our other foreign industrial centers." Wilson and his secretary of state, Robert Lansing, already inclined toward nonrecognition, agreed, and they discounted pragmatic recommendations to negotiate with the new Russian government.

As an anti-Bolshevik bloc cohered among American foreign policymakers, Gompers became a vigilant ally, ready to testify before Congress or mobilize businessmen through the National Civic Federation to shout down proposals to soften American policy toward Russia.[49] In the coming years, AFL leaders would flesh out their denunciations of the Bolshevik regime with details of its mistakes and crimes. But the facts only confirmed what they believed from the beginning.

European workers were not inclined to accept Gompers's interpretation of the events going on around them. Gompers's "grand junket" in Europe made few inroads among them. In Italy, the Confederation of Labor boycotted Gompers's reception; in France, journalist Ray Stannard Baker reported, Gompers's meeting with the Syndicalists broke up after he "tersely told them they were traitors to the cause of the people of France."[50] As an emissary for Wilson, Gompers accomplished little. (Much as the *Nation* expected: Gompers "goes abroad as neither an observer nor a prophet, nor has he the first qualification for either role.") Nevertheless, the experience gave AFL leaders a taste of statecraft and a wider view of the world. They would not get another chance to act as agents of American foreign policy until the next great war.[51]

Gompers was on his European mission when Postmaster Burleson's inspectors flagged the derisive *Nation* editorial. To Gompers, labor's ascension to respectability seemed complete. By turning the AFL into labor's loyalty patrol, labor conservatives gained a stature that would have been unimaginable just a few years earlier. The war years taught them to see the state differently. Federal policy could be the most efficient tool for organizing workers, and federal police the most effective way to eliminate radical challengers. Civil liberties seemed less important to labor conservatives as they lost interest in protesting against the government and instead joined the international battle against kaiserism and Bolshevism.

Two months later, a swift armistice brought the war to an end. The federal government dismantled its wartime labor policy, abandoning its role as union organizer. But the new federal policing apparatus remained. Labor conservatives would soon have cause to revisit the question of civil liberties.

PART II

Becoming Commonsense Anticommunists

CHAPTER FOUR

Communism, Civil Liberties, and the Red Scare

As the nation demobilized, the AFL lost its privileged seat at the table of the federal government. Gompers's old cynicism about the potential benevolence of the state was richly confirmed as the wartime labor relations framework was summarily dismantled. A huge postwar strike wave, driven by workers who had accepted wage freezes on behalf of war mobilization, provoked dramatic reprisals from employers and police. While the War Labor Board demobilized, the new federal police forces did not; the Department of Justice and the Military Intelligence Division supplied intelligence and agents to help coordinate the crackdown.

A new civil liberties movement emerged from the public outrage at government repression. Prominent lawyers such as Zechariah Chafee and Felix Frankfurter helped organize the arguments of citizens' groups into a coherent doctrine of free speech. Having seen firsthand how federal authority could be abused, the AFL reversed its wartime position and helped organize the fight against reauthorizing the Espionage Act. On the merits of the federal Bureau of Investigation, however, the AFL remained silent. Behind the scenes, AFL officials continued to collude with the BI's repression of troublesome radicals, including members of the new American Communist Party.

Examining the AFL's role in the Red Scare suggests the complexity of popular motives for antiradicalism. The Red Scare is customarily described as a comeuppance for the AFL, a bitter lesson showing that collaboration with the wartime state was a foolish bargain. Historian Robert Murray, for example, finds it "ironical" that the AFL cooperated with reactionaries in "digging its own grave" by trying to distance itself from revolutionary politics.[1] Certainly the elimination of wartime labor protections harmed the AFL. But the brunt of federal repression fell on the federation's radical rivals, and AFL leaders were more often collaborators than victims of federal crackdowns. For the postwar federation, a gap opened between word and deed, as AFL leaders publicly denounced and surreptitiously aided antiradical repression.

The Red Scare

The declaration of armistice in November 1918 undermined the justification for wartime labor policy, but the congressional midterm elections a few weeks earlier had already wiped out the political impetus. Republicans had swept the Congress, and within a few months they had begun to dismantle the new federal labor regime by slashing agency budgets. As the war ended, employers withdrew from federally supervised negotiations with their workforces, while their employees let loose complaints and demands they had stifled for the duration.[2]

In January 1919, radical workers orchestrated a general strike in Seattle, kicking off a wave of walkouts that continued all year. Five months later, a postal clerk intercepted sixteen mail bombs addressed to Supreme Court justice Oliver Wendell Holmes, capitalist John D. Rockefeller, Attorney General A. Mitchell Palmer, Immigration Commissioner Anthony Caminetti, and other enemies of radicals. The bombs were apparently intended to explode on May Day. Foiled, the bombers began again. On June 2, bombs exploded at the same hour in eight different cities, targeting, among others, a federal judge, a textile manufacturer, the mayor of Cleveland, and again Attorney General Palmer. Two of the bombers died. The warnings of the patriotic societies no longer sounded so outlandish.[3]

Over the next several months, a wave of reaction swept the nation. State legislatures banned red flags, and idle comments endorsing radicalism could get citizens arrested. The Department of Justice led the way, orchestrating a series of coordinated national sweeps of raids and arrests, picking up suspected radicals and seizing records of Communist and ethnic radical groups. In many cases, Justice Department agents did not bother to seek warrants in advance, or even to charge detainees with any crime. These "Palmer raids" culminated with a massive sweep in December 1919. Federal agents picked up thousands of radicals and loaded 249 resident aliens on the *Buford*, a ship with a secret destination. Once asea, the captain opened a sealed envelope that contained orders to land in Finland. American soldiers met the *Buford* at a Finnish port and escorted its prisoners to the Russian border. Emma Goldman, one of the detainees, remained defiant. "It was melodrama to keep it secret," she said of the cloak-and-dagger deportation.[4] There was no shortage of melodrama in the crackdown that later came to be known as the "Red Scare."[5]

For labor conservatives, the Red Scare presented continuing opportunities for discreet collaboration with the BI. Attacking the IWW remained an AFL priority. In December 1919, a UMW district president in Illinois named Frank Farrington wrote to alert Attorney General Palmer that the mining camps of southern Illinois were "a prolific field for the Department of Justice which, as I understand it, is making an effort to clean up the I.W.W.s and other rabid elements who would destroy our American Institutions." Farrington promised Palmer that the "law abiding 100% American citizens" of the Illinois UMWA would do whatever they could to help the Justice Department "operatives" and asked Palmer to keep the communication confidential. Palmer replied with warm thanks and assurance that he had referred the matter to the BI.[6]

A month earlier, Charles Moyer, president of the International Union of Mine, Mill and Smelter Workers wrote Gompers complaining that the IWW had continued to hold "propaganda meetings," "unmolested by the authorities," causing thousands of men and women to have their "minds poisoned against bonafied [*sic*] unionism, and all government." In the past, Moyer wrote, the Mine Mill union had gotten valuable information from an undercover agent who had worked as a "special employee" for the Justice Department and "furnished the Department the first information that resulted in the activities of the Department against the I.W.W." Moyer wanted Gompers "to use your influence" to have the agent reappointed by the Justice Department and detailed to the Mine Mill.[7] Other AFL union leaders similarly sought the BI's help in rooting out Wobblies from their ranks. The secretary of the California State Federation of Labor sent a list of names of Wobblies to the bureau in early 1919, hoping to see the Wobblies get "their just deserts"; and the president of the Connecticut Federation of Labor likewise offered to share intelligence with the BI.[8]

In March, New York state senator Clayton Lusk convened a committee to investigate Bolshevism's spread. Archibald Stevenson, a New York attorney and leader of the patriotic Union League, took a job as committee counsel. The Lusk Committee kicked off its work in June with a dramatic raid on the left-wing Rand School and the New York offices of the IWW and the Socialist Party. Forty former American Protective League members helped Stevenson and state police cart away files.[9] Over the summer and fall, the Lusk Committee charted the spread of red webs of radicalism in the labor movement. In March, Ralph Easley arranged for a lunch meeting at a Fifth Avenue club for Archibald Stevenson to share his "very important data" and "plan for dealing with the situation" with "four or five labor representatives." "Remember," Easley said, "No reporters!" In attendance were AFL staffers Hugh Frayne and Chester Wright, along with Robert Maisel from the American Alliance for Labor and Democracy and Timothy Healy, the president of the Brotherhood of Stationary Firemen (a railway union).[10]

After the June raids, Easley convened another luncheon, this time to discuss with Stevenson "how to use effectively certain material that the Lusk Committee has secured." The president and vice president of the United Textile Workers Union came to this meeting.[11] NCF records do not reveal what occurred at these sessions. It is clear, though, that labor conservatives and antiradical strategists had established formal channels for trading information. In its final report, the Lusk Committee took care to "distinguish the labor organizations which are led by conservative and constructive leaders, such as the American Federation of Labor," from the subversive labor groups, "which are founded upon the principles of industrial unionism."[12]

Labor conservatives continued to caucus with other antiradicals through the fall of 1919, and they complained that insurgencies were destabilizing relations with employers. At a National Civic Federation dinner in October 1919, called to discuss "a comprehensive campaign against Socialism and Bolshevism," Longshoremen's union president T. V. O'Connor said that a New York waterfront strike currently underway was "a rebellion in our organization." It was led by IWW radicals who had recruited Italian, Lithuanian, and Spanish workers who "hate everything American and anything that smells like an American." Stationary Firemen president Timothy Healy agreed that "it is very hard to satisfy the men right now," but he urged employers to negotiate with "the A.F. of L. men who try to do the right thing, men who are conservative and represent conservative organizations." O'Connor and Healy particularly denounced strikers' defiance of collective bargaining agreements. Contractualism was central to labor conservatives' view of proper union behavior. Radicals in the rank and file—whether anarchist, IWW, or Communist—humiliated their conservative leaders by flouting their authority (and often the majority vote of the membership) and forcing them to "break the word pledged by our organization," as O'Connor said.[13]

The Palmer raids marked the high tide of the Red Scare. In late November, the Justice Department swooped down on the offices of the Union of Russian Workers, arresting several hundred people, and in January 1920 Palmer coordinated an even larger raid on leftist and Communist organizations in thirty cities, sweeping over 6,000 people up in the dragnet. Palmer basked in glowing praise from the press and prepared to make a run for the presidency.

The National Civic Federation registered its admiration for his bold action with a telegram sent by Easley the morning after the raids: "Congratulations on wonderful clean-up. That is the only way to deal with Bolsheviks. Their sympathizers in parlour and editorial sanctum will begin crying 'more persecution.' It would be welcome if they themselves could be given a taste of the same methods."[14]

Retrenchment

Responsible trade unionism precluded radicalism, labor conservatives insisted. When "employers prohibited men from organizing in the A.F. of L.," the "radical element" organized "quietly." Employers were the radicalizing force, not unions. Labor conservatives had made this argument before, but in 1919 they reiterated it constantly, even casting employers as Bolsheviks. At another session with Archibald Stevenson and the NCF, Textile Workers president John Golden told attendees that "by cutting off all negotiations with a trade union that is 100% American, and a part of the A.F. of L., [employers were] doing more to encourage and foster and build up Bolshevism in this country than any other movement that I know of."[15] Gompers had floated this idea earlier, saying that "Bolshevism is manifested in the concerted effort on the part of some employers to create discontent and trouble in the ranks of labor, by lowering wages, throwing men into idleness and employing detectives to arouse the ire and passions of the workers." The AFL, on the other hand, was a "constructive force," "opposed alike to Bolshevism amongst employers as well as among employes [sic]."[16] Other unionists echoed this sentiment. "There are two kinds of Bolsheviki," according to the Cigar Makers union. "One is the wild-eyed and impatient red radical; the other is the despotic, grab-it-all employer and financier."[17]

Comparing employers to Bolsheviks was a stretch, and no one outside the labor movement picked up the analogy. But the notion that conservative unions and contractual labor relations curbed radicalism gained real currency. The Russian Revolution had sharpened the distinctions among varieties of workers' struggles. Increasingly, political leaders and social thinkers echoed labor conservatives' insistence that trade unions could forestall other, more militant social movements. In February 1919, a former member of the wartime United States Shipping Board expressed this idea clearly. "Organized labor in this country, as represented by the American Federation of Labor is one of the great conservative influences in the nation. Making allowances for many of its abuses of power, I can say that the Federation is anti-Socialist, anti-anarchist, and anti-Bolshevist," he said. "But it is in danger of attack by the Bolsheviki."[18]

Still, the AFL's wartime collaboration with the state and its new conservative credentials yielded few lasting gains. The federation's competitors had been weakened, but neither the government nor employers saw the AFL as a "constructive force." Strikers were outlaws, no matter the acronym on their banners, and the notion of unions as social stabilizers was honored mostly in the breach. Throughout the grueling year of 1919, the AFL saw the tide of employer opposition rise around them. When Boston policemen struck for recognition as an AFL affiliate, the mayor of Boston and the governor of Massachusetts agreed to fire them all. Coal miners struck in November, and Attorney General Palmer sought and received a federal injunction against UMW officials. Five years earlier, Woodrow Wilson had backed labor's exemption from federal injunctions in the Clayton Act; now his administration resurrected labor's bête noire. It was obvious to everyone that federal policy had changed. Wilson's secretary Joseph Tumulty commented, "If there is any class in the country to which we have been overgenerous it has been labor. I think this class owes us more than they have been willing to give."[19]

The great steel strike was symptomatic. The steel industry had been a nonunion bastion since Andrew Carnegie crushed the Homestead strikers in 1892. For decades, AFL unions had quarreled about whether and how to sign up workers in the vast mills. Part of the difficulty arose from the multitude of jobs inside the mills; numerous craft unions claimed jurisdiction but rarely attempted to actually organize. After his success organizing packinghouse workers, William Z. Foster set his sights on steel as the United States entered the war. The moment was propitious, as government demand for industrial output made a steel strike particularly inconvenient. John Fitzpatrick and the Chicago Federation of Labor negotiated with Gompers and the AFL to set up an organizing council of craft unions in 1918, and over the next year Foster coordinated a massive, methodical effort to rally thousands of steelworkers across the country. He won the admiration of both his corps of organizers and Gompers, who found him "a man of ability, a man of good presence."[20]

Foster needed all his diplomatic skills to deal with the twenty-four unions represented on the campaign leadership council, which required constant consultation for every decision and expenditure but demurred on requests for funding and staff. Internal squabbling among union leaders frequently threatened to scuttle the whole effort. By the time the steelworkers were ready to walk out, in late September 1919, newspapers denounced strikers as Bolsheviks. When the strike began, the government stood by as strikebreakers smashed picket lines. Foster's old radical ties gave fodder to claims that Communistic impulses drove strikers: "Beware the agitator who makes labor a catspaw for radicalism," read newspaper advertisements taken out by U.S. Steel.[21] In the mill districts, strike meetings were simply forbidden by local police. In Gary, Indiana, army troops moved to protect U.S. Steel's strikebreakers and plants. The steel strike collapsed quickly.

In the tense days of 1919, newspapers and steel executives were quick to paint the strikers red: an "experiment in Bolshevizing industry," said one editorial. Samuel Gompers and William Z. Foster went together to Capitol Hill to pledge that the steel strike was not a Bolshevik plot. Senators reminded Gompers of Foster's history as a syndicalist Wobbly and his past ties to international socialist movements. Was Foster "working right now to become the head of the American Federation of Labor and control it along radical lines?" they asked.[22]

Gompers protested that Foster deserved "something better than a mistaken past . . . held up to the contumely of the world." Foster had changed. When questioned, Foster agreed. "The word syndicalism merely means unionism," he said. "I think the method and system being pursued by the American Federation of Labor are those best calculated to improve the lot of American workingmen." For his part, Gompers reminded the committee that he had recently been "rather busily engaged in trying to help the Government of the United States and our allied countries to win the war." He might also have mentioned his service to the Department of Justice in identifying radicals. Had his loyalty counted for nothing?[23]

By late 1919, it did not count for much. In Washington, President Wilson had convened a postwar National Industrial Conference to tackle the labor problem. Employers, AFL officials, and representatives of the Wilson administration were to caucus on potential solutions. Gompers floated a resolution affirming the right of "wage earners" to "bargain collectively." The conferees voted it down. "It is hard to believe we are still in America, dealing with the same administration that we were cooperating with and aiding only a year ago," the streetcar union president wrote plaintively to Gompers. "It begins to look as though they were using us, that they only wanted our cooperation in the time of trouble."[24]

As AFL leaders had learned to live with Wilson's regulatory framework, their longtime skepticism of state power had eased. The war labor agencies had demonstrated the benefits of state restraint of employers while not overly impairing AFL unions' autonomy. But with the postwar retrenchment and the government's moves against strikers, old fears flared up. One thing seemed clear: the Espionage and Sedition Acts were dangerous for traditional unions as well as radical ones. "The right of public assemblage is guaranteed by the Constitution of the United States," Gompers told the Senate steel investigating committee. With the Espionage Act in place, that right had been suspended.

Labor conservatives held more complicated views on the emergent state policing power centered in the Justice Department. For decades, unionists waged armed battles with National Guardsmen, fought street fights with policemen, and tried to purge union halls of undercover informants. They fully appreciated the Justice Department's repressive function. During the war years, however, labor conservatives glimpsed its potential utility. When their targets overlapped, labor conservatives and government police could collaborate. While the Espionage Act's suspension of constitutional rights was a problem, the Justice Department's relentless pursuit of radicals was often helpful. As they reconsidered their stance on civil liberties in the aftermath of the war, labor conservatives continued to collaborate with the Bureau of Investigation even as they critiqued the legal basis for its antiradical repression.

Civil Liberties

As soon as the wartime Sedition Act expired in 1919, antiradical groups started lobbying to reenact a peacetime version. The American Legion and the NCF lined up with Attorney General Palmer to back a strict ban on advocating the overthrow of the government or interfering with the work of federal officers. Seventy such bills flooded the 66th Congress and were eventually consolidated into the Graham-Sterling Bill in January 1920.

A new civil liberties movement emerged to fight these laws. Whereas the prewar civil libertarians were isolated and iconoclastic, the new movement was rooted in the network of progressives who were shocked by the war "hysteria." Organized in groups such as the National Civil Liberties Bureau and the National Popular Government League, many of the new civil libertarians had opposed U.S. entry into the war and protested the crackdown on antiwar speech. In a dialogue carried out in intellectual journals and court briefs, people such as professors John Dewey and Felix Frankfurter and Supreme Court justice Oliver Wendell Holmes began to work out the contours of a new theory of civil liberties. The First Amendment should guarantee democracy, they argued, and protect the rights of citizens to voice competing political beliefs. Free-speech rights need not be balanced by obligation to the common good, as older traditions required; nor were all forms of expression equally worthy of energetic defense. Pornographers and anarchists perhaps had a right to expression, but people such as professor Zechariah Chafee did not feel compelled to take on their cases. As the cause of free speech took on new respectability, its new defenders narrowed its scope.[25]

After having defended and even participated in federal repression of the IWW during the war, the AFL now saw the danger posed by the Espionage and Sedition Acts. In the context of the Red Scare, a labor version of civil liberties suddenly appeared that differed from the strain developed by progressive lawyers and activists. In June 1919, delegates to the AFL convention backed a resolution calling for the repeal of "all laws in any way limiting or infringing upon the right of free speech, or a free press, and freedom of assembly, which were enacted as war measures." But they declined to support a number of convention resolutions calling for the pardon of political prisoners convicted under those laws. "There are undoubtedly many instances where the sentences imposed were fully justified," said the resolutions committee. In 1919, an undertone of Americanism and civic duty hummed through the AFL's debates on civil liberties.

A delegate from the Garment Workers chided his comrades that "it is our duty to see that [political prisoners] are not kept in prison. It shows a feeling of vengeance to keep them there, and I do not like to see that in the labor movement."[26] But a Typographical Union member said that the prisoners "defied the law and they defied the people of the United States," and a Musicians' union member agreed, saying the resolutions were "an insult to every man who wore the uniform." The apparent ingratitude of immigrants who criticized the American system vexed several delegates. "You talk about your constitutional rights! What was it that brought some of you people over here?" cried the musician. "You got it into your benighted minds that liberty and license are synonymous terms, but they were [not] and they never will be in the history of the American nation."[27] Delegates invoked a traditional understanding of civil liberties that balanced rights and responsibilities. Wobblies and draft resisters who shirked their duty forfeited the privilege of protected speech.

Gompers seemed to believe in free-speech rights, but he worried that his membership did not. Lucy Robins, a young anarchist dedicated to winning amnesty for imprisoned Wobblies, sought out Gompers to gauge his position in early 1919. "I believe every man must have his liberty," he told her. But he preferred to husband his political capital for other issues. Gompers "would not actively campaign for amnesty," he told Robins, "until she convinced many more union members to back the idea." Gompers let Robins lobby for amnesty at the AFL's 1919 convention but said nothing from the floor as the delegates voted it down, waiting to "speak out for an idea only when it already enjoyed a visible momentum," as historian Ernest Freeberg puts it.[28]

Robins took seriously Gompers's admonition that she organize support for the cause of free speech. She found allies among the New York garment workers' unions, which gave her an office and seed money, and she called herself the "Central Labor Bodies Conference for the Release of the Political Prisoners." Robins wrote to every AFL union local, enclosing a draft amnesty resolution and asking for their support. While numerous locals rejected the measure out of hand, many others grappled with the question, carving out their own position on the matter, some agreeing on amnesty but drawing the line at coming to the aid of those who advocated violent revolution. As union locals produced their own resolutions and petitions, Robins "orchestrated the delivery" to "key figures in state and federal government," thus creating a counterforce to the pressure for a new sedition law as Congress reconsidered these measures.[29]

Robins's campaign gave Gompers political cover. To fight the sedition bill, the AFL and the progressive civil libertarians joined forces. Jackson Ralston, a leading figure in the National Popular Government League, had been Gompers's lawyer in the Buck's Stove case. He brought Judson King, another good-government progressive, to caucus with Gompers and AFL staffers. Together, they coordinated a plan to defeat the bill. Ralston would orchestrate a hearing before the House Rules Committee, at which Gompers would be the leading witness. Ralston would also enlist other groups, especially the farmer lobby, to come out against the proposed act. This would be a potent combination, far more impressive than simply lining up lawyers to criticize the bill. Given the AFL's previous support for sedition laws, Gompers's statement would make waves.

At the hearing in February 1920, the new free-speech coalition made its first appearance. Jackson Ralston and Judson King testified against extending the Espionage Act, and so did Benjamin Marsh from the Farmers' National Council and Archibald Grimké from the NAACP. Gompers declaimed, with characteristic bombast, that the law would "take the reverence out of the hearts and souls for the spirit of America." Echoing Ralston and King, he made little mention of obligation, instead using the absolutist language of progressive civil libertarians: "A free government has no right, in my judgment, to deny the right of citizens" to activities "for the purpose of procuring changes" to the social order.[30]

But Gompers also insisted on labor's loyalty, reminding congressmen of his wartime service and denouncing Bolshevism at length. "Russia stands before our gaze like a flaming torch of warning," he said. To Gompers, it could happen here—and industrial democracy was the best defense. "Were there an American Federation of Labor in Russia there could have been no Bolshevism," he told the Senate in 1919.[31] And he hinted at a new, voluntarist theory of civil liberties that the AFL would refine over the next few years. Better to let radicals have their say, because upright citizens could easily discredit them. "Much as we are disturbed by any so-called radicalism, it is better that it should be permitted and be counteracted by other influences," he said, than "attempt to throttle it." The AFL, he argued, was uniquely positioned to play this role, as it stood on the front line of defense against radicalism, and "we are contending against it more effectually than any other known group of which I am aware."[32] Regular people were better at policing sedition than the state.

The other witnesses did not pick up this argument. Rather, they articulated a straightforward claim that the government had no right to limit political speech and pointed to the abuses by the state during the war. For progressive civil libertarians, the notion that the AFL would squelch radical speech was not particularly appealing. Many progressives would have preferred that radicals had more say in the affairs of the federation as well as the nation. On this point, labor's voluntarist theory of civil liberties diverged from the progressive view. Nevertheless the broad coalition for civil liberties succeeded in quashing the move to extend the Espionage Act.

A few months later, the National Popular Government League organized another volley, this time to critique the creation of a rogue federal police force. Distinct from the problem of sedition laws was the problem of lawless agents in the Department of Justice. Twelve lawyers, including Ralston, Frankfurter, and Frank Walsh, issued a report on the "Illegal Practices by the United States Department of Justice." They described the department's mass arrests of suspected radicals without warrants, violent assaults on prisoners, and distribution of antiradical reports and propaganda to newspapers and vigilant groups. The Bureau of Investigation was out of control, they argued. "It is a fallacy to suppose," they wrote, that "any servant of the people can safely constitute himself their ruler."[33] It was the first comprehensive analysis of the problems inherent in creating a domestic federal police force. Attorney General Palmer stammered badly as he tried to defend himself. His candidacy for the Democratic nomination for president was permanently damaged, but neither the Congress nor the Wilson administration took any action to rein in the Department of Justice. Although the statutory basis of wartime repression was removed, the bureaucratic apparatus remained.

It is notable that the AFL did not join these protests of the Justice Department. The organization's collusion with BI agents may have caused AFL officials to hold their tongues. In practice, the BI rarely attacked AFL unions or strikers; it was the Wobblies and anarchists who attracted its attention. The progressive critique of the Justice Department, lacking a broader coalition, could not gain traction. While the sedition law expired, the new federal police force remained intact, without the legal authority for repression that justified its recruitment. As a result, in the early 1920s the potential for abuse of federal police power was fully realized. American Communists would become the main targets for that abuse.

Soviet Russia and American Communism

While Gompers testified before Congress, denouncing Bolsheviks and their sympathizers, many AFL members cheered the Russian revolutionaries. The International Ladies' Garment Workers' Union expressed admiration for the "first great working class republic," and the Seattle Central Labor Council leafleted the coast with Lenin's speeches.[34] Gompers did not speak for them, and they challenged him at union conventions and in the pages of their periodicals. Radicals and many moderates pushed for recognition of Russia, aid to Russian famine victims, and liberal trade relations to bolster American industry. Pro-Russia advocates could never muster enough votes to compel Gompers to change AFL policy, but they forced Gompers and his allies to defend their anti-Bolshevik stance in convention speeches and the pages of the AFL's magazine. Thus, beginning around 1919, AFL members received a catechism of anticommunism grounded in a critique of conditions in Russia.

"Lenine [*sic*] is as great an enemy of democracy as the Czar," declared the *American Federationist* in 1919.[35] AFL anticommunists found ample evidence of Bolshevik autocracy, beginning with the party's failure to hold a mass election to legitimate its rule. In 1919, the AFL convention voted to urge the United States to withhold recognition of Russia "until such time as a duly constituted popular legislative body elected by the people" voted in a government, and subsequent conventions upheld this test. Arguing that Bolshevik militias prevented popular political expression, John Frey remarked that such elections would likely only occur if "the Communist Party were overthrown"—a tacit endorsement of the American occupation of northern

Russia then underway.[36] "Until the Soviets have repudiated Sovietism and surrendered unconditionally to their deadly enemy, Democracy," American labor must not waver, urged William English Walling.[37]

These criticisms reiterated an emerging anticommunist conventional wisdom and could be heard at the State Department or an American Legion meeting. For the AFL, though, Bolshevik labor policy was just as bad. During the Russian civil war, the Red Army conscripted peasants into "labor detachments" to take the places of soldiers at the front. After the war, factories remained militarized, controlled by foremen "dictators" using techniques of scientific management and crude force. To Gompers, "compulsory labor" coerced by the state was an outrage, as "the workers must work whether they wish to or not and they must accept wages and working conditions fixed arbitrarily by a military government."[38] Worse, trade unions had been eviscerated under the new regime, "transformed into organs of the soviet government." All workers were obliged to join mass unions that lacked the right to strike or elect their own officers, organizations whose members often "do not realize they are members of trade unions and do not even pay dues."[39]

This bill of particulars was essentially accurate—indeed, most of it came from speeches delivered by Lenin and Trotsky. The Bolsheviks thought of participation in industrial organizations as a way for workers to learn to manage themselves and their own factories, a step toward proletarian self-rule; but for Gompers and American union leaders who saw unionization as an end unto itself within liberal democracy, subordination of unions was anathema. Labor conservatives' suspicion of centralized state power made them into early critics of the Bolsheviks' statist regime, and they discerned its potential for authoritarianism well before many liberals and progressives.[40]

Some radicals came to similar conclusions. Many IWW members were alarmed by evidence of Bolshevik autocracy, as historian Kenyon Zimmer has shown; as Wobblies heard reports of centrally controlled factory councils and anarchists exiled or imprisoned, Russia no longer seemed to be the "workers' paradise that it had been pictured in the early elated reports." IWW members voted against joining the Red International in late 1920, despite the urgings of top Bolshevik leaders.[41] Anarchists were similarly dismayed, and their concerns mounted as the Red Army swiftly repressed strikes such as the sailors' mutiny at Kronstadt in 1921. The Kronstadt sailors had been stalwarts of the Bolshevik Revolution, but when they protested the new government's authoritarian measures and demanded civil liberties, Bolshevik leaders bombarded the port and crushed the uprising. Emma Goldman, who watched the Kronstadt crackdown from her hotel in Petrograd, remarked, "'A school for

Communism,' said Lenin in the famous controversy on the functions of the trade unions. Quite right. But an antiquated school where the spirit of the child is fettered and crushed."[42]

Radicals such as Goldman had also criticized the AFL's wartime alliance with the state, especially the no-strike pledge given by Gompers, who had "join[ed] the howl of the military clique."[43] It was ironic that just as American unions grappled with their proper relation to the state, the Russian Revolution suddenly presented a competing scenario of ostensible workers' control. American employers and industrial-relations authorities had warned that "industrial democracy" contained the seeds of a creeping Communism. Now Trotsky styled Russian soviets as "democracy in the matter of production." The AFL executive council scoffed at this "strange perversion of language," which was "entirely typical of the usual bolshevist inversions."[44]

After the revolution, then, AFL officers systematically campaigned at home and abroad against the Bolshevik government, squelching union member drives for Russian recognition and trade relations and pushing European labor leaders to join the International Labor Organization and stay out of the Third International. As they sought to quarantine Bolshevism in Russia and prevent its spread to Europe, they showed little concern that the infection would spread to the United States, where "industrial, social and political freedom" would prevent Bolshevism from "secur[ing] even a footing."[45] From their perches, the Communist movement in the United States seemed negligible.

This was a reasonable estimation. Already fractured and much reduced by clashes over the war, in 1919 American socialists had split again over the Russian Revolution. The fault line roughly followed nativity: most native-born socialists congratulated the Bolsheviks but doubted that Americans were ripe to join a global revolution. Elated foreign-born socialists, mostly Russian and eastern European, clamored to convert the party membership into revolutionary cadres. Their differences were irreconcilable, and the largely native-born Socialist Party leadership moved quickly to sever ties.[46]

At the end of the war, the Socialist Party had about 110,000 members (although it polled much higher in elections). Over the summer of 1919, as the party's left wing prepared to join Lenin's Third International, SP leaders expelled 70,000 party members and branches for radical and syndicalist tendencies. Undaunted, expelled leaders immediately organized two competing American Communist Parties, and about 25,000 people enrolled in one or the other. The new Communists were overwhelmingly eastern European and Russian; less than 10 percent spoke English as a primary language, according to CP estimates.[47] Shortly after the Communists' founding conventions, the Lusk Committee raided New York party offices, and over the next few months, the BI arrested thousands of suspected Communists. Within the year, party membership had dropped by at least half.[48]

Little wonder, then, that AFL leaders were sanguine about the domestic Communist menace. When Gompers worried about "destructionists" who would "rush our people into a mad whirlpool of impractical doctrines," he was thinking of the IWW, not the CP.[49] Wartime raids had decimated but not completely obliterated the Wobblies, and they remained a force in the Pacific Northwest. To AFL leaders, "the nearest thing to bolshevism in our country is the I.W.W. movement with its proposal to control the political, economic, and social affairs of the state."[50] This comparison was not unwarranted. Wobblies tended to approve of the Bolsheviks' militant action, though they balked at their party-centered state bureaucracy. Moreover, many of the native-born Americans moving into the new Communist Party had passed through the IWW, from organizers such as James Cannon and Earl Browder to intellectuals such as John Reed and Louis Fraina. Big Bill Haywood, out on bail while he appealed his criminal syndicalism conviction, joined the CP, and in early 1921 he bolted for Russia.

The Bolsheviks, for their part, had only contempt for the AFL. In his broadside "Letter to American Workmen," published in late 1918 to explain Brest-Litovsk and rebut Russia's critics, Lenin allowed that "it may take a long time before help can come from you, comrades, American Workingmen." But eventually help would come, as "workingmen the world over are breaking with their betrayers, with their Gompers and their Scheidemanns."[51] It was the first salvo in a long stream of invective issued from Moscow and St. Petersburg toward the AFL. Soon, however, Lenin shifted from anticipating insurgency in the AFL to encouraging it. For Gompers, this was an alarming change. Suddenly, the AFL's vanquished enemies had a new patron, Bolshevik Russia, and that patron had a large treasury and a mighty army.

In November 1920, Gompers told the members of the AFL executive council that the *Washington Post* was reporting that "the command has gone forth from the headquarters of the soviets of the world that the first thing necessary to be done is the destruction and disintegration of the American Federation of Labor." Whether the Bolsheviks intended that AFL leaders be "actually, physically destroyed" remained unknown, he said.[52] For the past five years, Gompers had fretted that enemies plotted to undermine the AFL. Socialists, German spies, Wobblies—he saw schemers everywhere. In this case, he was right again. Lenin had issued a call to American Communists to join AFL unions, agitate for change, and ultimately depose conservative and reformist leaders—by stealth and trickery, if necessary.

Bolshevik leaders, caught by surprise (like most people) by the Russian Revolution, had banked on a wave of revolutions sweeping Europe in the aftermath of the war to fortify Russia's borders with a bulwark of new socialist states. Surveying the wreckage of these uprisings in 1920, they resigned themselves to sustaining socialism in one country, and altered their directives to Western Communist Parties accordingly. Sectarianism and secrecy had been the Bolsheviks' trademarks. To survive under czarist repression after the 1905 Russian Revolution, the party scrupulously policed its own members, cultivating cells of seasoned and disciplined revolutionaries prepared to seize leadership when unrest rumbled.

The Bolsheviks' unexpected success elevated this tactic into dogma for radicals around the world, who restyled themselves "professional revolutionaries" responsible for directing the masses once the uprising began. For many new American Communists, politically marginal and often socially isolated, embracing the Bolshevik model made a virtue of these seeming deficiencies. The party "cannot afford to attempt to get 'contact with the masses' at the expense of sacrificing Communist principles and tactics," argued Communists concentrated in the foreign-language bloc. Political repression hastened their dive into underground organizing, and party members adopted pseudonyms, shredded documents, and winnowed out dilettantes. An opposing faction, led by native-born Charles Ruthenburg, insisted that the CP should also "participate in the every day struggles of the workers and by such participation inject its principles into these struggles."[53] How, they asked, could the CP possibly build a workers' revolution without any contact with workers?

In the summer of 1920, party leaders in Moscow settled the debate. In his pamphlet *Left-wing Communism, an Infantile Disorder*, Lenin instructed Communists to work "wherever the masses are to be found," and in Western countries that meant parties and unions. As the United States lacked a mass workers' party, Americans had to focus on unions. However much Communists might prefer to form their own pure and revolutionary workers' organizations, they were obliged to work with "the human material bequeathed to us by capitalism," no matter how "narrow-minded, selfish, unfeeling, covetous, pettybourgeois 'labour aristocracy,' imperialistically-minded, and bribed and corrupted by materialism" the unions might be.[54] Lenin thus resurrected the old socialist device known as "boring from within," or working to change an organization from the inside. Take on the AFL leadership, he urged: "The struggle against the Gomperses" must be waged "ruthlessly," "until all the incorrigible leaders of opportunism and social-chauvinism have been completely discredited and driven out of the trade unions." In other words, the tiny American Communist Party could grow by accreting the membership of the AFL.

This was a bitter prospect for many new Communists, especially former Wobblies who were accustomed to deriding unions from the outside, not working to change them from the inside. In Moscow, they protested to the Profintern, the agency created by the Communist International to direct international strategy within the trade unions. Bill Haywood "drew a dark picture of the corruption of the craft unions in the American Federation of Labour" and insisted that these "job trusts" could never be revolutionized. Solomon Lozovsky, head of the Profintern, patiently expatiated: "But what do you think we mean by a union?" he asked. "Is it the leaders, the bureaucracy, the house, the cashbox, the books, the tickets? Or, when we speak of a union, do we mean the millions of organised workers, constituting it? What do you wish to destroy? The form or something else?" Communists were obliged to work within the world as it was; and as things stood, the trade unions were the biggest working-class organizations in the United States. It was easier to start working within an existing group than to try to mobilize a new one.[55]

William Z. Foster was thinking the same thing. Unemployed after the defeat of the steel strike, Foster retreated to think through his next steps. The wartime strikes, despite their ultimate defeat, had convinced him that determined and wily militants could work inside the creaky old unions to build new ones. He reflected that "a mere handful of syndicalists" had managed to commandeer the AFL to run strikes involving "over half a million workers — native and foreign born, Negroes and whites, skilled and unskilled, women and youth," in the toughest industries in the country, despite the "crassest incompetency, indifference, and downright sabotage of the AF of L leadership."[56] It was possible, he believed, to "revolutionize the AFL," but it would require a brigade of disciplined radicals like himself, fanned out through the unions and working systematically.

Foster set up the structure for such an organization, calling it the Trade Union Educational League (TUEL), in late 1920. He was unaware that Lenin had just issued a call for American Communists to follow exactly this strategy until an old friend, Earl Browder, came to see him. Foster had supported the Bolshevik Revolution but, busy with union organizing, paid little attention to the organization of the American Communist Party, which was enamored with Wobbly separatism. American Communists had mocked Foster's efforts to organize for the AFL and dismissed the big strikes as misguided reformism. Now, as Browder explained, the party's strategy would be to organize militant cadres within AFL unions. He urged Foster to join the party and help lead the effort. Foster traveled to Russia in the spring of 1921 and spent several months in Moscow, seeing the revolution for himself. By the end of the summer, Foster had agreed to affiliate his Trade Union Educational League to the Comintern.

For labor anticommunists, this was alarming news. William Z. Foster was the best organizer in America. And Lenin was no wild-eyed dreamer, but a head of state with an army and a treasury. Just as the Red Scare was subsiding and popular concern about Communism ebbed, American union leaders faced a new red siege. The expiration of the Espionage Act meant that no federal law impeded Communist organizing. Without a federal statute, the Bureau of Investigation had no authority to police Communists. Luckily for the AFL, the bureau did it anyway.

Labor conservatives emerged from the war years with a political program grounded in three principles: antistatism, Americanism, and antiradicalism. Since the state was the most powerful antiradical agency, these principles were bound to be in tension. In the early 1920s, Communist organizing and BI repression forced labor conservatives to confront the contradictions between their fear of state power and fervent desire to be free of radical challengers.

CHAPTER FIVE

Secrecy and Surveillance

Anticommunism and the Bureau of Investigation

Official Washington was laughing at Samuel Gompers. His stature in the nation's capital, so dizzyingly elevated during the war, when President Wilson solicited his advice on matters foreign and domestic, had plunged. Republicans swept the 1920 elections, sending Ohio banker Warren G. Harding to the White House. A humiliating skit at a Gridiron Club dinner showed Gompers's reduced circumstance. A seer, gazing into a crystal ball, divined Gompers returning the White House key to Harding. Harding sent it back with a note: "May I not, my dear Mr. Gompers, ask you to keep this key as souvenir. I have changed the lock."[1]

The AFL's demotion was underlined in late July 1921. Gompers got a phone call from Harry M. Daugherty, the new attorney general, inviting him to an urgent meeting at the Justice Department. Gompers caught a cab and arrived at Daugherty's office within twenty minutes. Daugherty greeted him "cordially" then told Gompers that he intended to name detective William J. Burns to head the Bureau of Investigation, because "he knew Burns and thought well of him." "It would be a public scandal and would bring discredit to the department and to the Government of the United States if any such man was appointed to such a post," Gompers retorted. Burns was a sworn enemy and strikebreaker who had once called Gompers a "bunko man who has been deceiving his followers for years."[2] To even consider appointing Burns to head the BI was an open insult from the new administration.

But Gompers needed Burns and the BI. As it turned out, Burns had been keeping an eye on the international Communist movement. William Z. Foster was on his way back from Moscow, and his Trade Union Educational League was about to throw the American labor movement into new turmoil. Foster's

Communist members worked hard to follow Lenin's instructions and infiltrate AFL unions, which drove federation leaders mad and sparked a campaign to purge Communist organizers. Figuring out exactly who was a Communist and who was merely a radical unionist was not easy, though, especially as the TUEL embraced popular labor-reform issues. By collaborating with the BI, AFL leaders could corroborate their suspicions.

In the early 1920s, labor anticommunism matured from antipathy to ideology. Conservative labor leaders bound their critique of Soviet Russia to attacks on domestic Communist radicals, and, increasingly, they collaborated with a new network of antiradical crusaders outside of the labor movement. But even at the height of anticommunist purges, labor anticommunists took care to substantiate their attacks on Communist organizers. Under William J. Burns, the Bureau of Investigation showed less care in investigating radicals, often indiscriminately labeling strikers and protestors as Reds. Burns operated the bureau as an extension of his private detective agency, deploying federal agents on cases with dubious legality. During Burns's tenure, civil libertarians became increasingly aware that political freedom could be imperiled by unregulated federal police.

The AFL under Siege

Everything was going wrong for Gompers in the summer of 1921. The Republican electoral sweep and postwar retrenchment the previous November had pushed labor back to the sidelines. President Harding named William Howard Taft, a longtime AFL adversary, to be chief justice of the U.S. Supreme Court. The Taft Supreme Court handed down a series of decisions rolling back Wilson-era legislative gains, including union immunity from antitrust prosecution. Taft's court invalidated the Clayton Act's labor provisions, and the court also struck down state laws forbidding labor injunctions. Alert to the changing climate, employers across the country lined up for a massive open-shop onslaught. Between 1920 and 1923, AFL membership fell from 4 million to less than 3 million, a 25 percent decline that wiped out most of the wartime membership increase.[3]

At the 1921 AFL convention in June, a bloc of unions fed up with Gompers's leadership caucused to challenge him for the federation presidency. Since the armistice, the AFL's steadfast conservatism seemed increasingly antiquated to many unionists, and so did Gompers. As his opponents charged, "he is reactionary and he is slipping."[4] An early sign of restiveness came in 1920, when the AFL convention overwhelmingly overrode the executive council's recommendation to endorse the railroad unions' Plumb Plan, which called for federal ownership of the railroads. Frustration also mounted with the AFL's hostility toward state-provided health insurance and unemployment insurance. And a sizeable bloc of unions credited the United Mine Workers' argument that recognizing Russia would open trade relations and relieve the postwar U.S. recession.[5] The Mineworkers and the Machinists, whose membership included sizeable socialist contingents, led the effort to unseat Gompers, with Mineworker president John L. Lewis at the top of the ticket. They also called for nationalizing the railroads and mines, national health and unemployment insurance, and old-age pensions. It was a bold challenge to Gompers's leadership, especially since the powerful Carpenters swung their support to the insurgent ticket.

Yet despite this show of force, Gompers trounced his opponents by a two-to-one margin. Gompers won in part because he and his allies controlled the resolutions committee. But the vote also showed the abiding weakness of progressives in the federation and within even the most progressive unions. Gompers and other labor conservatives certainly used parliamentary maneuvers to maintain power, but they were consistently reelected by votes of the membership. Many historians have echoed William Z. Foster by casting labor conservatives as "misleaders of labor." But "no one," as Eric Foner has commented, "has satisfactorily explained how and why a presumably militant rank and file constantly chooses moderate 'misleaders' to represent it."[6] AFL members stuck with the conservative leaders and policies they had chosen for decades. Nevertheless, dissent within the ranks was obvious.[7]

Burns's Bureau of Investigation

Having survived a rebuke from his members, Gompers was blindsided by President Harding. Over Gompers's protests, Harding and Attorney General Daugherty announced the appointment of William J. Burns to the directorship of the Bureau of Investigation, saying that Burns was "as high-class a man as could be secured" to head the department.[8] To many observers, though, neither Daugherty nor Burns had distinguished themselves as "high-class" men. Harry M. Daugherty was a charter member of the "Ohio Gang," President Warren G. Harding's clique of friends. A veteran Republican political fixer, Daugherty learned his craft in the hardball Ohio arena dominated by Mark Hanna in the 1890s. After losing his own bids for the Ohio governorship and a congressional seat, Daugherty turned to lobbying for utilities companies and managing other people's political campaigns. Harding's candidacy was his greatest achievement. Daugherty recruited Harding, engineered his nomination at the Republican convention in 1920 from a suite in a Chicago hotel, and ran Harding's campaign operation. After his lopsided victory, Harding offered Daugherty any cabinet position he liked. Daugherty picked the attorney generalship.

Daugherty's reputation as a partisan operative discomfited even loyal Republicans. "You're not qualified, Harry, to be Attorney General," one of his old friends told him; "you've been a lobbying lawyer."[9] But Daugherty took the job, and he surrounded himself with cronies who searched the Justice Department for spoils. While they met nightly in a K Street house to play poker and drink, Daugherty's friends sold civil service jobs, trafficked in newly illegal liquor, and offered bootleggers and other nervous criminals immunity from Justice Department prosecution in exchange for payoffs. It was unseemly, even for Washington.

William J. Burns fit right in. Burns got his start as a detective in Columbus, Ohio, in the 1870s, and he and Daugherty became friends while Daugherty sat in the Columbus statehouse during the 1890s. After a long stint with the U.S. Secret Service, Burns launched his own detective agency in 1909, trading on a reputation for courage and integrity that he cultivated with lavish attention to Hearst newspaper reporters. Reputation mattered most in the crowded detective field; anyone could hang up a shingle as a sleuth, and detective agencies proliferated in the peculiarly American system that left crime control mostly to spotty municipal authorities with little federal intrusion. Detective agencies such as the Pinkertons descended like crows when a big crime occurred, angling for a piece of the investigation from overtaxed local police. As a freelancer, Burns used his press savvy to grab the limelight and the business in big cases such as the Leo Frank murder trial in Atlanta in 1915 and the Wall Street bombing in September 1920. He also built up a substantial business in labor espionage, supplying undercover agents to employers to help them identify union agitators and subvert strikes.[10]

Burns made his name, though, busting AFL union leaders after the 1910 *Los Angeles Times* bombing. When the *Times* printing plant exploded, killing twenty-one pressmen and passers-by, suspicion immediately fell on the city's unions, who had recently endured a bitter open-shop campaign directed by the city's leading businessmen and promoted by the *Times*. Burns rushed to Los Angeles to get the *Times* bombing job and, over six months, painstakingly built his case. He then arrested John McNamara, head of the Structural Bridge and Iron Workers, and his brother James at union headquarters in Indianapolis, where he also found bomb timers and letters discussing previous dyna-

William J. Burns, between
1910 and 1920. Library
of Congress, Prints and
Photographs Division.

mitings. Burns's arrests were illegal—he seized the McNamaras and shipped them off to California before extradition had been approved.[11]

The AFL erupted in fury, with Gompers leading the defense. It was a frame-up, he thundered. Over the next year Gompers and the AFL executive council led national labor protests of the McNamara arrests, screening a special film defending the brothers and raising funds with AFL-issued commemorative coins to fund Clarence Darrow's fees for the defense. Burns was a particular target of their outrage. At a speech in Los Angeles, Gompers roared, "After this trial is over we will attend to Mr. Burns. We haven't finished with him yet." While Gompers spoke, a rumbling noise came from the front of the hall, startling the audience. Gompers joked, "They want to know if there was any dynamite in my satchel. I told them there was not—the last time I looked in it."[12] His blithe humor evaporated when in the middle of their trial the McNamaras suddenly confessed to the bombings.

"We had every cause to accept their innocence as fact," Gompers pleaded, but Burns seized the upper hand.[13] "Mr. Gompers knew all the time that the prisoners were guilty," he told reporters. Pressing the attack against Gompers gave Burns personal satisfaction and professional advantage. "Gompers is unfit to be at the head of organized labor," Burns said. "I am going to continue my fight against him until the public comes to recognize what I know."[14] Burns kept the issue in the papers, insisting that Gompers and other AFL leaders were at least aware of the McNamaras' guilt and the Bridge and Iron Workers' proclivity for dynamite. Indictments would soon follow, Burns implied, though he never had the evidence for a criminal case against Gompers.

Ten years had passed since the debacle of the *Times* bombing. Gompers and the AFL had built a close working relationship with the Justice Department and the BI in Wilson's administration. Since then, their contacts had declined. The expiration of the Espionage Act left little statutory authority for the Justice Department to track radical political movements. Being a Communist or an anarchist did not violate federal law. The Immigration Act of 1920 had authorized the Labor Department to deport radical enemy aliens who had already been convicted under the wartime Espionage Act, but the law did not apply to native-born radicals. The amnesty campaign tried to prevent these deportations, thwarting what little federal authority remained. The federal criminal code set a high bar for prosecuting seditious or treasonable conspiracy against the state, and the often inept American Communist movement did not manifest "a specific and definite agreement" to overthrow the government, as a Justice Department lawyer explained. The BI had no business investigating people who simply held radical ideas.[15]

Nevertheless, the antiradical investigating team was still in place at the BI, headed by twenty-four-year-old J. Edgar Hoover. In 1917 Hoover had started out in the Justice Department working for the War Emergency Division, under Rintelen prosecutor John Lord O'Brian. Hoover had just graduated from law school. A short stint as a cataloguer at the Library of Congress had taught him how to manage masses of data. Hoover's assiduous recordkeeping impressed Palmer, who promoted him to head a new Radical Division of the BI in the summer of 1919. The Radical Division maintained a vast bank of reports and card files on Communists, anarchists, and other suspected insurgents to support the deportation of foreign-born radicals. The Department of Labor's Immigration Bureau had jurisdiction over deportations, so the BI used its information to goad immigration agents and local police into action. Information sharing was central to the Radical Division's work from the start.[16]

Hoover escaped the censure that A. Mitchell Palmer incurred for the Justice Department's misconduct during the Red Scare. He was junior enough to avoid public notice, but well-known within the Justice Department as a skilled and sophisticated manager. He had the good sense to rename the Radical Division; in 1920, its name became the General Intelligence Division. Hoover and the Justice Department red hunters carried on with their recordkeeping, even as their budget dried up. When Burns came on, he named Hoover as his deputy.[17]

Burns was eager to put Hoover's information to work. Although he had turned the presidency of the William J. Burns Detective Agency over to his son Raymond, Burns maintained close ties with his former clients. Having worked with the Bureau of Investigation during the war to chase slackers and radicals, he understood how sharing information helped federal and private detectives identify and harass agitators. Documents purloined by the Wobblies showed that when the Burns Detective Agency got an account to help Arizona copper companies fight an IWW campaign, BI Director Burns detailed a BI agent to the case and consulted regularly on it.[18] The appointment of a private detective as head of the BI illustrated the porous boundary between state and private authority, a permeability Burns was glad to perpetuate.

In the past, the AFL had been in the information-sharing loop, although the pace of intelligence exchange slowed dramatically after the war's end. Now, Lenin's alarming threats suggested that the AFL needed the BI more than ever. But the personal rancor between Gompers and Burns, as well as Burns's record as a labor spy, made cooperation awkward. In this situation, the AFL's old ally Ralph Easley stepped up to help. Easley's National Civic Federation had brokered relationships between corporate and government leaders and union officials, especially Gompers, in the past.

Immediately upon Burns's appointment, Easley reached out to congratulate him and set up a meeting. Easley ventured a hope that Burns would retain J. Edgar Hoover, as "he has no equal," and he advised Burns that the prominent radical hunter Archibald Stevenson, formerly of the Lusk Committee, was on the NCF staff. Signaling that the NCF had the interest and capacity to collaborate with the BI, Easley put himself forward as a proxy for the union leaders listed on his letterhead. Burns responded warmly. "Drop in," Burns encouraged Easley, and they could go over "some very interesting work we have in mind."[19] A frost remained between the BI and the AFL, but a backdoor connection had been established. Gompers no longer volunteered tips and intelligence to the BI, directly or through Easley. But on his behalf Easley solicited and received valuable material from BI files on Communist organizers and their plans.

Fighting Communists

William Z. Foster and his Trade Union Educational League obsessed the AFL and the BI alike. Foster's Communist organizers operated differently than other labor radicals. The TUEL adopted the old socialist tactic of "boring from within," but with a twist: they tried to keep their Communist allegiances secret. Whereas socialist borers used traditional political strategies such as making speeches and writing pamphlets, Communists dissembled, using proxy issues and attempting to take over unions by subterfuge. This dissimulation was singularly unsuccessful (in part because it was never secret — Lenin had published the plan in *Left-wing Communism*), and always more aspired to than accomplished. But it incensed union officials.[20]

When he came back from Russia, Foster got to work recruiting militant members of AFL unions. The TUEL's formal agenda was to "amalgamate" existing craft unions within industries such as railroads or construction into single, industry-wide unions uniting skilled and unskilled workers; to stir up dissenters within AFL unions to oppose and depose elected officials; and to mobilize newly active unionists into mass strikes and a labor party. This program attacked AFL unions head on, as Foster explained: the TUEL aimed to "revamp and remodel from top to bottom their theories, tactics, structure and leadership" by "campaigning against the reactionaries, incompetents, and crooks" at the head of AFL unions, "striving to replace them with militants."[21]

Worse for Gompers, the TUEL's proposals immediately attracted a slew of supporters. The ideas of amalgamation and a labor party were popular among radicals and many moderate unionists alike, who had seen the costs of dividing workers among unions and parties in the broken strikes and electoral reverses of 1919 and 1920. Foster's old allies in Chicago hosted a conference on amalgamation in May 1922 to spread the word, and over the next year and a half, thousands of local unions and labor councils endorsed amalgamation — according to historian James R. Barrett, "representing perhaps half of organized labor in the United States."[22] Chicago unionists also spearheaded a drive to resuscitate the Farmer-Labor Party movement, while the railroad brotherhoods caucused with the Socialist Party to create the Conference for Progressive Political Action — not a third party, but the foundation for a unionist electoral bloc. Foster knew how to organize within AFL unions better than anyone, and he quickly assembled diverse clusters of disgruntled members into a loose coalition.

As the TUEL stepped up its activity, the Civic Federation turned to the BI for help. In March 1922, Easley asked Burns "if the Department would not get the [*sic*] inside of the Foster organization in Chicago and let us have any information that we could send on to these labor men," including "all the names" of TUEL supporters to "enable the unions to kick them out." Burns readily agreed. He had already assigned agents to tail Foster and join the Communist Party, and he told Easley, "I think it is a wonderful idea and we will be delighted to help out."[23] Over the next six months, Easley corresponded regularly with Burns and J. Edgar Hoover, sharing gossip and reports. Easley advised Hoover that the Department of Labor was "full of 'Reds,'" and urged Hoover to "do something to expose" them.[24] Burns sent along an informant's report on a TUEL meeting in Chicago, including names of TUEL organizers, and intelligence on philanthropic Russian relief efforts.[25] Easley passed the material on to union officers to use as they saw fit. Teamsters president Daniel Tobin printed articles based on the TUEL material in the union magazine, intending "to get this information to our membership before any of those agents or apostles of either Foster or Lenine [*sic*] get on the inside of our organization."[26]

Union officials also solicited information on specific questions. Chester Wright, head of the AFL's Information and Publicity Service, asked Easley to find out who was orchestrating a campaign to get city central labor councils to publicly favor U.S. recognition of the Soviet government.[27] With the NCF as proxy, union leaders could maintain an arms-length relationship with the Burns-era BI. Easley was only one of many people given access to BI files. Hoover cultivated leaders of other patriotic groups such as Richard Whitney of the American Defense Society, doling out documents to seed stories in the press. For a period in 1922, Whitney had his own desk in Hoover's office.[28]

This collaboration with union leaders did not make Justice Department officials friendly to unions, especially striking unions. The BI continued to treat strikes as seditious, and big strikes in mining and the railroads shook the country in 1922. Soft prices and overproduction had plagued midwestern bituminous coalfields since the war. Six hundred thousand coal miners walked out in April 1922. Miners stayed out all summer as coal shortages threatened, and Harding threatened to send the army to reopen the mines. UMW president Lewis called his bluff, and Harding backed down, allowing Lewis to declare victory when the UMW and the coal operators cut a deal in early August 1922.[29]

Just as the miners' strike wound down, trouble flared on the railroads. While members of the running trades—conductors, engineers, and other workers operating trains—had wrested concessions from the railroads, the shop-craft workers who repaired and maintained train cars and track saw their work eroding as the railroads contracted out jobs to nonunion workers. On July 1, 400,000 shop-craft workers struck with immediate effect; railroads began curtailing and canceling service right away. Harding pleaded for a quick resolution, while the railroad executives stood firm, believing that strikers' resolve was waning.[30]

William Z. Foster had nothing to do with starting the big strikes, but he hurried to the picket lines to sign up activists. Among the Mineworkers, frustration with Lewis's heavy-handed leadership built over the summer. TUEL organizers helped knit Lewis's dispersed opponents into a coherent opposition group demanding direct election of union officials, shorter working hours, and reinstatement of radicals expelled from the union by Lewis. They had less success recruiting shop-craft workers but managed to attract hundreds of frustrated strikers to a national conference on union amalgamation in late 1922.[31]

Throughout both strikes, TUEL organizers leafleted workers with broadsides attacking union leadership and urging solidarity. These leaflets attracted less attention from strikers than from BI agents, who reported to headquarters that Foster's TUEL "was gaining a foothold among all the radical labor unions in this part of the country."[32] This imputation of radicalism frustrated, and endangered, unionists. After "one of Mr. Daugherty's sleuths" discovered "wholesale quantities of communist literature and propaganda and detailed plans for sabotage attacks," the *Locomotive Engineers' Journal* remarked, "the average reader of the morning's news doubtless execrated the strikers as criminals, dangerous radicals, and conspirers." Meanwhile, an Illinois judge authorized local police to deputize civilians to put down the strike and prevent the spread of "Communism, Bolshevism, and anarchy."[33] Strikers were accustomed to accusations of Communism, but, in their efforts to distance themselves from the radical element, the TUEL's literature did not help.

For the BI, it was hard to distinguish between Communist hyperbole and fact. Talking among themselves, union leaders often took a more measured view of the Communists' penetration of AFL unions. "In one or two places they have had some success," John Frey remarked in 1923, "but I do not feel that the Reds have made any serious breach in our organization."[34] AFL leaders insisted that "those who dream of destroying" the AFL and "substituting for it an organization controlled by an agent of Moscow have forgotten that American workers will belong to no organization in which they can not have a vote, that they will tolerate dictation from nobody."[35] Still, the Communists' effrontery was galling.

Foster's caginess about his Communist ties infuriated AFL leaders. Foster dissembled in part to defer the discussion of Communism with his recruits. Following Lenin, he wanted to remake AFL unions into fighting forces, seasoning workers for struggle through mass strikes and militant action, and then, after workers had tasted proletarian power, introduce them to Communist ideas. Moreover, police harassment helped convince American Communists to operate secretly whenever possible. The extent of Communist spycraft is striking. Members "adopted aliases, wrote to each other in code, and held secret meetings."[36] To encode their communications, party leaders used a blank postal order form as a key, with each letter represented as a fraction, the numerator indicating the line on the order form and the denominator being the position of a letter in a line.[37]

Max Eastman, a progressive in the 1920s, found this cloak-and-dagger culture silly and counterproductive, arguing that Communists had "formed an elaborately conspiratorial organization excellently adapted to promote treasonable and seditious enterprises, although they have no such enterprises afoot." (To his mind, it was "not so much the ruthlessness of the American capitalists, as the romanticism of the American Communists, which accounts for their being underground.")[38] Sam Darcy, a Communist Party leader, similarly recalled that "there was a great pull towards doing everything secretly. Not that in my concept we did anything illegally but to do it in a conspiratorial fashion." To Darcy, "it was ridiculous! Even as young as I was, I felt it was unreal, the phoniness." This debate raged until April 1923, when the Comintern ordered the underground party to disband.[39] William Z. Foster publicly announced his membership in the Communist Party that spring, right after his acquittal in the Bridgman trial, where he had vehemently and falsely denied any Communist ties, and other labor Communists such as William Dunne followed suit.

Red-Baiting

AFL leaders took care to investigate and substantiate charges of Communism. Simply voicing pro-Bolshevik sentiment or advocating union amalgamation did not get union members expelled. Federation officials tried to determine whether suspected Communists actually were Communists, and they proceeded with expulsion only after confirming party membership or allegiance. In Detroit, Seattle, and other cities, AFL staffers interviewed local unionists and questioned suspected Communists to figure out whether its members had merely embraced radical ideas or actually allied with the Communist

Party. As an AFL official later explained, "Our officers in the National unions and in the local unions are constantly watching for them, and where we find that they are avowed Communists, engaged in trying to commit the organization to Communism, charges are filed and they are given a trial, and if the evidence is strong enough, they are found guilty and expelled."[40]

These proceedings generally involved an inquiry led by a union committee or governing board to substantiate charges of Communism. If members were found to be Communist, they were ordered out of the union, and if local union leadership balked, the local's charter could be revoked by the international union. In the Carpenters union, for example, where a TUEL faction had gained a foothold in Detroit, a committee dispatched by the national union to investigate discovered "bedlam," and a union riven by charges of "deception, intrigue, dishonesty, obstinacy, trickery, playing politics, and so forth." The Detroit local was directed to expel the lead TUEL activist or else lose its union charter.[41]

Unionists and central labor councils found to be merely radical were simply ordered to forswear "extremism" and permitted to remain in the federation. It is notable that unionists rarely protested their expulsions as unfounded. By and large, the AFL accurately identified actual Communists.

This probative approach generally prevailed, with a glaring exception: the Mine Workers' 1924 pamphlet "Attempts by Communists to Seize the Labor Movement." This document rivaled the most sophisticated examples of "red web" journalism to show "the scope and purport of the hostile and inimical movement" attacking the UMWA and the nation. Behind the pamphlet was an ignoble motive, though. The UMWA hoped to blame Communists for instigating a riot at a southern Illinois mine. Facing public obloquy for the Herrin Massacre, as the episode was known, the UMWA tried to deflect attention away from its members and onto the Communist Party.

It was a tough sell. Herrin lay in the heart of "Little Egypt," a region in southern Illinois rich with bituminous coal and solidly under UMWA control. William Lester, a Cleveland engineer, bought a small strip mine in Williamson County, near Herrin, in 1921, just months before the UMWA launched a nationwide strike in April 1922. Like other Little Egypt mine owners, Lester operated union before the walkout, and he got special permission from the UWMA to continue mining during the strike, as long as he made no effort to load and sell the coal. But strike-inflated coal prices tempted Lester. In June 1922, Lester fired his UMWA miners and spirited a crew of mine guards, steamshovel operators, and trainmen into the county.

His temerity astonished the citizenry. Thirty thousand UMWA members lived in the surrounding area; a UMWA officer represented the region in the state senate; and local sentiment strongly favored the union. Williamson County's storied history of murderous family feuds and violent strikes had earned it the nickname "Bloody Williamson." On June 16, Lester shipped a carload of coal out. Four days later, the UMWA held a mass meeting in town, where members read a telegram from John L. Lewis advising that the local was "justified in treating this crowd as an outlaw organization." The next afternoon, a mob armed with rifles surrounded the mine.[42]

Frantic, the mine superintendent phoned for help. But the county sheriff (a member of the UMWA) and his deputies had suddenly disappeared, and the local official of the Illinois National Guard shrank from deploying guardsmen to protect the mine. While town officials dithered, the shooting started. The mine superintendent, deputy superintendent, and strikebreakers hid under empty coal cars overnight and traded gunfire as the crowd of unionists shot up mine outbuildings and blew up the water tower. Finally, after daybreak, the superintendent and staff surrendered. The mob marched the captives toward town, taunting and pistol-whipping them. Those who survived were marched to a schoolyard, where they were forced to crawl on hands and knees, and then to a cemetery, where they were tortured and finally killed. Twenty-two men died, including three union miners.

Public outrage exploded across the country. From newspaper editorial pages to the floor of Congress, denunciations condemned the Herrin Massacre. On the day of the killings, William J. Burns cabled his St. Louis office, detailing an agent to Herrin to investigate and "ascertain if any radicals are responsible for this action." Agent Charles Fisher proceeded to Herrin, where he visited "pool rooms, soft drink parlors, and questionable houses" in search of leads. He found the locals to be taciturn, unwilling to discuss the incident except to say, "the radicals had nothing to do with the troubles at the strip mine." On the other hand, "all expressed themselves as being sure that the larger proportion of those who participated in the rioting came from other towns." Fisher remarked, "This statement Agent is inclined to doubt."[43]

Fisher's other interviews produced much the same information. An injured strikebreaker recalling the attack said that "there didn't seem to be anyone in particular acting as the leader, everyone seemed to be doing as they pleased," but in any case he saw no evidence of radical involvement. The local UMWA officials insisted that while they did not know anyone in the mob, they were certain no radicals were involved. On the question of who did march on the mines, Fisher learned little, as everyone from the police force to the store-keepers were "deaf, dumb, and blind during this trouble."[44] The BI concluded that the Herrin Massacre was a strictly local affair.

So did the state's attorney, who stepped in after the Williamson County coroner's jury found that the coal company, not the mob, was responsible for the deaths of the strikebreakers and mine officials. As demands for prosecutions poured in from President Harding and Army general John Pershing, the UMWA voted a special assessment on its membership to fund the defense, while the Illinois Chamber of Commerce issued a fundraising appeal to subsidize the prosecution. Stung by the outcry, the county convened a special grand jury that indicted 214 local men for murder, riot, and conspiracy. That November, five of the indicted men stood trial for murder. "There is no tinge of 'red' about them. They are not of the bolshevik persuasion," a *Chicago Tribune* reporter wrote. "They are not 'wild, ignorant foreigners.'"[45] After a month-long trial, the jury took a day of deliberations to acquit all defendants. In April 1923, another jury acquitted seven more miners. Exasperated, the state's attorney dismissed all the remaining indictments. Throughout, the UMWA stoutly defended its members. "We shall leave nothing undone" to fight for "the lives and freedom of innocent men," declared Illinois UMWA president Frank Farrington.[46]

So it came as a surprise when John L. Lewis suddenly blamed the Herrin Massacre on the Communists. At the UMWA convention in May 1923, Lewis said that "in every instance where there has been any disorder or disturbance of the public peace in the mining regions there has been there secretly men of this type," aiming to "prejudice and inflame the minds of men and create disorder." The UMWA had learned that "prior to the Herrin riots there were nineteen organizers of the Communist party of America stirring up hatred and fomenting discord and preaching violence in that coal field for more than thirty days before the trouble occurred."[47]

Within a few months, the *United Mine Workers Journal* laid out the case. In a series of six articles, the UMWA offered an "expose of the Communist revolutionary movement in America" and the "fight which the miners' union is waging to stamp it out." The *Journal* described the structure of the American Communist Party, the strategy of the TUEL, and the "interlocking arrangement" uniting fifty-two red agents in forty-five organizations from the ACLU to the Federated Press. Moscow gold, $1.1 million worth, funded the whole campaign. And although the UMWA "has been mercilessly attacked and condemned for the Herrin Massacre," the *Journal* insisted that, "in fact, the miners' union was in no manner responsible for what took place. This revolting, inexcusable, terrible crime was fomented, promoted, and caused solely by the Communists."[48]

According to the UMWA, sixty-seven Herrin mineworkers were Lithuanian Communists who formed a "nuclei" in Herrin, "holding its meetings secretly in the Lithuanian language, but taking its instructions from the agents" of the Communist Party in Chicago. "Quietly and stealthily they worked among the idle miners at Herrin, preaching insurrection and armed attack." Meanwhile Communist organizers agitated among striking miners around the country, hoping to organize a great "armed insurrection, having for its purpose the establishment of a Bolshevik regime or dictatorship in this country."[49] When Lewis's telegram arrived, the Communists struck, "shrewdly twist[ing]" his words into a call to arms. The Herrin Massacre was a cautionary tale showing what Communist stealth could accomplish: "This is one occasion when labor and the employer might very well join hands and fight together instead of fighting each other," the series concluded.[50]

Coal operators scoffed. John C. Brydon, president of the National Coal Association, said that "it was no Lithuanian, it was John L. Lewis" who instigated the massacre. The United States Coal Commission agreed, saying that "it is true that Communists have made efforts to establish organizations in that county," but "there is no evidence that this had any relation to this lamentable and horrible occurrence."[51] So did the *Wall Street Journal*, calling the claims "propaganda" and an attempt to "get out from under the burden of reproach the union bears" for the episode.[52] Few took the UMWA's charges seriously. After all, no one from the prosecution or the defense—or the union, for that matter—had mentioned any Lithuanian Communists before. It was hard to believe that Williamson County had closed ranks around foreign-born revolutionaries.

Nevertheless, the UMWA was onto something. Ellis Searles, editor of the UMWA journal and Lewis's liaison to armchair antiradicals, wrote the series of articles. As Searles later explained in a congressional hearing, he undertook to research the Communist movement inside the UMWA in February 1923, at the height of the TUEL's successful organizing among miners and other workers. Searles "went over to the Department of Justice and had a talk with the Assistant Attorney General," and also with BI head of General Intelligence, "Mr. Hoover," and "they offered me all the assistance that they possibly could." Searles stationed a clerk with a typewriter in the Justice Department file room, "a very unusual procedure," and the BI "instructed the employees there to lend my man every assistance possible and to furnish to him all of the documents, reports, and everything they had there."[53]

After six weeks of searching, the UMWA's staffer found a wealth of incriminating material. Much of it came from police raids on the Workers' Party offices in Pittsburgh in April and May of 1923, which served as a base for organizing among Pennsylvania coal miners.[54] In his exposé, Searles described the Communist Party's plans to amplify coal strikes into general strikes, "in spite of" the officials of the UMWA, and the assistance in free-speech fights lent to the party by Roger Baldwin and the ACLU. Searles quoted liberally from the most grandiose statements of Communist organizers: miners would be "forced into armed insurrection" by employers' retaliation, and "a social revolution and the workers' republic" were within reach. Using a rhetorical sleight of hand, Searles linked radical Communist rhetoric from party leaders to rioting in southern Illinois coalfields.

But Searles also unearthed claims by Communist organizers that their recruits were at the center of the Herrin uprising. On the day after the massacre, Nick Dozenberg, a staffer on the Communists' Chicago journal, *Voice of Labor*, bragged to his colleagues that the party had sixty-seven Lithuanian members in Herrin. Searles quoted Dozenberg: "Our people working among the miners used clever tactics in assisting them, and are using the party tactics to influence the public officials." This was risible. Communist Party organizers had little traction in southern Illinois in the early 1920s. Such claims were typical of Communist organizers, who longed for sparks of radical insurgency and often took credit for blowing them into flames. All other evidence suggests that, whatever the truth of the CP's claim to a Lithuanian nuclei in Herrin, the town and the union protected the rioters because they were homegrown. Searles and Lewis undoubtedly understood this as well as the Herrin townsfolk.[55]

But it was delicious to have the CP on record taking credit for the embarrassing incident. In Washington, Lewis and Searles held a luncheon with Ralph Easley's National Civic Federation as the articles came out. Easley asked Lewis about the matter. Lewis insisted that "they have the goods," but Easley remained privately doubtful. "At any rate, I think we will all agree that it is a wholesome thing that the United Mine Workers are making this onslaught on the Communists," Easley told a correspondent.[56]

Bridgman

Not long after BI agents judged the Communists innocent of conspiracy in Illinois, they orchestrated a mass raid on the party in Michigan. With the greatest secrecy, Communist leaders had scheduled a national convention. It took delegates three days to reach the site of their national meeting in 1922. Participants were first sent to a meeting place in Philadelphia then directed to a spot in Cleveland, where someone else sent them on to Detroit; in Detroit, they were told to leave for Grand Rapids, where train tickets to St. Joseph, Michigan, awaited them.[57]

When Communists finally arrived at the meeting site in Bridgman, Michigan, in August 1922, they settled in to debate, among other questions, whether the party should renounce some of its secrecy. As they talked, a BI agent set up a stakeout in the woods outside, waiting for the local police to help him raid the camp, and another undercover agent—the section organizer in Passaic—sat among the delegates, listening carefully. Suddenly Foster spotted the agent lurking about. Delegates fled, burying the party's records in a cracker barrel in the woods, but the undercover agent led arriving police right to the records. Michigan had passed a law outlawing criminal syndicalism in 1919.[58] The BI agents helped Michigan police sweep up seventeen delegates hiding in the woods, and BI agents tracked down Foster at the TUEL headquarters in Chicago a few days later. Michigan charged eleven Communist leaders, including Foster, with criminal syndicalism, and BI agents remained in Michigan to oversee the prosecution.[59]

Roger Baldwin knew Foster from the 1919 steel strike, when Baldwin had briefly volunteered for the strike committee, and he immediately offered the ACLU's lawyers and public relations staff to the defense.[60] Baldwin noticed something strange right away. He wondered what the BI, charged with enforcing federal law, was doing in Michigan prosecuting violations of state law. In fact, the bureau's statutory authority to intervene in state cases was altogether unclear. BI director Burns and Attorney General Daugherty regularly trumpeted their close cooperation with state antiradical proceedings in appearances before Congress requesting bigger appropriations. But when pressed about the matter by ACLU lawyers, the Justice Department scrambled. Burns downplayed the BI's involvement in the case publicly and, on the advice of DOJ lawyers, temporarily terminated BI staff working on the case. Meanwhile, the county prosecutor's office in Michigan balked at the escalating expense of trying the cases, especially after the Communists' lawyer, Frank Walsh, won a court ruling obliging each case to be tried separately.[61]

Anxious to sustain the prosecutions, Burns turned to Ralph Easley for help. Easley hosted a luncheon for Burns in October with the purpose of finding "some way to help finance the cost" of the Michigan prosecution. An old hand at fundraising, Easley quickly began working his lists, writing to Howard E. Coffin of the Hudson Motor Company in Detroit to solicit money for the county prosecutor and explaining that funds were needed because "under the Michigan law, the Federal Government cannot touch it."[62] Alarmed by the prospect of bad publicity, the BI reined Easley in, advising him to quit fundraising and keep the NCF's role secret, as it "would do more harm than good" if the word got out. Instead, Easley offered his staffer, Archibald Stevenson, to help with the prosecution. Burns sent a letter to the Michigan Commissioner of Public Safety introducing Stevenson and asking the commissioner to "look after" him. Easley also arranged for Coffin to introduce Stevenson "to a few important people and interest them in this matter."[63]

The assistance of Easley and Stevenson did not help the case much. When Foster stood trial in the spring of 1923, he again denied being a member of the Communist Party, and the government could not prove that he was. Nor could the state prove that the Communist Party was a criminal conspiracy, and after a long trial, the jury deadlocked. The case became a cause for progressive labor and civil libertarians. Baldwin and the CP created a Labor Defense Council to raise funds and recruit popular support for the defendants, and they drew on the ongoing amnesty campaign for a rallying cry. The Chicago Federation of Labor jumped to Foster's defense, his stature secure from his years organizing in packinghouses and steel. Even the Michigan Federation of Labor, which had been accused of helping to pass the state's criminal syndicalism law, now backed repeal of the syndicalism statutes. For the CPUSA, Bridgman turned into a triumph.[64]

For the BI, Bridgman became a headache. Baldwin's ACLU kept track of Burns's misdeeds, and the Bridgman episode headed the list. It was becoming apparent to people such as Baldwin that simply repealing repressive laws was not enough. Curbing repressive federal agents was also necessary. Civil libertarians had not spent much time thinking about the problem of government bureaucracy, for good reason. Before the war, the federal government had few police and little role in regulating political speech. The sprawling Bureau of Investigation was a wartime creation, deriving its authority from the wartime Espionage and Sedition Acts. In the postwar backlash against the Red Scare, the new civil liberties movement denounced the autocratic abuses of the BI; as the National Popular Government League said in 1920, the "arbitrary power" exercised by the Department of Justice contravened the "fundamental American theory of the consent of the governed."[65]

With the expiration of statutory authority for political policing, the Bureau of Investigation should have ceased its political surveillance. Now, two years later, it was clear that the bureau continued to conduct political policing operations anyway. Baldwin's ACLU began to focus on the BI's actions as another form of civil liberties abuses. The AFL, compromised by its collaboration with the BI, did not adopt this analysis, remaining silent as evidence of bureau misdeeds mounted. Given Gompers's longstanding suspicion of state bureaucrats, it was an ironic position. Over the next two years, the contradictions in the AFL's civil liberties stance would become more uncomfortable.

CHAPTER SIX

Surveillance Scandals and the Downfall
of the Bureau of Investigation

During the Harding administration, the AFL was embroiled in fights on all fronts, attacking Communists, the attorney general, and the ACLU. Behind the scenes, AFL leaders were colluding with the Bureau of Investigation. Poking around the offices of "professional patriots" such as the National Civic Federation and the American Defense Society, veteran journalist Sidney Howard figured out the connection. In a series of articles for the *New Republic*, published in August and September 1924, Howard charged that "the militant patriots were publicity agents for Mr. Burns," the head of the federal Bureau of Investigation. Ralph Easley of the National Civic Foundation was the worst offender, according to Howard. Easley's contacts with Burns "provided, one surmises, a convenient link between sworn enemies, Mr. Burns and Easley's pal Sam Gompers; provided, too, a convenient source of A.F. of L. propaganda against renegade unions." Howard's explosive allegations threatened to expose the whole network of collusion between the AFL and the BI.[1]

By the time Howard's articles came out, however, the relationship between the BI and the AFL had ended. Burns had been fired in the spring of 1924, replaced by a temporary director, J. Edgar Hoover, who promised to shut down the BI's channels of communication with the professional patriots. Howard described a scandal that had already run its course. Roger Baldwin, whose lobbying against the BI's "spy system" helped drive Burns from office, was delighted with the new BI director. The new bureau "meets every suggestion we could possibly make," he told his colleagues at the American Civil Liberties Union. The AFL's confederate in the fight against Communism was gone.

To the federation, it was just as well. Labor anticommunists had grown increasingly wary of the concentration of federal power in the Department of

Justice. The BI's collusion had sometimes been helpful to the AFL, but Burns's agents had attacked AFL unionists as well, and the potential for the BI to abuse its authority had been amply demonstrated. Moreover, the Communist threat to AFL leaders had subsided. Strategic missteps cost the party its closest labor allies and discredited Communist credibility with potential recruits. By the summer of 1924, labor leaders no longer needed the BI's help. The AFL had come to agree with its old adversary, the ACLU: protecting civil liberties required restraints on federal police powers.

Impeachment

In September 1922, the huge railroad shopmen's strike entered its second month. The shopmen built and maintained railcars, performing skilled work as blacksmiths, electricians, and the like. Over 400,000 shopmen struck all the nation's major railroads after managers imposed wage cuts and company unions. The railroads refused to concede the shopmen's demands for restored seniority rights on the strikers' return to work. Instead they attempted to run the repair shops with strikebreakers. As railcars backed up in the repair shops and irate strikers ripped up track lines, train service slowed.

Harding was desperate to end the strike. Burns warned that Communist agitators were behind the walkout, and he had good reason to think so. William Z. Foster had been active in the Railway Carmen's union, and his TUEL had attracted many supporters of union amalgamation among the railroad unions, although few railroad workers knew of Foster's Communist ties. BI agents tailed Foster on his TUEL speaking tours and reported that "Foster was gaining a foothold among all the radical unions in this country."[2] Attorney General Daugherty counseled a hard line against the strikers. On September 1, Daugherty traveled to the federal courthouse in Chicago, presided over by Judge James Wilkerson, appointed by Harding to the bench two weeks earlier. Wilkerson granted Daugherty a restraining order first. Then he issued a sweeping injunction that banned strikers from picketing, giving newspaper interviews, or holding meetings. It also enjoined them from interfering with road operations or strikebreakers and declared the strike itself an illegal act. It was the most dramatic judicial attack unions had ever seen.[3]

Unionists howled in fury. "To hell with the injunction," said the president of the Railway Carmen. "Most outrageous!" Gompers said. "Mr. Daugherty may find he has stirred up a hornet's nest."[4] In New York, a Machinists' union officer called Daugherty "the most monumental ass who ever lived." In September 1922, as the strike collapsed, the AFL executive council unanimously voted to seek the impeachment of Daugherty. Unions and central labor councils across the country joined in the effort. "Resolved: that we will do all in our power to bring success to the effort to sustain the impeachment of Harry M. Daugherty," voted New York City unionists in October 1922, so that "the Department of Justice may be purged and purified of an influence which has besmirched it."[5]

Of course, union officials had no standing to impeach an attorney general. A curious reporter inquired as to who might introduce the impeachment, and AFL vice president Matthew Woll replied that "we do not expect to have any difficulty of finding a man to speak for us."[6] Soon they found a willing surrogate: Congressman Oscar E. Keller, elected in mid-1919 on a Farmer-Labor ticket in Minnesota to fill a seat vacated by death. Keller had been public works commissioner in St. Paul, and he was new to national politics. Having backed his campaign, the AFL called in their chit.[7]

On September 11, as the federation's executive council met, Keller stood up in the House and announced, "Mr. Speaker, I impeach Harry M. Daugherty, Attorney General of the United States, for high crimes and misdemeanors." Keller accused Daugherty of abridging freedom of speech and of the press and of the right of people to assemble, using "the funds of his office illegally," and failing to prosecute lawbreakers. "Where is your proof?" inquired the Speaker of the House. Keller replied, "I have it, but I am not ready to present it." Judiciary Committee members pressed him, insisting they could not report out an impeachment without more specifics. A person sitting next to Keller murmured in his ear, recommending he ask for more time to substantiate the case, and a congressman asked, "Who was that gentleman who just spoke to you?" Keller said, "I do not know," causing the man to speak up: "I am Mr. McGrady, representing the American Federation of Labor." After advising Keller and Edward McGrady to produce some facts to back up their charges, the Judiciary Committee adjourned, the proceedings having cemented the perception that the impeachment had been engineered by angry unionists.[8]

Having fired this volley across the Justice Department's bow, the AFL retreated to cobble together a case. It took several months. Keller did not file his impeachment specifications until December 1, but he returned with a scatter-shot blast of accusations. Keller charged Daugherty with failing to prosecute trusts among timber firms and builders in New York and Washington, retaining a U.S attorney in southern Illinois who had been reprimanded by the Illinois bar, failing to prosecute war-fraud cases, and showing favoritism toward J. P. Morgan. Buried in the list of thirteen specifications was a charge of "perverting the legal processes of the United States" by seeking the shopmen's strike injunction. Also buried was a claim that Daugherty had failed to pursue the fraudulent grant of mining rights to Standard Oil on U.S. Navy reserves in California, near Teapot Dome. Keller also charged that the Bureau of Investigation had improperly assigned federal agents to the Bridgman trial, and attacked William J. Burns as unfit for office because he had engaged in jury fixing in an Oregon land case while working for the Secret Service in 1905. It was quite an indictment.[9]

In the intervening months before the hearings, Gompers and the AFL continued to stump for the impeachment, declaring October 1 "impeachment day" and railing against the injunction.[10] The congressional midterm elections emboldened Daugherty's opponents. The Republicans lost seventy-seven seats in the House and six in the Senate, retaining a slim majority but losing the ability to control the congressional agenda. The Conference for Progressive Political Action (CPPA), an electoral alliance seeded by the railroad unions and the Minnesota Farmer-Labor Party, took some of the credit for helping elect progressive Republicans and Democrats such as Burton Wheeler to the Senate.[11] Flush with victory, they pressed their advantage by pushing the Daugherty impeachment back onto the House floor.

But its blatant partisanship irremediably tainted the proceedings. As the *New York Times* editorialized, "While Mr. Daugherty is vulnerable at many points, the move for his impeachment seems patently political," thinly veiled revenge for the railroad strike injunction.[12] Thus, although many of the charges against Daugherty pointed to real malfeasance, such as the Teapot Dome scandal (apparently fed to the impeachment team by Senator Robert La Follette, who had started investigating the oil leases in the Senate earlier that year), the Judiciary Committee never took the case seriously.[13]

Keller's pratfalls did not help. Gompers had hired Jackson Ralston, the longtime AFL lawyer, to manage the impeachment effort, and Ralston coached Keller through the proceedings, to the mirth of Judiciary Committee members who periodically inquired who exactly had written the bill of particulars (Ralston: "Mr. Keller has gotten assistance from many sources"), and who retained Ralston (Ralston: "Mr. Gompers, and no question was raised as to compensation.") Overall, the hearings were an undignified affair that degenerated rapidly into farce, or "comic opera," as Judiciary Committee chair Andrew Volstead called it.[14] Although the AFL demonstrated the political muscle to attack its enemies, derision rained down on the organization and its congressional front man.

Several days into the hearings, Keller, "white and tense," demanded to

interrupt testimony to read a statement complaining of abuse and humiliation. Lawmakers had made Keller a figure of fun by holding meetings and
making decisions without him. Though he was the chair, Keller withdrew
from the hearings altogether. In response, the Judiciary Committee promptly
subpoenaed Keller to testify in defense of his own impeachment charges, a
summons which he flouted, retreating to his home to suffer a nervous break-
down. By January, the impeachment inquiry had turned into a hearing on
whether the House could compel one of its own members to testify in a hearing. In the end the House relented, declining to persecute "a poor little dupe"
who was merely the "catspaw" of the AFL.[15]

Why did the AFL stumble so badly? The federation was generally considered to be a sophisticated lobby, savvy about congressional strategy. Perhaps
the din of outrage within labor circles deafened union leaders to the partisan
tone of their accusations. And perhaps they were simply deranged by the revival of the hated labor injunction and temporarily took leave of their political senses. "The labor injunction is the greatest menace to Constitutional government that has yet been devised," warned the Brotherhood of Locomotive
Firemen, and the "Daugherty injunction is only a maneuvering" by the Harding administration "to pave the way for anti-strike and compulsory arbitration legislation."[16] Enraged by this dire scenario, union leaders misjudged the
viability of their impeachment gambit.

Of all the charges, the Judiciary Committee seriously considered only one.
Gompers himself appeared to make the case. He produced a report written
in 1912 for George Wickersham, then attorney general under President Taft,
alleging that in 1905 Burns, then head of the Secret Service, had fixed a jury
in Oregon. Committee members were dubious, suggesting that perhaps the
McNamara incident was the real cause of Gompers's concern. Gompers ada-
mantly denied any personal animus, and he also denied having anything to
do with launching the impeachment proceedings. Burns brushed the accusations off, remarking that Gompers had "hounded" him for years. Burns
received unexpected support from Senator Hiram Johnson, who testified
that Burns was "one of the ablest detectives I have ever known."[17] Johnson, a
staunch progressive who had been governor of California during the McNamara case, cut the AFL's case from under them. So did Thomas Stevenson,
lawyer for the Brotherhood of Locomotive Firemen, who testified that the
attorney general had worked hard to address railcar safety and, in his judgment, did not warrant impeachment.[18] All in all, it was a debacle.

Roger Baldwin and the ACLU were baffled by the Burns charges. Why reach back to 1912 for evidence of malfeasance when Burns's BI had broken the law earlier in the year? The Bridgman case was a clear-cut example, and the ACLU had the proof. Baldwin reached out to Sam Evans, an ally at the Machinists' union, to explain the BI's illegal intervention in the Bridgman case and to urge the AFL to add the incident to the impeachment charges. The impeachment team balked: "it was objected to by nearly everyone here as dragging the Communist thing into these proceedings and thus damaging our case." But Evans prevailed on attorney Samuel Untermyer, a prominent lawyer brought in to help with the case who had little experience working with the AFL. Untermyer insisted on including the charges, and Evans turned to Baldwin to supply the evidence. Within a few days, Baldwin had sent affidavits affirming the Bridgman charges to Jackson Ralston.[19]

The National Civic Federation also had ample proof of the BI's illegal involvement in the Bridgman case, of course, in the form of letters signed by Burns. But divulging the letters would have disclosed the relationship between the BI, the NCF, and the AFL. Gompers likely suppressed the affidavits and the Bridgman allegations. Revealing their antiradical collaboration with the BI would have raised uncomfortable questions: how could the AFL denounce BI repression and collaborate in it at the same time? During the impeachment hearings, Keller mentioned the Bridgman incident but produced no evidence to back up his charges. When asked about it, Burns simply stated that "we had a perfectly legal right to do all that we did in the matter," and the committee left it at that.[20] As Untermyer recognized, the Bridgman intervention was a significant breach of federal law, and had they pursued the charges, the impeachment could have turned into a serious case. The AFL's compromised position impaired its ability to attack Burns and Daugherty and constrained its capacity to speak out for civil liberties.

Communist Organizing

After the impeachment effort, exchanges between the NCF and the BI on labor matters died down for a while. But for the AFL, the Communist challenge escalated. Foster's acquittal in the Bridgman case was a great victory for the party, and he announced his CP membership soon after. His Trade Union Educational League continued to agitate among miners, machinists, and carpenters, with Chicago as its strongest base. Foster sat on the Chicago Federation of Labor's organizing committee. The Seattle labor federation continued to call for recognition of the Soviet Union and push for industrial unionism, and TUEL candidates won scores of union offices in the International Ladies' Garment Workers' Union (ILGWU). To AFL officials, the radical tide seemed to be rising.[21]

Beginning in the spring of 1923, Gompers orchestrated a crackdown. He cut the budget of the Chicago federation and sent operatives to investigate the central labor councils in Seattle, Detroit, Tacoma, and Los Angeles. The AFL would no longer tolerate divergences from federation doctrine on Russian recognition, domestic Communism, or third-party politics; radical leaders such as James Duncan in Seattle stepped down or were forced out.[22] Rarely did members or leaders defend Communism, in principle or practice, and anticommunist resolutions generally sailed through. But unionists frequently defended the principles of amalgamation and labor parties, showing that the TUEL's agenda reflected real concerns among rank-and-file members. "We are not caring anything about this radicalism, this bolshevism, this red propaganda. We don't care what they do in England or in Russia; we are traveling under the American flag," said a mineworker at the Illinois AFL convention in September 1923. "We have more kings than any other country in the world—meat kings, cotton kings, corn kings, and coal kings. These kings are amalgamated. The commercial interests are amalgamated and if we do not amalgamate they will destroy our organizations."[23]

The popularity of many Communist proposals led AFL leaders to relentlessly emphasize the foreign pedigree of radical labor politics and the duplicity of Foster. "I have the official word of the organ of the Workers' Party, which is the cover for the Communist Party and so stated openly, that Mr. Foster is connected with that outfit," said Victor Olander, vice president of the Illinois federation. "I say there is an insincerity in the sort of campaign that has been carried on that is appalling."[24] The basic truth of these charges—most remaining members of the Communist Party were in fact foreign-born, and Foster's TUEL had indeed devised a disingenuous organizing strategy—made it hard for anyone, Communist or otherwise, to defend the TUEL.[25]

The conflict came to a head at the AFL convention in the fall of 1923. William F. Dunne, a Bohemian radical who joined the electricians' union in Montana and got elected vice president of the Montana State Federation, had joined the Communist Party in 1919. Dunne's position thus gave him an official credential to vote at the AFL convention. Dunne used it to introduce a resolution calling for union amalgamation, which caught the attention of AFL officials. Wanting to move against Dunne but needing to be sure they had all the facts, an AFL staffer cabled Ralph Easley from the convention. "Please wire any information you have on William F Dunne Radical Labor Man of Butte Montana would anyone in Department of Justice know about him." Easley and his contacts immediately got to work. By the next day, they had nailed it. A return cable reported: "William F Dunne arrested in Bridgman raid and under indictment. . . . Correspondence seized in Merrick's office Pittsburgh shows Dunne active comrade in all that work. He and Engdahl signed to whom it may concern letter certifying that Merrick was authorized to act as correspondent for Worker. Washington says Dunne member Executive Committee."[26] This exchange is the clearest evidence of the proxy function played by the NCF for the AFL. Asking Easley to check with the Department of Justice indicates that AFL officials understood exactly where Easley got his information.

At the convention a few days later, William Green of the Mineworkers took the podium to announce, "I impeach this man in the name of the workers of America, before the great bar of trade union power and authority." In this impeachment, the AFL came off quite a bit better than in the Daugherty affair. Charging Dunne with being a "traitor to organized labor," the federation held a roll call vote on whether to expel him from the hall. The vote was 27,837 to 108 to banish him. "I will meet you at the barricades," Dunne retorted on the way out.[27] The silence of Dunne's putative allies from the TUEL was a gauge of the group's real weakness, as historian David Montgomery notes. Under pressure, AFL members sided with their unions with little protest. To the *New Republic*, the TUEL failed because "leaders misread the minds of the rank and file and because they were inexpert in playing the game of practical politics."[28]

David Saposs, a progressive economist sympathetic with radical unionists, remarked in 1926 that "never before in the history of the labour movement has there been such a wholesale expulsion of members. . . . We are today witnessing a desperate struggle for control and domination where the usual rules of the game are discarded and war measures are invoked."[29] Labor economists Selig Perlman and Philip Taft, who watched the drama from the sidelines, believed that the conflict helped ensconce conservative leadership in the AFL. Progressive unionists were "driven to come to the old leadership for aid against the undermining tactics of their Communist foes," they wrote. "Moreover, when attacked from the left, with their own slogans and articles of faith turned against them, 'progressives' often lost heart as well as following."[30]

Likely Perlman and Taft were thinking of John Fitzpatrick, lion of the Chicago labor movement. Ham-fisted political maneuvering by Communist organizers had begun to alienate progressive and radical allies such as Fitzpatrick, president of the Chicago Federation of Labor. Fitzpatrick had flouted the authority of the AFL by defending William Z. Foster and endorsing the program of the TUEL. Under Fitzpatrick, the Chicago Federation became a bustling forum for radical and progressive laborites to plan organizing campaigns, fight for Irish self-determination and diplomatic relations with Russia, and, above all, forge political alliances in service of a new Farmer-Labor Party. In 1922, the prospects for fusion seemed propitious. Disillusionment with both the Democrats and Republicans drove socialists, railroad unions, and the Minnesota Farmer-Labor Party to convene the Conference for Progressive Political Action (CPPA) as a step toward a new third party. The CPPA refused to seat Communist delegates, over Fitzpatrick's protests, and when the CPPA wavered over the timeline for the new party, Fitzpatrick and Foster bolted to launch the Farmer-Labor Party themselves.[31]

Within a few months, though, Fitzpatrick regretted his decision to team up with Foster. Union support was melting away as AFL leaders pressured unionists to repudiate the Farmer-Labor Party, but New York Communist leaders insisted that Foster press ahead, over Fitzpatrick's pleas for patience. At the Farmer-Labor Party conference in July 1923, Communists won floor votes with strategic delegate placements and took control of the new Federated Farmer-Labor Party, to the dismay of all their progressive allies. A humiliated Fitzpatrick disavowed the effort. Surveying the wreckage, Gifford Ernest, a Chicago newspaperman and unionist, issued a pamphlet titled *William Z. Foster: Fool or Faker?* Although unable to resolve his title's question, Ernest warned unionists that in no circumstances could Communists be trusted in the house of labor: "Theirs is an under cover movement and, like all similar movements, it is underhanded as well. They are not out in the open and honest. They intend to survive and thrive by trickery and stealth."[32]

The situation only worsened with time. Minnesota Farmer-Laborites, locally powerful, still hoped to salvage the party by running the popular senator Robert M. La Follette for president in 1924. Again at the behest of the New York party leadership, Foster demanded that La Follette endorse the Communist program in exchange for the Federated Farmer-Labor Party's support. When La Follette declined without hesitation, Foster named himself as the party's presidential candidate. The promise of the Farmer-Labor movement had degenerated into farce.[33]

This episode irreparably spoiled Communists' relationship with progressive unionists such as Fitzpatrick. Nathan Fine, a longtime progressive activist, wrote to Fitzpatrick that "so far as the W.P. or the T.U.E.L. are concerned, they have buried themselves beyond all recovery, and have themselves been their worst enemies, have destroyed all hope of accomplishing their own program . . . they are a bunch of loose-tongued, venomous, impossibilists."[34] Fitzpatrick went farther, denouncing the "every-day practices of the modern communists," which were "betrayal, corruption, deception, lying, stealing, hypocrisy, cruelty, physical force and law-breaking. We must rid our movement of them."[35] Communist scheming permanently embittered Fitzpatrick, who renounced progressive politics in favor of AFL-style nonpartisanship and undermined the position of progressives across the labor movement. Gompers and the conservatives pressed their advantage. "The cleavage has been made," Gompers crowed at the AFL convention in October 1923. "This is an American labor movement, a movement of the workers, for the workers, and by the workers, and not any so-called intelligentsia."[36] Communists were effectively shut out of most unions for the next decade.

The garment workers unions were among the few exceptions. The needle trades were dominated by Eastern European and Russian immigrants steeped in Bundist socialism; they greeted the Bolshevik Revolution with joy and organized Communist cadres in their workshops long before the creation of the TUEL. Sidney Hillman's Amalgamated Clothing Workers Union, exiled from the AFL since 1914, managed to mediate arguments between socialists and Communists within the union through skilful maneuvering. Hillman championed the Bolshevik revolution, organizing famine relief and industrial reconstruction projects in Russia, and in exchange won support from Communist unionists for his campaign to impose uniform production standards across the union. When socialist clothing workers decried Hillman's centralizing program, Communist clothing workers shouted them down. Hillman expressed his gratitude with a donation to the TUEL. The relationship unraveled with the La Follette fiasco, and Hillman publicly distanced himself from the domestic Communist Party. But Hillman never attacked the CPUSA or shared the anticommunist agenda of AFL leaders.[37]

The Ladies' Garment Workers, on the other hand, fractured into a virtual civil war between socialists and Communists in the 1920s. Socialist ILGWU leaders such as Benjamin Schlesinger and David Dubinsky had backed the Mensheviks' struggle for power in 1917, and they doubted the benevolence of the Bolshevik regime. But their naysaying annoyed radical rank-and-file members, who followed their counterparts in the Amalgamated in resisting the leadership's efforts to rationalize work rules and practices across the industry. Communist insurgents and their anarchist and syndicalist allies seized leadership of several New York locals in 1922, extending their reach to Chicago and Philadelphia by 1924. Facing a far larger and more popular Communist challenge, ILGWU leaders tried expulsions and purges, but a backlash quickly coalesced. In 1925, 40,000 workers rallied at Yankee Stadium to protest the crackdown, and by the end of the year Communist slates controlled 70 percent of the union's New York shops. It looked like the conservative leadership had been routed.[38]

But again, Communist leaders fumbled their opportunity. Cloak makers had been fighting for a new contract since 1924, when New York governor Al Smith appointed a special committee to recommend terms to labor and management. In the summer of 1926, the committee issued a report rejecting the forty-four-hour week and other key demands, inflaming cloak makers. The national leaders of the Communist Party, reduced to this labor redoubt, angled for a say in the strike plan. Over the five-month strike, William Z. Foster and Jay Lovestone jockeyed with each other over bargaining strategy, while the cloak makers' position deteriorated. Finally, they struck a deal for terms worse than those recommended by the governor's committee. Support for the Communist leadership plummeted. ILGWU officers moved fast, kicking out Communists and reorganizing all the Communist-led locals. But unlike other AFL unions, the ILGWU did not purge Communists permanently; instead they offered amnesty to expelled members after a year. The CP was reduced to a vocal faction in the union.[39]

For conservative and progressive unionists alike, one lesson was clear: Communists were likely to sabotage their own recruitment campaigns and alienate workers even without the help of their enemies. Communist organizers were most successful when they adopted and amplified the concerns of rank-and-file unionists and when they downplayed radical politics in favor of practical, day-to-day concerns. But most union members rejected the premises of Communist ideology, especially the doctrinaire Bolshevist version espoused by American Communists in the 1920s. Years of catechizing AFL members about Soviet autocracy helped instill this aversion. To squelch Communist drives, union leaders reasoned that a simple strategy would suffice: exposure. Communist organizers lost traction among unionists when their true identities and purposes were revealed. Simply identifying and naming Communist organizers usually dispelled their influence. Federal repression, on the other hand, often aroused sympathy for Communists, especially among progressive civil libertarians.

Civil Liberties Coalition

Roger Baldwin's American Civil Liberties Union was a case in point. Born in Wellesley, Massachusetts, in 1884 to a family tracing its lineage to Plymouth Colony, the Harvard-educated Baldwin took up social work in St. Louis on the eve of World War I. A lecture by Emma Goldman electrified him, and he drifted gradually leftward until the American entry into the war thoroughly radicalized him. Baldwin organized a committee to assist conscientious objectors and defend protestors accused under the Espionage Act, which he led until his own imprisonment for refusing to register for the draft. On his release, Baldwin turned his committee into the American Civil Liberties Union. He assembled a board of famous progressives such as Helen Keller and Oswald Garrison Villard and a roster of liberal lawyers to defend dissenters and lobby to roll back statutes criminalizing political radicalism.[40]

Ralph Easley deplored the ACLU, and the rancor was mutual. From his Manhattan office, Easley lobbed salvos at the ACLU's headquarters in Union Square. Easley scorned the ACLU's "pretended effort to protect the pacifists, Socialists, Communists and their ilk in the 'right' to say what they please at any time and place." For his part, Baldwin regarded the NCF and other patriotic groups as "the lunatic fringe of reaction."[41]

In many ways the two men were alike—both were energetic progressives and skilled organizers who built networks of elites to support workers' struggles. Thirty years older, Easley represented the first wave of progressivism that saw transformative potential in associational politics. Easley maintained his faith in the benevolence of both AFL unionism and industrial employers, despite all evidence to the contrary, but his dream of social harmony hardened into a hatred of dissent. Roger Baldwin started on the other side of the progressive learning curve. His early idealism was roughened by the domestic wartime crackdown and the inadequacy of right-thinking associations when arrayed against concentrated power. Baldwin also dedicated himself to workers' struggles, but he backed the Wobblies and industrial strikers, militant action and mass organizing—confrontation, not compromise.

In the universe of labor, the NCF and the ACLU marked two different orbits. Both linked workers' organizations with sources of influence and money. Easley brokered connections between union leaders and grizzled authorities in business and the state, such as onetime Republican presidential candidate Alton B. Parker or Columbia University president Nicholas Murray Butler. His influence waned in the 1920s as the postwar open-shop drive and indifferent Harding and Coolidge administrations made mediation seem futile. By the 1920s, the NCF was little more than a publicity vehicle for Easley and his small coterie of labor conservatives. As a manager at General Electric explained to a BI agent, "Easley will do or say any thing which he thinks will bring [him] into the lime light and keep him before the public." Employers and civic leaders, the NCF's old constituency, drifted away, leaving only antiradical unionists.[42]

As the NCF declined, the ACLU flourished. Baldwin's ACLU put elite lawyers and activists in service to radical workers outside the AFL—mostly Wobblies and Communists—and attracted AFL dissidents such as A. J. Muste. Baldwin had his own wealthy patron in Charles Garland, a railroad heir who turned his fortune over to Baldwin. With the proceeds Baldwin formed the Garland Fund for Public Service and distributed the money to causes including the NAACP, the Rand School, and the Federated Press, a radical news bureau. The ACLU's relationships formed a branch of the networks that would become the Popular Front in the 1930s.

The ACLU's close ties to the Communist Party reflected Baldwin's increasing radicalism. Baldwin and Foster met in 1919, when Foster invited Baldwin to work in the steel mills and see the great strike firsthand. Baldwin invited Foster to sit on the ACLU's board in 1920, and the ACLU defended Communists in numerous criminal cases. To Baldwin's frustration, however, the CP showed little interest in protecting the free speech of non-Communists. In the mid-1920s, Baldwin argued with party secretary Earl Browder about Communist heckling of socialists, scolding him, "You don't encourage the support of people who believe in free speech by denying to others the rights which you demand for yourselves." Browder scoffed, saying that the actions of a private group such as the CP could not be compared to official repression by a state, and insisting that workers' demands in the fight against capitalism trumped any liberal concern about civil liberties.

Baldwin's misgivings reflected the contradiction between the radical ethic guiding an avowedly revolutionary movement and the liberal values that underlay the postwar civil liberties movement. Members of the ACLU's executive board such as Morris Ernst and Arthur Garfield Hays knew where they stood: they were civil libertarians, not foot soldiers for the revolution. Roger Baldwin was not so sure. The diminishing status of the Communist Party in the 1920s deferred internal ACLU debate on these questions until the 1930s.[43]

The AFL took note of Baldwin's friendly relationship to the CP and regularly attacked the ACLU as a puppet of the party and Baldwin as a silly intellectual. Baldwin "likes to puddle around dilettante fashion, in pools of social turbulence, mostly where it is neither wanted nor needed," commented the *American Federationist* in October 1923. Baldwin and the ACLU regarded the AFL as a hopelessly reactionary body, but one that could be prodded into action nevertheless.

In the spring of 1924, Baldwin suddenly saw an opportunity to draw the AFL into defending labor radicals. How? By threatening to reveal the Justice Department's illegal repressive tactics. Baldwin clearly did not understand the extent of Gompers's collusion with the BI. Meanwhile, Gompers was simultaneously planning his own exposé of Soviet domination of the American Communist Party. A rapid turn of events suddenly upended both their plans.

Teapot Dome

Senator William E. Borah, progressive Idaho Republican and chairman of the Foreign Relations Committee, had begun planning an inquiry on U.S. recognition of Russia. Throughout his tenure, President Harding had wobbled on the recognition question. Secretary of State Charles Evans Hughes, a dedicated anti-Bolshevik, "bombarded" Harding with memos and missives to stiffen his spine, insisting that recognition would bolster an illegitimate regime. Hughes's State Department staff echoed the secretary, as did Russian explorer and diplomat George Kennan, numerous corporate executives, and figures such as Father Edmund Walsh of Georgetown University.

But Harding also listened to advocates of recognition such as Raymond Robins, unofficial envoy to Russia during the revolution, and former Indiana governor James Goodrich, who argued that nonrecognition only "delay[ed] the economic reconstruction and the political development" of Russia. It took determined lobbying to keep Harding in line. One frustrated recognition advocate complained to Borah that "whenever there was any hint in the press or if there were just rumors" that the government considered easing its anti-Bolshevik hard line, "all the Czarist propagandists from Bakhmeteff and Brazol on down would get very busy. It usually culminated in a protest by Mr. Gompers or the National Civic Federation."[44]

In August 1923, Harding died suddenly while on a speaking tour, leaving the presidency to Calvin Coolidge and perhaps an opening to push for a policy change. At the AFL convention, Photoengravers Union president Matthew Woll warned of the risks: "Establish trade relations and you establish consular relations, not alone in Russia, but in our own midst, and that which Soviet Russia is now compelled to do through secret channels she will be enabled to do by open means, by making men like Dunne their consuls within this country."[45] To Woll, diplomatic recognition of Soviet Russia conferred political legitimacy on Communists. AFL leaders defeated a delegate resolution calling for Russian recognition at the convention "by a very large majority," but Borah was a tougher opponent. AFL publicity man Chester Wright had been keeping tabs on Borah for several years. In 1922, he told Ralph Easley he suspected Borah of "playing with both extreme ends of the

Russian situation, dealing on the one hand with the Communist crowd and on the other hand with the old monarchist outfit." If they could get evidence, "it might make Mr. Borah uncomfortable at an opportune moment."[46] It is not clear how Borah was "playing with both ends," but the AFL was looking for ways to discredit him.

Once the Senate Foreign Relations Committee hearings were announced, the AFL got busy preparing its own testimony. The forum offered an opportunity to indict Foster and the TUEL for their attacks on the AFL, and Gompers's staff prepared a thousand-page briefing, "a complete and astounding record" of the AFL's "uncompromising warfare against Communism," showing "with an amazing wealth of detail the picture of Communist intrigue."[47] They asked Easley to look through his files to find helpful documents and sent him to the Rand School bookstore in New York to collect pamphlets. Hearings began in January 1924, with State Department staffers presenting the case against recognition. Coolidge announced that he would await the committee's findings before reconsidering administration policy toward Russia. Eager to testify, Gompers issued an open letter to Republican senators, complaining, "It is impossible for me to avoid feeling that in the Communist inquiry there is not being shown that aggressiveness which is essential to the protection of American interests." As "one of the most powerful voices opposing recognition" in the country, Gompers was a formidable force.[48]

But Gompers never got the chance to testify. In another committee room at the Capitol, a witness had just admitted loaning $100,000 to Albert Fall, secretary of the interior, after Fall granted him oil-leasing rights to Teapot Dome. The Senate and the nation grew transfixed by the unfolding scandal as oilmen and administration officials begrudgingly acknowledged paying huge sums to Republican and Democratic politicians alike for oil rights and political access. The issue of Russian recognition paled in comparison. After the first round of witnesses, the Borah committee suspended, then cancelled, future sessions. Chester Wright tried to reconvene the hearings with a private committee made up of representatives from the American Legion, the Daughters of the American Revolution, and the National Civic Federation, but the idea faded.[49] With the end of Borah's inquiry, organized pressure to alter U.S. policy toward Russia dwindled, and nonrecognition remained policy until 1933.

For Gompers and the AFL, Teapot Dome helped scuttle the threat that the United States would diplomatically sanction Bolshevism. But Teapot Dome also set into motion the dismantlement of the BI's domestic political police force, on which the federation had relied for intelligence and anticommunist repression. Harry Daugherty had had little to do with Albert Fall's misdeeds, but attention naturally turned to the attorney general, given his scandal-ridden past. The dominos began to fall when Montana senator Thomas Walsh, chair of the Teapot Dome hearings, passed on damning evidence against Daugherty to fellow Montanan Burton Wheeler. In February 1924 Wheeler demanded a full investigation of the Justice Department, with himself at the head. Roxy Stinson, a flamboyant divorcée, kicked off the hearings by revealing that Daugherty and her ex-husband Jess Smith, a fixer from Harding's hometown, caroused on K Street with hundred-dollar bills delivered by oil graft and bootleggers' bribes.

For weeks, witnesses recounted incredible tales of perfidy in the attorney general's office, and William Burns's BI featured prominently. Gaston Means, a Burns hire already under indictment for bootlegging and graft, testified that BI agents rifled the offices of senators investigating Daugherty and Burns. Witnesses confirmed that Burns's BI agents worked as labor spies. A Columbus detective reported that BI agent Herbert Little traded information from BI files for introductions to Ohio union leaders. Little was on the payroll of the BI and U.S. Steel simultaneously and was in town to squelch a rumored steel-organizing drive.[50]

Daugherty was fatally compromised. He darkly implied that Communist plotting lay behind the hearings. After "the communists failed in their efforts to capture the labor organizations," Daugherty said, they began planning to "cripple the government of the United States," with the connivance of Senator Wheeler. When Daugherty refused to "contribute to a treasonable cause" by testifying at the hearing, Wheeler hounded him in Congress.[51] A skeptical President Coolidge asked for Daugherty's resignation at the end of March. Burns's downfall was not far behind. Senator Wheeler called him back in May to answer questions about the BI's investigation of Wheeler. Burns acknowledged sending agents to look for dirt. Two days later, Burns also resigned.[52]

Roger Baldwin and the ACLU saw an opportunity to strike. Since the Bridgman incident, Burns and Baldwin had traded barbs, with Burns calling Baldwin a Soviet agent and Baldwin calling Burns a "son of a bitch."[53] In February 1924, well before the Daugherty hearings, Baldwin proposed the idea of calling for a congressional investigation into labor spying. Journalist Sidney Howard had recently published a series of articles in the *New Republic* on the growth of labor-spy agencies, implicating the William J. Burns agency along with others. A public airing of the sordid practice would besmirch Burns and help unions fighting open-shop drives. Baldwin enlisted labor lawyer W. Jett Lauck to act as chief investigator.[54]

Attorney General Harry M. Daugherty interviewed by newsmen as he leaves cabinet meeting, 1924. Library of Congress, Prints and Photographs Division.

Once the Daugherty investigation opened, information flooded out. Baldwin heard from committee investigators that the BI had a file on the ACLU, and when the new attorney general, Harlan F. Stone, offered to open DOJ files to Wheeler's staff, Baldwin and Lauck conceived of a different idea: why not investigate the BI and expose "the general spy system centering in the Bureau of Investigation"?[55] A frontal attack on the BI could challenge its entire approach to political policing. The campaign could achieve broader ends as well. In an internal memo, the ACLU listed "the objects of the attack on the spy system" to include "divorc[ing] organized labor from the National Civic Federation" and "begin[ning] to unite all the forces in the labor movement in the defence of their common rights so that even the A.F. of L. will respond to the challenge of the defence of the left elements."[56]

The ACLU lined up support for an inquiry focusing on the BI's antiradical drives, especially its "huge expenditure of money with only a small showing," the BI's "spy system" and its collaboration with the "so-called patriotic organizations" and employers, and Burns's continued ties to his detective agency.[57] Burns's sudden resignation in early May obviated the latter question, but Baldwin and Lauck pushed to continue anyway. They issued an open letter to the Senate Appropriations Committee calling for a "material" reduction in the BI's budget and the elimination of the BI's "secret police, engaged primarily in combating political radicalism."[58] Attorney General Stone moved fast to head off this campaign. He invited Baldwin and Lauck to submit a brief "on what kind of a policy we want and what kind of man we desire as head of the bureau," and Stone promised to clean out all the Burns operatives.[59] In the meantime, Stone named J. Edgar Hoover as the interim head of the BI.

Baldwin and Lauck met with Hoover and Stone in August to talk the matter over. Hoover told them that the BI was being thoroughly reorganized and that "the department dealing with radical activities has been thoroughly abolished. There is not a single man in the department especially assigned to that work." Moreover, "the practice of giving out confidential information in the Bureau's files has been wholly discontinued."[60] Baldwin had been quite skeptical, recalling Hoover's years at the head of the Radical Division. But Hoover encouraged Baldwin to call him directly if the ACLU learned of any BI improprieties, and Baldwin soon felt that the ACLU had erred in its initial assessment of Hoover.[61]

As for Gompers and the AFL, they were lucky. Stone's swift appointment of Hoover forestalled a congressional investigation that would have focused on the BI's collaboration with organizations such as the NCF. Had the BI opened its files, the AFL would have been humiliated. As things stood, progressive activists suspected the worst. Sidney Howard had guessed the basic outlines of the relationship, as he detailed in his *New Republic* articles. But Howard confessed that he had "no direct evidence to back up these implications." Gompers and Easley were spared the public airing of such evidence by Hoover and Stone.

In December 1924, Gompers died at the age of seventy-four, having presided over the AFL for virtually its entire existence. He died at a low point in the federation's fortunes. Membership had fallen by 1.5 million since the end of the war, and AFL unions represented only about one in ten workers. Organized labor's influence had faded, in politics and in civic life. In his last days, Gompers comforted himself with the knowledge that he had built the AFL "in conformity with what we believe to be the original intent and purpose of America." The postwar years had shown "the dependability of voluntary institutions assuring individual initiative." Neither state nor party could be counted on to ensure workers' liberty. During the remainder of the 1920s, this legacy held firm at the AFL.

Gompers's fundamentalist faith in unionism as the sole bedrock of workers' liberty led him and the AFL into an instrumentalist politics that sometimes undercut other forms of political liberty. As the scope and power of the state swelled in the early twentieth century, many Americans reconsidered the meanings of civil liberties. The mobilization for the Great War and the repression of protest recast popular understanding of freedom of speech and the right to political protest. The Red Scare crackdown by a powerful new federal police force aroused demands for freedom from state surveillance and repression. Throughout these years, labor activists and allies insisted that the right to organize and strike was central to workers' freedom.

For Gompers and AFL leaders, unionism trumped other forms of civil liberties, and when confronted with a choice between advancing the interests of the AFL and defending civil liberties, they chose the AFL first. Thus the AFL backed wartime repression of civil liberties and collaborated with the Justice Department, especially when radical labor activists were targeted. But just as liberty could spread like a contagion, so could repression propagate like a virus, and colluding with crackdowns on radicals did not inoculate AFL unions from attack. Over time, Gompers and other AFL leaders adopted an instrumentalist civil liberties program. Unionism still headed the list, but the AFL also backed the freedom to speak and associate without government surveillance, even for radicals. It was a hard-won lesson.

PART III

From Commonsense Anticommunism to Red-baiting

CHAPTER SEVEN

Commonsense Anticommunism
and Civil Liberties

J. Edgar Hoover was in a delicate spot. Since his appointment as director of the federal Bureau of Investigation in 1924, Hoover had worked hard to rehabilitate the BI's reputation. Under his predecessors, the BI had swelled into a loosely supervised force of freelance agents for hire, skilled in political skullduggery and labor espionage. Charged with cleaning up the corruption, Hoover fired crooked agents and shut down the BI's political policing operations while beefing up the bureau's crime-fighting forces. Enforcing federal law, not chasing radicals, became the BI's policy. Now, in the spring of 1927, Ralph Easley was trying to undo Hoover's work. Easley had been a regular patron of the old BI, relying on its intelligence as political capital, and he badly wanted the BI to resume tracking Communists and radicals. Easley proposed to engineer a change in the language of the BI's congressional budget appropriation to create a back-door authorization for countersubversive surveillance.

Hoover prepared a carefully worded letter, marked "personal and confidential," to explain his view on the matter "personally, not in my official capacity." Not only did he doubt "the practicability of accomplishing such a change," Hoover wrote, "I am in fact doubtful as to its desirability." It was the process that was the problem. "If there is a radical menace existing in this country, and the American people feel that it should be handled by the Federal authorities, then through their properly elected spokesmen in Congress they should seek specific legislation for that purpose." Hoover intended to protect his BI's new bureaucratic autonomy from the antiradical clientele who had conspired with the BI in past scandals. The BI would "vigorously enforce any legislation enacted by Congress," Hoover said. Groups such as Easley's NCF, he made clear, would no longer call the shots.[1]

Easley's appropriations gambit failed, but he did not give up on the effort. Through the mid-1930s the NCF agitated for the BI to resume political policing and, in 1930, helped mount a special congressional inquiry into the matter. These efforts failed. After the first Red Scare subsided and the Teapot Dome scandal wiped out the BI's remaining political investigative units, professional patriots such as Easley lost the capacity to marshal federal raids on radicals.

Moreover, Easley's NCF had also lost the support of labor conservatives, who no longer supported his campaign to resurrect the old freewheeling Bureau of Investigation. Now labor conservatives articulated a common-sense anticommunism, based on a practical assessment of the revolutionary potential of the American Communist Party. As AFL president William Green explained of American Communism in 1930, "At the present time I do not regard it as of a serious nature or of a serious character." The federation had demonstrated its ability to police itself. This level-headed view, based on unionists' experience with actual Communists, differed from the wild "counter-subversive imagination" of people such as Ralph Easley. Armchair anticommunists like Easley favored muscular federal intervention to contain the vast red conspiracy they conjured. Through the late 1930s, the AFL's voluntarist approach to containing Communism helped foil federal policing of political radicals.

The fervor of labor anticommunism had not diminished, and AFL leaders fiercely attacked whenever Communists reared their heads inside AFL unions. Increasingly, Communist sectarianism and Stalinist orthodoxy turned once-tolerant socialist and liberal union leaders into anticommunist allies of labor conservatives. The ACLU, meanwhile, moved closer to the party. ACLU director Roger Baldwin became an ardent defender of Soviet Russia and American Communists, often to the dismay of fellow ACLU leaders. The ACLU and the AFL were uneasy allies, but their shared stance on civil liberties helped preserve newly won civil liberties from attack.

G-Men

When Attorney General Harlan F. Stone ordered the BI to cease political policing, Hoover shut down the bureau's antiradical division, reassigned its officers, and adopted the ACLU's interpretation of federal law. Ralph Easley was startled to find out about the BI's reorganization. In May 1925, Easley had requested that the BI send an agent over to the AFL headquarters to brief staffer Hugh Frayne. The BI refused. As Easley explained to Frayne: "The Department of Justice has suspended all its investigations of radical activities and has fired the men who did that work. 130 in all. This was brought about by the infamous American Civil Liberties Union exerting its influence upon Attorney General Stone during his incumbency and he issued the order."[2] Hoover cut the BI's staff in half, closed field offices, and restructured the agency.

There were lapses, to be sure. Hoover had launched his career as an antiradical crusader, and he had close ties to the remnants of the red-hunting network. Hoover advised the network and his agents that the BI could accept submissions of intelligence on radical activities and keep them in the BI's files. This allowed the BI to amass intelligence from other sources. Historians have debated whether the ban was more illusory than real. Scholars' difficulty in obtaining post-1922 BI records contributes to the confusion; many BI files remain classified or difficult to access. BI historian Athan Theoharis discovered several scattered instances in which the BI investigated Communist and radical groups after 1924, and he argues that these episodes show that the BI never stopped policing radicals. In a scrupulous study, historian Regin Schmidt assesses the evidence and finds that "most of the Bureau's political activities were, in fact, curtailed as a result of Stone's ban and that only a bare minimum of surveillance was maintained with the Justice Department's knowledge."[3]

Beyond the bureau's files, substantial evidence suggests that the ban was real. One measure is the frustration of antiradical collaborators such as Easley, who were accustomed to sharing information with the BI. Another indicator is the freedom from federal harassment Communists enjoyed after 1924. State sedition laws and city red squads still threatened the CP but, by and large, the party no longer contended with BI agents dogging their footsteps. Communists faced the sharpest surveillance in the South, where, in the late 1920s, they began organizing in earnest and fighting for African American liberation. Mass arrests and long prison sentences hobbled the party in Gastonia, North Carolina, after black and white textile workers marched together under a red banner.[4] But in places such as New York City, Chicago, and San Francisco, longtime havens for radicals, Communists opened recruiting offices and bookstores, marched in public squares, and published newspapers calling for the overthrow of capitalism and the American republic. The withdrawal of the BI gave party organizers some breathing room for the first time since 1919.[5]

Hoover devoted himself to professionalizing the bureau. He developed a

J. Edgar Hoover, 1924. Library of Congress, Prints and Photographs Division.

fingerprint database, set up an office to track crime statistics, and created a training academy for BI agents. A national wave of bank robberies and gangsterism, coupled with the explosion of bootlegging after Prohibition, gave Hoover's agents many new federal crimes to solve. With the help of a canny publicity agent, Hoover transformed the bureau's public image. The "G-Man" became an iconic figure, representing integrity, discretion, and bravery, and gangsters, not radicals, were the bureau's favored public enemy.[6]

The AFL in the Lean Years

Labor anticommunists received the news of the BI ban with equanimity. With the death of Gompers in late 1924, a new generation of leaders took over the AFL, but the federation's politics remained unchanged. The conservatives who headed the major unions in the AFL—the Carpenters, the Mine Workers, the Machinists, and the building-trades unions—had moved right, along with Gompers, in the years after the war. A "spiritual exhaustion" pervaded the labor movement in the 1920s, in the eyes of many observers. Welfare capitalism and company unions spread rapidly, while the AFL's membership continued to decline, hitting a postwar low of 3.4 million members in 1929; membership in company unions swelled to 1.5 million workers in the same years.[7] In this context, cooperation seemed like a better tack. AFL leaders experimented with cooperative union-management efficiency programs and rediscovered the virtues of voluntarism. In the 1920s, the federation shunned the growing movement to create a government program of old-age pensions. Instead, the AFL sponsored its own life insurance company, to give workers "a policy with a union label." To sociologist Selig Perlman, writing in 1928, the federation was "without illusions with regard to the actual extent of labor solidarity." Lacking a militant working class, the only option for the AFL was to "disarm public suspicion" and "commend itself as a constructive force."[8]

New AFL president William Green embraced this task. Green, an Ohio-born coal miner, was an amiable bureaucrat seasoned by years of service in the UMWA. He had none of the fiery passion of Gompers, but he shared the same commitment to preserving the AFL above all other goals. Thus the fight against Communist "wreckers" aroused him to fervor. Anticommunism was woven into Green's presidency from the start. In 1927, he declared, "Organized labor has two tasks. The first is to use its strength to advance the interests of workingmen and the second is unalterable opposition to Communism and all other isms." Like Gompers, Green received regular updates from Ralph Easley, and he appreciated the intelligence Easley supplied.[9]

But the AFL's relationship with the NCF cooled. As a member of the Mine Workers, Green was bound by the union's 1911 ban on membership in the NCF, and he never developed the same sort of partnership with Easley that Gompers had enjoyed. Another AFL official, Matthew Woll, took on that role. Woll was a member of the minuscule Photoengravers' union, and he had become close with Gompers during the war years, when he served as Gompers's deputy on the Council of National Defense and acted as Gompers's proxy on some overseas missions. Woll had been passed over for AFL president, despite Gompers's endorsement, perhaps due to his overbearing personality and reputation as a "champion publicity seeker." Woll was the architect of many of the AFL's cooperative schemes, and he became acting president of the National Civic Federation from 1924 through 1935. As ever, the NCF connection raised hackles for progressives; in 1929, the *Nation* asked, "Is Matthew Woll, then, a friend of labor?" (The answer was "No.") Woll used the NCF as a platform to elevate his own stature much as Easley did.[10]

John P. Frey also rose to prominence after Gompers's death. Born in Minnesota in 1871, Frey worked a series of odd jobs from the age of twelve until he found an apprenticeship in an iron foundry. Frey became a molder, one of the best-paid crafts in manufacturing. He read voraciously in his spare time and got involved in local Republican Party politics in Cincinnati, Ohio, where he moved in 1903. Labor politics proved more accessible, though; he joined the molders' union in 1897 and rapidly moved up to a national vice presidency in 1900, leaving the foundry behind forever. Fastidious, precise, and intellectual, Frey joined a Cincinnati literary salon and served on his local school board; after his hopes of being appointed professor of industrial relations at the University of Cincinnati fell through, he took a post as president of the Ohio Federation of Labor. In the late 1920s, Frey moved to Washington and joined the AFL leadership as secretary and later president of the Metal Trades Department, where he remained until his retirement in 1950. A master of union convention rules and an assiduous record keeper, Frey made himself indispensable to the conservative union presidents who made up the AFL executive council.[11]

Green, Woll, and Frey became the federation's leading strategists in the fight against Communism and radicalism. Increasingly, they relied on their own sources of intelligence. Frey cultivated a particularly useful informant, a freelance reporter named V. R. Tompkins. After an AFL convention, Frey recalled, Tompkins approached him. They chatted about "the progress of the Communist Party and its efforts to secure a foothold in the American trade union movement." Tompkins had been "watching Frey for several years," he confessed, "to see whether [he] could be trusted." Tompkins began to share with Frey "specific record[s] of Communist activity, saying that it was confidential."[12]

Tompkins's background is murky. Years later, he described himself as a reporter who began his career reporting on Emma Goldman's antiwar lecture tour in 1915. According to Frey, Tompkins worked as a freelance journalist and published under a pseudonym. Tompkins collected piles of party documents and assembled dossiers on radicals, and he vied for opportunities to share his research. Whether and how Tompkins also worked with Catholic anticommunists remains unknown. Tompkins became a key source of current information about CPUSA activity, replacing Ralph Easley as the AFL's most reliable informant.[13] Late in his life, Tompkins claimed to have worked for British military intelligence, the U.S. Office of Strategic Services (precursor to the Central Intelligence Agency), the U.S. Secret Service, and a huge array of employers' associations and red squads.[14]

Organizing from Without

For most of the 1920s, the AFL's anticommunist campaigns were mild because there was not much of a Communist "menace" to attack. American Communists continued to flounder, despite yet another change in strategy in 1927. American Communists were to abandon efforts to penetrate the hopelessly corrupted AFL and instead form new mass unions that would be revolutionary from the start. There would be no more boring from within. The CP had already experimented with this idea at Botany Mills in Passaic, New Jersey, in 1926, where a force of 10,000 textile millworkers rather unexpectedly revolted against wage cuts and staged a mass walkout. A young Communist organizer, Albert Weisbord, had been running his own organizing drive among the millworkers, without approval by the party. The AFL's moribund United Textile Workers (UTW) union, despite having failed to even attempt organizing its putative industrial jurisdiction, immediately called foul, and so did the CP leadership, which disapproved of Weisbord's unauthorized organizing. The Communist Party abandoned the strikers to the AFL's UTW, just before the new Comintern directive came down. But the incident underlined an argument made by many Communists and labor radicals: craft unions had little capacity or interest in capitalizing on the vast unrest among the nation's unskilled factory workers.

Over the next several years, the CP's new Trade Union Unity League (TUUL) sniffed out disquiet at textile mills in Gastonia, North Carolina, and New Bedford, Massachusetts, that the UTW had long ignored. Rather than working within existing unions, the TUUL launched new industrial union drives among longshoremen, machinists, and miners, though with less success. Historian Bert Cochran said that after 1927, "the Communist party resembled the prewar IWW to the extent that it supplied leadership for workers abandoned or ignored by AFL officials."[15] William Z. Foster bitterly opposed the change in party strategy. He had spent twenty years arguing that isolating radicals from the AFL weakened both. Now he was obliged to renounce his old platform or face charges of "Right deviation" from Stalin's lieutenants.

The massive drives launched by the TUUL were not very successful in their own right, but they won the admiration of radical American intellectuals such as Theodore Dreiser, John Dos Passos, and Richard Wright, who liked the Communist Party's "revolutionary rhetoric, outlaw status, and confrontational tactics."[16] In the late 1920s the CP earned a reputation among radicals for militant advocacy for neglected masses. Communist activists' real commitment to organizing among black workers in the South, and their growing reputation as fearless militants in local struggles against Jim Crow, also won the party admirers among progressives.

What intellectuals saw as the CP's principled militancy, though, AFL leaders saw as irresponsible adventurism. Each of the big textile strikes collapsed as quickly as they exploded, leaving behind no enduring union structure, no permanent shop-floor gains, and a chastened workforce. The strikes were textbook examples for the reasoning behind craft unionism: unskilled workers who were easily replaced could not sustain challenges to employers' power for very long. And except for scattered locals of mineworkers and longshoremen, few AFL unions had bestirred themselves to support black workers' fights for political rights, while many actively fought black workers' demands for equal access to union jobs.[17]

Visions of Russia

This official shift away from organizing within AFL unions confirmed what federation leaders believed: Communists could make themselves a nuisance within most AFL unions but were not a viable threat to the federation. Nevertheless, the AFL kept its guard up. As the CP turned to building its own unions and internal challenges to AFL leaders abated, federation officials remained alert for international threats.

The AFL's biggest concern was the reinvigorated campaign calling for U.S. diplomatic relations with the Soviet Union that arose in the mid-1920s. A stream of American scientists, agronomists, and intellectuals visited the Soviet Union to observe the Bolshevik experiment and were impressed with what they saw. Labor radicals organized their own such delegation in 1927. Albert Coyle, editor of the *Locomotive Engineers' Journal*, hoped to enlist moderate union officials for a fact-finding trip to the Soviet Union. The AFL vehemently opposed the project. Fierce protests from AFL leaders reduced Coyle's delegation to a rump faction of progressive unionists including James Maurer, socialist president of the Pennsylvania Federation of Labor, and John Brophy, a longtime rival of John L. Lewis in the Mineworkers union. A large complement of intellectuals joined the trip, including Paul Douglas, economist at the University of Chicago and future Illinois senator, and Rexford Tugwell, a Columbia University economist and future New Deal staffer.[18]

In Moscow, the group met with Joseph Stalin and held an extraordinary colloquy on labor and politics. The Americans asked whether the Comintern directed the policy of the CPUSA. "Absolutely untrue," Stalin answered; the Comintern had better things to do than "sit around all day writing instructions." Stalin wondered why American workers had no labor party. The Americans explained that the direct primary system in the United States allowed workers to "get responsible positions and command influence" in the major parties. Stalin also talked at length on the value of principled dissent: unionists should continue to "criticiz[e] the cowardice and the reactionary policies of the reformist labor leaders," because "such criticism can serve only to stimulate and strengthen the labor movement."[19]

On their return, delegates presented their findings to a meeting of 6,000 at Madison Square Garden. Americans had been "duped" by anti-Soviet propaganda, they argued; the workers' state was as democratic as the United States. Douglas distanced himself from the American Communist Party but urged the United States to open diplomatic relations with the Soviet Union, as "it would be an act of treason to mankind to let the Russian experiment go down."[20] The meeting was a harbinger of growing popular affinity for the Soviet Union that would swell in the 1930s.

Labor conservatives countered with their own Russian colloquy. In 1927, AFL executive council members met with Menshevik revolutionary leader Alexander Kerensky, who expressed hearty approval of the AFL's campaign against American diplomatic recognition of the Soviet Union. "It is of immense help to the democratic forces of Russia that the democratic labor forces of the United States are against recognition," Kerensky told them.[21]

Around the same time, Kerensky talked with Edmund A. Walsh, dean of Georgetown University's School of Foreign Service. In the mid-1920s, Walsh emerged as the leading anticommunist organizer among American Catholics. While the Catholic Church officially condemned the Bolshevik Revolution, anticommunism was a minor concern for American Catholics in the 1920s. Walsh had been in Russia in 1922 and 1923 on a papal famine relief mission, where he witnessed the Soviet crackdown on Russian churches. After closing Catholic churches and expropriating their property, Soviet leaders arrested Catholic priests and the Russian archbishop and tried them for counterrevolutionary activity. Walsh frantically sought a visit with the condemned priests to administer last rites, but the deputy archbishop was executed unshriven. Seared by the experience, Walsh returned to the United States determined to raise the alarm. He turned the School of Foreign Service into an anti-Soviet research center and traveled constantly to lecture on the Soviet menace. Warning that American Communists aimed to import atheism and autocracy, Walsh insisted that the United States must never recognize the Soviet Union as a legitimate regime.[22]

Walsh praised the AFL as a "stabilizing element against revolution" and often appeared with AFL leaders on the program at public debates and lectures on Communism. But neither Walsh nor the Catholic Church made special efforts to include American workers or trade unionists in their anticommunist work in the 1920s. Some Catholic unionists such as Peter Collins, an Electrical Worker official from Boston, used their unions as platform to propagandize against Communism and the Soviet Union, and Catholicism underlay the anticommunist animus of some union workers and leaders. By and large, though, Catholic anticommunism was a diffuse sentiment rather than an organized program among AFL unions in these years.[23]

Among Jewish workers, the lines were sharper. Working-class Jews remained the greatest champions of the Soviet Union, and despite their conflicts with American Communists, union leaders such as Sidney Hillman and David Dubinsky defended the Russian experiment. Throughout the 1920s, both the ILGWU and ACWA conventions called for Soviet recognition, over the protests of the prosperous leaders of the American Jewish Committee, which had long fought socialism and the Soviet Union. Abraham Cahan, socialist editor of the *Forward*, became a vociferous opponent of domestic Communism and critic of the Soviet Union in the early 1920s. Cahan often waded into political disputes in the garment unions, siding with socialists and using his newspaper to castigate Bolsheviks and American Communists alike. In the hothouse of the Lower East Side, garment unions, political parties, and cultural institutions formed a continuous and contentious Jewish civil society, and debates over socialism and Communism spilled from the street into the workshop.[24]

While church and union remained distinct in the rest of the labor movement, no clear division can be drawn between Jewish institutions and Jewish unionism in this period. Jewish anticommunism often arose from sectarian loyalties or experiences of political conflict with the Communist Party rather than the antiradicalism shared by other AFL leaders. The case of J. B. S. Hardman is instructive. Hardman, born Jacob Salutsky, had been exiled from Lithuania for his radical activities in 1908. In New York, Salutsky became editor of a radical Jewish newspaper and a leader of the Jewish Socialist Federation.

In the dizzying years after the Bolshevik Revolution, Salutsky and other radicals tried to navigate a middle course between the moderation of the Socialist Party and the uncritical embrace of Bolshevik tactics by the early founders of the American Communist Party. While they shared the radical aims of the Communists, Salutsky and his allies disliked the party's conspiratorial practices and crude political judgments. Rather, Salutsky "envisaged an America in European revolutionary garb, but with coffee on the breakfast table and a bathtub in every house—a revolution with modern American improvements."[25] In historian Tony Michels's words, Salutsky "wanted the impossible: a party at once revolutionary and pragmatic, pro-Soviet and attuned to American conditions."[26]

In 1921, Salutsky and his allies warily negotiated a merger with the Communist Party, but within a few years, Communist Party functionaries took over the Jewish Socialist Federation and its newspaper, and veteran leaders such as Salutsky were expelled. Salutsky later changed his name to J. B. S. Hardman, and he remained a dedicated trade unionist and leftist for the rest of his life, working as the education director for the Amalgamated Clothing Workers of America and as an editor and journalist. Hardman was also a life-long critic of the Communist Party, and particularly its labor organizing. In 1930, Hardman wrote a series of articles on American Communism for the *New Republic*, and his inside experience made his critique especially withering. The Communist Party "went on the rocks because of the inability of its leadership correctly to read developments and trends in American reality," Hardman said. No radical movement could "thrive on a foundation of canonized truth and canned reasoning, and under the tutelage of political puppets manipulated from the distance of 7,000 miles."[27]

This practical sensibility underlay the anticommunism of Jewish labor leaders such as Hardman, Dubinsky, and Hillman. Their experiences in the socialist Jewish labor movement made them sympathetic to leftist politics but pragmatic about the possibilities of political change, and impatient with what Hillman called the "revolutionary phrase-mongering" and "dreamy ultimatums" of American Communists.[28] But Jewish labor anticommunists were careful in their public pronouncements to distinguish between their critiques of American Communism and aspirations for Soviet Russia. Their knowledge of the oppressions of tsarist Russia convinced them that while American Communism was not viable for American workers, Soviet Communism was an improvement for Russian workers. Despite their differences on the nature of the Soviet Union or the viability of American Communism, Jewish anticommunists in the garment unions agreed with Communists and radicals on one question: the United States should recognize the Soviet Union. Diplomatic recognition would increase trade and prosperity for both Soviet and American citizens, and even sworn antagonists such as Cahan hoped to see the Soviet Union reform, not collapse.[29]

A word on anti-Semitism and labor anticommunism. Though working-class Jews were divided on the question of diplomatic recognition, the AFL tended to lump all of them into the pro-Soviet camp. In public statements and private papers, AFL leaders insisted that prejudice never colored their views. But among the largely Christian officials of the AFL, pronouncements about Jewish workers sometimes carried an anti-Semitic and nativist undertone. In his 1930 testimony to the Fish Committee, William Green confided, "you know about the Jewish temperament and the Italian temperament; and the Communists find there a sort of sympathetic and responsive field. It was easier for them to impose on these unsuspecting people in the garment trades than it would be the carpenters or the printers or the musicians or the skilled tradesmen."[30]

Correspondence from union members was often more explicit. An anonymous member of the Typographical Union told John Frey that "the International Jewish bankers and Zionists are using Communism as a wedge to form a Jew World Oligarchy under which we should all work in Jewish sweatshops—if any Christian laborers should still be living!"[31] Many labor anticommunists likely shared the anti-Semitic sentiments rampant in 1920s culture.

At the same time, there is little evidence that anti-Semitism was the motive force for many anticommunist union leaders. Gompers was Jewish, and he never saw radicalism as a particularly Jewish problem. John Frey, in private letters to his old friend W. A. Appleton, the secretary of the General Federation of Trades Unions of Great Britain, expatiated on the peculiarities of American radicalism and immigration. Frey saw "non-English speaking aliens" as a "a most fertile field for the extreme radicals," but not because of any inherent racial or ethnic character. Rather, immigrants "have been exploited from the time they left their native shores. They have realized this and they feel that they owe nothing to our country and their socialist theories lead many of them to feel that they owe nothing to our trade-union movement."[32] There is little hint of anti-Semitism in these remarks; the experience of abuse, not ethnic descent, was the source of radicalism, in Frey's view.

Ralph Easley, on the other hand, showed a proclivity for blaming Jews for the rise of Bolshevism and Communism. During World War I, Easley sometimes circulated materials suggesting that Jewish conspiracy lay behind Lenin's trip from Germany to Russia, and he developed a close relationship with the German propagandist George Sylvester Viereck. In the early 1930s, Easley was impressed with the Nazi attacks on the German Communist Party, and he got back in touch with Viereck to organize an effort to reverse American boycotts of German goods. When Easley reached out to the American Jewish Congress for help, they declined, incredulous. Easley tried to mobilize his anticommunist labor allies in this effort and to sign labor conservatives up for expressions of support for the Nazis' anticommunist initiatives. Labor anticommunists refused to endorse Easley's efforts. While Easley vehemently denied any anti-Semitic sentiment, this campaign suggests otherwise. At the same time, Easley's inability to enlist any union leaders in overtly or covertly anti-Semitic work undermines the notion that anti-Semitism was a primary motivation for many labor anticommunists.[33]

Armchair Anticommunism

But anti-Semitism pervaded the growing network of antiradical activists that emerged in the 1920s. During the wartime loyalty campaigns and postwar Red Scare, patriotic organizations such as the American Legion and the Daughters of the American Revolution functioned as both clearinghouses and proving grounds for a generation of anticommunist activists. They shared a politics of militant nationalism and aggressive nativism and deplored the social leveling and secularism of Bolshevism and Communism. While popular anxieties about anarchism and Bolshevism died down by the mid-1920s, especially after the 1924 restriction of immigration, the anticommunist network stayed on alert. Historian Ellen Schrecker describes this anticommunist network as a sort of "lunatic fringe" that was derided by contemporaries for its often-ludicrous claims. But they managed to "keep the countersubversive ideology alive" in the 1920s and early 1930s, and their notes and contacts seeded the shock troops of McCarthyism in the 1940s.[34]

But unlike labor anticommunists, these antiradicals had little occasion to contend with actual Communists in their daily life. Elizabeth Dilling, author of the book *Red Network*, was a "University of Chicago educated, conservatory trained concert harpist."[35] Harvard graduate Richard M. Whitney had been a newspaper reporter for the *Los Angeles Times* and *Associated Press* when he wrote his 1922 book, *Reds in America*.[36] They both learned about Communism through reading about it.

I call them armchair anticommunists, because they worked like armchair detectives, collecting stacks of documents and bits of intelligence like magpies and building vast libraries of literature. From their armchairs, they pored over their collections and pieced together clues about political movements far removed from their experiences. It was not very difficult to find material. The CPUSA published prolifically, putting out a monthly magazine, innumerable weeklies, broadsides, and pamphlets. Government investigations such as the Lusk Committee produced multivolume reports that reproduced party documents, testimony, and the findings of previous government investigations. Well-connected armchair anticommunists had sources in police red squads and, before 1924, the BI. People such as Whitney, Dilling, and Walter Steele of the *National Republic* looked for patterns and found vast red webs connecting far-flung radical movements to liberal organizations to progressive politicians.[37]

For the armchair anticommunists, the international Communist movement was a Trojan horse carrying social anarchy. Elizabeth Dilling called on her readers to "ask yourself if in recent years sex, pacifistic, atheistic, and socialistic propaganda has increased in America and why."[38] Communist calls for African American liberation were particularly threatening, and a strong current of nativism ran through the armchair anticommunists' literature. Their meticulously documented research, full of charts showing linkages among radical and liberal organizations, came in handy for such reactionary organizations and movements as the Ku Klux Klan, antifeminism, and immigration restriction in the 1920s.

By linking diverse social movements and cultural phenomena, from settlement houses to the Harlem Renaissance, armchair anticommunists imagined the CPUSA as the domestic agent of a vast international conspiracy to derange traditional American social relations and power structures. To their opponents, anticommunists looked like a similarly structured conservative conspiracy. In his 1927 exposé, *Professional Patriots*, journalist Norman Hapgood constructed his own "spider-web chart" showing ties between groups such as the National Civic Federation, the American Legion, and business and government officials.[39]

Commonsense Anticommunism

From their direct experience combating Communism, AFL officials drew different conclusions from the armchair anticommunists. First, they saw American Communism as a political program, not a cultural tendency. While an antiradical such as Elizabeth Dilling glimpsed "Communistic" undercurrents in labor strikes, antilynching campaigns, and Christian pacifism, union leaders saw Communism as a much more delimited phenomenon that was manifest in Communists' observable activities organizing workers and activists into parties and unions. Moreover, they regarded the CP as unsuccessful, having failed to organize or retain many adherents, surviving only because of financial support from the Comintern. Second, this clear-eyed assessment of the actual state of American Communist organizing convinced union leaders that as an ideology, Communism held little appeal for Americans. The CP's danger lay in its capacity to co-opt popular issues and foment unrest in established institutions such as the AFL, not in the ideal of Communism per se.[40]

Following from these premises, labor anticommunists insisted that exposure was the way to fight Communism. Simply telling potential recruits about conditions in the Soviet Union, or showing them Lenin's writings, generally sufficed. When the CP proceeded by stealth, tactics such as unmasking CP front groups and organizers worked well. Invariably, labor anticommunists added that desperation was the breeding ground of radicalism. Autocratic employers were the CP's best organizers.

I call this approach "commonsense anticommunism." I use the term "commonsense" in two seemingly incongruous senses, to convey both practical simplicity and ideological complexity. In the first sense, I use the term in its plain meaning, to suggest that this style of anticommunism relied on a rational analysis grounded in facts and expressing widely held views. Labor conservatives' rejection of radical political visions and reservations about centralized state power reflected mainstream opinion, and their judgments about the nature and reach of Communism comported with the actual condition of the party.

In the second sense, commonsense beliefs do not simply register an uncontested reality but function as an ideological worldview that appears "natural and self-evident." Writing in an Italian prison in the late 1920s, Communist leader Antonio Gramsci struggled to understand the appeal of Fascism and unpopularity of Communism for Italian workers and peasants. One explanation was "common sense": a sort of collective consciousness that was a complicated blend of contradictory political tendencies, both radical and reactionary. In the main, however, the "common sense" tended to rationalize existing political and economic hierarchies and rebuff revolutionary ideas. Labor anticommunists embodied a similar swirl of political views— sometimes militant, sometimes conservative—and this "common sense" ideology was organic and often unpredictable.[41]

The AFL's commonsense anticommunism put them at odds with the red network. Their growing estrangement from Easley's National Civic Federation was an early sign of this divergence. In 1923, Easley circulated articles by armchair anticommunist Fred Marvin to union officers. John Frey was skeptical. "I know something concerning their unscrupulous methods," he wrote Easley, but Communists "exercise no such influence as Mr. Marvin seems to imagine."[42]

At the same time, AFL leaders developed their own dossier. The federation had direct experience with Communist organizing on a regular basis. Their organizers and union locals regularly confronted actual Communists. They did not need to read the *Daily Worker* to find out what the party was doing in the trade-union field. Leaders and organizers seasoned by fights such as the cloak-makers' strike or the Farmer-Labor Party episode had first-hand accounts of Communist tactics, broadsides and leaflets from organizing drives and strikes, and ranks of disaffected workers to draw on. This was local knowledge, unavailable to people such as Richard Whitney or Elizabeth Dilling, and it had national scope, unlike the intelligence collected by city red squads. Their years in the trenches fighting Communists made AFL leaders into authorities on the Communist Party with no equals after 1924.

Commonsense Anticommunism and the BI

With labor anticommunists' own intelligence and their ability to self-police, who needed the BI? Ralph Easley saw the situation differently. Despite his increasing isolation from the labor movement, Easley continued to lobby against Communism in the late 1920s. Reversing the ban on BI surveillance headed his wish list. Self-interest surely motivated him; without his old pipeline to the BI, Easley's intelligence and his usefulness dwindled. The problem was that seditious speech and organizing was no longer a federal crime. Short of a new sedition law, Easley proposed to reinterpret the Constitution. Archibald E. Stevenson, the former counsel to the Lusk Committee and Easley's longtime staffer, came up with a workaround. Stevenson argued that syndicalism and criminal anarchy "are attacks against the republican form of government in the several states," and thus the federal government had a "constitutional obligation" to investigate radicalism. No sedition law was needed; the Congress could merely "give effect" to the constitutional duty by appropriating funds for the BI to commence its work.[43]

Delighted with this new theory, Easley took it to the Department of Justice in the spring of 1927. J. Edgar Hoover swiftly demurred. Stevenson's argument "was a view point that I had never considered," he told Easley in his confidential letter. But regardless of the merits of the idea, Hoover opposed the idea of furtively slipping a new antiradical appropriation into the BI's budget. "If the people of the United States are desirous of having the Federal Government combat radical activities, there should then be, on the Statute book, specific legislation making such activities a crime." Hoover volunteered that, in his personal opinion, the best form for such a law would make it a crime to "advocate the overthrow of the United States by force and violence." But Congress would have to decide whether such a law was constitutional or favored by voters.[44]

Undeterred, Easley and Stevenson continued to circulate their proposal. Asked his opinion in 1927, AFL president William Green equivocated on the question, promising to give the idea "thoughtful and serious consideration."[45] But some old allies rejected the notion. Louis Marshall of the American Jewish Committee sent a blistering critique. "A long arm would reach out from a secret bureau located in Washington, for the purpose of seizing those who may meet the displeasure of the little bureaucrats invested with tremendous power," he wrote. "My advice is to stop this pernicious propaganda."[46] To resurrect the old BI, it seemed, Easley and Stevenson would have to revive the Sedition Act. Demonstrating the existence of seditious conspiracies would be the first step.

By early 1930, Easley thought he had proof: documents proving that the Soviet Union was instigating revolution in the United States. Easley loved skullduggery and secret operations, and, ever since his first foray into detective work during the Great War, he had been an easy target for self-styled Russian princesses, intelligence agents, and ex-Communists looking to sell their stories. In 1929, Gaston Means, a veteran con man, found his way to Easley's office. Means had worked for William J. Burns's corrupt BI and served a prison term for bootlegging. Now he claimed to know where to find a stash of secret documents proving that Amtorg, the Soviet Union's trade office in New York, was financing strikes. Easley, eager to demonstrate his value to his old union allies, took the bait. He paid Means thousands of dollars to track down the incriminating documents, and, for months, Means cabled Easley for more funds, claiming to have just missed an elusive Soviet agent. As Richard Gid Powers has shown, the Amtorg revelations turned into a debacle. Easley had been duped, conned out of lavish sums by Means, whose promises of a warehouse full of documents turned out to be an empty locker. But, somehow, Easley got his hands on another set of papers purporting to show that Amtorg was planning a massive demonstration for May Day, 1930. Easley convinced New York City police chief Grover Whalen that a riotous uprising was imminent, and he shared his intelligence with Congressman Hamilton Fish.[47]

Revolution was in fact in the air. The Depression had been throwing people out of work in New York and across the world. Unemployed workers, already restless, flocked to meetings and rallies organized by the Communist Party. The Comintern designated March 6, 1930, as "International Unemployment Day," calling on Communists to lead marches in cities around the world. The response was remarkable: 35,000 New Yorkers marched in Union Square;

75,000 people gathered in Detroit; and smaller crowds massed in Seattle, Los Angeles, and Boston, joining marchers in Paris, London, and other European cities.[48] A backlash erupted immediately. On March 6, Hamilton Fish rose in Congress to call for an investigation into the Communist Party, its propaganda and strategy, and its campaign to "advocate the overthrow by force or violence of the government of the United States."[49]

Easley saw his opportunity. In the initial debate over convening a congressional investigation, Fish made no mention of sedition laws or the BI's lack of investigative authority. Once Fish's committee had been authorized, Easley jumped into action, sharing his files and his ideas. By the time the Fish Committee convened a few months later, the question of the BI's countersubversive authority had risen to the top of its agenda. As Fish explained in his opening statement, "the Federal Government has practically no power to deal with the activities or propaganda of any of the Communists in the United States"; and the Department of Justice "has no agents that are following up on the activities of the Communists" and "no authority to act." His congressional colleagues expressed their surprise about this state of affairs: "That is certainly news to me," said one.[50] Behind the scenes, Easley had engineered an inquiry into his pet project.

Over the next year, the Fish Committee took testimony from antiradical activists, union leaders, urban red-squad officers, and Communists on Communist organizing, Soviet espionage, and civil liberties. Roger Baldwin from the ACLU was there, and so were representatives from the American Legion. Armchair anticommunists such as Walter Steele testified alongside Communist leader William Z. Foster, and J. Edgar Hoover appeared in a closed session. A large contingent of union leaders, from William Green to John L. Lewis, appeared as well. The Fish Committee hearings offer a snapshot of the styles of American anticommunism at the beginnings of the 1930s, before the heyday of American Communism.

Virtually all of the witnesses were hostile to Communism; only the ACLU and Communists themselves defended the party or its principles. On the question of civil liberties, though, a clear divide separated anticommunists into two camps. The armchair anticommunists such as Walter Steele and American Legionnaires uniformly backed a new sedition law and expansion of the BI's political policing authority. Labor anticommunists and the ACLU opposed the criminalization of Communism and political speech. Their stance on state power showed the split between reactionaries who saw Communism as a proxy for a broader repressive agenda and antiradicals who saw

Communism as a despicable but legitimate political movement and a repressive state as a real menace.

Walter Steele, various American Legionnaires, and a representative from the Daughters of the American Revolution showed up with stacks and stacks of files they had collected on Communism. They read into the record testimony from old congressional hearings, newspaper articles, and Communist Party tracts, often repeating each other and prompting pleas for brevity from congressmen. The armchair anticommunists formed a chorus of support for an expanded BI. The committee must enact "some proper authorization for adequate defensive action by our Government," said Steele.[51]

Ralph Easley did not testify. But he arranged for a letter from Elihu Root, a former secretary of war and conservative Republican, to be entered as evidence. The letter backed Easley's BI plan. "An assault is being made by secret means, supported by the resources of a great empire," Root wrote, "and we find that the Federal Government has no police force available for our protection. Of course, such a force ought to be provided."[52] Leading Catholic anticommunist Edmund Walsh denounced the menace of Soviet collectivism and the international reach of the Comintern, but no one asked him his view on domestic political policing, and he did not venture an opinion.

As for the BI's position on the matter, J. Edgar Hoover testified in closed session, where he reiterated to the Congress what he had told Ralph Easley: if Congress wanted the BI to police Communists, it would have to come up with a law banning Communism. Hoover agreed that Communism was a serious domestic problem, sketching out the party's agitation among workers, African Americans, and the unemployed, but emphasized that Communist organizing did not violate Federal law. He ventured his view that legislation "that would make it a crime for any individual or any group of individuals to advocate the overthrow of the Government of the United States by force or violence" would be "perfectly proper." But Hoover urged Congress to take care in crafting any such legislation, as "no one wants any legislation that abridges the freedom of the press or the freedom of speech, or the right to strike, or any inalienable right."[53] Without explicit congressional authority, there was "no law applicable and no appropriations available" for BI surveillance of Communists.[54] Both Hoover and Assistant Attorney General Oscar Luhring insisted that the BI had halted anticommunist policing in 1924.[55]

Roger Baldwin echoed the BI officials' view that political radicalism was perfectly legal. Asked whether the ACLU upheld "the right of an American citizen to advocate force and violence against the government," Baldwin shot back, "Certainly, in so far as mere advocacy is concerned." Repression was more likely than radicalism to produce revolutions, Baldwin told the committee, and outlawing Communism or creating a federal "secret police" would "drive the movement into underground channels, with the inevitable tendency to secret conspiracies and to violence."[56] This was a classic statement of the civil liberties credo developed in the early 1920s.

The ACLU and the American Legion responded predictably, in accord with past public statements. But Fish and the other congressmen seemed surprised by the labor anticommunists' stance. Their hostility toward Communism was well known, and so was the AFL's often-expressed antipathy for the ACLU. Likely Fish thought that union leaders would back his proposals. Instead, William Green sounded more like a civil libertarian. There was no need for expanded state authority, he argued. Private organizations such as the AFL could deal with the problem. The AFL preferred to treat Communism as an internal union problem, using organizational tools such as trials and membership bans to keep avowed Communists out of unions. Strong trade unions were the best defense against Communism, AFL president William Green told Congress in 1930, as they permitted working people "to express themselves through organizations of their own choosing." Free citizens could assess Communism for themselves, and union workers initially gulled quickly realized that Communist "doctrine is not on a sound basis, and they soon see what it all means, and then the Communist is done; he is driven out."[57] Several labor leaders reported success in expelling Communists from their organizations: A. Philip Randolph, head of the Brotherhood of Sleeping Car Porters, testified that his union had "grappled with the communists, and we routed them and practically destroyed their movement." He said, "They do not molest us any more now."[58]

Labor anticommunists expressed this sentiment repeatedly in the Fish hearings. Unions could handle Communists on their own. "We are not afraid of them. We will deal with them," Green told the committee. "We have served notice on them that the fight is on, and we will meet them wherever they are."[59] There was no need for new federal legislation, or for an enlarged BI. John L. Lewis, a veteran anticommunist, said that "the very idea of a Federal or secret police force in this country is obnoxious to me personally and I am quite sure would be opposed by the members of the United Mine Workers of America."[60] Even Matthew Woll temporized on the question of expanding BI surveillance, on the grounds that "legitimate trade unions and trade-union leaders have been arrested and hunted under the assumption that they were Bolsheviks."[61] No Jewish union leaders appeared at the hearings, nor any Jewish leaders at all, for that matter. Their well-known support for Soviet recognition, and Louis Marshall's opposition to Easley's BI proposal, likely kept the Fish Committee from inviting them.

Commonsense anticommunism carried the day. In its final report, the Fish Committee proposed to outlaw the Communist Party, cancel the citizenship of party members, deport resident alien Communists, and ban Communist publications from the mail, but Congress declined to even consider most of these recommendations (although the House Immigration Committee favorably reported a bill to exclude alien Communists). The ACLU immediately organized against the Fish report. As a fallback, Fish sought legislation to simply grant the BI special authority and funds to investigate Communists, but that bill went nowhere, too.[62] Fish complained, "If this empowerment of the Department of Justice and the provision for deportation of alien Communists were submitted to the American public throughout the country, I am convinced that they would be carried in a plebiscite or referendum, 99 to 1."[63] The Congress's disinterest in the matter suggests otherwise. William Green likely came closer to conventional wisdom when he said of Communism, "I do not want to exaggerate the importance and influence of Communism in our country. At the present time I do not regard it as of a serious nature or of a serious character. It is, perhaps, true that the most serious aspect of it is its potential possibilities."[64]

As a result of the actions of the AFL, the ACLU, and J. Edgar Hoover, the United States entered the Depression without a sedition act and without a federal antiradical police force. Communist organizers enjoyed an open field wherever local authorities let them organize. Over the next decade, Communist organizers experimented with new approaches modeled on their successes mobilizing unemployed workers and supporting African American insurgencies. In Chicago stockyards, Alabama cotton fields, and the City College cafeteria, the Communist critique of commonsense political and economic relations helped Americans imagine alternative ways to structure the state.

As Communist organizing escalated during the Depression, AFL leaders had occasion to regret their restraint. Over the course of the 1930s, the AFL gradually abandoned its commonsense anticommunism, but by then, it was too late. Communists got their chance to remake the world, and AFL leaders would have a smaller place in it.

CHAPTER EIGHT

Labor's Counter-Reformation

The American Federation of Labor and the End of Reform

In early November 1933, Maximilian Litvinoff, the foreign affairs commissar of the Soviet Union, arrived in Washington to negotiate a deal with the new U.S. president, Franklin Delano Roosevelt. In the depths of the Depression, business leaders pleaded with Roosevelt to restore diplomatic relations with the Soviet Union and allow American companies to resume trade with Russian firms. The heads of General Motors, International Business Machines, Curtiss-Wright, and the Pennsylvania Railroad eagerly waited for word as Roosevelt's State Department negotiated with Litvinoff.[1]

William Green, the AFL president, fretted. The AFL had opposed recognition of Russia since the October Revolution, but now it seemed inevitable. Green issued a public "memorandum" to Roosevelt, outlining the sordid history of Communist incursions in American institutions; it was "information that ought to be catalogued in the home of every American," Green wrote, "a blacklist of hated interlopers and destroyers." Reminding Roosevelt of the AFL's extensive experience as "the first line of defense" against Communism, Green aimed to show "the imperative necessity, in Labor's opinion" of demanding guarantees from Litvinoff that "none of the various agencies of international Communist propaganda will function in the United States."[2]

The United States recognized the Soviet government, as Green expected. Roosevelt extracted a promise from Litvinoff that the USSR would cease Communist propaganda in the United States, as Green had requested. Still, neither government seemed to take the pledge very seriously. In fact, Communist organizing escalated sharply, as the Communist Party's new legitimacy burnished its appeal for many Americans. The episode was symptomatic of the

AFL's relationship to the Roosevelt administration. Frequently FDR and his staff gave AFL complaints a polite hearing but little credence, especially when they concerned Communism. Stymied by New Dealers, labor conservatives sought new allies in Congress.

The AFL joined conservative capitalists and farmers in protesting the incursions of the New Deal state. They voiced a common critique: technocratic officials, insulated from popular pressure and insensitive to local conditions, arrogated authority from rightful leaders and deranged settled social and economic relations. Labor conservatives who had limited say in the creation of New Deal labor policy also came to deplore the meddlesome officials appointed to administer it. Within months of the passage of the Wagner Act, the AFL fractured into two hostile camps. Unionists who opposed the AFL's conservative leadership split off from the AFL, forming a Committee of Industrial Organizations. With powerful backing from the New Deal state, the CIO thrived. Those who remained behind in the AFL seethed. Labor conservatives felt increasingly alienated from the coalition of industrial workers, liberals, and radicals committed to an interventionist welfare state that was coalescing in the Democratic Party. In a few short years, the nation's political economy had been transformed, and the AFL's place in it seemed much smaller.

Feeling isolated and embattled, labor conservatives reached out to other opponents of the new regime who sought to hem in the New Deal, reduce progressives' congressional majority, and end reform. Labor conservatives criticized the Roosevelt administration's labor policy, backed Republicans and conservative Democrats in the 1938 midterm elections, and collaborated with the National Association of Manufacturers and the Liberty League to curtail the Wagner Act and the National Labor Relations Board (NLRB).

AFL attacks on Roosevelt gained little traction with union members or the general public, but their complaints about the CIO and the Communists struck a chord. In a strange coincidence of history, in 1935 the Communist Party resumed efforts to organize within mainstream unions, just as the CIO was forming. The emergence of a hostile Nazi regime in Germany frightened the Soviet Union into seeking alliances with liberals in governments and unions everywhere, and, accordingly, American Communists seized on the CIO and the New Deal. Communism thus became commingled with the CIO from its birth. This relationship enraged and astonished labor conservatives, as did the Roosevelt administration's evident unconcern about the matter. As the Popular Front Communist Party abandoned its old sectarianism and championed an expansive social-democratic vision, labor conservatives insisted that Communism was genetically totalitarian and anti-American. In the 1930s, this position put them at odds with the New Deal order.

Nevertheless, labor conservatives maintained their commonsense approach to civil liberties. The AFL still opposed efforts to reinstate the Sedition Act in 1935, reiterating their argument that voluntarist exposure and exclusion was the best way to contain Communism. But the frequent alliance of the National Labor Relations Board with the CIO challenged labor conservatives' reluctant toleration policy. As direct critiques of FDR's labor-policy regime failed to gain much purchase, labor conservatives tried another tack and attempted to whip up a new Red Scare aimed at rooting out Communists in the NLRB and the CIO. That strategy proved to be far more effective.

The State versus the Unions

Urban workers and coal miners helped Roosevelt sweep into office in 1932. AFL unions had little to do with the victory. The federation had maintained its customary nonpartisan stance, and several union leaders, John L. Lewis most prominent among them, endorsed Hoover. Roosevelt's support for protective labor legislation while he was governor of New York earned him the goodwill of many union leaders. But during his election campaign he had consistently displayed greater solicitude for the needs and votes of unorganized workers than of labor unions. Given the political impotence and small size of AFL unions, this was a risk-free strategy, as his election returns demonstrated.

Once in office, FDR signaled his indifference to the demands of the AFL with his first major labor-policy decision, the selection of the secretary of labor. A union official had held the office since the creation of the cabinet post in 1916, and several AFL leaders jockeyed for the nomination. But FDR picked Frances Perkins, a former lobbyist for the National Consumer's League and industrial commissioner for New York state. "Very unsatisfactory," AFL leaders grumbled.[3]

The AFL's grievances mounted. In contrast to their experience with the last labor-friendly president, Woodrow Wilson, few union officials were appointed to positions in the Roosevelt administration or played much of a role in formulating labor policy or programs in the New Deal. As political scientist David Plotke has argued, a cohesive political bloc of "progressive liberals" drove much of the New Deal's experimentation with new approaches to old problems such as cyclical economic downturns and labor unrest. People such as Felix Frankfurter, Senator Robert F. Wagner, and Heywood Broun, seeded throughout the government, the universities, and the media, functioned as a coherent leadership with shared progressive values, notably a belief in a strong central modernizing state using its authority to redistribute wealth and power equitably among citizens.[4]

A cadre of leftist unionists such as Sidney Hillman and John Brophy, scarred by the union wars of the 1920s, made up the labor wing of the progressive alliance. Progressives were familiar with the AFL's strenuously antistatist politics and defense of union autonomy, as well as its narrow membership and longstanding failure to organize the bulk of the working class. "While I was all for upholding workers' rights," recalled one Labor Department official, "I was not automatically pro-union. Far from it . . . I doubt[ed] the efficacy of any program designed to increase the strength of the A.F. of L."[5] Other New Dealers in key positions had no experience at all with unions or industrial work, for that matter. A key New Deal operative, Heber Blankenhorn, remembered the early labor board staffers as "young fellows whose hearts were more or less in the right place but whose ignorance of labor conditions was terrific."[6]

Thus, although labor and employment policy lay at the center of the New Deal project, the AFL played little role in creating it. In the White House and the Congress, progressive intellectuals and policymakers wrote labor legislation and programs, and AFL leaders jostled to amend or endorse proposed acts well after their outlines were established.[7] AFL leaders welcomed the New Deal's broad endorsement of unionization, but legislation increasingly included too much government oversight and too few guarantees of AFL preeminence for their taste.[8]

The first round of New Deal legislation showed the emerging conflict between AFL and New Deal views. The National Industrial Recovery Act (NIRA) required industry codes to acknowledge workers' right to unionize and elevated unions to parity with employers and the state in tripartite code governance. Although the AFL's modest membership meant that it could claim a role in only 23 of 500 industry codes, the federation lobbied unsuccessfully to be appointed as code representative for nonunion employees.[9] For the AFL, no prior relationship with workers was needed to establish its authority to speak on any worker's behalf. As the AFL argued in 1938, its affiliates "enjoyed a right to establish a bargaining relationship with an employer entirely independent of the provisions of public policy and irrespective of whether the union represented a majority, a minority, or indeed any, of its employees."[10] The Congress's demurral signaled that the notion of agency—that unions

derived provisional legal status as the agents of members and had to demonstrate that members actually wanted to join them—was becoming increasingly central to New Deal policy.[11]

The 1935 Wagner Act, also known as the National Labor Relations Act
(NLRA), took a more interventionist approach. An appointed government
board would adjudicate the validity of workers' claims to union representation. Rather than simply accept a union's assertion of jurisdiction over
a group of workers, the board would poll workers to assess whether they
wanted to be represented and determine the grouping of employees most ap-
propriate for recognition. To ensure support from southern Democrats, agricultural and domestic workers were explicitly excluded from the law's protection, effectively withholding labor rights from a majority of African American
and women workers. Industrial workers, not the AFL, would decide for themselves who represented them. The AFL objected and sought amendments that
assured its authority to choose who and how to organize, but the federation
was overridden. In the heady days of 1935, the AFL endorsed the bill anyway,
enticed by the sweeping new protections it conferred.[12]

While many labor conservatives felt dismay at the prospect of robust state
oversight, pragmatic unionists cheered. An early sign of restiveness inside the
AFL was rank-and-file agitation to reverse the AFL's longstanding opposition
to state unemployment insurance.[13] As thousands of unorganized workers,
recognizing the NIRA's section 7(a) as an unprecedented federal sanction for
unionization, spontaneously formed new unions, numerous union leaders
scrapped their reflexive cynicism about state oversight. UMW president
John L. Lewis exemplified the pattern: a lifelong Republican and supporter
of Hoover who shared the AFL philosophy of union preeminence as the best
guarantee of workers' welfare, he quickly shed his antistatist impulses and
began planning how to use the new law to organize entire sectors of the economy. He saw that existing unions could thrive under a strong state.

The ACLU versus the New Deal

Roger Baldwin also understood this fact. He spent several years fighting the
NIRA and the Wagner Act, on the grounds that state sanction of standard AFL
practices would privilege conservative AFL unions over radical unions such as
those organized by the Communist Trade Union Unity League (TUUL). Baldwin had been drifting closer to the Communist Party since the mid-1920s.
Like many American liberals, he was inspired by the example of the Soviet
Union as the first worker's state. Baldwin regularly defended the Soviet gov-

ernment against charges of repression, arguing that the exigencies of revolution were outweighed by the historical importance of the Soviet experiment.
Emma Goldman chided Baldwin for glossing over the tyrannies of the Soviet
dictatorship, but Baldwin was not much different from many other Americans who hoped that the Soviet Union could bring the socialist dream to life.
Having toured Russia in 1926, Baldwin returned as a self-described "notoriously pro-Soviet" advocate, publishing *Liberty under the Soviets*, an extended
vindication of the Soviet regime. Over the next few years, Baldwin's support
for American Communists deepened. Within the ACLU, Baldwin stood out,
as the group's leadership tended more toward socialism than Communism.[14]

As progressive and liberal activists streamed into Roosevelt's new government of "alphabet agencies," Baldwin stayed on the outside, dubious of this
burgeoning state power. Like other veteran activists, Baldwin remembered
how, during World War I, seemingly innocuous authority could swiftly turn
oppressive. What would prevent these new agencies from following the same
trajectory? To historian Judy Kutulas, this memory separated older civil libertarians such as Baldwin from younger activists who trusted the progressives
who filled Roosevelt's administration and, by extension, trusted the government. The NIRA and the Wagner Act made this tension clear. Baldwin feared
that the Wagner Act would be a "dangerous, fascist intrusion of government
into unions," intended to bolster conservative union leaders, much as federal
labor policy had done during the war.[15]

In September 1933, Baldwin escorted a small delegation to the White House
to make this case directly to Roosevelt. The delegation included William
Dunne, secretary of the TUUL, socialist A. J. Muste from the Conference for
Progressive Labor Action, and Louis Weinstock, a Communist member of the
Painters' union. Baldwin draped these radicals with his own political credi-
bility, orchestrating what was surely the first and only meeting between an
American president and Communist organizers about labor policy. Baldwin's
American Civil Liberties Union helped usher the Communist Party into the
mainstream of American politics.[16]

Together, Baldwin and the CP fought Wagner's proposed labor legislation.
Labor "wins its rights to organize and bargain collectively not by dependence
on governmental agencies," Baldwin wrote, "but by its own organized power."
He sounded a lot like Communist leaders. In the early 1930s, the Communist Party was locked in an ultra-leftist phase, and for party leaders, the main
enemy was neither conservatives nor capitalists but New Dealers, whom they
called "social-fascists." According to the CP, New Dealers misled the working
class into dead-end bourgeois democracy: the NIRA was an "industrial slavery

act," and Roosevelt was comparable to Mussolini. A Communist Party official testified before the Senate, for example, that the law aimed to "enforce compulsory arbitration directly under the control of Government agencies," and he deplored the "time-serving economists and pretentious social-welfare workers" who administered New Deal programs.[17] "We see no hope in the present tendency of the administration either for impartial enforcement," Baldwin wrote to Wagner in early 1935, "or any assurance that labor's rights will be enhanced."[18]

The reaction was swift. Progressive allies such as W. Jett Lauck and Morris Hillquit had already tried to dissuade Baldwin from joining the CP's campaign against the Wagner Act; now his board revolted. Liberal ACLU board members such as Arthur Garfield Hays organized a referendum of the national ACLU membership on the question of the Wagner Act, while several local ACLU affiliates publicly disavowed the opposition to the bill. ACLU members' overwhelming support for the Wagner Act forced Baldwin to backtrack.

The Communist Party switched its position the following year. In Moscow, the Comintern reacted to the rise of European fascism by ordering international affiliates to join forces with liberals and form a Popular Front. American Communists balked, but pressure from the Comintern obliged them to mute their criticism of Roosevelt in early 1936 and actively support the Democrats in the run-up to the 1936 presidential election. Party membership shot up to 75,000 by 1938. The CPUSA changed from a sectarian splinter group into the left wing of the Democratic alliance. Championing the Wagner Act became a platform of the Popular Front party. Heber Blankenhorn, a staffer in Wagner's Senate office, witnessed the turnabout. In the winter of 1937, some reporters came by his office with a CP pamphlet called "Save the Wagner Act." Blankenhorn remembered, "As they read out parts of it, you would have gathered from that pamphlet that the real father and the only true friend" of the Wagner Act "from the very beginning was the Communist Party. We sat there and laughed."[19]

Inalienable Rights

As ever, Baldwin's Communist associations rankled the AFL. So did the CP's ascension to political respectability. But the federation held fast to its civil liberties policy. Labor conservatives opposed efforts to revive federal laws restricting advocacy of radical ideas and kept its distance from the resurgent antiradical network.

In the early years of the New Deal, armchair anticommunists redrew their charts of red webs to include Roosevelt's brain trust. In 1934, Elizabeth Dilling published *The Red Network*, which linked Rexford Tugwell, Frances Perkins, and Eleanor Roosevelt to a global Communist alliance. Was President Roosevelt "stupid, blind, badly-informed, and played-upon by radicals," Dilling wondered, "or well-informed and deliberately playing the Red game?" Irate businessmen and sidelined Democrats joined in, organizing the Liberty League to fight FDR and imputing Bolshevist designs to initiatives such as the National Recovery Administration.[20]

Congressional conservatives responded with a rash of new antiradical legislation. Seven federal sedition bills were introduced in Congress in 1934 and 1935. Several of these bills originated in efforts to control Fascist speech and expanded to include Communism only after antiradicals intervened. The House Special Committee on Un-American Activities exemplified the pattern: originally launched to investigate Nazism, the committee's purview widened to include Communism as well, thanks to determined lobbying by Ralph Easley and other armchair anticommunists. Congressman John McCormack chaired the panel, but Congressman Samuel Dickstein maneuvered to reorient its focus. Dickstein invited Easley to organize a panel of witnesses to testify on the Communist menace in late 1934, and Easley arranged for Archibald Stevenson to make his case for ordering the Bureau of Investigation to resume antiradical surveillance. Remarkably, Easley's recent humiliation in the Gaston Means debacle did not seem to impair his credibility with the committee.[21]

Easley lined up the usual roster of patriotic organizations, including the Better America Foundation, the American Legion, and the Veterans of Foreign Wars. Matthew Woll appeared on behalf of the NCF, in his role as acting president. He supported Stevenson's call for a new sedition act and renewed political policing, with the caveat that labor organizations should be specially exempted. As a vice president of the AFL, Woll's presence implied labor support for the proposal.

But William Green dispelled that notion. In lengthy remarks, Green restated his reservations about federal restrictions on political speech. "Freedom of speech, freedom of the press, and freedom of assembly are cardinal principles in a democracy," he said. And he "had never been very much in favor of giving the Government power to conduct undercover investigations." It was better to "rely on a healthy and aroused public opinion." The AFL had dedicated itself to making "an exposé" of Communism for just that purpose. Chairman McCormack told him, "Mr. Green, I am very much interested in your views," given Green's well-known antipathy toward Communism. Green impressed him with the "difficulty of reaching this evil by legislation."[22] In the committee's final report, McCormack called for a stripped-down sedition law, but declined to endorse expanded authority for the Justice Department.[23]

Roger Baldwin was impressed too; he wrote to Green to say that "this is precisely the position we take" at the ACLU. The ACLU organized a mass rally at Madison Square Garden in April 1935 to protest the "gag rule trend." Fifteen thousand people heard Baldwin, a Methodist bishop, and Congressman Vito Marcantonio, among others, denounce the proposed sedition bills. Francis Gorman, the vice president of the Textile Workers' union, appeared as well. The AFL-affiliated Textile Workers had fought Communists as vigorously as other unions. But, Gorman said, "We have gained for American workers certain recognitions of rights which are now supposed to be inalienable. The organized labor movement must stand solidly against any infringement of the civil liberties of American citizens in these matters."[24]

William Green reinforced the AFL's position when queried by affiliated unions. When a concerned member of the International Typographical Union asked about the AFL's appearance before the committee, Green assured him that "the American Federation of Labor has always been opposed to sedition laws." The Pocatello, Idaho, Central Labor Union inquired about a petition being circulated to support the sedition laws. Green reassured them, "you were right in not signing the petition," and remarked that "very dangerous legislation" was often proposed "in times of hysteria."[25]

Thus even as the Communist Party approached its greatest popularity in the United States, AFL leaders sustained the lessons learned in hard times: state repression was a dangerous force that could easily be unleashed against anyone, including them. As historian M. J. Heale comments, "The mid-1930s red scare never gained general credibility."[26] The AFL deserves some of the credit for containing the "hysteria" William Green warned of.

Yet one antiradical bill received their muted support: a proposal to exclude and expel alien fascists and Communists. Dickstein's Immigration Committee proposed to amend the Alien Act of 1920 by including Communists and Fascists, along with anarchists, among the categories of people who could be deported or refused entry. In April 1935, just as the Madison Square Garden assembly met, an AFL lobbyist appeared to back the bill, saying that "under our Bill of Rights, we may criticize anyone in office. This liberty has been abused by certain people as a sort of license to foment trouble." No one pressed him to explain the nuance in the federation's approach, and the AFL never publicly advocated for the bill or otherwise pressed it. The bid to exclude alien Communists failed, like the other sedition proposals.[27]

For many union officials, conservative and liberal alike, restricting immigration was a central and uncontroversial strategy for gaining some control of labor markets. Racism and ethnocentrism mingled with pragmatic economic considerations: unskilled immigrant workers could undermine hard-won labor standards, and "unassimilated" workers from Asia, southern Europe, or South America destabilized the northern European racial order that prevailed in most unions. Excluding Communist aliens was an easy extension of this thinking.[28]

Brother against Brother

In the summer of 1935, though, bigger legislative changes were afoot. Roosevelt was at war with the Supreme Court after its *Schechter Poultry* decision voided his early New Deal policies. Rather than backing down, Roosevelt promoted even more sweeping social legislation. One of the first planks of his second New Deal was the Wagner Act. Roosevelt signed the Wagner Act in the summer of 1935, but it was a virtual dead letter as a Supreme Court reversal seemed assured. Employers flatly refused to recognize the NLRB's authority, and there was thin popular support for the law as little public discussion had preceded it. At the NLRB, board agents hunted for examples of extreme employer repression to shore up their Supreme Court test case. Heber Blankenhorn, veteran publicity agent, argued for congressional hearings publicizing employers' most nefarious conduct to whip up public sentiment in support of the law. Blankenhorn recruited Senator Robert La Follette to convene a special committee to investigate employers' repressive practices and, in Blankenhorn's words, "let the country, through public hearings, judge what these great industrialists really want when they declare the Labor Relations Act 'unconstitutional.'"[29]

Inside the AFL, meanwhile, a bloc of progressive unionists and John L. Lewis argued that it was time to act fast and organize the huge factories. It made no sense to dither about parceling out workers in advance among various unions; mass recruitment of entire factories and industries must begin at once. When a majority of unions in the AFL voted against industrial organizing drives, Lewis famously punched the Carpenters' union president in the jaw, stalked out of the AFL convention, and announced the founding of a Committee for Industrial Organization. The AFL suddenly had a viable competitor.[30]

The CIO launched ambitious drives in the auto and steel industries, hoping that the Wagner Act would survive but not waiting to find out. Meanwhile the

John Frey told the Dies Committee that before the AFL's 1937 Convention in Tampa this "welcome card" was posted around the city by an organizer for the CIO's Agricultural Workers union. Box 5, folder 83, Papers of John P. Frey, Library of Congress.

La Follette Committee functioned like the publicity department for the CIO, inviting organizers and workers in the midst of organizing drives to the floor of Congress to testify about employer abuses. As workers sat down in auto plants and steel companies sent in strikebreakers and spies to head off insurgency, the CIO brought NLRB agents to the factory floor to investigate, and NLRB agents invited strikers to Congress to finger strikebreakers and spies before the La Follette Committee. CIO organizers, congressional Democrats, and NLRB agents worked together to enforce labor's new rights regardless of their statutory legitimacy. Their success helped convince the head of U.S. Steel that the political climate had been irreversibly altered. Roosevelt's overwhelming victory in the 1936 election buttressed his New Deal with a popular mandate. In February 1937, General Motors bowed to the sit-down strikers and negotiated an agreement with the United Auto Workers. The election

returns and momentum of the auto strikes drove U.S. Steel into negotiations with Lewis, and they privately negotiated a deal for U.S. Steel to recognize the CIO in March. When the Supreme Court reversed itself and upheld
the Wagner Act a few weeks later, on March 29, the decision confirmed an
already-transformed reality.

For its part, the AFL also thrived, recruiting over 700,000 new members in
its affiliate unions in 1936 and 1937, albeit in less-spectacular fashion: as in the
past, groups of workers organized themselves and approached the federation
for a charter, mostly in smaller workplaces in transportation, construction,
and telephone and electrical work. This sort of organizing frequently proceeded by pressuring employers, via boycotts or sabotage, to bargain with the
union, rather than rallying workers to demand industrial rights.[31] At the same
time, most AFL affiliates represented craft workers within industrial factories
along with groups of less-skilled workers. These hybrid units blurred the lines
between craft and industrial unionism. At the moment that the AFL and CIO
split, ostensibly over the question of structure, all the major unions were becoming structurally more alike. And many of the unions that defected from
the AFL to the CIO could hardly be considered "industrial"; New York subway
operators and garment workers worked in sectors with employers more susceptible to traditional political and economic pressure characteristic of AFL
organizing.[32] They joined the CIO because they shared a political vision, not a
union structure.[33]

Ultimately, the debate about craft versus industrial unionism signified
deeper divisions among union leaders and members, and the split set off a
reordering of organized labor around two new poles: the AFL as the conservative defender of traditional values and union preeminence, and the CIO as
the progressive champion of the unskilled masses and ally of Roosevelt and
the Democrats. Especially in sectors with substantial union presence prior
to the 1930s, the flurry of organizing in the New Deal years often disordered
settled relations and sparked new tensions among workers and employers.

These local conflicts were complex and varied, but fundamentally the
same issues underlay them: shifting conceptions of solidarity among workers.
At the same time some workers were linking arms in general strikes in San
Francisco and Minneapolis, others kept working when colleagues walked out.
Subway motormen valued their "confidence and dignity" and declined to join
forces with the train repairmen and conductors, preferring to remain in their
own union with their own separate break rooms in the train terminals. The
long effort to unite San Francisco waterfront workers into a single maritime

union was scuttled when the seamen cut a deal and returned to work during a strike, leaving longshoremen hanging. In a Milwaukee foundry, leaders of AFL locals of the Electrical Workers dissolved their union and led the drive for a wall-to-wall organization but could not convince many of their former craft-union brothers, who considered themselves an "upper crust," to join it.[34] These rivalries were not universal—in Philadelphia, "the unions in the A.F. of L. were delighted to see finally some activity occurring," according to the head of the CIO there—but they were frequent.[35]

National leaders fought viciously. During the final negotiations of the General Motors sit-down strikes, AFL president William Green wired Michigan governor Frank Murphy to insist that the AFL claimed the craft workers and that an exclusive bargain with the CIO-affiliated UAW, whom Green urged Murphy not to recognize, would be "a direct attack against the American Federation of Labor."[36] The International Brotherhood of Electrical Workers rushed to sign sweetheart deals with employers, such as the "perpetual" labor agreement negotiated with Consolidated Edison, on behalf of workers recruited into the union by Consolidated foremen to block the CIO's United Electrical Workers.[37] The AFL sent an organizer to persuade ILGWU strikers to return to work during a 1937 strike in Cleveland.[38] CIO leaders mocked the AFL mercilessly; the 1936 UMW magazine featured a cartoon of William Green as a timorous old woman.[39] To furious AFL leaders, the CIO's very existence was betrayal enough. But CIO unions generally refrained from undermining AFL strikes or negotiating corrupt contracts.

Escalating hostilities led the AFL to seek a preemptive amendment to the Wagner Act in April 1937 that would oblige board officials to certify craft units, in factories or elsewhere, on the request of a majority of craft workers.[40] The effort failed, and five days later the Supreme Court upheld the law and, by extension, the second New Deal. The National Labor Relations Board hired a swarm of staffers to handle an onslaught of petitions for union recognition; nearly 10,000 cases were filed in 1937.[41] Initially, the NLRB directed its staffers to stay out of internecine conflicts among unions, but this proved impossible. Most contentious were cases in which a CIO union requested an NLRB election for an entire workplace, skilled and unskilled workers alike, and an AFL affiliate demanded that the craft workers vote separately for their own union.

The Wagner Act charged NLRB agents with determining which workers properly belonged in a single union, and as many NLRB staffers were avowed leftists and advocates of industrial unionism, they often ruled in favor of the CIO. Moreover, when the AFL and CIO both appeared on the ballot, workers voted for the CIO in eight out of ten cases. Conflict also flared when board

"Measuring the Results of the Latest Peace Efforts." A 1938 Herblock cartoon, copyright by The Herb Block Foundation.

agents insisted on polling workers when they suspected sweetheart deals. The AFL took particular umbrage when the NLRB invalidated the Electrical Workers' contracts with Consolidated Edison, claiming the NLRB sought to "restrict us in the making of contracts."[42] Investigative procedures designed to detect undue employer influence uncovered improper collusion between unions and employers.

To the AFL, it looked like the NLRB favored the CIO, resulting in "union development under Government patronage." Echoing conservative capitalists and farmers who deplored encroaching state power as a menace to liberty, labor conservatives increasingly couched their complaints about the NLRB in a broader critique of the New Deal. The AFL warned that as "government intrudes its commanding hand" into internal union affairs, this way lay tyranny: "a future dominated by dictatorship."[43] Early on, conservative leaders became convinced that this new regime was intolerable. "For the last few months about everything the administration could do is being done to cut the ground from underneath our feet," John Frey told his AFL colleagues in February 1937. "It is time we begin to defend our rights as a trade union movement and decide what we are going to do to protect ourselves."[44]

Communism and the CIO

As the federation enrolled new members, AFL leaders tried to keep Communists out; the AFL's Steel Workers union president commented in 1932, "we have some of these snakes in our organization and we are trying to fasten something on them so we can throw them out bodily."[45] In Detroit auto factories, a CIO stronghold, a strong core of Communist skilled tradesmen had agitated since the 1920s. When the AFL granted a federal charter to auto workers in early 1935, Green took a heavy hand in selecting their new officers, sidelining Communists and radicals and obliging their convention delegates to denounce Communist "meddling."[46] AFL officials watched for signs of apostasy and policed affiliates; in 1935, for example, when the central labor council in Reading, Pennsylvania, signed up for a CP-organized "Continental Congress for Economic Reconstruction," the AFL ordered it to resign, warning that "your central body is either a part of the American Federation of Labor or it is out of it."[47] Federation leaders relied on familiar tactics to manage a familiar problem.

This was easier when the CP was organizing separate radical unions. But the party's Popular Front approach extended to the Communists' trade union work as well, and in 1934 the CPUSA dissolved its revolutionary unions, directing their members to join AFL affiliates. Many veteran party organizers applauded the change, having concluded that workers' resistance to Communism made it impossible to build viable alternative unions. So the party returned to its old strategy of "boring from within" existing unions as a fallback maneuver. (William Z. Foster, who had long advocated this strategy, was sidelined for the debate. He had suffered a heart attack in 1932, and his slow recovery prevented him from returning to an active leadership role in the party until the late 1930s.)[48]

As in the 1920s, Communists aimed to cloak their party affiliation so as not to scare off potential recruits. It appears that many Communist union organizers resumed the practice of subterfuge in the 1930s instinctively, "almost automatically." In 1934 Chicago organizers had reverted to disguising their Communist identity in a pre–Popular Front campaign among African American dress workers, hoping to "first build the union" and later convert its members into Communists, and CP organizers did the same in a Detroit auto strike that year.[49] This tendency became common practice for CP labor organizers in the Popular Front years. To Communist organizer Sam Darcy, this was a risky tactic, as "sooner or later the issue before the people will be,

'Are you liars or are you telling the truth? Are you really communists or are you something else?'"[50]

The AFL was fully briefed on the change in party policy. As usual, party leaders debated the strategy in the pages of their published journals, and documents leaked regularly; the AFL circulated an internal CP "Report on Trade Union Work" describing party plans to support CIO organizing within months of its preparation.[51] In response, AFL leaders advised members again that the CP aimed "to get control of the unions and the entire labor movement" and proposed an amendment to the AFL's constitution banning from membership any union or local labor assembly headed "or controlled" by Communists. The ban passed at the federation's 1935 convention, over the protest of several Communist delegates. John L. Lewis told the convention that the Mine Workers supported the ban, as "we have probably had more trouble with the Communists than any other organization in the movement. We know their objectives, we are not in sympathy with them."[52] That same day, Lewis socked William Hutcheson of the Carpenters' union and set the split within the AFL in motion, but on the question of Communism, labor unity prevailed.

Secretly, Lewis met with CP leaders sometime in early 1936 and struck a deal to use party organizers in the steel campaign. Within months, fifty CP organizers were on the CIO payroll.[53] Why did Lewis change his mind? His politics were an idiosyncratic amalgam of reactionary and progressive tendencies. Lewis was foremost a canny and aggressive unionist, and he needed lieutenants and ground troops to carry out the massive job of organizing the steel and auto industries. Rank-and-file unionists often proved to be poor staffers. The UMW sent "three or four elderly United Mine Workers" to help organize Philadelphia breweries and textile mills. "All of them [were] good guys," recalled the director of the Pennsylvania CIO, but "all of them were absolutely and conspicuously unfitted for activities in organizing workers outside of their own particular areas. They fumbled the ball." Young Communists, on the other hand, had "sophistication, some education, some training" in organizing tactics, and more important, discipline.[54] Lewis and his colleagues structured the CIO and its new unions as centralized, hierarchical organizations run by professional staff—a model not dissimilar to the Communist Party.[55]

Lewis's alliance with Communists floored his former colleagues in the AFL. In July 1936 John Frey passed around copies of CP correspondence directing organizers to join CIO organizing campaigns. Knowing nothing of Lewis's

deal with the CP, Frey told the AFL executive council that he "was not assert-
ing that the c.i.o. had combined with the Communists, but that the Communists are combining for the purpose of helping the Congress for Industrial
Organization." By February 1937, Frey had figured out much of the story. He
told the executive council that "among the first people put on the c.i.o. or
Steel Workers Organizing Committee was one member of the Communist
Party and very soon there was an army of members of the Communist Party
working as organizers of the steel industry."[56] Outraged labor conservatives
felt betrayed. William Green told reporters in August 1937, "No longer does
John Lewis associate with the conservatives that were his friends. He lives
with the radicals. He has become a radical himself."[57]

With his excellent inside information on Communist activity, John Frey
stepped forward as a leading spokesman for the AFL. His old informant, V. R.
Tompkins, fed him material, and Frey had other useful contacts as well. He
had met officers in the army's Military Information Division on AFL delegations to Europe during World War I and used these credentials to make contacts in the State Department. According to Frey, the State Department employed "a man whose sole duty was to follow up Communist activity, at home
and abroad, and keep the records." Frey shared information with him until
the State Department abolished the agent's position after establishing diplomatic relations with the Soviet Union in 1933.[58] Frey's papers at the Library of
Congress contain his source documents, sometimes with attached, unsigned
notes, but no evidence as to their provenance.[59]

Labor anticommunists had long maintained the nation's most comprehensive intelligence on the activities of the CPUSA. Most of their information
about party activities came from confronting Communists in disputes over
union organizing and strikes—that is, by observing Communists in action. In
contrast, Frey's sources supplied a pipeline into the inner circles of the party.
Beginning in November 1935, Frey received periodic timely recaps of Central
Committee meetings, copies of instructions to party organizers, and lists of
meeting delegates and attendees. This material gave labor conservatives accurate, current information on the party's strategy, its relationship to the CIO,
and its assessment of its strength in both AFL and CIO unions. Their mounting
anxiety about Communist penetration of U.S. unions was grounded in fact,
not paranoia.[60]

Accuracy mattered. Anticommunists had been discredited in the 1920s
and early 1930s by their outlandish claims of elaborate conspiracy. The lunacy
of armchair anticommunists such as Elizabeth Dilling convinced few readers
and repelled many more. The anti-Semitism and nativism of much popu-

lar anticommunism—especially the version broadcast weekly on the radio by Father Charles Coughlin—rendered both its claims and its proponents incredible to many. The burden of proof was on the anticommunists, and without solid evidence, their warnings could fall on deaf ears. When a Hearst reporter wrote Green in 1934 to ask for the names of "every Communist" in the AFL, Green demurred, explaining, "I wish the leaders of our local organizations, as well as of the National and International Unions, could not only name but publicly proclaim the names of Communists who constitute the cells created in the unions organized by the American Federation of Labor. Many times our leaders feel sure that certain members are Communists, but, if called upon to prove and establish the fact that those who they believe are Communists are really Communists, they would be unable to do so."[61] AFL anticommunist leaders were careful to check their facts, and their caution gave them credibility inside the labor movement and outside.

Indiscriminate and unsubstantiated accusations were ineffective, as the example of the International Longshoreman's Association president Joseph Ryan showed. Ryan's union had split beneath him, as militant California longshoremen threw off their corrupt leadership and formed a West Coast longshoremen's union, affiliating with the CIO. Left with his East Coast base, Ryan watched as Atlantic shipboard workers in the moribund Seamen's Union followed suit, forming the National Maritime Union (NMU) and infecting his turf with the spirit of insurgency. While Harry Bridges and Joseph Curran, leaders of the seceding longshoremen and seamen, denied Communist Party membership, both their organizations had substantial Communist leadership.

But Ryan could not prove it. The Senate's Commerce Committee, headed by conservative Democrat Royal Copeland, held hearings in early 1938 to consider broad changes to merchant marine law. Copeland gave ample floor time to Ryan and other labor conservatives to attack the CIO. Ryan tried to explain that Communist organizers had "got control" of the insurgent unions, that he believed Curran and Bridges to be working closely with the party, and that "Communist direction" was responsible for "all the trouble" in the ports. Copeland and Senator Vandenberg, clearly sympathetic, asked Ryan repeatedly to substantiate his charges: "Where did you get that information?" They pressed him, "Could you prove it if you had to?" Ryan explained, "We hear it from men" in the union.[62] Ryan's accusations hardly made a splash, even though most of his information was correct.[63]

John Frey supplemented his clandestine intelligence with information reported to him by leaders and members of unions, frequently from AFL affiliates recently departed for the CIO. In the NMU, a large faction of members formed a "Mariners Club" as an explicitly anticommunist opposition group in 1938, and they ran an anticommunist slate to challenge Curran for the presidency. As ballots were being counted, a delegation of the Mariners Club carrying baseball bats visited the Communist Party's waterfront section offices, where they were met by a party member carrying a rifle. In the ensuing melee, the Mariners Club trashed the offices and ransacked the CP's files. Within a few days, Frey received a list of more than one hundred CP members of the NMU, along with their aliases and ship departments.[64] A former leader of the AFL's Auto Workers union, deposed early in the leadership fights, promised Frey a full dossier on the "Communistic gang of racketeers" that had taken over the UAW.[65] A lumber worker from Eureka, California, wrote to John Frey to say that "outside 'uplifters'" had come to Eureka, started a "Communist-inspired 'Rank and File' movement," and got a charter from the Carpenters union. He demanded an investigation into how the Carpenters "issued these reds a charter in the first place enabling them to cloak their Communist organizing schemes under an A.F.L. Charter."[66] Anticommunism was bleeding into local struggles among workers over the form and structure of their unions.

AFL leaders reworked their anticommunist critique to focus on the CIO. A number of AFL unions had Communist factions before and after the split with the CIO, but AFL leaders had rarely mentioned this fact in their denunciations of Communism in labor. Indeed, when competing with the CIO to affiliate unions, the AFL welcomed members of Communist-organized unions recently liquidated by the party, such as the Transport Workers union, various machinists and foundry workers absorbed by the AFL Machinists union, and New York hotel workers.[67] In their public and private statements, AFL leaders strategically red-baited the CIO — sometimes in league with employers. When the New England Shoe and Leather Association wrote to Frey in March 1937 seeking information on the "radical beliefs and activities" of CIO leaders John Brophy, Powers Hapgood, and Adolph Germer, Frey sent along records of their 1920s expulsions from the UMWA and advised that Brophy had visited Russia and Hapgood was "an active associate of Communist officials."[68]

The AFL also reactivated old alliances with patriotic organizations, reaching out to the Daughters of the American Revolution and the American Legion to enlist them in the fight against the red CIO. Communists had "attempted to penetrate the ranks of the American Federation of Labor," Mrs. Vinton Earl Sisson told her sisters in the DAR in April 1938. "It is a cause for rejoicing that on the whole American labor will have nothing of radical dictatorship."[69]

State and local AFL bodies followed suit. The California Federation of Labor unanimously approved a resolution denouncing the CIO as an effort "supported by every radical, subversive, unpatriotic and Communistic element with the avowed purpose of enforcing minority and undemocratic rule on the workers of the nation."[70] In early 1938, the Wisconsin federation issued a "solemn warning" to beware "conspiring destructionists." "Some of them are direct emissaries of the Communists," and "still others represent the C.I.O."[71]

At the same time, a small but growing number of leaders defected from CIO unions, complaining of heavy-handed Communist direction. Anthony Uccello, president of a CIO local in New Britain, Connecticut, resigned after the party put him on the *Daily Worker* mailing list.[72] In Los Angeles, four unions walked out of the CIO's local Industrial Union Council in August 1938, angered that leader Harry Bridges was "subordinating the interests of the C.I.O. and trade unionism to the Communist Party." The unions—the UAW, the Rubber Workers, the Ladies' Garment Workers, and the Shoe Workers— were mainstays of the CIO, and their departure augured mounting resistance to the Communist presence in the CIO.[73]

In their anticommunist campaign, AFL union leaders made speeches and passed resolutions at conventions, met with leaders of other national organizations, and worked behind the scenes with employers and politicians. Meanwhile, the Catholic Church developed a grassroots approach to working-class anticommunism: they began organizing. In the 1920s and early 1930s, the Catholic Church had concentrated its American anticommunist work on opposing American diplomatic recognition of the Soviet Union, and the clergy continually reminded parishioners of Soviet repression of Catholicism. As urban Catholic workers streamed into CIO unions, church leaders fearful of secularization struck a middle ground: support the CIO, but fight Communism. In February 1937, American Catholics created the Association of Catholic Trade Unionists (ACTU) to train and mobilize anticommunists in the industrial unions.[74]

The New York Irish Catholic workers who started ACTU aimed to build a Catholic counterweight to Communist and radical influences in the new industrial unions. AFL and CIO ACTU members supported striking workers and denounced bosses and corrupt union leaders in what they called a "united front" for social justice. But a January 1938 confrontation in Jersey City forced underlying tensions to the surface. Mayor Frank Hague, longtime machine boss, and the local AFL collaborated in beating back the "red army" of CIO textile strikers with the support of the local Catholic leadership, to the shock of progressive ACTU activists. The next month, ACTU progressives called a referendum to resolve their debate with conservative hardliners over a local political endorsement. The hardliners won handily, two to one. Rank-and-file conservative ACTU activists, with institutional support from the church, took the reins and reorganized ACTU around a strong anticommunist, antiradical program. They rapidly established new branches in Boston and Detroit from which they launched factional fights within unions such as the UAW. Anticommunist workers eager for support flooded the group, including supporters from the largely Jewish Amalgamated Clothing Workers and Ladies' Garment Workers.[75] While AFL leaders caucused with elites, the ACTU organized isolated surges of labor anticommunism into a coherent movement.

Labor Conservatives Fight Back

In 1936 and 1937, then, labor conservatives grew increasingly disaffected with the New Deal order that promoted intrusive federal bureaucrats and alternative forms of unionism. Disgruntled allies abounded. Employers despised the "G—D—Labor Board," and Roosevelt's Democratic congressional bloc was showing signs of strain. Militant strikes aroused dismay among broad swaths of the voting public. A May 1938 Gallup poll found that 62 percent of respondents believed the Wagner Act should be amended or repealed, and that proportion increased to 81 percent in the industrial states of Ohio, Indiana, Michigan, and Illinois.[76]

Congressional Republicans and conservative, mostly southern, Democrats, found common ground in denouncing labor militancy and the NLRB. Democratic congressmen Howard Smith of Virginia and Edward Cox of Georgia led the pack. Their protests against New Deal measures grew more vehement as the 1930s progressed, and labor rights aroused their particular ire.[77] In the spring of 1937, the congressmen reached out to AFL leaders, offering to join forces to cut the appropriation and clip the power of the NLRB. The offer was tempting: as AFL lawyer Joseph Padway told an NLRB official, "if things got bad enough, and the Federation was double-crossed, there would be nothing left for them to do but play ball."[78] Later that year, Padway reiterated the threat directly to Roosevelt, warning that Congressional Republicans hoped to bring "labor into an alliance with a future block composed of Republicans and reactionary Democrats."[79] Roosevelt's union support was about to wobble.[80]

Labor conservatives took on Roosevelt and the CIO head-on, by fighting his labor legislation and opposing his candidates in the midterm elections.[81]

The first legislative skirmish arose in mid-1937. Roosevelt had developed a proposal to set minimum wages and hours by federal law—an initiative with the potential for far broader impact than the NLRA, as it would benefit non-union workers, who comprised the great majority of the workforce. Sidney Hillman helped draft the legislation, which provided for a minimum wage and a quasi-judicial Labor Standards Board to set maximum hours for each industry. Roosevelt was taken aback when the AFL came out against the bill, disapproving especially of the creation of a new governmental board with authority over labor, and Lewis echoed their critique (revealing that his old voluntaristic impulses lingered).[82]

The AFL, of course, had opposed such laws for male workers for decades and reiterated that stance in its 1936 proposals for both Republican and Democratic Party platforms. AFL concerns about the law grew out of well-established AFL policy, but federation leaders turned the debate into a forum for their quarrel with the CIO and the NLRB. Their opposition helped kill the bill in committee in the summer of 1937, obliging Roosevelt to reintroduce it during the special congressional session he called later that year. Although Lewis compromised and the CIO backed the law, the AFL dug in, accusing Roosevelt of favoring the CIO by rejecting the AFL's proposed amendments. The AFL was "fed up with boards," Green said.

After five months of haggling, Congress finally passed the Fair Labor Standards Act (FLSA) in May 1938, rejecting many of the AFL's amendments but excluding workers in agriculture, domestic service, transportation, retail, and the communications sector. Ironically, most women workers, for whom the AFL had always supported wage and hour legislation, were not covered, along with the vast majority of African American workers in the South and Mexican workers in the Southwest. Indeed, union members were more likely to be covered than nonunion workers. The federation had shown its muscle and reminded Roosevelt that labor conservatives' support was contingent, not guaranteed, and that union preeminence, not working-class power, was its main goal.[83]

The Wagner Act was next in the AFL's sights. AFL unions enjoying explosive growth recognized that the NLRB regime created the most auspicious climate for collective bargaining in memory. Labor conservatives and AFL partisans thus took care to distinguish their attacks on the administration of the law from their endorsement of its basic premises. "We believe the act itself is sound and constructive," Green said in the summer of 1938. But the law had been implemented "in a way we never dreamed of, clearly out of accord with its letter and spirit, by those with authority to administer it."[84] This critique corresponded to the federation's old suspicion of state bureaucracy and administrative discretion.[85] Its subtleties proved difficult to convey for some union leaders, who struggled to finesse their attacks.

The rancor was sometimes startling. In October 1937, Roy Horn, president of the Blacksmiths union, took aim at Frances Perkins: "First, we get a Secretary of Labor that none of us wanted and none of us ever heard of before we got her and now she tells us what union we shall belong to. If they get away with that, they will soon tell you how to vote and what church you shall worship in." Horn expressed his preference for the autocracy of "Hitler and Mussolini," because "a little dictator with a wisp of hair under his nose . . . is much preferable to me than one who wears a skirt."[86] Horn conveyed a clear distaste for bureaucratic autonomy, especially when wielded by women; he also conveyed a much broader resistance to government of any sort. In this, he struck the same chords as the employers in the Liberty League.

After losing a case before the NLRB in which the board awarded sole jurisdiction over West Coast longshoremen to the CIO, AFL leaders abandoned hopes that NLRB agents would ever see things their way. In June 1938, AFL attorneys secretly began meeting with lawyers from the Liberty League and the National Association of Manufacturers to draft a full-scale revamping of the Wagner Act. Among other changes limiting the power of board agents, they sought especially the statutory preservation of craft units and a severe curtailing of the NLRB's power to invalidate contracts.[87] If the election broke their way, a new Congress would look more favorably on their proposals. Publicly, Green denounced the NLRB in numerous forums, and the Massachusetts and New York federations declared their support for a revision of the law. But there was also opposition in the ranks of the AFL. An AFL official was shouted down at a 1938 Labor Day picnic in Omaha when he tried to rally the crowd against the NLRB.[88] Frey and his fellow conservatives "put President Roosevelt in a delicate position," a retired carpenter wrote Frey. "Should the mass strikes become lost, the principal cause will be the stand that the A.F. of L. is taking. The A.F. of L. will become a body of scabs."[89]

Despite the tumult in local union fights, union members overwhelmingly supported the Wagner Act. Their loyalties to the Democratic alliance were less reliable. The AFL reinforced the message in the midterm elections. The CIO had created a political arm, Labor's Non-Partisan League, to mobilize working-class voters for Roosevelt in 1936. Its great success attracted various AFL locals and leaders who enrolled in the league, maintaining the political independence characteristic of the old AFL. In April 1938, Green ordered all AFL locals to quit the league and announced the launch of the federation's own get-out-the-vote program to work for the "defeat of those who are out of sympathy with" the AFL. Green told reporters that CIO support would be "one thing against a candidate," thereby declaring that "the labor vote would be divided."[90]

Troubled by the growing rebelliousness of conservative Democrats, Roosevelt tried to drive them from the party in the summer of 1938, backing progressive challengers to conservative Democrats in party primaries and gubernatorial races. His purge backfired, turning local races into referenda on Roosevelt and the New Deal, and only one of his targets lost his seat. In several races, the AFL stood with the Copperheads, backing Ed Smith in South Carolina, Guy Gillette in Iowa, and Martin Dies in Texas.[91] The AFL also campaigned against some Democrats that Roosevelt supported, including Maury Maverick in Texas, and declined to support Robert Bulkeley in Ohio. (Maverick had publicly backed CIO organizing drives, causing William Green to say, "We will support no one who gives aid and comfort to the C.I.O. . . . even if he has a perfect voting record.").[92]

In some cases, the AFL's endorsement corresponded with Roosevelt's, such as William McAdoo in California and Alben Barkley in Kentucky. But the federation acted independently of the administration. After the primaries, William Green explained to reporters that this "nonpartisan policy" showed that "labor's political strength could be used as the balance of power."[93] To some observers, the balance looked rather one-sided. A headline in the *Nation* read, "A.F. of L. into G.O.P."[94]

AFL backing shaped state and local politics as well. In Minnesota, the AFL helped block the adoption of a state "little Wagner Act" in 1937, fearing it would "favor the C.I.O."[95] In Pennsylvania, the split between the AFL and the CIO helped cost Democrats the governorship. The AFL had protested angrily when the CIO tried to win the nomination for a UMWA official, and AFL support helped carry Republican Arthur S. James into the statehouse.[96] In Columbus, Ohio, the state labor federation reversed its Democratic endorsements when the AFL "forced the resignation of the [Columbus Federation of Labor]'s progressive leadership" and instead backed Republican James Rhodes for local office.[97] Craft workers in Akron and anti-CIO rubber workers swung the vote for the Republican mayoral candidate in 1938.[98]

The AFL's impact should not be overstated. The AFL's voter-organizing skills were creaky, as the federation had largely abandoned electoral turnout decades earlier, and the CIO's giant presence on the electoral field overshadowed the AFL.[99] Labor conservatives registered their discontent at the voting booth, but they claimed their biggest victim through an indirect move.

Michigan governor Frank Murphy lost his seat in the fall of 1938, in a shocking reversal, after Martin Dies's House Un-American Activities Committee held special hearings focusing on his role in the GM sit-down strikes.[100] Labor conservatives were about to learn that anticommunism was their most effective tool.

Turning to Martin Dies

For years, William Green and other labor anticommunists insisted that if Communist organizers and ideology were exposed, workers would shun them. The CIO's success suggested otherwise. On the other hand, labor conservatives' worst suspicions about the perils of state power had been confirmed. To AFL leaders, it looked like the NLRB had a thumb on the CIO's side of the scale, giving CIO organizers an unfair advantage. Attacking the NLRB was one strategy, although risky. A congressional investigating committee was another. John Frey had mountains of material on labor and Communism; now he saw a way to use it.

The AFL had a good relationship with Congressman Martin Dies of Texas. A conservative Democrat from Beaumont, Texas, Dies came into office in the early 1930s, and he cultivated the AFL. In March 1937 he met with an AFL lobbyist to share the intelligence that "the entire state of Texas and particularly the Oil Workers," a CIO affiliate, "are opposed to the c.i.o."[101] The following month, Dies sponsored the AFL's first package of NLRA amendments. This friendly cooperation led the AFL to campaign for Dies's reelection in the 1938 Democratic primaries, and in May 1938, the two found a new way to work together.

Dies had convinced his colleagues to let him chair a committee to investigate the spread of un-American ideologies in the United States. Although Dies and his supporters insisted that they would focus on Communism and Nazism, several congressmen warned that Dies and other conservatives sought "to investigate the New Deal, as he claims it is un-American."[102] Congress authorized the special investigative committee but appropriated only $25,000, a modest sum, for its work. To collect data and conduct research, Congress directed that federal agencies detail staff to assist the committee, a common arrangement. But Dies complained that the executive branch refused to cooperate. As a lordly gesture, La Follette offered to loan staff from his own committee to help Dies out. But Dies smelled a rat. He said that he received "a telephone tip that they were Communist Party members." He sent the staff back, and La Follette would soon have reason to regret his offer.[103]

The FBI was no more helpful. Dies and his staff repeatedly requested that the FBI detail investigators to the committee, but J. Edgar Hoover told the attorney general that "it will be obviously impossible for the Bureau to devote any time" or staff to the Dies Committee. Nor would the FBI permit committee staffers to interview FBI agents or consult bureau files.[104]

Indeed, as everyone suspected, Dies did intend a broader inquiry, and he needed the AFL's assistance. In May 1938 Dies told the AFL's lobbyist that his intent was to "go into the Communist tie-up between the Communists and the C.I.O.," and he asked whether the AFL "will aid and testify before the Committee."[105] John Frey was enlisted to help. Later, Dies cast Frey as the architect of the strategy. "John Frey came to me and said he wanted to testify," Dies told reporters. "I asked him about what. He said Communism. I said, Communism where. He said, oh, Communism in lots of places, and especially the CIO."[106]

Over the summer, Frey prepared carefully. That August, Dies opened the first hearings of the House Un-American Activities Committee, and Frey took the chair as the second witness. He later confessed to a friend that "the subject got under my skin to such an extent that it was difficult to go to sleep for the evidence kept dancing before my mind." Frey declared that Communists had invaded the labor movement and dominated the CIO, following "Moscow's instructions to 'bore from within' the American labor movement." He named 280 organizers in CIO unions, 185 of the "leading Communists in our country," and the members of the "national Committee of the Communist Party in the United States." Frey found that testifying "was much like going in swinning [sic] the first time at the beginning of the season, and feeling the temperature of the water with my toes, but after the initial plunge I rather enjoyed the experience."[107] The next day, newspaper headlines blared, "Communists Rule the CIO"; Frey resumed his seat and his incriminations; and HUAC began its long career.

The year 1938 marked the beginning of the "end of reform," in historian Alan Brinkley's phrase, a narrowing of New Deal aspirations for wholesale social transformation enforced with robust federal authority.[108] Historians have shown how a range of actors, from industrialists resisting regulation to southern growers fearing African American liberation, mobilized to contain popular uprisings and constrain state bureaucracies. Organized labor's role in this backlash has received far less attention. The ascension of the liberal CIO has obscured the persistence of a conservative labor politics centered in the AFL that exerted a rightward pull throughout the 1930s and 1940s.

The New Deal state transformed working life for many Americans, creating a new structure of laws and bureaucracy to regulate working conditions and fostering new unions to govern workplaces. Millions of workers gained new protections that were simply unavailable in the pre–New Deal years. By organizing new unions, backing passage of laws such as the Fair Labor Standards Act, and campaigning for Roosevelt's reelection, many workers were "making a New Deal," in the words of historian Lizabeth Cohen.[109]

But the state's muscular new labor institutions jostled the old order of the AFL. The institutional interests of the labor federation were often at odds with the individual and collective interests of its members and nonunion workers alike. The New Deal state dramatically weakened the AFL's power to govern the labor movement and define the labor-policy agenda. For some members of AFL unions, the floods of new unionists threatened their traditional hegemony at the workplace and in the labor movement. By disrupting existing power relations within the labor movement, the New Deal state created enemies. In reaction, the AFL led its own "counter-reformation" against the New Deal order.[110]

The relative weakness of labor conservatives in the broader political landscape forced the AFL to rely on its lobbying skills. Effective lobbying did not require popular mobilization or political consensus. All the federation needed was a political strategy and a compelling issue. Direct critiques of the New Deal labor policy gained limited purchase in the mid-1930s. But by 1938, labor conservatives figured out that an oblique attack, using anticommunism as a proxy issue, could work. Over the next few years, labor conservatives would dedicate themselves to painting the New Deal red.

CHAPTER NINE

Anticommunism, the Dies Committee, and Espionage

In June 1938, Ralph Knox walked into the Detroit field office of the FBI to complain that Communists had kicked him out of the United Auto Workers. Knox was a door fitter at Briggs Manufacturing in Detroit, and he had helped organize the Briggs local and served as its president. Knox told the FBI that after a plant shutdown, Communist infiltrators took over the local and convinced Briggs not to rehire him. The UAW was "entirely controlled by members of the Communistic group," he said, and reporting them to the FBI was his "patriotic duty." Knox had written a 2,500-word report explaining the entire situation.

The FBI agent in charge advised Knox that "there appeared to be no Federal violation involved" and thanked him for the information. Knox was not satisfied. He "called frequently to inquire whether any action would be taken." To mollify Knox, the FBI solicited a written opinion from the local U.S. attorney that disavowed any interest in the case. Knox persisted, continuing to call up the agent regularly and offering to "make himself available at all times" to the FBI to share "any information regarding Communistic activities." The exasperated agent filed his report "only because of Mr. Knox's insistence."[1]

By October, Knox had found a more sympathetic audience. He testified before Martin Dies's House Committee on Un-American Activities about the "Socialists, revolutionary workers, Trotskyites, and so forth" in the UAW, who "seemed to have the idea that when we have the revolution they are going to be the leaders. They think they are the intelligent group." Knox listed dozens of radicals, giving their names and aliases, the plants where they worked, and whether they were "Arab or Bulgarian or something like that." His words tumbled out. "Please do not talk so fast," Dies asked. It was hard to get the story straight with so many details, and when Dies pressed Knox to explain why the union expelled him, Knox finally said, "They were just a bunch of fools."[2]

Knox seemed like the fool to many observers (*Time* magazine dryly described him as someone "whom his former associates would like to put in a psychopathic ward.")[3] His excitable demeanor undermined the basic truth of Knox's testimony. Briggs had been a Communist beachhead since the early 1930s, with a reputation for uncommon militancy.[4] The Dies Committee offered a freewheeling arena for people such as Knox, who saw Communism and "Communistic tendencies" at work in their unions, their communities, and their government. Lightly staffed and loosely managed, the Dies Committee functioned like the FBI of the World War I era. It depended heavily on freelance antiradicals for intelligence, giving people such as John Frey considerable ability to stage-manage its activities. J. Edgar Hoover's FBI, on the other hand, displayed far more rectitude in its investigation of alleged Communist activity. In several cases Hoover and his agents refuted false red-baiting claims and refused to harass or repress Communists and radicals, despite pressure from labor anticommunists like Knox and Frey. In the years before Pearl Harbor, Hoover's FBI helped protect union activists against spurious charges of treasonous Soviet intrigue.

Despite the Dies Committee's effort to root out Communists, the CPUSA built a large espionage operation in the United States in the 1930s. Soviet and American archives definitively establish that American Communist leaders cultivated hundreds of informants to collect intelligence from well-placed posts in the federal government, scientific labs, and the left-wing and mainstream press. Given the scale of Soviet espionage, some historians have judged Hoover's FBI insufficiently alert to the actual risks of Communist intelligence operations. Hoover's FBI had resumed secret political surveillance in 1936 with the approval of President Roosevelt, but the bureau focused on German and Japanese suspects rather than Communists. To some historians, the FBI's failure to detect Soviet spying was a "catastrophic" error.[5]

Looking at the FBI's role in policing labor offers a new angle on this debate. With the help of Dies, labor anticommunists repeatedly alleged that CIO unionists were disloyal Soviet emissaries, using false smears to gain advantage in union rivalries. Hoover's FBI debunked these allegations and prevented unwarranted repression of the CIO, despite Hoover's longstanding antiradicalism. To date, the archival evidence vindicates Hoover and the CIO: none of the significant espionage rings involved union activists, with the exception of the highly skilled engineers in atomic research. Soviet espionage was largely a white-collar business. The FBI accurately absolved union activists of charges of subversion and protected the civil liberties of Communist unionists. By taking care to investigate charges of labor-based espionage, the FBI helped avert civil liberties abuses that HUAC and labor conservatives tried to inflict.

The AFL, the CIO, and the ACLU did not know about Soviet espionage operations. Indeed, Soviet statecraft made people such as Roger Baldwin uneasy. In 1939, when American Communist leaders switched their stance to conform to Stalin's separate peace with Germany, Communist allies and enemies alike began to wonder whether the Communist Party of the United States was in fact an agency of the Soviet government. Their fears led them to reconsider their ideas about free speech. Civil libertarians in and outside the labor movement began questioning whether Communists deserved the same toleration as other radicals. In the late 1930s, in other words, the ACLU moved closer to the AFL's brand of anticommunism.

The Dies Committee

John Frey learned in July 1938 that he "would be the principal first witness before the Dies Committee."[6] On August 13, Frey began three days of electrifying testimony. The Communist Party had "failed to secure a foothold in an American trade-union movement," he said, "until the CIO was organized. Since then the Communist Party has become a definite factor in the American labor movement." Communists swarmed "every sitdown strike, every mass-picketing venture," and they "fostered violent disturbances" in the steel and auto industry. Their vehicle was the CIO, where Communists occupied senior positions, despite John L. Lewis's "thorough knowledge of the danger" of Communist influence. Frey then offered the names of "some 280 organizers in CIO unions, under salary, who are members of the Communist Party," the names of "185 of the leading Communists in our country," and "the names of the new national Committee of the Communist Party in the United States." Chairman Dies underlined the point: the AFL had "information that perhaps no other organization in America has, does it not?" he prompted Frey.[7]

Throughout his testimony, Frey used the imagery of infiltration to describe Communist organizing. He dwelled on the spycraft used by "Communist undercover men and espionage agents," the "spies, the disrupters, the agents provocateur," who "carry out Moscow's instructions to 'bore from within' the American labor movement." This language harkened back to the 1920s, when anticommunist unionists decried the "secrecy and stealth" of the "agencies and forces behind the Communist International." Frey did not imply that Communist unionists engaged in international espionage, stealing state or industrial secrets, and his listeners did not infer from his remarks that Communists in unions functioned like traditional spies. Communist union organizing, not Communist espionage, worried labor anticommunists and their allies.[8]

In his introductory remarks, Frey said that Communists attacked their critics as "red baiters," implying that opponents were driven by "prejudice" and spoke without "logic or facts; perhaps a professional opponent of impure motive." He had been called a red-baiter, Frey said. But he intended to make a case that was "factual to the hilt, and it will require something more than cunningly contrived and misplaced adjectives in answer."[9] Frey was careful to distinguish between card-carrying Communists and fellow travelers, which permitted him to name people such as John Brophy, "not a member of the Communist Party, but he consorts with Communists continually," and Francis Gorman, who "married a Communist," along with confirmed party leaders such as William Z. Foster and Jack Stachel.[10]

Denials flooded his mailbox, many from people such as Transport Workers Union (TWU) president Michael Quill, who declared, "At the outset I deny that either I or any of the other leaders of the Transport Workers Union of America, named by you, are members of the Communist Party." In fact, Communists did dominate the leadership of the TWU, and, according to his biographer Joshua Freeman, Quill was almost certainly a party member.[11] So were virtually all of the people Frey named. For instance, Frey identified as a Communist James Matles, a veteran organizer for the Communist Trade Union Unity League and an official of the United Electrical Workers. Matles wrote Frey repeatedly to ask that his name be withdrawn from Frey's list of Communists, and he suggested that Frey's testimony was "a sensational display to distract the attention of your membership from the failures of your organization." Frey promised that if Matles would "submit to me any facts or proof," he would quickly "file a frank correction with the committee." Matles complained that he could supply "little in the way of 'evidence,' save for a personal denial," yet he did not make such a denial, and Frey did not withdraw Matles's name.[12] "You are the Benedict Arnold of the American labor movement," Quill told Frey. Unfortunately for Quill and other labor Communists, Frey was also the Inspector Javert of the labor movement, and his public statements were generally accurate.

A contemporary observer thought that Frey's testimony helped shape HUAC's mission: "It was probably the very success of the Frey testimony as an experiment in publicity that awakened Dies and his associates to a full realiza-

U.S. Representative Martin Dies speaking to reporters, February 17, 1940. Library of Congress, Prints and Photographs Division.

tion of the potentialities of the political gold mine that they had struck. From Frey on it was catch as catch can with no holds barred. No patrioteer was too wacky to be taken seriously."[13] Other congressional committees had investigated Communism and radicalism, but they tended toward a more sober exploration of the matter. Dies subpoenaed hostile witnesses, interrogated them impertinently, and threw the committee open to wide-ranging allegations of all sorts of subversion, especially in New Deal agencies. Dies created a new platform for a "cross-party conservative coalition" in the Congress to attack the White House and the New Deal under the banner of countersubversion. Enormously popular in the polls, Dies's committee won reauthorization and generous funding for the next six years. Roosevelt and the Democratic leadership were blindsided.[14]

Despite the committee's new funding, it depended more on the information witnesses volunteered than it did on its own investigations. In the summer and fall of 1938, the Dies Committee had only two investigators on staff dedicated to researching Communism, neither with strong connections inside unions. (One investigator was a former labor spy who had been exposed by the La Follette Committee.)[15] Yet HUAC did not have to go digging for labor movement witnesses, because they tended to recruit themselves. In some cases, informants such as Ralph Knox literally walked in off the street. For frustrated anticommunist unionists in the CIO, the committee gave them an accessible forum to complain about and challenge the Communist leadership of their unions. Shortly after hearings began, a UAW member and Joint Council delegate from Detroit's Ternstedt plant—Walter Reuther's local— appeared in the office of the Dies Committee's investigator and "offered to give us names"; he returned the next day with the local's former vice president.[16] Dies Committee investigators regularly met with union officials and rank-and-file workers who eagerly volunteered their time and testimony.[17]

During the committee's first round of hearings, very different workers— New York subway operators, California seamen, Detroit autoworkers— testified. Many were onetime party members, and many had been voted out of union office or lost elections to CP unionists. They voiced a common set of complaints. CIO Communists were undemocratic; they dissembled about their affiliation and purposes; and they pursued party goals at the expense of workers' interests. Communist unionists were undemocratic, these witnesses said, because they manipulated parliamentary procedure and secret caucuses to coordinate apparently spontaneous deliberations and decisions at union meetings. Richard Eagar, a machinist working for General Motors, said, "The average man working in the plant has not any organization at the back of him, and they have got key men throughout the various sections of the plant, and their men then campaign for a certain slate."[18]

In part, what these unionists described was the problem of faction in any democratic polity and the advantage that experienced organizers had in a contest with willing but inexperienced candidates; Democrats and Republicans tend to have the same advantage over third-party or unaffiliated candidates. But Communists pressed their troops beyond the boundaries of legitimate debate, according to the witnesses. If their coordinated speakers could not carry the motion, Communists resorted to "filibustering," according to the UAW's Zygmund Dobrzynski, "until the honest-to-goodness members of the organization become disgusted and walk out, go home, after 3 or 4 or 5 hours of constant heckling, filibustering; leaving the meeting in the hands of this disruptive element."[19] This description of CP strategy echoed accounts from the 1920s of the methods Communist organizers used to take over the Farmer-Labor Party.

Compounding the problem of Communist factions, CP members disguised and denied their affiliation to the party, further distorting the function of democracy in the union, witnesses said. Sam Baron from the ILGWU argued, "Where a trade-union official is taking his orders from the Communist Party and carrying out its political line inside that trade-union, in all honesty these people should get up and say, 'I am a Communist, and I stand for this,' and stand on their own feet, so that the public will know and be able to decide. But they do not do that. In the trade-unions these Communists will deny they are Communists, and then they will put forward their propositions, and so the members will not be able to consider the propositions on their merits."[20] Communists' antidemocratic practices violated unionists' sense of fair play. John Murphy, a subway station agent and onetime party member, called the CP "reactionary, in the sense that it does not practice what it preaches. It used to talk about democracy, but it does not practice it."[21]

According to Dies's witnesses, CP unionists sought to advance the party's interests at unions' expense. However, witnesses provided little evidence of just how CP members harmed workers' interests. Edward Maguire testified that the party leader in the TWU told him flatly, "'we are not building the transport workers' union; we are out to build the Communist Party.'"[22] William Harmon of the TWU said that the CP leaders devoted most of their time to organizing the Labor Party in New York, and gave scant attention to handling workers' grievances. "The companies are gradually taking away all they have given them, and these fellows are playing politics," he said.[23] But as he spoke, the TWU was winning the best wage increases and contracts that the subway workers had ever had. Likewise a National Maritime Union dissident said that CP union leaders had the ship owners "over a barrel," which would seem to be just where most unionists would want the employer to be.[24] When it came to explaining exactly what militant red unionism cost workers, anticommunist unionists were short on specifics. Rather, militancy and the culture of militancy sometimes sounded like the problem, as UAW member James Mitchell put it: "they make fun of everything; of Congress as a whole, and of the President, and of everybody."[25]

Still, the coherence of the Dies Committee witnesses' critique is striking. One explanation may be their involvement with the Association of Catholic Trade Unionists. Throughout 1938 and 1939, ACTU chapters popped up in industrial cities, using Jesuit high school and college teachers to train anticommunist unionists in "methods of combating Communist anti-union tactics" and strategies for ousting Communist union leaders. In 1938, 7,500 shop stewards and local union officers graduated from ACTU schools.[26] It does not appear that ACTU brought labor witnesses to the early Dies hearings, but at least some of the Dies witnesses attended ACTU sessions.[27] In most cases, anticommunist unionists found their own way to Dies.

Although labor anticommunists presented no evidence of ties between the USSR and the radical union members they opposed, their testimony helped construct what Ellen Schrecker has called the image of a secretive, "monolithic, Moscow-run party" that used trickery to further a Soviet conspiracy to overthrow the U.S. government.[28] Central to this image was the notion of domination. Witnesses compared, both implicitly and explicitly, Communist domination of unions to employer domination of unions. A key premise of the Wagner Act had been that employers' domination of workers' organizations undermined industrial democracy, and the La Follette hearings demonstrated just how employers exercised that domination, from establishing company-controlled unions to sending labor spies to manipulate union meetings. Progressives and radicals who authored the Wagner Act pointed to employers' abuses as the greatest risk to workers' free exercise of association and speech in the workplace and called for the state to rein employers in.

Now conservative unionists, along with anticommunist workers, argued that Communists, in league with the CIO, menaced not just workers but the nation with their stealthy domination of unions. Labor anticommunists undermined the hard work of the Popular Front CPUSA. By emphasizing the CP's stealth and sneakiness, the Dies witnesses rejuvenated old images of the party as an alien invader. HUAC's early labor witnesses focused on the micropolitics of their workplaces and unions, on matters such as the election of grievance chairs in their department of a factory. Their vehemence suggests the visceral anger that underlay rank-and-file anticommunism. Whether it arose from frustration with factionalism and cliquishness, distaste for Communist impertinence or militancy, or a religiously grounded rejection of Communism, this animus created popular support among union members in both the CIO and AFL for anticommunist initiatives.

Not surprisingly, the 1939 AFL convention voted to endorse the Dies Committee, as did the 1940 convention, and the AFL lobbied for its continuation on Capitol Hill through 1944. The Boston Central Labor Union, the Jefferson County, Ohio Trades and Labor Assembly, the California Federation of Labor, and other labor bodies issued public statements of support for the Dies Committee, echoing William Green: "Those who are with us need not fear, those who are against us ought to be exposed."[29]

There was opposition within the AFL as well. Some AFL unionists protested the committee's "hysterical" tone and worried that its investigation only exacerbated divisions among unions and emboldened their enemies. The Dies

Committee had "converted itself into a political club to blast any friends that organized labor may have," the Cascades County Trades and Labor Assembly said.[30] Charles Ickes, secretary of the Brotherhood of Railway Carmen in Brewster, West Virginia, gently chided Frey: "I have two Bro in the CIO and I don't think they are any more Communist than any other union. Just fighting for a living in life. I think if labor is to march on they will haft to make friend, not knock each other."[31] Voices of dissent within the AFL were audible but muted.

Frustration with Communist subterfuge challenged the civil liberties commitments of a wide swath of unionists. A. Philip Randolph exemplified the quandary of many labor leaders. Since founding the Brotherhood of Sleeping Car Porters in the 1920s, Randolph, a socialist, had tussled with Communists. Despite the CP's dedication to black liberation struggles in the 1930s, Randolph saw the party much as other labor anticommunists saw it: a disruptive force of invaders bent on capturing American unions to serve Soviet ends. The CP had taken over the National Negro Congress, to his great outrage. In April 1940, Randolph gave a fiery speech to the National Negro Congress, denouncing Communists' "allegiance to the Soviet Union" and their disregard for civil liberties.[32] The National Negro Congress leadership derided Randolph as a "frightened Negro petty bourgeoisie" and applauded his decision to step down from the presidency in 1940.

"Because of the behaviour of the Communists in the National Negro Congress," Randolph told William Green in May 1940, "I have altered my opinion, in some measure, of the Dies Committee and its usefulness." Earlier, Randolph had decried the Dies Committee for undermining free speech by attacking radicals, but by 1940 he had changed his mind. Randolph resolved that if Dies would "carefully observe the democratic rights of persons and movements" but "relentlessly and aggressively push its crusade to destroy every vestige of foundation for Trojan Horse and Fifth Column conspiracies against the American government, then it will be fulfilling an important public service."[33] Unable to beat back Communists within their organizations, some unionists saw the Dies investigation as a venue for continuing the fight.

Anticommunism in the CIO

Only a tiny fraction—less than 1 percent—of the CIO's membership belonged to the Communist Party. A substantial proportion of CIO union leaders and staff, however, were party members or closely aligned to the party. Unions including Mine Mill, the United Electrical Workers, and the Food and Tobacco

Workers were led by Communists, while the TWU, NMU, and International Longshoremen Workers' Union had officers who were closet party members, and unions such as the UAW and the Office and Professional Workers had sizeable Communist contingents among union leaders and staff.[34]

Although AFL leaders and members were divided on the merits of Dies's investigation, CIO leaders continued to denounce it. Yet by 1938 and early 1939, the CIO had also grown impatient with Communist unionists. Internal union factionalism and old sectarian allegiances underlay the developing conflict. In the UAW, plummeting auto-plant payrolls during the recession of 1937–38 washed a fifth of new members away and left a core of sit-down strike leaders to quarrel over leadership of the reduced union. Socialists and leftists, including the Reuther brothers, rallied with immigrant unskilled workers in the Unity Caucus, and they frequently relied on the support of Communists. Homer Martin's Progressive Caucus, backed by Protestant, native-born skilled workers, took a majority of seats on the union's executive board in 1937 and held power in part by freely denouncing Communists and radicals. Their fight for control of the UAW escalated until the summer of 1938, when Martin suspended his opponents on the executive board, including Reuther and the union's leading Communists.

At their trial that August, the Communists flipped their trump card: purloined letters between Martin, ILGWU president David Dubinsky, and ex-Communist Jay Lovestone, revealing the involvement of anticommunist Dubinsky in the UAW's leadership fight. Exasperated, Lewis sent Sidney Hillman from the Amalgamated Clothing Workers and Philip Murray from the Steel Workers to mediate. Although the Communist candidate enjoyed enormous popular support and could likely have won union-wide election, CP head Earl Browder nixed his candidacy, fearing that a too-prominent CP leader would further agitate anticommunist tensions in the UAW and the CIO. Communists kept a majority on the union's executive board, to the fury of Martin, who left for the AFL, along with a rump faction of 17,000 members.[35]

As a young City College intellectual Lovestone had been a star of the 1920s CP. But Stalin had sidelined him from CPUSA leadership in 1929, turning Lovestone from an ardent Communist into a lifelong anticommunist crusader. His work with Dubinsky and Martin marked his first foray into professional anticommunist strategy. When Lovestone came into the AFL, he brought new information about the CP to the federation, particularly in regard to foreign affairs. Over the next forty years, Lovestone became the United States' foremost authority on international anticommunist labor strategy.[36]

Lovestone found an eager listener in David Dubinsky of the ILGWU. Dubinsky had always been uneasy in the CIO, and the prominence of Communists in the organization was his main concern. A longtime conservative socialist, Dubinsky's enduring suspicion of the CP left him lonely for old allies in the AFL. When the CIO announced its constitutional convention for October 1938, intended to make the coalition a permanent federation, Dubinsky took the ILGWU out of the CIO and back into the AFL.[37] The Sailor's Union of the Pacific (SUP), the West Coast branch of the Seamen's Union, broke off negotiations to join the CIO in the spring of 1938, after the CIO chartered a coastal National Maritime Union. The charter of the NMU signaled the ascendance of the CP and the CIO's disregard for the SUP's craft autonomy. Meanwhile former SUP leader Harry Lundeberg, now the head of the AFL-affiliated Seafarer's Union, increasingly couched his critique of the NMU in anticommunist terms.[38]

By early 1939, then, conflict over Communism had driven one union from the CIO, caused the defection of an anticommunist faction in another, and prevented the affiliation of a third. Even in newly created CIO unions at the height of the Popular Front, when Communists dedicated themselves to building strong CIO unions, the Communist alliance with the CIO was unstable and contested. Communist involvement in power struggles within and between unions illuminated the party's factional coherence, undermining the CP's effort to blend into the labor movement. Such decidedly domestic conflicts likely would have recurred over the next several years as the CIO's unions developed. The CP would have been forced to either continue to forego union leadership roles, as it had in the UAW, or to assert its legitimate claim to operate in the CIO, forcing the fight with anticommunists. As it happened, international affairs intervened, remaking the conflict into a skirmish in a much larger arena.

In August 1939, Stalin and Hitler struck a deal. Germany and the Soviet Union agreed to a separate peace between the two countries. The Comintern sent the word down to its international affiliates: world war, not fascism, was the greatest threat to Russia, and keeping new belligerent states out of the war was the new task of Communist parties everywhere. The American party quickly regrouped, switching its "Communism is Twentieth Century Americanism" banners for new ones reading, "The Yanks Are Not Coming." Many of their Popular Front allies recoiled. Among the angriest were eastern Europeans, who watched in horror as the Red Army took Poland, Finland, and the Baltic states, and American Jews who were alarmed by the Soviet countenancing of Nazi pogroms across Europe. The policy switch permanently alienated many of the new allies the CP had won during its short-lived Popular Front period. And as pressure mounted for the United States to enter the war, the CP's Russian connection suddenly turned the party into an agency of a potential enemy state. Popular anger toward the Soviet Union and hostility toward American Communists escalated sharply in 1940 as Hitler steamrolled across Europe, seizing France in the summer of 1940.

Within the CIO, antiwar Communists found an unexpected ally: John L. Lewis, who strongly opposed U.S. entry to the war and who had grown to strongly dislike FDR. Lewis had always been an uneasy New Deal Democrat. His bond with FDR was an opportunistic alliance easily broken by their disagreement over the war and Lewis's frustration with the New Deal's shortcomings. While most of the CIO leadership grew more bound to and comfortable with the New Deal regime over time, Lewis remained suspicious of entrenched state power and autonomous state actors — quite like his old comrades in the AFL.

When FDR appointed Sidney Hillman, whom Lewis saw as a rival, to represent labor on the National Defense Advisory Commission, a wartime planning body, Lewis turned decisively against FDR. In late October 1940, Lewis astonished the CIO and the nation with a radio address announcing his endorsement of Republican Wendell Willkie in the upcoming presidential election, and his offer to step down as head of the CIO should the membership fail to back him. FDR swept industrial districts in his landslide victory, and Lewis made good on his promise to resign at the CIO's 1940 convention, held a few weeks after the presidential election.

Hillman, on the other hand, had grown more loyal to FDR's domestic program and shared his conviction that the United States must enter the war. CIO Communists stood in the way, however, and Hillman dedicated himself to containing them. In New York State, Hillman's representative fought CP proposals to form a CIO Industrial Union Council, and called for the expulsion of the NMU, the Newspaper Guild, and other Communist-led unions from the state CIO. But expulsion was a call for fratricidal warfare. The proposal went nowhere in New York, and Hillman did not repeat the effort elsewhere that year.[39]

Hillman and other CIO anticommunists instead turned to formal bans on Communist membership — an old tool used by the AFL. Bans were ineffective at preventing Communists from joining but gave the organization a pretext for later expulsions. And Communist bans functioned as a warning to the CIO Communists: blunt your partisanship and lay low if you want to remain in the CIO.[40] Philip Murray, elected as new president of the CIO at the 1940 convention, demanded a ban on CP membership as a condition of his presidency.

Communist delegates negotiated to dilute the requirement, and in the end the convention renounced "Communism, Nazism, and Fascism" as "foreign doctrines opposed to our concept of industrial and political democracy."[41] The next summer, the UAW's convention banned fascists and Communists from union office.[42] A string of unions followed suit, from the Laundry Workers Joint Board in Brooklyn to the Marine Engineers' Beneficial Association.[43]

Spy Catchers

While unions battled over the role of Communists within their ranks, the federal effort to investigate radicals in the labor movement secretly expanded. Hoover's FBI had resumed secret investigations of domestic subversion in 1936 at the direction of President Roosevelt. The rise of domestic xenophobic and fascist movements troubled FDR, as did the growing influence of the Communist Party. As late as 1930, Hoover had told the Fish Committee that Communists had little pull in the American labor movement, but the party's successful organizing in the Depression years changed his mind. Roosevelt and Hoover had an excellent relationship, grounded in mutual admiration and respect, and when Hoover argued that fascist and Communist subversion had become a real threat, Roosevelt listened. Hoover emphasized the growing influence of Communists in three unions: the Newspaper Guild, the Mine Workers, and the Longshoremen, and he warned that these unions— especially the last two—could "cripple" the U.S. economy. There was still no federal law prohibiting the advocacy of Communism or fascism by American citizens, but Roosevelt had a simple solution: in 1936 he issued a secret presidential order authorizing the FBI to investigate Communism and fascism. By fiat, the problem of FBI authority to conduct political policing was solved.[44]

At first Hoover did not do much with this authority. The secrecy of the order was one impediment. Hoover sent reports to the president on CP activities, but the FBI had little capacity to conduct investigations of subversive groups. No agents were dedicated to political surveillance in FBI field offices, and the bureau's jurisdiction was quite constrained. To take formal action that could stand up in court, the State Department had to issue a formal authorization to investigate, and the State Department could only approve investigations relating to charges of treason or threats to national security. Hoover's hands were still tied. In 1938, he pleaded for more resources, asking for 5,000 new agents and authority to oversee domestic countersubversion without State Department oversight. Roosevelt turned him down, giving him a modest budget increase to hire 140 new agents and allowing for the creation of a federal coordinating committee made up of agents from the Military Intelligence Division of the War Department, the Office of Naval Intelligence, and the State Department, along with the FBI. The result was weak. The legacy of the civil liberties movement of the 1920s was a straitened state surveillance apparatus.[45]

Hitler's invasion of the Soviet Union snapped the government to attention. Roosevelt issued a new executive order centralizing jurisdiction over investigations of domestic subversion—espionage, sabotage, and violations of U.S. neutrality—in Hoover's FBI. This dramatic expansion of the FBI's authority provided the justification for a massive increase in manpower and budget, and restored to the Bureau a sweeping authority to surveil "any suspicious groups." Ralph Easley, who died the day after the executive order's issuance, would have been delighted.[46]

Hoover could not plot his strategy in peace, however. Martin Dies dogged his steps. From the beginning, Dies and Hoover quarreled, with Hoover declining to help Dies with investigators or research and Dies wondering loudly, and often, why the FBI had failed to detect the Communist menace he had so easily discovered. To the press Dies suggested that Roosevelt blocked cooperation to undermine the committee. In internal memos defending his decisions, Hoover painstakingly recounted HUAC's ham-handed inquiries and illegal searches.[47] The secrecy of the bureau's resumption of political surveillance left the FBI wide open for grandstanding attacks by Dies.

German espionage concerned Roosevelt and Hoover more than anything else. In 1938 in an apparent replay of the run-up to World War I, the FBI discovered a German spy ring of engineers and doctors who collected military blueprints from installations such as the Boston Navy Yard. Hoover and the FBI devoted far less attention to potential Communist espionage, even after the Non-Aggression Pact. This relative unconcern persisted despite incidents such as the defection to the United States of a senior Soviet intelligence official, Walter Krivitsky. In 1939 Krivitsky published a series of articles in the *Saturday Evening Post* describing "Stalin's secret service," in which he revealed tidbits such as the fact that CPUSA head Earl Browder's sister Margaret had been traveling on a false passport, setting up a Soviet radio station in Berlin. Krivitsky claimed that the Soviets had 250 agents operating in New York alone.[48]

As voluminous research in Soviet and American archives has revealed, the Soviet Union indeed maintained a large espionage operation in the United States throughout the 1930s, and the lack of state surveillance made its work easier. Many of these agents were deployed directly from the KGB in Moscow, but the leadership of the American Communist Party supplied intelligence and support to this network as well. In the years before the Non-Aggression Pact, most of this intelligence gathering was dedicated to developing industrial information to support the Soviet Union's aircraft and other manufacturing industries. But the party succeeded in developing some well-placed sources within the government. Alger Hiss, who joined the State Department in 1936, is the most famous example of the small coterie of Communists who took jobs in the Roosevelt administration in the 1930s; Hiss went to the State Department in September 1936. Most other New Deal Communists ended up in more prosaic jobs, in the Agriculture Department and the NLRB.[49]

The subject of Soviet espionage in the United States is vast and complex, and beyond the scope of this book. For my purposes, however, a few observations are warranted. First, among the hundreds of people identified as Soviet espionage agents in decrypted Soviet communications and KGB files, there are very few union activists. An important exception, the Federation of Architects, Engineers, Chemists, and Technicians (FAECT), included several atomic spies among its members, including Julius Rosenberg. FAECT actively sought opportunities to spy by organizing technicians in army and navy bases and the atomic scientists at the University of California's Berkeley Radiation Laboratory.[50]

But it is an exception that proves the rule. FAECT represented highly skilled professionals who had privileged access to sensitive information. Other unions represented rank-and-file workers who had far less opportunity to collect such information. Based on the evidence we have at this point, it appears that the Communist Party and the KGB did not attempt to mobilize its mass unions, in any industry, in its espionage network. Certainly individual workers could have obtained particular documents, such as airplane design schematics, that would have been of use to the Soviet Union. But the relatively open and democratic nature of mass unions likely precluded any consideration of such a tactic, as the risks of exposing Soviet espionage outweighed the potential benefits.

To some contemporary observers, though, mass unions seemed to be a potential vehicle for sabotage. War mobilization gave Dies a new opportunity to bludgeon the FBI with questions familiar from the previous war: could enemy agents sabotage military preparation? During the Great War, German saboteurs had preoccupied leaders in the government and the AFL, and the AFL had helped uncover a German scheme to organize strikes in munitions factories. Two decades later, officials saw Communist-led unions as the most serious threat to military production.[51]

These fears were not unfounded. In September 1939, Benjamin Gitlow, a onetime Communist candidate for the U.S. presidency, warned the Dies Committee that a Communist-controlled union was "in a position to do tremendous damage . . . they can become a source of sabotage and espionage."[52] His warning seemed prescient in 1940, when the FBI's wiretaps picked up officials of the Mine Mill union discussing a "secret branch" of Communists within CIO-dominated munitions and war-production plants.[53] Meanwhile, the CIO and the AFL both launched vigorous organizing drives in booming defense industries. With the CP publicly opposing war mobilization and holding a leadership role in numerous manufacturing unions, fear of sabotage and slowdowns was reasonable.

Yet labor Communists were far less interested in sabotage than they were in union building, and they confined their antiwar campaign to protests in union newspapers and public marches. Rather than use their industry position to sabotage the war effort, they used the war effort to shore up their industry position, organizing airplane factories and winning contracts with suppliers such as General Electric. Indeed, several Communist-led unions, such as the West Coast Longshoremen, volunteered no-strike pledges and patriotic cooperation with the war effort, despite the USSR's demands. Historians have found no evidence of Communist coordination to sabotage or slow down production.[54] At the time, however, the burst of organizing and walkouts struck observers in the government as potentially treacherous. John Frey understood this dynamic well, having lived through it twenty years earlier during World War I. In 1938, labor anticommunists refrained from exploiting these fears for strategic advantage, as they had done with the IWW before. But their self-restraint quickly crumbled. By 1940, labor anticommunists figured out how to use the Dies Committee to falsely smear CIO competitors as seditious Communists.

Civil Liberties Dilemmas

While the Nazi-Soviet Non-Aggression Pact came as no great surprise to long-standing doubters of the Soviet project, it shocked people such as Roger Baldwin at the ACLU. Liberal and radical allies of the Communist Party had been proud of the Soviet stance against fascism. But it had been getting harder to ignore evidence of Soviet wrongdoing. Stalin had begun purging the party in 1936; many of the officials tried and executed for treason were known to American liberals. The persecution of Leon Trotsky particularly vexed the Popular Front. In exile in Mexico, Trotsky had agreed to appear before the

Dies Committee to testify about Stalin's crimes in late 1939. (Dies eventually declined the offer, as Trotsky also intended to use his appearance to exhort workers to unite in a global revolution against the coming war.)[55]

In August 1938, Dies had denounced the ACLU as "an instrument of Communism," and he had ample evidence to draw on. Baldwin had publicly pronounced his Communist affinities in the early 1930s, and the ACLU's obvious alliance with the CP in the years before the Popular Front spoke for itself. Liberal noncommunist and anticommunist ACLU leaders were furious with Baldwin. Arthur Garfield Hays took control of the situation. The ACLU's board had already voted that no one from the ACLU could appear before the Dies Committee unless subpoenaed, so Hays made a private deal to call the committee off of the ACLU. In March 1939, he arranged for Baldwin to submit a deposition swearing that no Communists had ever served on the ACLU board (which was false—Communist Elizabeth Gurley Flynn was at that time on the board), and Baldwin stated that he "was not now, nor have I ever been, a member of the Communist Party." Under fire, Baldwin locked arms with other ACLU leaders to protect the organization from outside attack.

Opposing the Dies Committee should have been uncontroversial for ACLU leaders. After all, Dies consistently called for restraints on free speech and a free press by demanding a new federal sedition law, and his investigators operated precisely like the "nationwide spy system" that the ACLU had deplored in the twenties. But the wearying fights between socialists and Communists had sapped the ACLU's energy by the late 1930s, and growing misgivings about Soviet Communism made Baldwin and others rethink their positions. In early 1939, the ACLU board resolved to support the continuation of both the La Follette investigation and the "legitimate portions" of the Dies Committee's work, in a move Baldwin's biographer calls "blatantly political." Baldwin himself testified in a closed meeting with Dies Committee investigators in March 1939, again to disavow Communist ties. The Dies Committee had clearly spooked the ACLU.[56]

What was the ACLU so afraid of? Baldwin and other leaders knew that the organization's ties to the CP were deep and longstanding. Likely they believed that exposure of these connections would erode the organization's newfound respectability. Moreover, many noncommunist ACLU leaders were becoming increasingly hostile to the party. They disliked the prospect of defending the ACLU for ties to a political party they found objectionable. Thus well before the Non-Aggression Pact fractured the Popular Front, the ACLU had already distanced itself from the CP. When the pact was announced in August 1939, the fissure deepened.

By the summer of 1939, the Dies Committee had been in operation for a year, and the Communist Party had lost some of its luster, but the civil liberties regime begun in 1924 remained mostly intact. No federal law banned the advocacy of radical ideas or membership in radical organizations, and the FBI had limited authority to police radicals. Despite their vehement anticommunism, labor conservatives agreed with liberals and radicals inside and outside the labor movement: changing the law was dangerous. Federal repression, once unleashed, could be turned against all of them. Over the next two years, though, labor conservatives changed their mind. They abandoned their civil liberties stance, backing the creation of a new regime of federal political policing. And labor conservatives learned how to strategically deploy that new regime against their enemies, in the process proving the case they had made all along.

CHAPTER TEN

Labor's Red Scare

The AFL and the Architecture of Anticommunism, 1939–1941

In 1941, William Bell, a junior assistant statistician in the Pennsylvania Department of Labor and Industry, got a taste of what, a decade later, would be called McCarthyism. His boss, the director of the Department of Labor and Industry, distributed a questionnaire asking employees whether they were members of the Communist Party or had ever signed electoral nominating petitions for Communist Party candidates. Bell replied no to both questions, but in fact he had signed a nominating petition on a Pittsburgh sidewalk in 1940. Bell had no idea that he was signing for Communists, he later explained: "I have on numerous occasions signed petitions, as a personal favor, taking the petitioner's word as to the contents of the petition." In November 1941, Bell was fired, for "giving aid and comfort to the Communist Party" with his nominating signature. Bell protested his firing, arguing that his membership in the CIO's State, County, and Municipal Workers union, not his petition signature, was the real reason for his termination.

Bell lost his appeal, but he was right. Lewis G. Hines, the director of the Pennsylvania Department of Labor and Industry, had seized on the Communist petitions as a pretext to fire CIO activists. Hines was no ordinary government bureaucrat. He was a longtime AFL union leader and right-hand assistant to AFL president William Green prior to his appointment as head of the Department of Labor and Industry. In Pennsylvania, AFL leaders motivated by partisanship hounded vulnerable government staffers with dubious charges of subversion, in a dress rehearsal for the abuses that came to be known as McCarthyism. Hines's red purge occurred at the end of a little Red Scare that erupted in the United States between 1939 and 1941. During these years, a new system of anticommunist laws and practices was created with the help of labor anticommunists.

Two strains of labor anticommunism emerged during this era, one liberal and voluntarist, the other conservative and statutory. Along with other liberal anticommunists in the ACLU, CIO leaders considered the CPUSA to be essentially a coalition of American radicals with internationalist sympathies, led by ideologues prone to sectarian excesses but hardly subversive. Thus they saw Communist containment and civil liberties as being in tension, and they tended to support ad hoc policing of Communist misbehavior while opposing statutory limits on political action. Conservative unionists, on the other hand, treated the CPUSA as an agency of the Soviet Union operating through subterfuge to infiltrate American social and political institutions, especially the labor movement. Its Soviet ties disqualified the CPUSA from the constitutional protections afforded other political parties. As a result, the civil libertarians stepped in unison to the right. Liberals in the ACLU and the CIO shifted into the stance previously held by labor conservatives. They adopted a voluntarist anticommunism that advocated self-policing, removing Communist leaders, and prohibiting Communists from holding leadership roles.

Labor conservatives also shifted. They moved into the position formerly occupied by armchair anticommunists and advocated for increased governmental powers to suppress sedition. They argued that the Communist Party was a unique threat due to its Soviet ties and stealthy practices, and thus the state was justified in placing special restrictions and stepped-up surveillance on the party. By the summer of 1941, a Communist exception had been carved out of the civil liberties platform.

Subversives in the NLRB

While the Dies Committee hunted for subversives in New Deal agencies, the AFL focused on the National Labor Relations Board. Emboldened by the elections of 1938 and polls showing a majority of voters supported amendment or repeal of the Wagner Act, AFL leaders insisted that the NLRB's pro-CIO bias required a legislative curb. Among a flurry of proposals introduced in Congress, the AFL and the National Association of Manufacturers backed a package of amendments aimed at improving the odds for craft unions when competing against the CIO's factory-wide units. Thus the AFL pushed to permit employers to openly support one union in the case of competing union claims, to compel recognition of separate craft units, and to limit NLRB agents' discretion.

John P. Frey (left) speaks with U.S. Representative Howard Smith, December 14, 1939. Library of Congress, Prints and Photographs Division.

While Democratic leaders of the House and Senate labor committees tried to stall the proposals, AFL ally Representative Howard Smith of Virginia commandeered the issue in his House Rules Committee and won a resolution for a special committee to investigate the NLRB. From December 1939 through March 1940, Smith hauled NLRB members and staffers before his committee to account for their decisions, ideologies, and supposed affinity for the CIO. As liaison to Smith's staff, John Frey fed them information and questions. In March, Smith proposed a radical reworking of the Wagner Act. When the House took up Smith's bill in early June 1940, William Green dropped a bombshell: the AFL announced its support for the Wagner Act overhaul, pending modifications that generally reverted to the AFL's initial proposals. Green's announcement rocked Washington, and his backing helped shift support for the bill in the House, which passed Green's revision of Smith's amendments by 258 votes to 129; the Democrats split evenly on the bill, while Republicans overwhelmingly backed it.[1]

Thereafter, the Smith-AFL legislation languished. The Senate never took it up, reflecting the continuing strength of the liberal Democrat-CIO coalition and the dissent within AFL ranks, as numerous AFL affiliates disavowed Green's lobbying campaign. Central labor councils in Denver, Cincinnati,

Omaha, and Salt Lake City, the state federations in Colorado, Nebraska, Iowa, and South Dakota, and locals from the New York Painters to the Machinists in Portland, Oregon, all spoke out against the amendments. Nevertheless, the silence of many AFL unions on the matter is equally striking. Of the major union leaders in the AFL, only Daniel Tobin of the Teamsters took a firm stand against the law's revision.[2]

When Congress again took up the question of revising the nation's labor policy in 1947, many of the Smith-AFL amendments became law in the Taft-Hartley Act. In 1940 the anti-NLRB campaign had two main effects: it convinced Roosevelt to replace crusaders at the NLRB with more moderate technocrats, and it branded NLRB officials, and by extension New Deal staffers, as Communist.[3]

In fact, the NLRB harbored more Communists than even John Frey could imagine. Edwin Smith, a member of the board, was a Communist, as was the board's secretary, Nathan Witt; and the NLRB staff held one of the most active Communist cells in the government. In September 1939, Whittaker Chambers made a special appointment with Assistant Secretary of State Adolf Berle to warn him about a group of midlevel Communist staffers in the State Department, the Treasury Department, and the NLRB, among other government agencies.[4] Apparently untroubled by this information, Berle kept it to himself until 1942—a measure of the generally benign view of the CP many liberals maintained.

As usual, John Frey had the best intelligence. He had guessed Edwin Smith was red back in 1937, when he received a photograph of a dinner party hosted by Smith and attended by the Russian Ambassador and John L. Lewis.[5] When Smith and Lewis both attended a pan-American labor conference in Mexico in 1938 that was also attended by Communist unionists, Frey added it to his bill of particulars. Frey testified repeatedly about Edwin Smith, first to the Dies Committee and later to the Senate hearings on the Wagner Act revisions.[6] William Green helped drive the message, declaring that "many employees of the Board are radical-minded, if not communistic," in a February 1939 article.[7] The AFL pushed hard to add subversion to the charges against the NLRB.

NLRB Communists were mostly lawyers who joined the CP during the Popular Front years. Most had worked at a number of alphabet agencies—the Agricultural Adjustment Administration, the Works Projects Administration—and several met while on the staff of the La Follette Committee. Herbert Fuchs, the cell leader, later said that seventeen NLRB staffers formally joined the party between 1937 and 1942. NLRB Communists dedicated most of their energy to organizing an NLRB staff union, and taking part in radical causes via this union—the NLRB union sent delegates to the American League for Peace and Democracy, raised funds for the Southern Tenant Farmers' Union and the Friends of Spanish Democracy, and marched against the European war.[8] Fuchs met regularly with cell leaders in other government agencies such as the State Department and the Labor Department. NLRB member Edwin Smith, a onetime personnel manager for Filene's department store and Massachusetts commissioner of labor, frequently made radical pronouncements in public forums, denouncing "fascist" strikebreaking and calling for support for the Spanish republic.[9]

Did Communists shape the policy or practice of the NLRB? Most scholars agree that NLRB staffers, Communist and noncommunist, generally favored industrial organizing over craft unionism and endorsed the CIO's approach as a rule. A number of staffers reported that the NLRB had a staff culture of "extreme liberalism" and believed that the CIO "had a pipeline into the board."[10] In other words, CIO advocates, CP members, and liberals all shared a common labor agenda, and it is hard to separate out a Communist thread. The NLRB office was a highly charged political environment, cliquish and ideological, and moderates and conservatives certainly felt uncomfortable there. David Saposs, the NLRB's chief economist and a veteran progressive laborite, found the partisanship alarming. Over lunch, he asked the seemingly clueless NLRB Chairman, Warren Madden, "Do you realize that you're surrounded by communists and pro-communists?" Madden brushed the question off; like Berle, he was a liberal who saw such charges as "witch hunting," Saposs said.[11]

Ironically, Saposs, not Smith, became the focus of red-hunting inquiries. Saposs was a graduate of the University of Wisconsin's labor economics program, and throughout his career he demonstrated the commitment to labor rights and industrial order characteristic of that school. Saposs's name first surfaced in November 1938, when Dies Committee research director J. B. Matthews mentioned that a Communist workers' school was reading Saposs's 1926 Columbia dissertation on left-wing unionism.[12] The Smith Committee picked up the charge and grilled Saposs in February 1940. They established that he had been a member of the Socialist Club while at Wisconsin and confirmed that he had a "strongly exaggerated social consciousness," but Saposs seemed pink at best. Historian Earl Latham remarked, "As the Smith committee was saving the 'capitalistic and democratic form of government' from David Saposs, who was not subverting it, it took sober testimony about the board's operations from some who were."[13]

Fuchs, Witt, Edwin Smith, and other Communists remained under the

Smith Committee's radar. Saposs did not betray them, even when a Wisconsin congressman attempting to defend him reported that he had heard Saposs complain about sectarian in-fighting on the NLRB staff. In an unkind cut, a disgruntled trial examiner also fingered Saposs as a radical when he quit the NLRB in March 1940 because board members "continue brazenly and openly to foster Communists and kindred radicals."[14] Many saw the charges against Saposs as groundless—the AFL's director of organization tried to step in, and *Time* magazine called Saposs "neither red nor useless, but a zealous watchdog of labor rights." Nonetheless, Saposs lost his job when Congress zeroed out the appropriation for the NLRB's staff economist. He was the only casualty of Smith's red hunt.[15]

Labor conservatives were not the only ones alleging that FDR's brain trust harbored Communists. The Federal Theater Project was a favorite target, thanks to its program of radical plays. But the NLRB received the most sustained scrutiny. In 1939, the NLRB hearings put the question of federal loyalty in the spotlight.

While Dies and Smith harried New Deal staffers for their ties to the CP and the CIO, other congressmen and -women went after New Deal agencies for their ties to Roosevelt. In the 1938 midterm elections, WPA workers were pressed into electioneering against Roosevelt's purge targets in Kentucky, Tennessee, and Pennsylvania. When the surviving conservative Democrats returned to Congress, they allied with Republicans to pass the Hatch Act, which barred political candidates from using federal relief funds or recipients in election campaigns, and also forbade federal employees from using their offices to support electoral candidates. The measure came to the House floor in July 1939, after Dies and Smith had kept the question of federal employee loyalty before the Congress for a year. At the last minute, an extra provision was tacked onto the bill, barring from federal employment anyone belonging to a political party or organization advocating "the overthrow of our constitutional form of government."[16] The drumbeat of anticommunist insinuations was starting to take shape.

The AFL publicly endorsed the Hatch Act. At its convention that fall, the federation held that "avowed Communists, actual members of the Communist Party, and active Communist sympathizers, have worked their way into important administrative posts in National and State Government." The convention called "for the immediate dismissal of such Communists and Communist sympathizers."[17] The AFL's traditional suspicion of state bureaucracy predisposed the federation to like any measure to limit civil service autonomy. Banning Communists from government jobs was a natural extension of this logic. The following summer, in 1940, Congress appropriated $100,000 to fund an FBI operation to investigate any federal worker suspected of subversion, and Dies sent Hoover a list of 1,121 names to start with.[18] Federal loyalty probes had begun.

Statutory and Voluntarist Anticommunism

Numerous other measures targeting Communist and Nazi subversives flooded the Congress. Many targeted immigrants and resident aliens, demanding the registration and fingerprinting of all aliens and denying WPA posts to noncitizens.[19] As pressure mounted for a peacetime sedition law, the AFL's position seemed solid: not only did the AFL refuse to back a ban on the Communist Party, but it defended the civil rights of resident aliens. Testifying before three separate subcommittees in the spring of 1939, the AFL's legislative representative, Paul Scharrenberg, reiterated the federation's support for immigration restriction but stood up against deporting resident aliens for political activity. Such a law would impair immigrant workers from striking or from getting involved in their unions, Scharrenberg said. Further, the federation feared legislation that banned advocacy of "any change in the American form of government," because "that is something that strikers are likely to do."[20]

The AFL's stance baffled Scharrenberg's listeners. Hadn't a stream of AFL witnesses recently appeared before Congress complaining about Communist subversion in their unions? Incredulous committee members pushed him to clarify, then one asked, "For whom are you speaking this morning? You do not represent the American Federation of Labor, do you?" Finally, Scharrenberg said, "I am here to oppose the bill before the committee. If you have any other language to submit, I will consult my superiors and tell you truthfully what their position is."[21] Their puzzlement is telling. After all, the AFL's position on sedition laws had not changed since 1924. But labor conservatives' constant complaints about Communism overshadowed the nuances in their policy platform. Even though AFL lobbyists had consistently objected to the letter of sedition laws, the tone of the federation's public statements seemed to provide justification for the spirit of legislation constraining Communists and radicals.

The AFL's defense of its members' civil rights put the federation in familiar company. The American Civil Liberties Union campaigned hard against the sedition bill, mobilizing a letter-writing campaign and organizing rallies. The CIO joined the ACLU's campaign, and moreover opposed immigration restriction as well, asking "if the First Congress had passed a bill such as this, just how many of us would be in this room today?"[22] The AFL limited its lobbying to public testimony, but its stance broke the unity of the antiradical lobby.

Congressman Howard Smith took the lead in shepherding antisubversive legislation through Congress, and by the spring of 1940 both houses of Congress agreed on an omnibus bill. Some of the most odious proposals had been stripped out, such as the establishment of camps to house immigrant radicals whom the United States could not arrange to deport. The law banned any person from advocating the overthrow of the U.S. government, whether individually or as a member of a group, by speech, writing, or any public display. The Smith Act, as the law came to be called, was breathtakingly broad. Smith brought the bill to the floor for voting in June 1940, as France was falling to Hitler. The Senate approved the bill by voice vote on June 15, and the House passed the measure by 382 ayes to 4 nays on June 22.[23]

Since 1924 the AFL had consistently supported a broad definition of civil liberties, arguing that the risk of state repression outweighed the risk posed by Communist subversion. Suddenly in 1940 the AFL's position changed. As the bill sat on Roosevelt's desk, the AFL weighed in again. Now the federation came out in support of the Smith Act. In a speech on June 26, Green laid out his argument: "This is not hysteria. It is plain common sense. The Communist Party and the Nazi Bund in this country are anxious to keep their secret operations unhampered. The moment they are exposed and rooted out, they fill the air with shrieks about civil liberties. Let us not be deceived." After the windup, Green delivered his peroration: "The time has come for us to identify the traitors in our midst. I believe the Communist Party and the Nazi Bund should be outlawed."[24] Green reiterated his new position at a speech at the FBI's National Police Academy a few days later. He added a swipe at the CIO, remarking, "we consider it shameful that a labor group, not affiliated with the American Federation of Labor, bitterly opposed these measures, and lent itself to underhanded attacks on the Federal Bureau of Investigation."[25]

FDR signed the bill, and at the AFL's convention in the fall of 1940 the federation went even further. A delegate from the California State Federation of Labor introduced a resolution arguing that since "the Communist Party does not represent a party but is an agency of a foreign Government," the AFL should support laws not only outlawing the Communist Party but also prohibit[ing] it from appearing on the ballot in any state." By unanimous vote, the convention passed the resolution.

What changed suddenly in 1940? No AFL official publicly explained the shift. One explanation may lie in the bill's sponsor. Congressman Howard Smith was moving the federation's NLRB amendments through Congress at the same time that the eponymous Smith Act was pending. Perhaps there was some sort of quid pro quo.[26] It is also likely that labor conservatives believed that the political climate made the Smith Act less dangerous to unions. After years of evangelizing about the evils of Communism and the loyalty of the AFL, the events of 1939 indicated that political leaders in Washington saw the CP in the same way as labor conservatives: a unique political organization that was utterly unlike other radical movements or workers' organizations. Meanwhile the Wagner Act had established the legal legitimacy of unions, strikes, and labor protest. The most likely reason for the shift, though, is the apparent inevitability of the bill's enactment. FDR seemed inclined to sign the Smith Act, and continued opposition would be fruitless. Continuing to stand up for the rights of Communists and fascists could also undermine the AFL's reputation for loyalty and unleash red-baiting attacks that the CIO was already enduring. Backing the Smith Act was an act of realpolitik for the federation.[27]

The CIO vehemently opposed the Smith Act, as did the ACLU, which called 1940 "the crisis year" of "liberty's national emergency."[28] But the Dies Committee was an ongoing source of internal conflict. Liberal anticommunists inside the ACLU relished the committee's humiliating excoriations of Communist enemies: ACLU board member John Haynes Holmes, active in the group since 1915, "gloated" that Dies was "getting the goods on some of our friends and associates."[29] Union lawyers Morris Ernst and Arthur Garfield Hays met privately with Dies in the fall of 1939 when Harry Ward, the chairman of the ACLU board, was due to testify about his involvement in the Popular Front American League for Peace and Democracy.[30] When Dies went easy on Ward, many ACLU activists suspected a deal. Ernst later said that his relationship with Dies "saved the Civil Liberties Union."

The ensuing uproar forced a crisis in the ACLU. In early 1940, anticommunists and CP allies fought over the ACLU's relationship to the party and to Dies. Anticommunists pushed to issue a report supporting the Dies Committee and tried to ban Communists and supporters of other "totalitarian" doctrines from leadership roles in the ACLU; radicals decried Dies and denounced political litmus tests for leaders. By February, the anticommunists prevailed. The ACLU leadership passed a resolution barring any board member who displayed "inconsistency" in the defense of civil liberties; supporting "totalitarianism" abroad was an automatic disqualification. Harry Ward resigned, but Elizabeth Gurley Flynn forced the ACLU to kick her out. In a six-hour trial in May 1940, the ACLU board debated what to do with Flynn, but the outcome was unsurprising: she was expelled from the board.

The ACLU thus permanently severed its old relationship with the Communist Party and embraced a politics of civil liberties stripped of its revolutionary aspirations. Ironically, the ACLU adopted the AFL's old voluntarist approach to Communism. The organization would maintain its traditional opposition to state policing of radicals, while policing itself for red influences. Nevertheless, the ACLU could not entirely shake its radical aura. As Judy Kutulas writes, "The ACLU was not antifascist enough to satisfy liberals, progressive enough to satisfy progressives, or anticommunist enough to satisfy anticommunists."[31]

In many ways, the CIO faced the same dilemma. CIO unions had begun to turn on Communists in their ranks, instituting bans on Communist Party members and periodically denouncing Communist sectarianism. The CIO and the ACLU thus learned to police themselves, much as AFL unions had done since the early 1920s. In practice, their position looked a lot like the voluntarist anticommunism outlined by Gompers and Green. State repression would only breed rebellion. Give labor enough liberty, and its members would reject revolutionary doctrines on their own. But the AFL was taking a new tack, embracing statutory repression of the Communist Party.

Labor's Red Scare

With the legal architecture of federal anticommunism in place, AFL conservatives moved quickly to use it. A series of defense-industry strikes in 1940 and 1941 attracted particular concern as potential Communist-led conspiracies. The UAW was involved in all three: Vultee Aircraft in late 1940, North American Aviation in spring 1941, and Allis-Chalmers, also in spring 1941. Federal officials and union leaders collaborated in increasingly sharp crackdowns on these strikes, ordering strikers back to work at North American Aviation and sending federal troops in to reopen the plant at Allis-Chalmers. Historians have described the repression of these strikes as steps in the construction of a "new corporatist regime of laborite cooptation," in the words of Nelson Lichtenstein.[32] A closer look at these strikes expands our understanding of the origins and outcome of the defense-industry strike wave. In all these strikes, the AFL-affiliated International Association of Machinists (IAM) unsuccessfully competed with the UAW for the loyalties of workers, and in each case the Machinists helped devise and spread charges that their UAW rivals were both red and subversive. Rival unionists thus played a key role in creating the

R U S S I A *in the making!*

C *oercion, then*

I *nsurrection, then*

O *ppression!*

This flyer, found in the papers of the California Federation of Labor, carries the distinctive "union bug" in the bottom left corner, indicating that it was printed by a unionized printer, and was likely created by an AFL affiliate. Box 11, folder 12, California Federation of Labor Papers, Labor Archives and Research Center, San Francisco State University.

specter of labor disloyalty. Moreover, as during World War I, union officers built new relationships in the U.S. Army and War Department as they collaborated in policing labor disloyalty. By 1941, union leaders in the AFL and CIO had a hand in creating a new regime for policing radicals in industry.

An episode at a Boeing factory in Seattle reveals the pattern. Aircraft manufacture exploded in the 1930s, and national employment in the industry jumped from 30,000 in 1937 to 200,000 in 1941. Seeing no reason to respect the IAM's jurisdictional claims, the United Auto Workers launched its own organizing drive in 1937.[33] By 1940, the UAW had begun to make headway, stirring consternation inside the IAM headquarters and interest among the Machinists at Boeing.

The 8,000-member lodge at Boeing had organized in 1936, and its leaders were well-known locally as leftists. (Several leaders of the local were Communists as well.) This reputation probably encouraged African American activists in Seattle to push the Machinists to support a fair-employment drive at the plant. (From its founding, Boeing had refused to hire African Americans.) In late 1939, African American community activists, led by a black former CP district head, called on Boeing to lower the color bar, but Boeing blamed the IAM's whites-only membership policy. The Boeing Machinists pleaded for time, arguing that "progressive locals like our own" had been fighting within the IAM to eliminate the whites-only oath and that, as a recent affiliate, they could hardly be blamed for either Boeing's or the Machinists' policy. In July

1940, the Boeing Machinists promised to demand repeal of the policy at the IAM's September convention.[34]

Meanwhile, the local was embroiled in its own months-long fight with management, protesting mandatory overtime with pickets and one-day strikes. Most ominous for the IAM leadership, rumors had reached Washington that their Boeing local was contemplating a switch to the CIO.[35] Machinist president Harvey N. Brown called John Frey for help.

Frey worked his confidential sources, who advised that the entire leadership of the Boeing lodge were Communists. But there were other sources of intelligence. In Seattle, Boeing manufactured B-29 bombers for the army and patrol boats for the navy. Procurement officials from the War Department and the services thus closely monitored production and took notice of the industrial turmoil. Undercover FBI and Seattle police agents were placed in the factory that spring. Frey visited Seattle in late July, where he met with the local head of the FBI, the immigration inspector, and the army contracting officer. The War Department believed that Communist workers had orchestrated a production slowdown. But the FBI, which had received "several charges of espionage and sabotage" and "thoroughly investigated," assured Frey that carelessness or lack of training, not sabotage, lay behind production delays.[36]

Frey reported his findings to the IAM, and met with Boeing's president, P. O. Johnson, whom he gently chided for failing to show "the necessary strength and determination" to deal with the Communists. Johnson complained that he had asked the FBI or the army to "rid him of the Communists, for should he attempt to discharge the ringleaders it might precipitate a strike and would in all probability lead to a case against him under the NLRB." The refusal of Boeing and the FBI to intervene left the matter in the hands of the Machinists, Frey concluded.[37]

Frey's machinations surpassed anything dreamed up by earlier labor antiradicals. Here, Frey, an official of the AFL, was attempting to entice both an employer and the federal government to surveil and fire members of an AFL-affiliated union based merely on the suspicion that the members were considering a move to the CIO. Both the FBI and the company president declined the opportunity to repress radical workers, invoking regulatory limits on their authority. But no such limits bound the AFL or the IAM.

As for the civil rights demands, IAM documents and private letters among Frey, Brown, and the War Department make no mention of African American agitation for jobs.[38] It seems likely that the Boeing Machinists dropped the issue as relations heated up with the international; at the IAM convention, the Seattle Urban League president watched with anger as the lodge "did little if anything by way of fighting for the proposed change."[39] But the Boeing lodge's alliance with African American activists, especially Communists, likely confirmed IAM officials' suspicions about the sympathies of the lodge leaders.

So did the demonstration of rank-and-file support for their officers. Members stalled the lodge's formal investigation and forced the IAM leadership to travel to Seattle in April 1941. At unruly lodge meetings, members booed the trial committee and shouted down Brown and the international officers. Nonetheless, the IAM's executive board tried and expelled sixty-eight members of the lodge. Only eleven members were expelled for Communism, however. The remaining fifty-seven members were expelled for "advocating secession" from the IAM and for "attacking the character, impugning the motives, and questioning the integrity of the Officers of the Grand Lodge, Local Lodge, and the Executive Council." The IAM split the Boeing lodge into six separate lodges, as "orderly and democratic meetings" had become "impossible," and appointed an international representative to remain in Seattle and oversee the local. With this move, the IAM broke the back of the secession movement and the radical opposition in its Boeing lodge.[40]

The Boeing incident shows how the IAM tried to use the renascent domestic-security state to weight the scales in its competition with the UAW. The Machinists union red-baited its own members to quell dissent and head off secession and lured federal police to repress dissident members in its own ranks by charging sabotage and Communism. The Machinists even reported on their own local officers to their employer. They were so vociferous in alleging Communism and disloyalty that the FBI sometimes acted as a check on their more outrageous claims.

As the Machinists fought the UAW for dominance of the burgeoning defense industries, the IAM used these tactics next in southern California, the emerging center of American aircraft manufacture and a place where the IAM had little presence. When Wyndham Mortimer, an avowed Communist, arrived to organize aircraft workers for the UAW in the summer of 1940, he found low wages and restive workers. At Vultee in Los Angeles, Mortimer petitioned the NLRB for an election of the plant's 400 workers. When the election was held three months later, 4,000 workers were on the voting list. After a few months of contentious bargaining, Vultee workers struck for twelve days, inciting Martin Dies to charge subversion and question why the FBI had failed to intervene. Attorney General Robert Jackson defended the FBI by joining the attack: the FBI had "already investigated" and "identified those leaders of the strike who are either members of the Communist Party or affiliated with the Communists."[41] But neither the FBI nor any other federal agency intervened in the strike. The IAM apparently had nothing to do with these charges at Vultee.

The Machinists moved aggressively at the UAW's next target. North American Aviation in Inglewood employed 5,500 workers to make fighter planes. The UAW and the Machinists had been jockeying for two years over the plant. In 1938, the UAW first filed a request for recognition at North American, and the Machinists intervened, claiming to have seven members in the plant. Both unions began organizing aggressively. Finally, at an NLRB hearing in the summer of 1940, the UAW presented petitions and membership cards signed by about 2,500 workers, while the IAM had the signatures of about 1,200 workers. It took until the following January for the NLRB to order an election at the plant. The Machinists then proceeded on two fronts. Its activists inside the plant alleged sabotage by German workers, aiming to get antiunion German workers fired. At the same time, its organizers at the plant gates passed out leaflets attacking the UAW and CIO as Communist organizations.[42]

Some of the Machinists' most active members sought out the union for its conservative reputation. Thomas Lally, a leadman at North American, had previously been a member of the UAW, but he grew frustrated at union meetings when he found "Communist literature in the seats," and when some unionists "walked out of the hall" rather than pledge allegiance to the American flag. Lally had already taken his suspicions to the local FBI office, which told him, "Lally, we have not got any money appropriated to take care of anything like that," and sent him to the Los Angeles police red squad instead. In 1940, Lally called the AFL organizer and signed up with the Machinists.[43]

Rumors of German sabotage in Los Angeles aircraft factories had circulated since mid-1939, but Dies's investigators had been unable to pin the facts down.[44] Then in November 1939, a mechanic named Charles Hollingshead hired on at North American. He had previously worked at Douglas Aircraft during a short-lived sit-down strike organized by the UAW, and he told his new coworkers that he left because he could not abide the Communist domination of the UAW. An investigator for Dies, James Steedman, had been working in Los Angeles, with the "close cooperation of the local AFL," and soon he met Hollingshead. Once Hollingshead signed on as an informant to "furnish information to the Dies Committee on espionage and sabotage activities," Steedman notified the North American personnel director of Hollingshead's new role, to make sure Hollingshead did not get fired. Over the next year, other IAM activists, including the local lodge president, also began supplying information to Dies.[45]

First, they warned that a German clique in the plant planned "acts of sabotage." Dies Committee member Jerry Voorhis made a special visit to Los Angeles in October 1940 to hear their testimony. Their warnings appeared to come true in November. One of North American's prototype jets crashed, and Hollingshead and his colleagues, along with a plant inspector, fingered several German mechanics, saying they had removed bolts and tampered with the plane's gauges. Within days, Dies told a convention of sales managers in Albany about a German "wave of sabotage in our defense industries, particularly on the West Coast."[46]

Irate, Hoover sent a crew of FBI investigators to the plant to check the story out. They found the charges of German conspiracy to be meritless, but the FBI did uncover the relationship between the IAM and the Dies Committee. North American's chief inspector told them that "the Germans in the plant still refused to join a union" and that he believed the "the union was behind this agitation and the charges to the Dies Committee in order to force the company to fire the Germans." It turned out that several of the antiunion "Germans" in the plant were not German at all, but native-born. Eventually the plant inspector renounced his charges, telling the FBI that "he had been taken advantage of by the union."[47] The president of North American Aviation, J. H. Kindleberger, agreed. Kindleberger had received numerous "anonymous letters" and complaints alleging "communistic" and Nazi sympathies among his workforce. "In each case I have checked," he said, "I have found they were personal gripes and piques and little feuds." With the FBI's intervention, allegations of German sabotage died down.[48]

IAM red-baiting escalated nonetheless, and the union's organizing campaign was still going strong. In January 1941, the NLRB finally ordered an election to be held in March. Competing organizers from the IAM and the UAW ringed the plant, passing out flyers and union newspapers. The Machinists "had just one argument, like a fellow trying to play a tune on just one string," Wyndham Mortimer later recalled. "That one thing was Communism—the CIO was a Communist organization, Harry Bridges was a Communist, Wyndham Mortimer was a Communist, John Lewis was a Communist. Everybody connected with the CIO was tinged with Communism." To catch workers' attention, the unions stepped up their efforts. The Machinists brought in a sound truck; the UAW passed out lollipops with tags reading "Don't Be a Sucker—Vote CIO." Just before the election, to counter the Machinists' Americanist rhetoric, Mortimer hired men in Native American costumes, complete with tomahawks, to stand at the plant gates. Their leaflets read simply, "This leaflet was handed to you by real 100% *original* Americans." Mortimer recalled, "This, I think, was what clinched the whole thing; it made the Machinists' Red-baiting argument look so silly."[49]

Still, the Machinists had made huge organizing gains. In July 1940, the UAW held an edge of more than 1,000 supporters, but by the election in March 1941 the UAW's margin had nearly evaporated. The final vote was 3,043 for the UAW, 2,973 for the IAM.[50] Despite the fact that the FBI had exonerated the UAW, the Dies Committee investigations and IAM red-baiting helped shift support away from the UAW. The Machinists and the AFL, along with their ally Dies, had cast doubt on the UAW's loyalty.

Warfare in Wisconsin between the UAW and IAM at another defense contractor may also have influenced the vote. At Allis-Chalmers, a Milwaukee heavy-machine and tooling factory, workers had been locked in battle since the mid-1930s. A core of skilled craftsmen, many German and Catholic, had fought to maintain a separate union with its own contract against a growing majority of less-skilled southern European immigrant workers, who had joined the UAW in 1937. The factory floor was unusually politicized—along with the UAW and IAM, Allis-Chalmers had a Communist cadre organizing in the plant since the early 1930s and an independent union, which supported industrial organization but opposed the Communist leadership now concentrated in the UAW.[51] These factions had been fighting for several years, with the Machinists often undercutting mass strikes and the UAW insisting that it held sole jurisdiction over the plant.

In December 1941 the conflict exploded into a plant-gate fistfight between IAM and UAW partisans. The UAW, led by Communist Harold Christoffel, insisted that Allis-Chalmers fire the IAM men involved in the fight and bargain solely with the UAW. Allis-Chalmers refused, and in January 1941 the UAW walked out. Months of bargaining, with mediation by Sidney Hillman and the National Defense Advisory Commission, could not resolve the question of union security, as Allis-Chalmers refused to grant the UAW a closed shop. By the end of March, the IAM led a back-to-work movement, with a new patriotic organization called the American Workers for Defense. Thousands of workers crossed the UAW's picket lines with the protection of Milwaukee police. Strikers cut streetcar cables and fought to block returning workers. After seventy-seven days, the National Defense Mediation Board finally brokered a deal: the UAW would return to work, without a union security clause but with an impartial referee to adjudicate claims of "undermining the union."[52]

As part of the return-to-work movement, Dies and the AFL raised the specter of Communist sabotage. In late March, Martin Dies remarked on

Christoffel's Communist affiliation on the House floor, and in mid-April AFL president William Green called the strike a "Communist-inspired walkout" that amounted to "nothing less than sabotage."[53] Allis-Chalmers shared voluminous information with FBI and Army Military Intelligence Division investigators about the UAW and Christoffel, leading administration figures from FDR to Secretary of State Cordell Hull to decry Communist influence in the strike.[54]

Meanwhile the UAW and North American Aviation could not agree on contract terms and scheduled mediation with the National Defense Mediation Board (NDMB), a new body created to speed resolution of labor disputes with defense contractors. As the NDMB mediation proceeded in Washington, Dies kept up the attack—and now, anticommunist unionists from the CIO materialized to help. In late May 1941, a former president of a UAW General Motors local and several Ford workers returned to the witness table to repeat their old charges of subversion at North American Aviation, and they came up with an elegant new formulation: Communists were working with the German-American Bund to undermine production. The North American UAW local president appeared in the hearing room to demand equal time, but a staffer produced a telegram revealing that he had registered as a Communist voter. The committee promptly subpoenaed him to testify that afternoon, and he was obliged to admit that he had registered as a Communist in early 1938.[55] For the UAW and the CIO, embroiled in their own fights with the Communist Party and working hard to ensconce labor at the center of war-mobilization planning, Wyndham Mortimer and North American Aviation had become a big headache.

A few days later, a crew of North American Aviation workers, tired of waiting, walked off the job in June 1941. Elated, Mortimer called a plant-wide strike. UAW vice president Richard Frankensteen was furious, and so was Hillman at the NDAC; the strike suggested their inability to discipline their own membership and instantly reinvigorated the issue of subversion. Frankensteen flew out to Los Angeles to order strikers back to work. In a public statement, he condemned the strike on behalf of the UAW and the CIO and added a warning: the "vicious maneuvering of the Communist Party" was apparent in the strike, and in the future they must "keep their hands off the policies and affairs of the aircraft division."[56] Frankensteen fired Mortimer; North American fired all the union leaders; and Roosevelt sent 2,500 troops to oversee the return to work.[57]

In the aftermath of the North American Aviation episode, the Roosevelt administration and labor officials started looking for ways to forestall both subversion and charges of subversion in defense industries. Officials in the FBI and the unions believed that CP-organized sabotage of war production was possible, but their investigations had not turned up any actual evidence of such plots. On the other hand, employers, politicians, and union rivals were prone to lob baseless charges, and the army's military intelligence branch tended to label all strikers as Communist. In June 1941, the FBI proposed the creation of a special unit to investigate defense industry employees, who would be deprived of their draft deferment if they engaged in wildcat or subversive strikes. Union officers could use an FBI blacklist of "dangerous employees" to bar subversives from union office, and defense industry contractors would fire them. Sidney Hillman backed the idea, but various constitutional difficulties apparently led the Justice Department to abandon the plan.[58]

The story of the aircraft-industry strikes demonstrates how the FBI often mitigated the excesses of Red Scare politics by insisting on actually investigating and substantiating charges of subversion. Although enterprising antiradicals could mobilize the Dies Committee to chase specious red claims, upright FBI agents protected accused workers and curbed the wild claims of conspiracy emanating from Dies's hearing room. Hoover's FBI remained deeply suspicious of Communist intentions and wary of the potential for sabotage. Hoover's antiradical sentiments had not changed. But in the aircraft strikes the bureau upheld the rule of law, relying on its professional capacity to distinguish between radical rhetoric and subversive action. Whereas in 1919, the FBI accelerated the Red Scare, between 1939 and 1941, the bureau often slowed it down.

Testing the Smith Act

The distinction between radical rhetoric and action was less clear in the case of the Trotskyist Minneapolis Teamsters. Since the mid-1930s, a crew of veteran radical organizers had been leading organizing drives for the Teamsters in Minneapolis and across the Midwest. Ray, Grant, and Miles Dunne (younger siblings to William Dunne, who had been expelled for Communism from the AFL's 1923 convention) had broken with the Communist Party and allied with its Trotskyist opponents, helping to form the Socialist Workers Party (SWP) in 1937. While Popular Front politics modulated Communists' revolutionary sloganeering, the SWP remained militant throughout the 1930s and aimed to drive out both the "reactionary trade union leaders" and the "Stalinists" from American unions. In the early 1930s, the Dunnes and local

Trotskyists had strategically chosen the Minneapolis Teamsters local, a weak union with a broad jurisdiction, for a base. They succeeded brilliantly, organizing tens of thousands of truckers over the 1930s and ensconcing SWP organizers at the head of the local.[59]

Teamsters president Dan Tobin appreciated the membership gains but disliked the politics of the Minneapolis leaders. Eye-popping wage gains secured members' loyalties, though, and Tobin's hands were tied until early 1941, when disgruntled members of Local 544 began complaining that union leader Farrell Dobbs was urging them to donate to the SWP and to prepare to muster into a workers' Red Army. Other conflicts also underlay the complaints, such as dissatisfaction with the terms of a recently settled brewery contract. But the discomfort of some Teamster members with revolutionary sentiment mirrored the unease in many Communist-led union locals across the country. FBI agents in Minneapolis, alerted to the conflict by a local detective with an extensive union-surveillance business, began to investigate, and numerous union members eagerly shared information with bureau agents.[60]

In June 1941, Tobin asked the Teamster executive board to trustee the local to remove "subversive" leaders, citing member complaints and FBI reports. But he discovered that Dobbs had already contacted the CIO, which agreed to charter the Minneapolis Teamsters into a new CIO union. Irate, Tobin telegraphed to President Roosevelt that "Bundists, Stalinists, and Trotskyists" were overrunning his union, thanks in part to Tobin's endorsement of Roosevelt in the 1940 election. Roosevelt ordered the Justice Department to investigate, and within weeks FBI agents descended on Local 544 with search warrants. In July 1941, Dobbs, the Dunne brothers, and several other officials of Local 544 were charged with violating the Smith Act. That December, eighteen union officers were acquitted of sedition but convicted of conspiracy to foment insubordination among the armed forces. Two years later, a federal appeals court upheld the conviction, and the Smith Act stood as settled law.[61]

Why did the Roosevelt administration prosecute the Minneapolis Teamsters but leave Communist unionists alone? Some historians have argued that Roosevelt attacked the Trotskyists to curry favor with Tobin, and surely there is some truth to that explanation. But the pleas of other AFL union leaders for federal repression of their Communist members were ignored, even though they also backed Roosevelt's reelection in 1940. Other historians see the crackdown as part of a domestic war mobilization and argue that the Communists were spared because of their prowar flip after Hitler's invasion of Russia, while the Trotskyists remained antiwar, but this explanation is lacking. As Donna Haverty-Stacke has shown, the FBI had been covertly investigating Local 544 for months before Hitler's invasion, just as it had investigated other unions since 1936, and the CPUSA's Pact–era isolationism surely offered enough reason for prosecution. Hoover and the Justice Department had already begun pursuing the Minneapolis Teamsters well before Hitler's invasion on June 22, 1941.

Attorney General Francis Biddle's inexperience also mattered. He had been named acting attorney general just a few weeks earlier, in early June 1941, and Biddle later disavowed the decision to proceed with prosecution, explaining that he intended the case as a test of the Smith Act's constitutionality and expected the courts to strike down the law. Biddle had not been involved in reviewing evidence of Communist activity in unions, unlike his predecessor Robert Jackson, and thus he was not able to compare the activities of the Minneapolis Trotskyists to Communists in other locales.[62]

Hoover's FBI had been investigating all the alleged cases, of course, and the FBI judged the Minneapolis Teamsters to be dangerous radicals. In fact, they were more militant than the Communists organizing within the CIO. In the defense-industry strikes, Communist organizers dedicated their energies to agitating workers to demand workplace gains such as wage improvements, and they rarely interjected Communist dogma directly into shop-floor struggles. The Minneapolis Trotskyists, on the other hand, were far more forthright than Communists about their revolutionary aims. For example, in consultation with Trotsky himself, they organized a 600-member Union Defense Guard in 1938. (In various writings, Trotsky called for "armed workers' detachments" and advised organizers to "drill and acquaint [workers] with the use of arms.")[63] Local 544's Defense Guard organized target practices with pistols and rifles, and marched in downtown Minneapolis. Union members also reported that union leaders often discussed revolutionary plans for stationing militants strategically to "paralyz[e] all forms of communication, power, industry." The Union Defense Guard provided the fodder for the first count of the indictment: fomenting rebellion.[64]

At trial, the defendants argued that the Defense Guard was organized to protect unionists against fascist Silver Shirt mobs and downplayed the revolutionary rhetoric, and none of them were convicted on the Union Defense Guard charge. Nevertheless, by mustering an armed guard of union members, the Minneapolis Trotskyists had gone much further than any American Communist organizer had dared. In this light, the prosecution looks less surprising. As the appeals court held, "This record leaves no doubt that force was the ultimate means to be used by the Party in the overthrow of the Government by the 'proletariat.'"[65] Moreover, the union's leaders continued to oppose U.S. entry to the war through the fall of 1941. Their undisguised militancy made the Minneapolis Trotskyists a much easier target than Communists who, far from defending their fellow revolutionaries, applauded the "exterminat[ion] of the Trotskyite Fifth Column."[66]

Red-baiting in Pennsylvania

Meanwhile, in Pennsylvania state politics, where the FBI had no reach, labor conservatives such as Lewis Hines learned how to use the new loyalty oaths against their enemies. Lewis Hines had been a labor man for most of his life. Born in Philadelphia in 1888, he worked at a series of skilled craft jobs, first as a glass blower in Salem, New Jersey, and later as a pipefitter at the Baldwin Locomotive Works in Philadelphia and a polisher at Eastman Kodak in Rochester, New York. By his early thirties, Hines had moved into union leadership and Pennsylvania labor politics. He became the business agent for the Philadelphia Metal Polishers union and began moving up in the local Republican Party. His political connections helped him get a job with the state government as a mediator with the Pennsylvania Department of Labor and Industry in 1925, even as he remained the vice president of Philadelphia's Central Labor Union. Hines lost his mediation post when progressive Republican Gifford Pinchot beat Hines's candidate for the gubernatorial nomination in 1931, but an old friend, former U.S. secretary of labor and then U.S. senator from Pennsylvania James J. Davis got Hines a new federal position as state director of the United States Employment Service. But the Depression soon caused the elimination of the agency, and Hines again lost his job. In 1933, he went to work as a representative for the national AFL, and by 1937 Hines had been appointed as a special assistant to AFL president William Green.[67]

Hines proved to be a loyal AFL operative. In the early years of the New Deal, Hines helped the Metal Polishers and other AFL unions navigate the new federal labor bureaucracies and organize under the Wagner Act. As fault lines began to emerge in the AFL in the mid-1930s, Hines had no trouble picking a side. When Philadelphia metal workers starting talking about forming an industrial union, Hines tried to stop the movement and keep the Metal Polishers out of the nascent United Electrical Workers. In 1937 he suspended CIO-friendly delegates to the Philadelphia Central Labor Union, vowing to purge it of Communists and the CIO. Early the following year, when the state AFL refused to expel unions affiliated with the CIO, the AFL removed all its officers and installed Hines as temporary president.[68]

The 1938 elections became a flashpoint of conflict for Pennsylvania labor.

Two critical seats were up: the governorship and a Senate seat. Republicans had dominated Pennsylvania state and municipal politics for decades, but in 1934 a Democrat, George Earle, won the governorship, and Democrats also won a U.S. Senate seat and substantial gains in the statehouse. Earle earned the loyalty of Pennsylvania's workers with a raft of "little New Deal" initiatives, including the elimination of the repressive Coal and Iron Police, teacher tenure, and a forty-four-hour week for women. But Earle could not run for reelection, as the Pennsylvania constitution limited governors to a single term. Earle thus turned his eye to the U.S. Senate seat held by incumbent Republican Senator Davis. Republican Arthur S. James, a sworn opponent of the New Deal, ran to replace Earle as governor on the Republican ticket.

But the split between AFL and CIO scrambled the strategy for the Democrats in the primaries and the general election for both the Senate seat and the governorship, as the CIO pushed its own candidates for each seat and the Pennsylvania AFL backed a different slate. After divisive primary battles, the CIO's candidates lost. Both the Pennsylvania AFL's preferred candidates won: Charles Jones took the Democratic nomination for governor, and George Earle won the Democratic nomination for senator. Thereafter, Pennsylvania union leaders united behind the Democratic ticket.

In the general election, however, the national AFL stepped in, and Pennsylvania became a front in the national battle against the CIO and the New Deal. The CIO and Pennsylvania AFL leaders supported Democrats Earle and Jones, and the national AFL backed Republicans Davis and James. It was a dizzyingly complex situation. "Regardless of who comes out on top," remarked one observer, "the beneficiaries are going to be the Republican nominees."[69]

Hines and Green devoted strenuous effort to convert the state AFL officers to the Republican slate and, when that failed, simply campaigned in Pennsylvania against both the state federation and the Democratic candidates. They appealed to trade unionists on an explicitly anti-CIO program. As a campaign operative reported to Hines, "I cannot emphasize too strongly the success of a campaign of propaganda that Mr. Hines and I started several months ago regarding the sell-out of the Democratic administration to the C.I.O. organization."[70] John Frey helped out from Washington at the Dies Committee hearings, sharing Communist Party meeting minutes that reported that "in the anthracite coal region, the Communists can certainly get their people in many offices by entering the Democratic primaries" for Earle.[71]

The Republican Party reaped the rewards on election day. Senator Davis retained his seat, and Arthur James won the governorship by 279,000 votes. The election reversed a seeming Democratic ascendancy in Pennsylvania and cooled the climate for labor in the state. During his term, James lobbied for a state ban on sit-down strikes, sent state troops to break a strike by the Steel-workers' Union at Bethlehem Steel, and enacted an Emergency Coal Act to force conciliation between coal miners and operators.[72] As promised, James moved strongly against the CIO.

As a reward, Hines got a plum job in the James administration: director of the state Department of Labor and Industry. Almost immediately, Hines ran into trouble with his own employees. Workers in the Pennsylvania De-partment of Labor and Industry had been organizing into competing public employees unions. Of his 4,000 workers, Hines estimated that half supported the AFL union, the American Federation of State, County, and Municipal Em-ployees (AFSCME), and the other half backed the CIO-affiliated State, County, and Municipal Workers (SCMW). The SCMW had split off from AFSCME just a few years earlier, and several of the union's national leaders were CP members or were closely allied with the party. (Like most CIO unions, though, it had few Communist members.)[73] Although public employees were not covered by the Wagner Act and no state law obliged Hines to deal with either union, Hines negotiated agreeably with the AFL's AFSCME, developing "a splendid relation-ship"—but not with the CIO's SCMW. Within a few weeks of taking office he notified the SCMW that he would not meet with them.[74]

The SCMW had little affection for Hines either, a fact he knew well, since he had state police monitoring their meetings beginning in October 1939. These reports kept Hines apprised of the identities of union activists and their criti-cisms of Hines "and his attitude toward Civil Service persons," and of the union's plans to introduce a convention resolution denouncing him. Hines also learned the prosaic details of union proceedings, from who stacked the chairs to how much union buttons cost.[75] Several months later, Hines sent another state policeman to investigate whether SCMW members in the unem-ployment division had been copying the names of unemployed workers for local CIO affiliates to contact. The business agent for the AFL's Cement Finish-ers union, seeing several "colored men" in his union with letters inviting them to an organizing meeting for a CIO construction workers' union, had asked Hines to check it out.

After working undercover in the unemployment office for a few days, the policeman could find no evidence to substantiate the charge, and he reported that he believed "the complaint was made through prejudice on [the busi-ness agent's] part that a rival labor union was attempting to stir up his em-ployees."[76] As a seasoned labor leader, Hines knew a great deal about union-busting tactics, having seen them firsthand. While the La Follette Committee continued to meet in Washington, hearing testimony about employers' use of labor spies and detectives, Hines deployed his own detectives to spy on union workers.

Relations between Hines and the SCMW continued to deteriorate while a Red Scare bloomed in Pennsylvania. A reporter for the *Pittsburgh Press* had published a series of dramatic investigative reports on the local Communist Party workers' school and CP electoral organizing, producing rich material for the Dies Committee. Dies investigators raided the Pittsburgh and Philadelphia offices of the Communist Party in early 1940, and Dies subpoenaed Pittsburgh Communist leaders in the spring of 1940. Then in the summer of 1940, James's administration seized on a fertile new source for identifying red sympathizers: CP nominating petitions for electoral office, submitted to the commonwealth's secretary. Fifty-nine thousand signatures, complete with addresses and occupation, appeared on the petitions (at a time when Pennsylvania and Delaware combined had only about 3,600 registered Communist party members). Newspapers printed the names of some signers, many of whom insisted they had been tricked by canvassers who claimed the petitions called to keep the United States out of the war. The state convicted thirty Communist leaders for election fraud in 1940.[77]

The Red Scare gave Hines a new angle for undermining the SCMW. In November 1939 he wrote to William Green: "I took advantage of an opportunity to brand this organization as Communistically-dominated, and more concerned with promoting the tenets of Communism than with the welfare of the employees in this department."[78] Starting in the summer of 1940, Hines moved beyond red-baiting to purging. In July 1940, the Department of Labor and Industry began submitting lists of names of employees to the state police for investigation as potential Communists. Around the same time, Hines distributed a questionnaire for all department employees to complete. When David Kanes, local president of the SCMW protested, Hines retorted, "You have reached the height of impudence when you question my right as Secretary of Labor and Industry to ascertain the status of employees of this Department with regard to their affiliation or non-affiliation with the Communistic, Nazi, Fascist, or Bund groups."[79] Hines checked David Kanes and another SCMW officer with the Dies Committee. An investigator confirmed that while Kanes certainly appeared suspicious, the other officer was "a very active Communist."[80]

As was the case with many CIO unions, the SCMW indeed had a strong core of Communist leadership. Whether the local leaders of the SCMW were also Communists is unknown. Undoubtedly Hines's anticommunist sentiment was heartfelt, and, as he told Kanes, nothing restrained him from exercising his authority to remove Communists from the civil service. Yet the timing of his purge, coming after a year of maneuvering against the SCMW, makes his partisanship abundantly clear.

Between the petitions and the police investigations, Hines had a comprehensive strategy. Hines gave the state police at least seventy names of staffers in offices with a strong SCMW presence to investigate. The state police turned up little, and only five of the targeted workers showed red tendencies. A typical report, such as the one on employee Reba Baskin, suggested the absurdity of the list. Investigators discovered that Baskin had worked as a stenographer for a number of machine-tool foundries, and her father owned a dry goods store; she was a registered Republican, and her neighbors said that she was a "good American citizen."[81] Whatever the politics of SCMW national leaders, the organization's members seemed like a moderate lot.

Hines's questionnaire offered more potential to trip SMCW loyalists up. It had only a few questions, including: Are you a citizen of the United States? Are you now or have you ever been a member of the Communist Party, or a member of any Nazi, Bund, or Fascist organizations? Will you agree to take an oath of allegiance to uphold the constitution of the United States and the constitution of the Commonwealth of Pennsylvania? On their own, these questions might have sent a chill through the office. But the real purpose of the questionnaire was the following question: Have you ever signed nominating petitions for any candidate on the Communist Party ticket? Hines had access to the CP nominating petitions. Virtually all respondents denied signing the petitions, but it did not matter what they answered. If their names appeared on a petition, Hines had them.[82] In the end, thirty-six employees were fired from the Department of Labor and Industry's Public Assistance Division for subversive activity.[83]

Four of the dismissed employees appealed their firings to the Pennsylvania Civil Service Board of Review, which found that nothing "bars an executive of the State Government from removing any employee, for the good of the service, as to whom he has any tenable evidence that he is either a member of the Communist Party or, even if legally not a member, that he has in any way given aid or comfort to that Party." The Pennsylvania Supreme Court affirmed the Civil Service Board, remarking that the state need not "supinely await an overt subversive act before it may discharge a Communist from its employ." In any case, in July 1941 the state legislature had formally banned employees who advocated "un-American or subversive doctrines" from the civil service.[84]

Reflecting on the outcome of the case, Hines told William Green, "I am more than gratified." Moreover, he said, "I have eliminated all traces" of the SMCW from the Department of Labor and Industry, while the AFSCME "has developed quite a strong organization and are going along nicely."[85] Green congratulated Hines for having shown "tact and great courage."[86] The SCMW did not give up so easily, however. The union worked its connections with the U.S. Department of Labor, which oversaw Social Security funds administered by Hines in Pennsylvania. Pressure from the Social Security Board obliged Hines to rehire four workers dismissed for "fomenting discord" and similar activities. He clashed repeatedly with the federal Department of Labor. As one Department of Labor representative pointedly noted, "funds granted by the Social Security Board are for the 'proper and efficient administration' of your law. It is conceivable that the Social Security Board might find that there is no 'proper and efficient administration' under the circumstances here."[87] In 1942, the Social Security Board withheld all funds from the state until "the Commonwealth adopted a rule giving civil service employees a hearing before dismissal."[88] Accusations of maladministration dogged Hines, and when Governor James left office, Hines was not retained by the new Republican administration. Hines had a job waiting for him nonetheless. He went back on the staff of the American Federation of Labor, where he remained for the rest of his career.

Hines's crusade against the CIO had made a lasting impact. The Pennsylvania Supreme Court decision upholding his termination of civil servants for Communist sympathies became part of public employment case law, cited by courts in California, New Hampshire, and New York.[89] More important than its legal precedent, though, was the legacy of strategic red-baiting. In the 1950s, dubious charges of Communism were used to expel gay civil servants from the State Department, black letter carriers from the Postal Service, and scientists from the Food and Drug Administration. In some cases, union activists were targeted for expulsion. In the past, AFL leaders had warned that federal sedition laws could produce just such politically motivated reprisals against activist workers. In the years before the Second World War, the AFL made those warnings come true.

In 1941, at the convention of the Pennsylvania Federation of Labor, Green spoke at length on Communism and the split within labor. "It is not the difference of industrial unionism as against craft unionism; it is a difference in political and economic philosophy and the different policies pursued by the two groups." The events of the past year had made this clear, he said, and "honest

American workers are given to understand as never before the Americanism of the A.F. of L."[90] Even as Green spoke, however, the Red Scare was ebbing. Hitler invaded Russia in June 1941, and within days the CPUSA reversed its position and offered full-throated support for U.S. entry to the war. FDR warmly welcomed the party into the Allied coalition, and fears of red subversion quickly dissipated as Communist unionists transformed into industrial-efficiency experts, urging war workers to hustle on the line and speed munitions to the battlefront. But the war years merely suspended hostilities in the labor movement. When the House reauthorized the Un-American Activities Committee in 1945, Green pledged his support, reminding Congressman Karl Mundt that "we felt [the committee] did some excellent work under the most adverse conditions and in the face of great opposition from some in high places."[91] As before, HUAC could count on the AFL.

Epilogue

By the spring of 1941, the legal structures of anticommunism and McCarthyism were in place. In the Congress, Martin Dies's House Un-American Activities Committee grilled witnesses about their Communist sympathies. J. Edgar Hoover's FBI was busy adding names to its list of subversives. Communists had been barred from federal employment by the Hatch Act, and the Smith Act made it a crime to advocate revolution. This "blackout of civil liberties" was merely a first step of an "organized attack which, if not checked now, will be directed, before long, against the democratic rights of labor and the entire people," warned Elizabeth Gurley Flynn.[1]

Significantly, it was Adolph Hitler who checked the anticommunist attack with his invasion of the Soviet Union in June. Betrayed by Germany, Stalin quickly turned to the Allies and joined the war recently denounced by Flynn as "Anglo-French imperialism." Roosevelt sent Harry Hopkins to Moscow to offer American assistance. In August, the United States cemented its support by delivering a hundred fighter planes to the Soviet Union.[2] The American Communist Party also reacted fast. Within a week of Operation Barbarossa, the party passed a "People's Program" that exhorted members to "defend America by giving full aid to the Soviet Union, Great Britain, and all nations that fight against Hitler!"[3] Almost overnight, American Communists became fervent patriots. In 1944, party head Earl Browder promised not to "raise the issue of socialism in such a form or manner as to endanger or weaken national unity," and dissolved the Communist Party altogether, reconstituting it as a "Communist Political Association" that would "cooperate in making [American] capitalism work effectively in the post-war period."[4]

During the war, the machinery of anticommunism ground to a virtual halt. Communists troubled the federal government far less than potential subversion on behalf of Germany and Japan. The Dies Committee met rarely, and Dies himself left Congress, choosing not to stand for reelection in 1944. The Justice Department dusted off the Smith Act to prosecute not Communists,

but anticommunist William Dudley Pelling, the leader of the pro-Nazi Silver Shirts, along with other isolationists and pro-Fascists such as Elizabeth
Dilling and George Viereck.[5] Hoover's FBI, flush with new funding from its
prewar designation as the state's counterespionage force, added thousands
of agents, and Hoover developed a massive network of factory informants in
defense industries. The FBI's wartime investigations concentrated on German
and Japanese subversion, and Soviet espionage dropped to a lower place on
the bureau's priority list.[6]

Likewise, anticommunist conflict within the labor movement died down.
The AFL and CIO continued to vie with each other to represent workers in war
industries, but in other ways the ideological gap between the two organizations narrowed during the war. As both federations grew rapidly under strong
federal rules protecting wartime unionism, the AFL grew more comfortable
with state oversight and the CIO grew less militant. Communist unionists,
for their part, turned into taskmasters on factory floors, harrying workers
to speed up production to aid the Soviet Union. Communists pushed for
incentive-pay plans (to the disinterest of employers growing rich on cost-plus
contracts) and aggressively enforced no-strike pledges in the CIO's defense-
industry plants. This new concern for industrial efficiency made Communists
a moderating force in the CIO, allowing unionists such as Walter Reuther to
organize militants into noncommunist coalitions. Ironically, during the war
Communists lost support among militant workers, long their most promising
recruits.[7]

Communist enlistment in the Allied cause helped forestall the sort of civil
liberties crackdown on radicals and war protestors that had occurred during
World War I. The government was determined not to reenact the repression
and censorship of the Great War. From Roosevelt to Attorney General Francis
Biddle to J. Edgar Hoover, the message was the same: the federal government
would not tolerate the "stupidities of the vigilante" or misuse of sedition laws.
The American Civil Liberties Union took some of the credit for this attitude.
"We have educated a whole generation of people, and this is now reflected
in the attitude of the government," said ACLU board member John Haynes
Holmes.[8] In the eyes of the civil libertarians, the state's wartime tolerance was
a testament to the justness of their cause.

But their vision was blinkered. Many civil libertarians failed even to recognize one of the most profound violations of civil liberties in American history,
the wartime internment of Japanese Americans, as it unfolded before their
eyes. The ACLU struggled to develop its views on the question. Its national
board first found the internment to be legal, then later helped internees such

as Fred Korematsu challenge their detention in court, while consulting closely with the Justice Department on strategy. Meanwhile old ACLU allies such as Walter Lippmann defended the internment. "There is the assumption that if the rights of a citizen are abridged anywhere, they have been abridged everywhere," Lippmann wrote, but "the enemy alien problem on the Pacific Coast" was a "very special case." Lippmann did not challenge the internment, and nor did the AFL, the CIO, or the Communist Party. The episode showed that civil liberties commitments were not universal or absolute, but predicated on deeper cultural and social prejudices.[9]

The wartime civil liberties consensus did not outlive the war itself. Even before V-J Day, old suspicions about Soviet intentions resurfaced. By 1943, the FBI had picked up scattered clues suggesting that American Communists were passing on industrial intelligence to Moscow, and Hoover stepped up surveillance of party members. In the spring of 1945, leaked American intelligence reports appeared in *Amerasia*, a small journal run by a Frederick Vanderbilt Field, a Communist (and descendant of tycoon Cornelius Vanderbilt). In June 1945, the FBI arrested John Service, a State Department officer on the China desk, for spiriting piles of classified documents to *Amerasia*. In August, Elizabeth Bentley walked unbidden into an FBI branch office, and by November 1945, she had named eighty people in the United States who were spying for the Soviet Union. Hoover, charged with investigating espionage, started to realize that the Soviet Union had a far more elaborate intelligence operation than anyone in the government suspected. Meanwhile the U.S. Army's Signal Intelligence service was working to decrypt Soviet diplomatic cables intercepted during the war. By the summer of 1946, the secret program, codenamed Venona, revealed that the Soviet Union was receiving technical information about the atomic bomb.[10]

Decades of warnings from armchair anticommunists, with their lists of suspected subversives and drawings of red webs, had made such accusations seem ridiculous. As Harvey Klehr writes, "A kind of Gresham's law operated: the more non-Communists who were branded Communists—whether from malice, confusion, or error—the greater the tendency to discount anyone named as Communist." This legacy shaped perceptions inside and outside the government of postwar accusations of Soviet espionage. Even President Harry Truman had a hard time taking the threat seriously at first. But as tensions mounted in Europe between the United States and the Soviet Union, and evidence accumulated that indeed some Americans had been passing information to the Soviets, anticommunism mushroomed. In late 1946, Truman's administration began investigating the loyalty of federal employees.

Former Communists such as Louis Budenz and Benjamin Gitlow became frequent witnesses before a proliferating array of congressional committees such as the Senate's Internal Security Subcommittee, and the FBI started chasing suspected atomic spies such as Julius and Ethel Rosenberg.[11]

Labor anticommunists, who had never dropped their suspicion of the Soviet Union, reacted much as they had before the war. Labor conservatives based in the AFL continued to endorse anticommunist repression, and liberals in the CIO tended to denounce federal initiatives such as loyalty oaths while also repudiating Communism. Dies's committee had survived his departure. Mississippi congressman John Rankin had convinced his colleagues to reauthorize the inquiry as a standing House Un-American Activities Committee. As ever, the AFL endorsed HUAC, praising its "excellent work in ferreting out those who believe in the overthrow of our form of Government by force."[12] The CIO did not support HUAC and found itself, as before, a constant target for HUAC investigations. But increasingly, CIO officials availed themselves of HUAC's assistance in internal struggles with Communists.[13]

The unstable alliance between the CIO leadership and the Communist Party had become increasingly untenable. After the war Communist unionists abandoned their patriotic Americanism and resumed working closely with Soviet handlers. The final straw: in 1947, Communist unionists lined up against the Marshall Plan and behind Progressive presidential candidate Henry Wallace. CIO head Philip Murray saw the Progressive Party campaign as a reckless gamble to ensure the election of an "ultra ultra reactionary government, and then the people will get sick of it and they will vote a liberal government into power four years from now." The *Washington Post* reported, "Wallace Sickle Cleaving CIO." The CIO began systematically sidelining Communist members. Once the 1948 elections were over, the CIO expelled eleven Communist-led unions from its ranks.[14]

This effort was easier thanks to a new provision in the National Labor Relations Act that withheld the law's protection from any union controlled by Communists. In 1947, the Taft-Hartley Act imposed sweeping restrictions on unions, including a ban on sympathy strikes. The law also required union officers to submit affidavits swearing that they were not Communists. The noncommunist affidavits had been added to the Taft-Hartley law as an afterthought, near the end of deliberations. Representative Richard Nixon floated the idea with AFL president William Green in a hearing on Taft-Hartley. "What would be your reaction to legislation," Nixon asked, "providing that no officer of a union should be a Communist, a member of the Communist Party?" Green said, "Well, I would not have any use for Communists or communism," but he was "rather doubtful" of the need for legislation. Nixon and his colleagues did see such a need, and it is not surprising. For twenty-five years, labor conservatives had warned Congress that Communist organizers were attempting to seize control of unions through subterfuge. Banning Communists from union leadership was an extension of the statutory anti-communism that the AFL had come to embrace.[15]

Unionists in both the AFL and CIO despised the Taft-Hartley Act, calling it a "slave labor law," and a chorus of union leaders from William Green to John Lewis refused to submit the affidavits. It was "insulting," said AFL counsel Joseph Padway. Hadn't they served as America's first line of defense against Communism since the Bolshevik Revolution? Why should conservative unionists have to profess their loyalty?[16] John L. Lewis called the affidavits "the first ugly active thrust of fascism in America." But some labor conservatives were less troubled by the affidavits, and skeptical of Lewis's outrage. George Meany, the secretary-treasurer of the AFL, reminded the federation's 1947 convention that Lewis had professed "uncompromising resistance to Communism" until 1935, when Lewis "made fellowship with Harry Bridges, Lewis Merrill, Michael Quill," and "all the other stinking America haters who love Moscow." "I was never a comrade to the comrades," Meany said. "I am prepared to sign an affidavit."[17] Within a year, most noncommunist union leaders in the AFL and CIO signed the affidavits.

The Supreme Court heard a challenge to the Taft-Hartley noncommunist affidavit provision in 1949. The officers of the American Communications Association, a small Communist-affiliated union, refused to sign the affidavits and appealed the NLRB's withholding of protection. Among the justices who heard the case was Robert Jackson, the former U.S. attorney general who had worked with J. Edgar Hoover on the defense-industry strikes in 1940 and 1941. As attorney general, Jackson had declined to order the FBI to pursue AFL allegations of Communism among CIO members at Boeing, and he had a reputation as a civil libertarian on the court, having recently written an opinion relieving schoolchildren of the obligation to salute the American flag.[18] Jackson's background seemed propitious for overturning the law.

But Jackson upheld the affidavits, arguing that "the Communist Party alone among American parties past or present is dominated and controlled by a foreign government," and "the most promising course of the Communist Party has been the undercover capture of the coercive power of strategic labor unions as a leverage to magnify its power over the American people." Jackson could have been quoting Samuel Gompers or John Frey. "I am aware," Jackson said, "that the oath is resented by many labor leaders of unquestioned loyalty and above suspicion of Communist connections, indeed by some who have themselves taken bold and difficult steps to rid the labor movement of Communists. I suppose no one likes to be compelled to exonerate himself from connections he has never acquired." But Jackson, along with Felix Frankfurter and a majority of the court, held that union leaders would have to sign the affidavit; only Hugo Black dissented. It was "not a civil-rights or a free-speech or a free-press case," but a matter of national security, Jackson wrote.[19]

The ACLU had filed an amicus curiae brief opposing the affidavits in *ACA v. Douds*, but the ACLU did little else on the Taft-Hartley question. Since the late 1930s, the ACLU had drifted away from labor issues. In its first decades, the ACLU vigorously defended radical unionists' right to organize. Once the ACLU's ties to radical labor broke in the conflicts over Communism, the ACLU's interest in labor organizing waned.

One union issue still attracted Roger Baldwin and ACLU lawyers though: the rights of individual union members to challenge their leaders. In 1943, the ACLU published a booklet called *Democracy in Trade Unions*, intended to propose solutions to the problem of union leaders' autocracy. "There is no union Bill of Rights" to "safeguard the right of free speech" in unions, the ACLU pointed out. Union democracy required "fair and regular elections," an end to discrimination within unions "on the grounds of race, sex, religion, politics, or national origins," and toleration of "honest opposition to union leadership." An impressive roster of people signed onto the document, including academics Mary Beard and Carl Becker, labor relations experts Selig Perlman and Jacob Bilikopf, and Freda Kirchway, editor of the *Nation*.[20]

The AFL and CIO took little notice of the proposal, but the ACLU continued to lobby for it, submitting it to Congress as a proposed amendment to the Taft-Hartley Act in 1947 and reissuing the document in 1952. In the late 1950s, the idea suddenly got traction. The Senate's McClellan Committee revealed an alarming collaboration between many union leaders and organized crime syndicates. In 1959, the Landrum-Griffin Act was passed to remedy the labor movement's "corruption, disregard of the rights of individual employees, and other failures to observe high standards of responsibility and ethical conduct."[21] Landrum-Griffin restricted unions' ability to boycott, strike, and picket, and the ACLU's "bill of rights" was incorporated in the law. Now unionists were obliged to guarantee their members' civil liberties. It would have been a boon to radical unionists, if there were many still around, but there was little radical activity in American labor by then.

Could it have been different? The AFL's early antiradical campaigns and immediate repudiation of the Bolshevik Revolution show that labor conservatives would have opposed Communists in any case. Yet Communists' tactical blunders and sectarian squabbling provided the fodder for a compelling critique and isolated them from the vast working class. In Europe and England, Communist parties operating openly attracted mass followings that granted Communism political legitimacy. American Communists remained marginal. The coincidence of the Popular Front with the formation of the CIO offered an opportunity for Communists and radicals to build a mass labor base. But it also created a volatile alliance that inflamed conservatives and dismayed many rank-and-file workers and voters at a critical moment when controversial new state powers disrupted settled authority. Had the Popular Front happened later or not at all and the CPUSA remained antagonistic to Roosevelt, the AFL, and likely the CIO, it would have been harder to smear the New Deal as communistic. Perhaps the New Deal state would have survived as a sturdier political structure. Such counterfactual scenarios make for good stories, but bad history. Any number of facts could have been different, but as things turned out, it is hard to imagine an alternate course of events.

The beginning of the Cold War pushed debates about Communism, loyalty, and civil liberties into the center of American politics, while within the labor movement, these debates were winding down. By the late 1940s, the labor movement's struggle with Communism was in its final stages. A general unanimity prevailed within both the AFL and CIO leadership: Communism was incompatible with unionism, and the only question was how to stamp out the remnants of Communist influence within the federations. The opening acts of mainstream American anticommunism—spy trials, loyalty oaths, and congressional hearings—coincided with the denouement of labor's anticommunist convulsions. The purges of CIO unionists took time, but the basic thrust of the program was in place by 1948, just as the "great fear" of anticommunism, and the practices of scurrilous red-baiting that came to be known as McCarthyism, began to spread. This unanimity helped smooth the merger of the AFL and CIO into a single organization in 1955.

As labor's domestic anticommunist campaign entered its finale, the Cold War created a new global arena for seasoned union strategists. Since the end of World War I, union leaders had played little role in U.S. foreign policy. After Yalta, the State Department began to see how labor anticommunists could combat Communism within European labor movements. Jay Lovestone, the former Communist leader now on the AFL's payroll, and Irving Brown, Lovestone's prodigy, led the AFL's international anticommunist program for decades. With funding and support from the State Department and later the Central Intelligence Agency, the AFL and later the AFL-CIO helped noncommunist and anticommunist unions and governments fight Communists in Europe, Central and South America, Africa, and Asia. This international campaign lasted far longer than the domestic fight. Irving Brown, who battled Communists in the French unions in 1945, was still working for the AFL-CIO in the mid-1980s, helping to organize anticommunist insurgencies in Central America. Perhaps in the end, American labor anticommunists made the greatest impact in these international campaigns, in countries where Communism was a much larger and more significant working-class movement than in the United States.[22]

Labor anticommunists were not the authors of Cold War foreign policy, nor did they create the antiradical animus that drove domestic anticommunism and McCarthyism. The impetus for domestic and international anticommunist policy and sentiment was diffuse, and many different actors and agencies, from presidents to preachers, had a hand in developing the distinctively American ideology of anticommunism. Rather, conservative labor anticommunists were often ineffectual, unable to convince the federal government to take the threat of Communism seriously. During the 1920s, the Justice Department withdrew from political policing; in the 1930s, Roosevelt resumed diplomatic relations with the Soviet Union over AFL protests, and the FBI resisted pressure to pursue Communists in the CIO. It was U.S. foreign policy that shaped most federal approaches to Communism, not pressure from labor or other anticommunists. Conservative labor anticommunists were most effective in peacetime, when they helped prevent the enactment of sedition laws and the authorization of federal political policing. As reluctant civil libertarians, labor conservatives helped ensure that Communists enjoyed the political freedom to organize against AFL leaders.

Nevertheless, by the late 1940s the AFL was in step with the prevailing spirit of federal policy and domestic political culture. After meeting with officials from the U.S. Air Force in early 1949, the AFL's Executive Council announced their support for increasing defense appropriations to fight the "cold war" with the Soviet Union. "The Stalin forces are convinced that once the free American way of life is overthrown there will be no effective resistance to the complete Communist enslavement," said the AFL leaders.[23] Such pronouncements reflected the distinctive politics of labor conservatism in the postwar era. For labor conservatives, the "American way" meant Keynesian economic policy, aggressive anticommunism at home and abroad, and, as always, an instrumentalist vision of union preeminence that prioritized unions' institutional interests. Most labor conservatives were reliable backers of the Democratic Party, but their political agenda, and their voters, often overlapped with the Republicans.[24] In the 1960s, this conservatism came into sharper view, when black liberation and women's liberation movements challenged the authority and autonomy of conservative union leaders, and student protesters challenged the AFL-CIO's support of the Vietnam War.

Today, veterans of those movements lead many American unions. The contemporary American labor movement is far more liberal, and far more uniform in its liberalism, than at any time in American history. As American politics has shifted right in the last forty years, the labor movement has shifted left, shedding its cold war alliances, embracing civil rights and immigrants, and making common cause with environmentalists and anticapitalist activists. Many labor activists look longingly back to the 1930s as an era when worker militancy and creative union organizing helped create a radical change in American politics. This nostalgia relies on a partial version of the 1930s that erases the role of conservative unions in containing radical change. Likewise, historians and political thinkers often point to the rise of the CIO and the Democratic Party in tandem in the 1930s, arguing that strong labor unions help drive liberal politics. But, as this book shows, unions could also be agents of conservatism, whose dedication to their own preservation could lead them into conflict with an inclusive progressive agenda.

In the decades after the 1960s, labor politics changed as the Soviet Union collapsed, free-market ideologies ascended, and American workplaces and unions were opened to formerly excluded women and people of color. As it recedes in political memory, the legacy of anticommunism comes into clearer view. The story of labor anticommunism told here does not validate either the caricatures of the Right or the shibboleths of the Left. Rather, it underscores the contingency and complexity of political action. Individual actors created labor conservatism, from leaders such as Samuel Gompers to rank-and-file workers such as Ralph Knox, the Dies Committee informant, just as individuals such as William Z. Foster created labor radicalism. None of them did so, in Marx's words, "in circumstances of their own choosing," and they were motivated, like most people, by a mix of principle and expedience. Ultimately, American unions were not inherently conservative, liberal, or radical, any more than were the workers who joined them.

American unionists today, faced with a punishing economy, a complex political field, and transformed workplaces, cannot choose their circumstances either. But their political choices are perhaps less constrained than those of Gompers or Foster. For much of the twentieth century, Soviet Communism and American anticommunism skewed American labor politics, subsuming other, older traditions like socialism and syndicalism. Conservative union-ism was buoyed when leaders could associate challengers with Communism. The end of the Cold War removed that skew, leaving American unionists, like their counterparts around the world, to imagine alternative ways to order the economy and polity in the interests of workers. To the old questions such as "What does labor want?" and "What is to be done?" it is time for new answers.

Notes

INTRODUCTION

1. For example, see Patterson, *Grand Expectations*, 201–2, who argues that McCarthyism "derived much of its staying power from the frightened and calculating behavior of political elites and of allied interest groups, not from the public at large." On this point, see Heale, "Beyond the 'Age of McCarthy,'" in Stokes, *State of U.S. History*, 139.

2. The most sustained treatment of labor anticommunism can be found in Ronald Radosh's *American Labor and United States Foreign Policy*. As the title indicates, Radosh describes union leaders' involvement in American diplomacy and covert operations from World War I through the 1960s, concentrating especially on AFL participation in efforts to undermine the early Bolshevik revolution and AFL-CIO support for CIA-organized coups in Latin America in the 1940s and 1950s. I follow Radosh in examining labor anticommunists' relationship to the state; my study fleshes out the domestic front of Radosh's story. Cochran's excellent *Labor and Communism* focuses mainly on Communism, rather than anticommunism, through the mid-1930s, carefully charting shifts in CPUSA labor organizing strategy, and picks up labor anticommunism in the late 1930s through Taft-Hartley. As for histories of anticommunism and McCarthyism, my account builds on Richard Gid Powers's *Not Without Honor* and Ellen Schrecker's *Many Are the Crimes*. I follow Powers in treating anticommunism as a coalition of diverse groups with distinctive approaches, rather than a transhistorical antiradical tendency. In this study I flesh out labor anticommunism, which is not prominent in his account. I rely on Schrecker's astute analysis of the effects of McCarthyism on its victims, and the often-duplicitous intentions that underlay red-baiting and McCarthyism. Schrecker has called for more study of unions' role in building American anticommunism, and my study responds to this need. I differ from Schrecker in seeing anticommunism as less continuous with an antiradical impulse arising out of American or western culture, and instead more as a political reaction to a political movement. I also see J. Edgar Hoover's FBI as a more contradictory force, sometimes containing reaction and sometimes fueling repression.

3. A quick word on terminology. In this book, I use "anticommunism" to refer to the broad range of ideological and political movements and policies that opposed Communism after the 1917 Bolshevik Revolution, and "McCarthyism" to refer to the regime of loyalty oaths and investigations in the period from the late 1940s through the mid-1950s. While many of the legal structures of what became McCarthyism were created before World War II, the scope and intensity of public and private anticommunist repression dramatically increased in the late 1940s. I use the word "red-baiting" to signify the use of false or specious imputations of Communist sympathies for political advantage. I capitalize "Communist" throughout, for readers' ease, although I acknowledge the complex con-

siderations underlying the question of capitalization; for a thorough treatment, see Filardo, "What Is the Case?"

4. On labor and early civil liberties, see Rabban, *Free Speech in Its Forgotten Years*; Pope, "Labor's Constitution of Freedom"; and Weinrib, "The Liberal Compromise." On radical labor movements and AFL collaboration with repression, see Dubofsky, *We Shall Be All*; Preston, *Aliens and Dissenters*. On AFL antiradical rhetoric, see Schrecker, *Many Are the Crimes*, 69–70; Powers, *Not Without Honor*, 121–22, 176–80.

5. Greene, *Pure and Simple Politics*; Sanders, *Roots of Reform*; Clemens, *The People's Lobby*. In this book I extend their reinterpretation of the political history of the AFL through the interwar years. Labor historians have heeded the call to "bring the state back in" to social history, with salutary results. We have learned how popular struggles shaped politics and policy, but most of this work has focused on militant workers' actions. We have much less research on the impact of conservative union leaders, who dominated the institutional labor movement, or conservative workers.

6. On industrial democracy, see McCartin, *Labor's Great War*.

7. Theodore Draper became the leading proponent of the traditionalist case with *Roots of American Communism* and *American Communism and Soviet Russia*. This debate culminated in a series of exchanges in May 1985 in the *New York Review of Books*, in letters responding to Draper's essays "American Communism Revisited" and "The Popular Front Revisited." Emblematic revisionist works include Naison, *Communists in Harlem during the Great Depression*; Ottanelli, *The Communist Party of the United States*.

8. Harvey Klehr and John Earl Haynes laid the groundwork for the espionage research with *The Secret World of American Communism*, and they continue to publish extensively on CPUSA espionage. Ellen Schrecker and Maurice Isserman have concurred that the archival record definitively demonstrates that the CPUSA was much more involved in intelligence gathering than had previously been suspected, in Isserman and Schrecker, "'Papers of a dangerous tendency': From Major Andre's boot to the Venona files," in Schrecker, *Cold War Triumphalism*. On the question of party autonomy, see Pedersen, *The Communist Party in Maryland*, for an effort to reassert the CPUSA's relative autonomy, see Storch, *Red Chicago*. Recent work exploring the role of the Comintern in directing CPUSA labor work includes Rosswurm, "Wondrous Tale of an FBI Bug."

9. See Delton, "Rethinking Post–World War II Anticommunism"; Powers, *Not Without Honor*; Plotke, *Building a Democratic Political Order*; Arnesen, "'No Graver Danger.'"

10. The growing social and political historiography of modern American conservatism includes McGirr, *Suburban Warriors*; Nicolaides, *My Blue Heaven*; Rymph, *Republican Women*; Perlstein, *Before the Storm*; and Wald, *The New York Intellectuals*. Alan Brinkley describes the political conservatism of craft unionists in the 1930s in *Voices of Protest*, 198–203. See also Brinkley, "Problem of American Conservatism."

11. On "union preeminence," see Mink, *Old Labor and New Immigrants*.

12. U.S. House, Special Committee to Investigate Communist Activities in the United States, *Investigation of Communist Propaganda*, pt. 2, 35–36; Fronc, *New York Undercover*; Capozzola, *Uncle Sam Wants You*.

CHAPTER ONE

1. Gompers, "Free Speech and the Injunction Order," 256, 262.

2. Schroeder, *"Obscene" Literature and Constitutional Law*, 146.

3. Ibid. On the IWW free-speech fights, see Dubofsky, *We Shall Be All*, 173–98; Rabban, *Free Speech in its Forgotten Years*, 77–126; Higbie, *Indispensible Outcasts*, 144–51.

4. Gompers, "Free Speech and the Injunction Order," 264; Rabban, *Free Speech in its Forgotten Years*.

5. *Los Angeles Times*, February 21, 1915.

6. Debs, "The Crime of Craft Unionism," and "Craft Unionism."

7. *The Double Edge of Labor's Sword*, 10, 94.

8. On Samuel Gompers, see Greene, *Pure and Simple Politics*; Kaufman, *Samuel Gompers and the Origins of the AFL*.

9. I am not entering the old debate on American exceptionalism here but merely describing the views of Gompers and other federation leaders, as well as union members, who repeatedly cited the franchise and workers' diverse party loyalties as the reason for a nonpartisan labor policy. On American exceptionalism, first articulated by Werner Sombart in 1906 in his book *Why Is There No Socialism in the United States?*, Eric Foner has produced the most complete analysis of the question in his essay "Why Is There No Socialism in the United States?" On the postwar electoral landscape, see Bensel, *Yankee Leviathan*. Victoria C. Hattam offers a rich account of workers' political dilemmas in the American context, focusing on the role of the American judiciary, in *Labor Visions and State Power*.

10. Archer, *Why Is There No Labor Party*; Katznelson, *City Trenches*; Leon Fink, "Labor, Liberty, and the Law." See also Martin Shefter, *Political Parties and the State*, 101–69.

11. Voss, *The Making of American Exceptionalism*; Leon Fink, *Workingmen's Democracy*.

12. Cooper, *Once a Cigar Maker*.

13. Greene, *Pure and Simple Politics*, 33–35.

14. Kaufman et al., *Samuel Gompers Papers*, 2:425.

15. Engels to Herman Schlueter, January 29, 1891, and Engels to Friedrich Sorge, January 6, 1892, in Marx and Engels, *Letters to Americans*, 234, 240.

16. *Gunton's Magazine*, February 1896, 134–38; Brooks, "Organized Labor in the United States"; *New York Times*, January 20, 1887; *Literary Digest* 12 (1895): 247.

17. DeLeon, "Blockhead Gompers," *Daily People*, September 5, 1908.

18. On the complexities of AFL governance, see Greene, *Pure and Simple Politics*, 36–47; Ulman, *Rise of the National Trade Union*; Brody, "Shaping a Labor Movement," in *In Labor's Cause*, 81–130; Fones-Wolf and Fones-Wolf, "Rank-and-File Rebellions."

19. On the 1894 convention, see Archer, "Unions, Courts, and Parties."

20. On the sharpening of political orthodoxy within the federation, see Brody, "The Course of American Labor Politics," in *In Labor's Cause*, 51–57.

21. On the Jewish labor movement, see Michels, *Fire in Their Hearts*. Michels reports that "by 1917 some 59,000 people belonged to the Arbeter Ring (Workmen's Circle) fraternal order and 250,000 to the United Hebrew Trades." *Fire in Their Hearts*, 3.

22. Laslett, *Labor and the Left*; Fones-Wolf and Fones-Wolf, "Rank-and-File Rebellions"; Gary Fink, "The Rejection of Voluntarism."

23. Clemens, *The People's Lobby*.

24. On the use of the boycott, see Andrew Cohen, *Racketeer's Progress*, 111–18. On the federal judiciary's approach to labor, see Hattam, *Labor Visions and State Power*, 30–75, 112–80; Forbath, *Shaping of the American Labor Movement*; and Orren, *Belated Feudalism*.

25. Greene, *Pure and Simple Politics*.

26. Ibid., 105–215. See also Karson, *American Labor Unions and Politics*, 42–74.

27. *Current Literature*, May 1906, 465.

28. *The Double Edge of Labor's Sword*, 100.

29. Sanders, *Roots of Reform*, 400. On these lessons, Forbath, *Shaping of the American Labor Movement*; Hattam, *Labor Visions and State Power*.

30. *Proceedings of the Thirty-Fourth Annual Convention of the American Federation of Labor* (1914), 421.

31. Wilson, *The New Freedom*, 155.

32. Recchiutti, *Civic Engagement*, 145–76.

33. *American Federationist*, February 1913, 132; Stromquist, *Reinventing "The People"*; McGerr, *A Fierce Discontent*, 134–35. On reformers' concerns about craft unionism, see Andrew Cohen, *Racketeer's Progress*, 121–57.

34. Debs, "Craft Unionism."

35. Stromquist, *Re-Inventing "The People,"* 90–92, 118–23; Recchiutti, *Civic Engagement*, 145–77; Skocpol, *Protecting Soldiers and Mothers*, 205–48.

36. On the National Civic Federation, see Marguerite Green, "The National Civic Federation"; Cyphers, *The National Civic Federation*; Mink, *Old Labor and New Immigrants*, 167–201; *Chicago Tribune*, November 14, 1894.

37. On the Murray Hill agreement, see Montgomery, *Workers' Control in America*, 48–82; Perlman and Taft, *History of Labor*, 115–16.

38. Marguerite Green, "The National Civic Federation," 150–55.

39. Kaufman et al., *Samuel Gompers Papers*, 9:135.

40. On socialism and the early labor movement, see Laslett, *Labor and the Left*; Michels, *A Fire in their Hearts*; Greene, *Pure and Simple Politics*, 189–91, 220–23.

41. Montgomery, *Fall of the House of Labor*, 281–90.

42. Laslett, *Labor and the Left*.

43. Two biographies of William Z. Foster provide the background for my analysis: Barrett, *William Z. Foster and the Tragedy of American Radicalism*; and Edward P. Johanningsmeier, *Forging American Communism: The Life of William Z. Foster*.

44. This passage relies on Barrett, *Tragedy of American Radicalism*, 9–70; and Johanningsmeier, *Forging American Communism*, 10–55.

45. On the stockyards organizing drives, see Halpern, *Down on the Killing Floor*, 44–73; and Barrett, *Work and Community in the Jungle*, 188–240.

46. Marguerite Green, "National Civic Federation," 170; Barrett, *Tragedy of American Radicalism*, 49. *American Federationist*, October 1911, 827; ibid., November 1911, 901; ibid., December 1911, 978.

47. Gompers to William Z. Foster, July 11, 1916, and August 2, 1916, in Kaufman et al., *Samuel Gompers Papers*, 9:453–54, 461–62. Foster apparently declined to write the article.

48. Hunt, *Front-Page Detective*; Lukas, *Big Trouble*, 750–51.

49. Rabban, *Free Speech in Its Forgotten Years*, 58.

50. On the Wobbly free-speech fights, see ibid., 173–98; Dubofksy, *We Shall Be All*, 183–90; Work, *Darkest before Dawn*, 20–34; Auerbach, *Labor and Liberty*, 16–18.

51. Gompers, "Free Speech and the Injunction Order," 264.

52. Schroeder, *"Obscene" Literature and Constitutional Law*, 146.

53. Gompers to Schroeder, February 19, 1909, box 9, Theodore Schroeder Papers, Southern Illinois University Library, Special Collections, Carbondale.

54. Emma Goldman, letter to the editor, *Lucifer the Light-Bearer*, December 11, 1902; *Mother Earth* 5, no. 6 (August 1910): 179. On conceptions of free speech in the Progressive Era, see Rabban, *Free Speech in Its Forgotten Years*; Graber, *Transforming Free Speech*, 17–74.

55. On industrial democracy, and the Commission on Industrial Relations, see McCartin, *Labor's Great War*, 12–38; Auerbach, *Labor and Liberty*, 13–18.

56. On the Clayton Act debate, see Sanders, *Roots of Reform*, 267–314; O'Brien, *New Deal Paradox*, 34–38.

57. Holmes to Frankfurter, quoted in Ernst, *Lawyers against Labor*, 190.

58. Sanders, *Roots of Reform*, 480 n. 69; *North American Review*, July 1914, 14.

59. Gompers, "The Charter of Industrial Freedom," *American Federationist*, November 1914, 962–72.

CHAPTER TWO

1. *New York Times*, June 16, 1915.

2. Quoted in Karson, *American Labor Unions and Politics*, 92.

3. Samuel Gompers to George Perkins, February 24, 1915, in Kaufman et al., *Samuel Gompers Papers*, 9:253.

4. On popular sentiment, see Link, *The Struggle for Neutrality*, 1–73.

5. Daniel M. Smith, *Robert Lansing and American Neutrality*, 32–34.

6. For an overview of the debate over preparedness, see Kennedy, *Over Here*, 15–24. On German American and Irish American agitation, see Link, *The Struggle for Neutrality*, 137–70.

7. Link, *The Struggle for Neutrality*, 164–68.

8. Woodrow Wilson, "Joint Address to Congress Leading to a Declaration of War Against Germany," April 2, 1917, Records of the Senate, Record Group 46, National Archives; Doerries, *Imperial Challenge*, for New York newspaper, 54–56; for Irish revolutionaries, 72–76; for passports, 144–46; for Mexico, 165–69; quote on p. 142. See also Provost, "The Great Game"; Tinnemann, "Count Johann von Bernstorff"; Link, *The Struggle for Neutrality*, 554–70. For more on Rintelen, see his Bureau of Investigation file in Investigative Case Files of the Bureau of Investigation, 1908–1922, Old German Files, National Archives, Washington, D.C. (hereafter BI Case Files), case #8000–174.

9. On the rise of propaganda as a weapon, see Stevenson, *Cataclysm*; Ferguson, *The Pity of War*, 233–57. On German spycraft, see Boghardt, *Spies of the Kaiser*.

10. On Germany and the Easter Rising, see Doerries, *Imperial Challenge*, 155–65; Doerries, *Prelude to the Easter Rising*; Beckett, *The Great War 1914–1918*, 507–8.

11. On the Ghadr case, see Doerries, *Imperial Challenge*, 146–55; Price, *The Lives of Agnes Smedley*, 56–74; Plowman, "Irish Republicans."

12. On Germany's relationship to the Mexican Revolution, see Michael C. Meyer, "The Mexican-German Conspiracy of 1915," 76–89; Tuchman, *The Zimmermann Telegram*; and Doerries, *Imperial Challenge*, 165–76. On the Plan de San Diego, see Benjamin Heber Johnson, *Revolution in Texas*.

13. Germany was not the only belligerent to consider fomenting munitions strikes in the United States. In August 1915, Austria-Hungary's ambassador to the U.S., Constantin Dumba, wrote to Austrian foreign affairs minister that "we can disorganize and hold up for months, if not entirely prevent, the manufacture of munitions at Bethlehem and in the middle west," in part because the "white slaves" employed at the factories were "working for twelve hours a day and seven days a week." After this letter was intercepted in September 1915, the U.S. demanded that Austria-Hungary recall Dumba. Few histories of World War I include this evidence of planned industrial sabotage; governmental concerns about

factory security make more sense in light of these cases. On Dumba, see "The Recall of Ambassador Dumba," *Washington Post*, September 8, 1915.

14. Reinhard Doerries's research relied primarily on German sources. For American accounts of the Rintelen affair, the LNPC, and German efforts to suborn labor radicalism, the federal Bureau of Investigation developed a case file of several thousand pages, found in BI Case Files, case #8000-174. A helpful overview of the BI's evidence can be found in the testimony of BI head A. Bruce Bielaski in the postwar congressional hearings into beer brewers and wartime propaganda, which helped lead to Prohibition: see Senate Committee on the Judiciary, *Brewing and Liquor Interests and German Propaganda*, 1570–78. The records of the U.S. District Court for the Southern District of New York, held in the National Archives, contain largely procedural documents relating to pleas of various defendants. Franz von Rintelen wrote two autobiographies, *The Dark Invader* (New York: Macmillan, 1933) and *The Return of the Dark Invader* (London: P. Davies, 1935). These memoirs, in the estimation of Doerries, alternate between fact and fiction, and therefore I do not rely on them in my account. See Doerries's introduction to *The Dark Invader* (1998).

15. Doerries, *Imperial Challenge*, 183–84. (It is not clear whether the $200,000 for munitions manufacturer strikes came out of the $500,000 budget or was a separate allocation.) For Lamar's obituary, see *New York Times*, January 14, 1934.

16. For David Lamar, see his obituary, *New York Times*, January 14, 1934; Senate Committee on the Judiciary, *Brewing and Liquor Interests and German Propaganda*, 1571–74; Cotter, *United States Steel*, 205–6. For a contemporary muckraking account, see French Strother, "Fighting Germany's Spies: The Tiger of Germany Meets the Wolf of Wall Street," *World's Work*, May 1918, 304–7.

17. On Buchanan, see his entry in the *Biographical Dictionary of the United States Congress*, http://bioguide.congress.gov/ (accessed May 4, 2011); Greene, *Pure and Simple Politics*, 116; and his obituary in the *New York Times*, April 19, 1930.

18. On Fowler and Buchanan, see *Biographical Dictionary of the United States Congress*, http://bioguide.congress.gov/ (accessed May 4, 2011).

19. *New York Times*, June 24, 1915. A preliminary public meeting in May had attracted Joseph Cannon of the Western Federation of Miners and John Golden of the Textile Workers, but neither union leader signed up to lead the LNPC. Montgomery, *Fall of the House of Labor*, 359. There is very little scholarship on the LNPC, and most accounts misconstrue the organization as a legitimate initiative. David Montgomery's brief mention of the LNPC makes no mention of its origins or later exposure as a German subterfuge. Elizabeth Sanders has a similar treatment of the LNPC in *Roots of Reform*, 403–5. Philip Foner discusses the LNPC at length in *History of the Labor Movement in the United States*, vol. 7, *Labor and World War I*, 40–52. However, Foner garbles the story badly, arguing, for example, that Buchanan founded the LNPC in 1914 as a bona fide pacifist organization. Simeon Larson describes the founding of the LNPC but not its exposure as a Rintelen front: Larson, *Labor and Foreign Policy*. Carl Weinberg has a brief but accurate mention of the affair in *Labor, Loyalty, and Rebellion*, 65–66.

20. Easley to Gompers's home address, June 10, 1915, box 49, folder 5, National Civic Federation Papers, New York Public Library, New York, N.Y. (hereafter NCF Papers).

21. Gompers aired these concerns in the *Washington Post*, July 19, 1915; see also *Independent*, August 9, 1915, 181; and *Chicago Tribune*, September 13, 1915. In his autobiography, Rintelen claimed to have actually instigated strikes among longshoremen: *Dark Invader*, 169–74. In his testimony to the Senate in 1919, BI chief A. Bruce Bielaski cast doubt on this

account, stating that "the proof in the direction and financing of that by the Germans was never absolutely clear, although we have no doubt that morally they were responsible for it. No prosecution resulted in that case." Senate Committee on the Judiciary, *Brewing and Liquor Interests and German Propaganda*, 1602.

22. Bucki, "Dilution and Craft Tradition," 107.

23. On Easley and the war, see Marguerite Green, "National Civic Federation," 364–66; for Easley's account of this discussion, see box 454, folder 6, NCF Papers; *New York Times*, August, 18, 1915.

24. Easley to Ambassador Cecil Arthur Spring-Rice, July 8, 1915; Spring-Rice to Easley, July 9, 1915, box 442, folder 1, NCF Papers. Spring-Rice likely knew, but did not reveal, that in June 1915 British intelligence agents had discovered Rintelen and organized a ruse to lure Rintelen back to Europe; see Link, *The Struggle for Neutrality*, 562.

25. *New York Times*, July 23, 1915.

26. Ibid., July 20, 1915.

27. Ibid., January 12, 1916.

28. Bucki, "Dilution and Craft Tradition"; Montgomery, *Workers' Control in America*, 127–34.

29. *New York Times*, July 24, 1915.

30. Gompers to Ernest Bohm, July 28, 1915, in Kaufman et al., *Samuel Gompers Papers*, 9:303–4.

31. *Chicago Daily Tribune*, December 7, 1915.

32. Ibid.

33. Report of agent W. L Furbershaw, August 23, 1915, BI Case Files, #8000–174.

34. On Robinson, see *New York Times*, November 5, 1908; ibid., January 8, 1914. Robinson died in 1918; see ibid., May 11, 1918.

35. See, for example, Easley to Gompers, September 15, 1915, box 49, folder 5, NCF Papers.

36. Box 435, folder 4, NCF Papers; box 456, folder 7, NCF Papers.

37. *New York Times*, August 10, 1915; *Washington Post*, August 10, 1915.

38. *New York Times*, August 11, 1915.

39. *Chicago Daily Tribune*, December 5, 1915.

40. Link, *Struggle for Neutrality*, 562–563.

41. *Washington Post*, December 22, 1915; *New York Times*, December 22, 1915.

42. *New York Times*, December 7, 1915; BI Case Files, #8000–174.

43. Senate Committee on the Judiciary, *Brewing and Liquor Interests and German Propaganda*, 1574.

44. *New York Times*, May 5, 1917; BI Case Files, #8000–174; Doerries's introduction to Rintelen, *Dark Invader*, xxiii–xxiv. The case was delayed for some time because Buchanan used his position as a member of the House of Representatives to impeach H. Snowden Marshall, the U.S. attorney for the Southern District of New York, in a retaliatory move intended to derail Buchanan's indictment. Buchanan charged Marshall with "subservience to the great criminal trusts," but most observers, including the New York City Bar Association, regarded the matter as an abuse by Buchanan of his congressional powers; see *New York Times*, December 14, 1915; *Law Notes*, July 1916, 63; see also House Committee on the Judiciary, *H. Snowden Marshall*. Marshall was ultimately cleared of the charges.

45. Gompers, *Seventy Years of Life and Labor*, 2:334, 342. Scholars should refer to the full edition of the autobiography for details of the Rintelen affair and the secret service bureau.

Most of Gompers's discussion of these matters is excised in Nick Salvatore's abridged edition, published in 1984 (Salvatore, *Seventy Years of Life and Labor*). Salvatore's treatment of Gompers's experiences with German espionage reflects a general tendency by historians to dismiss or downplay German subterfuge on the World War I home front. Indeed, Gompers's previous biographer, Ernest Mandel, similarly made light of Gompers's suspicions: Mandel, *Samuel Gompers*, 356. The upsurge of nativism and anti-German xenophobia in 1917 and 1918 surely accounts for historians' skepticism, along with the many specious accusations of subversion later launched during the war. Yet the existence of actual German subversion in 1915 and 1916, and the relatively mild public reaction to these early cases, suggests that the story of anti-German reaction warrants more research.

46. Box 454, folder 6, NCF Papers. In her excellent study *New York Undercover*, Jennifer Fronc describes the NCF/AFL investigations of anarchists and IWW members in New Jersey (yet makes no mention of the Rintelen case that sparked the investigation.)

47. Box 454, folder 1, NCF papers.

48. Box 437, folder 1, NCF Papers.

49. Box 454, folder 1, NCF Papers.

50. Box 54, folder 5, NCF Papers; box 456, folder 5, NCF Papers. The full extent of NCF investigations is hard to gauge. In March 1917, Easley informed the NCF executive board that the secret service bureau had agents in boot and shoe mills in Boston and silk mills in Paterson; he also claimed that employers were sharing information on subversive activity. There are many detective reports in NCF files whose provenance (and sometimes, subject) are impossible to determine, due to their elliptical language and lack of author identification. See Marguerite Green, "The National Civic Federation," 374 n. 29.

51. The investigator, L. Garland, used as a pseudonym "Oscar Greenhalge." BI Case Files, case #98-A.

52. Box 54, folder 1, NCF Papers.

53. Preston, *Aliens and Dissenters*, 70–71.

54. Dubofsky, *We Shall Be All*, 304–7.

55. Theoharis et al., *The FBI*; McCormick, *Seeing Reds*, 10–17; Powers, *Broken*; Schmidt, *Red Scare*.

56. On private detectives in the BI, see Schmidt, *Red Scare*, 208–9; McCormick, *Seeing Reds*, 14–19.

57. On the APL, see Jensen, *Price of Vigilance*. Easley proposed to organize a labor counterpart to the APL—a mass organization enlisting AFL members as volunteer agents. This "Bureau of Information" would "have its members keep their eyes and ears open for every utterance or suspicious action against the interests of this Government." In a letter to New York City police chief Theodore Bingham, Easley claimed that "this plan has been discussed with Mr. Gompers and other labor men and they are assisting with its organization," planning to name Herman Robinson as its head. Easley to Bingham, n.d. [1917], box 401, folder 8, NCF Papers. A similar proposal was made by Ralph Van Deman, head of the Military Intelligence Division, to the AFL in April 1918. Van Deman suggested that "each local union constitute itself an unofficial branch of Military Intelligence and forward to us, thru its secretary, all information that its members have or may hereafter learn relative to disloyalty or hostile activities, and any persons suspected thereof, and relative to labor conditions in their vicinity." MID officials met with Gompers and AFL secretary Frank Morrison to discuss the idea in May 1918, and Morrison sent an address list of AFL affiliates to the MID later that month. There is no evidence that the MID or AFL proceeded with

this plan. Van Deman to Frank Morrison, April 24, 1918, Kaufman et al., *Samuel Gompers Papers*, 10:434–36.

58. Powers, *Broken*, 92–94; Preston, *Aliens and Dissenters*, 102–18.

59. For examples of this information exchange, see Schmidt, *Red Scare*, 207–8.

CHAPTER THREE

1. *Nation*, September 14, 1918; Villard, *Fighting Years*, 354–55.

2. Villard, *Fighting Years*, 354–55; Gompers, "Free Speech and the Injunction Order," 264.

3. Montgomery, *Fall of the House of Labor*, 377.

4. *Public*, vol. 18 (November 12, 1915), 1092, quoted in Link, *Confusions and Crises*, 26; see also Rossinow, *Visions of Progress*, 60–86.

5. Gompers quoted in Karson, *Labor Unions and Politics*, 93–94; the federation's war declaration was reprinted in Gompers, *American Labor and the War*, 289–95. For a comprehensive view of the AFL during the war years, see McCartin, *Labor's Great War*. See also Dubofsky, *State and Labor in Modern America*, 61–83.

6. Grubbs, *Struggle for Labor Loyalty*, 20–34.

7. On the People's Council, see Rossinow, *Visions of Progress*, 69–78; Kennedy, *Over Here*, 27–29.

8. On the Russian Revolution and the Socialist Party, see Draper, *The Roots of American Communism*, 80–97; Weinstein, *Decline of Socialism in America*, 163–81; Michels, *Fire in Their Hearts*, 217–22.

9. Grubbs, *Struggle for Labor Loyalty*, 38–39; Radosh, *American Labor and Foreign Policy*, 55–72; Montgomery, *Fall of the House of Labor*, 386.

10. Radosh, *American Labor and Foreign Policy*, 59; Kennedy, *Over Here*, 29.

11. There is a large literature on Americanization and labor during the war; key works include Gary Gerstle, *Working-Class Americanism*, 43–48; Barrett, "Americanization from the Bottom Up"; and McCartin, *Labor's Great War*.

12. Grubb, *Struggle for Labor Loyalty*, 58–66.

13. Weinstein, *Decline of Socialism in America*, 45–53.

14. McCartin, *Labor's Great War*, 91–114; Barrett, "Americanization from the Bottom Up," 1009–10.

15. McCartin, *Labor's Great War*, 82; Lincoln Steffens memo, December 28, 1917, in Link et al., *The Papers of Woodrow Wilson*, 45:383.

16. Mink, *Old Labor and New Immigrants*, 25.

17. Union membership figures from Perlman and Taft, *History of Labor*, 410. On the balance of power between progressives and conservatives in the AFL during the war, see especially Joseph McCartin's *Labor's Great War*.

18. On the origins of the Espionage Act, see Stone, *Perilous Times*, 137–53; Rabban, *Free Speech in Its Forgotten Years*, 248–98.

19. House Committee on the Judiciary, *Espionage and Interference with Neutrality*, 37, 52.

20. Ibid., 27–29.

21. Ibid., 55–56.

22. Donald Johnson, "Wilson, Burleson, and Censorship," 46–58; *St. Louis Post-Dispatch*, September 24, 1918; Capozzola, *Uncle Sam Wants You*, 151–60.

23. *Proceedings of the Thirty-Eighth Annual Convention of the American Federation of Labor* (1918), 118–19.

24. Kennedy, *Over Here*, 83.

25. Chafee, *Freedom of Speech*, 193.

26. Ibid., 192.

27. Dowell, *History of Criminal Syndicalism Legislation*, 45–68. In the 1920s, in the aftermath of the Red Scare, state unionists took a much more active role in opposing new criminal syndicalism legislation. See also Heale, *American Anticommunism*, 50, 72–73; Dubofsky, *We Shall Be All*, 381–82.

28. Capozzola, *Uncle Sam Wants You*, 144–72.

29. Quoted in Gompers, *American Labor and the War*, 95–96.

30. Senate Committee on the Judiciary, *Brewing and Liquor Interests and German Propaganda*, 1574.

31. Investigative Case Files of the Bureau of Investigation, 1908–1922, Old German Files, National Archives, Washington, D.C., case #60221. It appears that the BI detail ended with armistice.

32. Ibid., case #8000-255851. Gompers also took the opportunity to report a private detective agency that compared labor unions to German subversives; see case #36437.

33. William C. Fitts to U.S. Representative Carl Hayden, January 31, 1918, in Dubofsky, *Department of Justice Investigative Files*. See also Fitts to Secretary of Labor William B. Wilson on the difference between the AFL-affiliated Mine Mill union and the IWW, "the Smelters' Union being good, and the I.W.W.'s being vicious." Fitts to Wilson, September 18, 1917, in ibid.

34. *Christian Science Monitor*, February 12, 1918.

35. *New York Times*, September 10, 1917.

36. Harré, *The I.W.W.: An Auxiliary of the German Espionage Service*, 19, 23.

37. Preston, *Aliens and Dissenters*, 93, 96.

38. Ibid., 122.

39. Samuel Gompers, "Memo," December 22, 1917, in Kaufman, et al., *Samuel Gompers Papers*, 10:297–98.

40. Ralph Easley to William C. Fitts, January 18, 1918, in Dubofsky, *Department of Justice Investigative Files*.

41. Dubofsky, *We Shall Be All*, 432–38.

42. Gompers, *Seventy Years of Life and Labor*, 2:336. Note that Gompers links IWW "preaching the doctrine of sabotage" as aiding the German effort to slow munitions traffic in 1915, but he does not directly say that the IWW worked deliberately on behalf of Germany.

43. Ibid., 2:378, 388.

44. *New York Times*, January 18, 1918.

45. Quoted in Radosh, *American Labor and Foreign Policy*, 167.

46. On the origins of the totalitarian image, see Markku Ruotsila, *British and American Anticommunism*, 54–62; Taft quote from ibid., 57. See also Maddux, "Red Fascism, Brown Bolshevism"; and Adler and Paterson, "Red Fascism."

47. Quoted in Foglesong, *America's Secret War against Bolshevism*, 35.

48. McKillen, *Chicago Labor and Democratic Diplomacy*, 96–99; McCartin, *Labor's Great War*, 80–82.

49. For the memo, see Samuel Gompers to Woodrow Wilson, February 19, 1918, in Link

et al., *The Papers of Woodrow Wilson*, 46:310–13; on Wilson's reaction to the memo, see Foglesong, *America's Secret War against Bolshevism*, 37.

50. Radosh, *American Labor and Foreign Policy*, 171, 176.

51. *Nation*, September 14, 1918, 283; Rosenberg, *Spreading the American Dream*, 83–84.

CHAPTER FOUR

1. Murray, *Red Scare*, 108.

2. On the demobilization, see McCartin, *Labor's Great War* 173–99; Kennedy, *Over Here*, 248–87; Perlman and Taft, *History of Labor*, 435–88.

3. On the bombings, see Gage, *The Day Wall Street Exploded*, 115–22; Murray, *Red Scare*, 57–81; Hagedorn, *Savage Peace*, 218–33.

4. *New York Times*, December 21, 1919; ibid., January 18, 1920.

5. On the Palmer raids and the deportations, see Murray, *Red Scare*, 190–222; Preston, *Aliens and Dissenters*, 181–237; Schmidt, *Red Scare*, 236–300.

6. Frank Farrington to A. Mitchell Palmer, December 30, 1919; Palmer to Farrington, January 7, 1919 (letter apparently misdated and should read 1920), Investigative Case Files of the Bureau of Investigation, 1908–1922, Old German Files, National Archives, Washington, D.C. (hereafter BI Case Files), case #202600.

7. Charles Moyer to Samuel Gompers, November 19, 1919; Gompers to A. Mitchell Palmer, November 24, 1919, BI Case Files, case #202600.

8. Schmidt, *Red Scare*, 130, 210.

9. Murray, *Red Scare*, 98–101; Jensen, *Price of Vigilance*, 275.

10. Box 410, folder 15, National Civic Federation Papers, New York Public Library, New York, N.Y. (hereafter NCF Papers).

11. Box 410, folder 21, NCF Papers.

12. New York Joint Legislative Committee to Investigate Seditious Activities, *Seditious Activities: Part II*, 3:2013.

13. Box 410, folder 25, NCF Papers.

14. Easley to Palmer, January 3, 1920, box 76, folder 5, NCF Papers.

15. Box 410, folder 31, NCF Papers.

16. *American Federationist*, February 1919, 153–54.

17. Quoted in the *Stone Cutters' Journal*, December 1919, 16. See also Mandel, *Samuel Gompers*, 456.

18. *New York Times*, February 14, 1919.

19. Quoted in Dubofsky, *State and Labor in Modern America*, 78.

20. Senate Committee on Education and Labor, *Investigation of Strike in Steel Industries*, 112. On Foster and the steel strike, see Barrett, *Tragedy of American Radicalism*, 83–102; Johanningsmeier, *Forging American Communism*, 111–50; Foster, *The Great Steel Strike and Its Lessons*.

21. Quoted in Murray, *Red Scare*, 143.

22. Senate Committee on Education and Labor, *Investigation of Strike in Steel Industries*, 853–54.

23. Ibid., 94, 112, 391, 394.

24. William Mahon to Samuel Gompers, November 1, 1919, in Kaufman et al., *Samuel Gompers Papers*, 11:21–23.

25. Rabban, *Free Speech in its Forgotten Years*, 2–9; but see Weinrib, "Lawyers, Liber-

tines, and Free Speech," in the possession of the author. Also see Stone, *Perilous Times*, 220–26; Rossinow, *Visions of Progress*, 78–86.

26. *Proceedings of the Thirty-Ninth Annual Convention of the American Federation of Labor* (1919), 392–94. Roger Baldwin of the National Civil Liberties Bureau helped orchestrate some of the debate on the Espionage Act. In May 1919 he wrote to James Maurer, the progressive president of the Pennsylvania Federation of Labor, suggesting that "it would be a grand and glorious thing" if the AFL "would pass resolutions opposing any peace-time sedition law," remarking that if the AFL "doesn't watch sharp the peace-time sedition law will be used against it." Robert M. Buck, editor of the magazine *New Majority*, reported back to the NCLB's Albert de Silver that he had written a resolution demanding "immediate repeal" of the Espionage Act, but the AFL delegates "chewed up" his version, adopting instead a resolution calling for a "restoration" of free-speech rights after the peace treaty was signed. Roger M. Baldwin to James H. Maurer, May 29, 1919, and Robert M. Buck to Albert de Silver, June 20, 1919, *American Civil Liberties Union Records* (microfilm), vol. 106.

27. *Proceedings of the Thirty-Ninth Annual Convention of the American Federation of Labor* [1919], 392–94.

28. Freeberg, *Democracy's Prisoner*, 167.

29. Ibid., 168–70.

30. House Committee on the Judiciary, *Sedition*, 246.

31. Senate Committee on Education and Labor, *Investigation of Strike in Steel Industries*, 135.

32. House Committee on the Judiciary, *Sedition*, 246, 252.

33. National Popular Government League, "Illegal Practices of the Department of Justice," 8.

34. Philip Foner, *History of the Labor Movement*, 7:53–56.

35. "This Thing Called Bolshevism," *American Federationist*, March 1919, 232.

36. *Proceedings of the Thirty-Ninth Annual Convention of the American Federation of Labor* (1919), 333; *Proceedings of the Fortieth Annual Convention of the American Federation of Labor* [1920], 369.

37. William English Walling, "The American Federation of Labor and the Soviets," *American Federationist*, August 1919, 703.

38. Samuel Gompers to the Chicago Federation of Labor, August 20, 1920, *American Federationist*, November 1920, 1025.

39. *Proceedings of the Forty-First Annual Convention of the American Federation of Labor* (1921), 92–93.

40. On liberals' reaction to the Bolshevik Revolution, see Lasch, *American Liberals and the Russian Revolution*; and Filene, *Americans and the Russian Experiment*.

41. On the relationship between the IWW and American Communists, see Dubofsky, *We Shall Be All*, 462–65; Draper, *Roots of American Communism*, 315–20; see also Conlin, *Big Bill Haywood*, for a detailed recounting of schisms within the IWW and conflict between the Communist Party and the Wobblies.

42. Zimmer, "Premature Anti-Communists"; Emma Goldman, "My Disillusionment in Russia," reprinted in Shulman, *Red Emma Speaks*, 390.

43. Emma Goldman, "Preparedness: The Road to Universal Slaughter," reprinted in Shulman, *Red Emma Speaks*, 353.

44. *Proceedings of the Forty-First Annual Convention of the American Federation of Labor* (1921), 94.

45. *American Federationist*, April 1919, 319.

46. On the early CP, see Klehr, *Communist Cadre*; Palmer, "American Communism in the 1920s"; Weinstein, "Radicalism in the Midst of Normalcy."

47. Draper, *Roots of American Communism*, 158, 188–93; Weinstein, *Decline of Socialism in America*, 177–233.

48. Draper, *Roots of American Communism*, 206.

49. *Proceedings of the Fortieth Annual Convention of the American Federation of Labor* (1920), 210.

50. *American Federationist*, April 1919, 320.

51. Lenin, *A Letter to American Workingmen*, 15. Philip Scheidemann was a prowar German Socialist leader and member of the Reichstag in 1918.

52. Boehm, *Minutes of the Executive Council of the American Federation of Labor* (microfilm), November 1920.

53. Draper, *Roots of American Communism*, 218–19.

54. Lenin, *Left-wing Communism*, 37, 35.

55. Wilkinson, "The Red Trade Union Congress," *Communist*, September 17, 1921; A. Lozovsky, "The First International Congress of Revolutionary Trade Unions," *Communist International*, October 1922.

56. Quoted in Barrett, *Tragedy of American Radicalism*, 100.

CHAPTER FIVE

1. *Washington Post*, December 20, 1920.

2. For Gompers's account of the meeting, see House Committee on the Judiciary, *Charges of Hon. Oscar E. Keller*, 172–73; *Washington Post*, December 8, 1911.

3. Taft, *AFL in the Time of Gompers*, 362. Note that overall union membership, including unions such as the railroad brotherhoods not affiliated with the AFL, fell from 5 million to 3.6 million over the same period; Bernstein, *The Lean Years*, 84.

4. *Proceedings of the Forty-First Annual Convention of the American Federation of Labor* (1921), 449.

5. William Appleman Williams, *American-Russian Relations*, 180.

6. Eric Foner, "No Socialism in the United States?" 68.

7. On the 1921 AFL election, see Taft, *AFL in the Time of Gompers*, 363–68; Montgomery, *Fall of the House of Labor*, 404–6.

8. *New York Times*, August 19, 1921.

9. Giglio, *H. M. Daugherty and the Politics of Expediency*, 118.

10. For background on Burns, see Gage, *The Day Wall Street Exploded*, 136–42; Hunt, *Front-Page Detective*.

11. On the McNamara case, see Adams, *Age of Industrial Violence*, 1–24.

12. *Los Angeles Times*, September 11, 1911.

13. Ibid., December 3, 1911.

14. *Washington Post*, December 16, 1911.

15. Preston, *Aliens and Dissenters*, 238–42; Belknap, "Uncooperative Federalism."

16. Gage, *The Day Wall Street Exploded*, 129–30; Preston, *Aliens and Dissenters*, 208–11.

17. Powers, *Secrecy and Power*, 67; Ackerman, *Young J. Edgar*, 338–46.

18. Howard, *The Labor Spy*, 131–50.

19. Ralph M. Easley to William J. Burns, August 22, 1921; Burns to Easley, August 27, 1921

National Civic Federation Papers, New York Public Library, New York, N.Y. (hereafter NCF Papers).

20. For a helpful contemporary account of the practice of boring from within, see Saposs, *Left-Wing Unionism*, 33–84; see also Joseph Kucher's essay, "If American Labor Is to Be Organized," in J. B. S. Hardman, ed., *American Labor Dynamics*, 303–10.

21. "The Principles and Program of the Trade Union Educational League," March 1922, series 6, box 35, Daniel Bell Research Files, Tamiment Library, New York, N.Y.

22. Barrett, *Tragedy of American Radicalism*, 126.

23. Ralph M. Easley to William J. Burns, March 30, 1922; Burns to Easley, April 4, 1922, NCF Papers. On BI infiltration, see Draper, *Roots of American Communism*, 366–69.

24. Easley to J. Edgar Hoover, April 7, 1922, NCF Papers.

25. Burns to Easley, May 4, 1922, and September 27, 1922, ibid.

26. Tobin to Easley, March 27, 1922, ibid.

27. Chester M. Wright to Easley, May 29, 1922, ibid.

28. Schmidt, *Red Scare*, 103–4; Powers, *Secrecy and Power*, 139.

29. On the 1922 coal strike, see Dublin and Licht, *The Face of Decline*, 53–55; Dubofsky, *State and Labor in Modern America*, 89–91.

30. On the coal strike, see Dubofsky and Van Tine, *John L. Lewis*, 62–71; on the shopmen's strike, see Davis, *Power at Odds*.

31. Barrett, *Tragedy of American Radicalism*, 129–30; Johanningsmeier, *Forging American Communism*, 183–85.

32. Quoted in Johanningsmeier, *Forging American Communism*, 183.

33. *Locomotive Engineer's Journal*, October 1922, 731; Davis, *Power at Odds*, 91.

34. Frey to Ralph Easley, June 28, 1923, NCF Papers.

35. *American Federationist*, May 1922.

36. Schrecker, *Many Are the Crimes*, 11.

37. Draper, *Roots of American Communism*, 367.

38. Max Eastman, "An Opinion on Tactics," *Liberator*, October 1921, 5–6. Eastman drifted toward Trotskyism until the mid-1930s, when he renounced Communism entirely and became a leading conservative intellectual. On Eastman, see Denning, *The Cultural Front*, 426–32; Diggins, *Up from Communism*, 17–74, 201–33. Samuel Darcy oral history, Oral History of the American Left, Tamiment Library, pt. 1, 30; pt. 2, 5–6.

39. On the twists and turns of this complicated debate, see Draper, *Roots of American Communism*.

40. House Special Committee to Investigate Communist Activities, *Investigation of Communist Propaganda*, 1:75.

41. Galenson, *The United Brotherhood of Carpenters*, 217.

42. Paul M. Angle wrote the definitive account of the Herrin Massacre in *Bloody Williamson: A Chapter in American Lawlessness*.

43. "Investigation of Rioting at Strip Mine," June 27, 1922, Herrin Massacre file, Federal Bureau of Investigation Papers, RG 65, Classification 57, box 15, National Archives, College Park, Md.

44. Ibid.; William J. Burns to M. C. Laughlin, June 22, 1922, ibid.

45. Quoted in Angle, *Bloody Williamson*, 46.

46. *New York Times*, August 31, 1922.

47. "Address of International President John L. Lewis in Connection with a Circular Distributed by Emissaries of the Progressive International Committee of the Mine Workers

of America," Friday, June 29, 1923, United Mine Workers of America Papers, President-District correspondence, District 1, box 1, folder 1, Pennsylvania State University, Historical Collections and Labor Archives, State College.

48. United Mine Workers of America, *Attempts by Communists to Seize the Labor Movement*, 1, 15.

49. Ibid., 16.

50. Ibid., 42.

51. *New York Times*, September 16, 1923.

52. *Wall Street Journal*, September 20, 1923.

53. House Special Committee to Investigate Communist Activities, *Investigation of Communist Propaganda*, 4:16–17. The articles comprise the only record of Searles's research. No trace of his materials can be found in the UMWA archives, which are only partially processed. His account of information sharing with Harry Daugherty's Justice Department comports with department practice in the early 1920s.

54. On the Pittsburgh raids and the BI's involvement, see Schmidt, *Red Scare*, 116–17. The discrepancy in the dates—Searles said he began researching DOJ files in February, but the Pittsburgh raids occurred several months later—may be due to an error in Searles's memory or may indicate that the DOJ continued to share files after the first research stint.

55. Twenty years later, the Dies Committee subpoenaed Dozenberg, who went on to work as an agent for the Soviet Union's military intelligence organization, the GRU, in Europe and the United States. Dozenberg left his post in the late 1930s as Stalin's purges reached the intelligence service, and he sought refuge in the United States. In his Dies Committee testimony, Dozenberg described his *Voice of Labor* articles on the Herrin strike as "absolutely from one end to the other, as far as I am concerned, just 100 percent lies." Dozenberg attributed the Herrin articles to a "publicity stunt." House Special Committee on Un-American Activities, *Investigation of Un-American Propaganda Activities in the United States* [1939–41], 13:8150; on Dozenberg, see Haynes and Klehr, *Venona*, 164–66.

56. Ralph M. Easley to John Hays Hammond, September 14, 1923, NCF Papers. John Hays Hammond was the president of the recently created United States Coal Commission, a fact-finding body convened by President Harding in the wake of the 1922 strike. Easley's letter looks like an attempt to interest Hammond's commission in pursuing the Communist allegations despite their dubious provenance.

57. Draper, *Roots of American Communism*, 367; Gage, *The Day Wall Street Exploded*, 297–303. As James Barrett notes, ironically, "at the precise moment that Communist leaders concluded it was essential to work openly, they were arrested." Barrett, *Tragedy of American Radicalism*, 132.

58. Walter M. Nelson, a liberal lawyer in Detroit, told Baldwin that AFL officials in Michigan and Washington "actually connived at [the criminal syndicalism law's] passage. . . . The idea of the Federation Craft and conservative unionists appears to have been that only the Communists, anarchists, and one big unionists would be persecuted." Nelson to Roger Baldwin, September 6, 1922, *American Civil Liberties Union Records* (microfilm). Nelson later helped defend Dr. Ossian Sweet on charges of shooting into a mob attempting to drive Sweet from his house in an all-white neighborhood; Boyle, *Arc of Justice*, 254.

59. Draper, *Roots of American Communism*, 362–75; Belknap, "Uncooperative Federalism," 27–31.

60. Cottrell, *Roger Nash Baldwin*, 111–12.

61. Belknap, "Uncooperative Federalism," 33–43.

62. Easley to Conde B. Pallen, October 13, 1922, NCF Papers. Easley lists attendees at the meeting, including Alton Parker, Archibald Stevenson, and William C. Redfield, who was Wilson's secretary of commerce. No representatives from unions are included in his list.

63. Burns to Easley, October 18, 1922; Easley to Burns, October 20, 1922. Regin Schmidt reports that Easley also helped arrange the hiring of Alexander Rorke, an experienced criminal-anarchy prosecutor from New York; Schmidt, *Red Scare*, 104.

64. Belknap, "Uncooperative Federalism"; Barrett, *Tragedy of American Radicalism*, 132–33. On the criminal syndicalism laws and the Michigan Federation of Labor, see Walter Nelson to Roger Baldwin, September 5, 1922, *American Civil Liberties Union Records* (microfilm), reel 30.

65. National Popular Government League, "Illegal Practices of the Department of Justice," 6.

CHAPTER SIX

1. Sidney Howard, "Our Professional Patriots: Ralph Easley, Dean of the Prodigy," *New Republic*, August 20, 1924, 346; and Howard, "Our Professional Patriots: Sweeping Up the Crumbs," ibid., September 10, 1924, 10.

2. Quoted in Johanningsmeier, *Forging American Communism*, 183.

3. On the strike and the injunction, see Davis, *Power at Odds*, 116–32; Giglio, *H. M. Daugherty*, 146–50; Dubofsky, *State and Labor in Modern America*, 91–97.

4. *Los Angeles Times*, September 2, 1922.

5. *New York Times*, September 8, 1922; *Wall Street Journal*, September 11, 1922.

6. *Chicago Daily Tribune*, September 15, 1922.

7. Boehm, *Minutes of the Executive Council of the American Federation of Labor* (microfilm), September 1922. On Oscar Keller's background, see Gieske, *Minnestota Farmer-Laborism*, 34–35.

8. House Committee on the Judiciary, *Charges of Hon. Oscar E. Keller*, 1, 13; *Washington Post*, September 12, 1922; *Chicago Daily Tribune*, September 19, 1922.

9. The effort to impeach Harry Daugherty is strangely absent from virtually all accounts of labor politics in the 1920s, from Selig Perlman and Philip Taft's surveys to David Montgomery's synthesis, *The Fall of the House of Labor*, to Dubofsky's *State and Labor in Modern America*. I speculate that the AFL's silence on the impeachment after its ignominious defeat is one reason; another may be the long shadow that Teapot Dome casts over the Harding administration, obscuring earlier events. Nevertheless, the affair was hardly hidden at the time; the impeachment and the AFL's involvement were frequently reported in AFL publications and major American newspapers. Regin Schmidt mentions the impeachment in *Red Scare*, 318.

10. *Baltimore Sun*, September 17, 1922.

11. On the 1922 midterm elections and the CPPA, see Montgomery, *Fall of the House of Labor*, 404, 434–43.

12. *New York Times*, December 5, 1922.

13. This was the consensus of the national press; see, for instance, *Baltimore Sun*, September 20, 1922 ("If every official in Washington who is either an ignoramus or a politician should be impeached, how many would be left to run the government?"); *Los Angeles Times*, September 15, 1922 ("The Attorney General has incurred the enmity of the labor union chiefs because he has refused to be intimidated by their threats and abuse.")

14. *Washington Post*, September 21, 1922.

15. *Congressional Record*, 67th Cong., 4th sess., vol. 64-a, January 25, 1923, 2424–25.

16. *Brotherhood of Locomotive Firemen and Engineers Magazine*, November 1, 1922, 2.

17. House Committee on the Judiciary, *Charges of Hon. Oscar E. Keller*, 221.

18. Ibid., 293.

19. Sam Evans to Roger Baldwin, December 10, 1922, and Roger Baldwin to Jackson Ralston, December 12, 1922, *American Civil Liberties Union Records* (microfilm).

20. House Committee on the Judiciary, *Charges of Hon. Oscar E. Keller*, 570.

21. Barrett, *Tragedy of American Radicalism*, 133–42; Johanningsmeier, *Forging American Communism*, 192–93, 202–7; Montgomery, *Fall of the House of Labor*, 431–33.

22. Frank, *Purchasing Power*, 178–90; Barrett, *Tragedy of American Radicalism*, 136–38.

23. Illinois State Federation of Labor Proceedings, Fortieth Annual Convention [1923], 367, Newberry Library, Chicago, Ill.

24. Ibid., 407.

25. It is very difficult to quantify the total numbers of union members expelled as Communists from AFL unions during this period. Some expulsions, such as the dramatic showdown with William Dunne, were highly public affairs. Most occurred more quietly, in local union meetings, and to my knowledge no central data tracking expulsions was maintained by either the AFL or the TUEL. TUEL reports tended to exaggerate both the popularity of the league and the ruthlessness of its suppression; for example, in the 1920s Earl Browder reported that TUEL "followers can be estimated at four to five hundred thousand," or about 15 percent of AFL membership, which surely overestimated its support dramatically. Browder did not enumerate expulsions, merely stating that "today there are expelled militants battling for re-admission to the unions in almost every industry, particularly among the miners, machinists, railroaders, carpenters, and in the city central bodies." Browder, "The Left-Wing in the American Trade Unions, 1921–1925," n.d., box 38, folder 2, Daniel Bell Research Files, Tamiment Library, New York University.

26. Telegram from O. E. Carruth to Ralph Easley, October 4, 1923; telegram from R. Montgomery to Chester M. Wright, October 5, 1923, correspondence files, National Civic Federation Papers, New York Public Library, New York, N.Y. (hereafter NCF Papers).

27. *New York Times*, October 9, 1923; *Los Angeles Times*, October 9, 1923.

28. Montgomery, *Fall of the House of Labor*, 434; "The A.F. of L. and the Future," *New Republic*, October 19, 1923, 95–96.

29. Saposs, *Left-Wing Unionism*, 56. On the expulsion campaign, see Taft, *AFL in the Time of Gompers*, 455–60, Perlman and Taft, *History of Labor*, 541–61; Montgomery, *Fall of the House of Labor*, 427–34; Frank, *Purchasing Power*, 163–90.

30. Perlman and Taft, *History of Labor*, 558. On this point, see also the *New Republic*: "To the onlooker, it is not hard to regard Mr. Foster and these leaders of the opposition as fellow conspirators who connive at keeping Mr. Gompers and his machine in power." *New Republic*, October 17, 1923, 196.

31. On the Chicago federation's leadership in this campaign, see especially McKillen, *Chicago Labor*, 192–213.

32. Ernest, *William Z. Foster*, 10–11.

33. This incident is recounted at length in Draper, *American Communism and Soviet Russia*, 77–126; other useful treatments include McKillen, *Chicago Labor*, 192–213; Barrett, *Tragedy of American Radicalism*, 135–47; Palmer, *James P. Cannon*, 177–88.

34. Nathan A. Fine to John Fitzpatrick, January 3, 1924, accession number 1997.46, folder 6, John Fitzpatrick Papers, Chicago Historical Society.

35. "Reflections and Observations as a Matter of Record, by J. H. Walker," box 28, folder "1928," Victor Olander Papers, Chicago Historical Society.

36. *American Federationist*, November 1923, 938.

37. On Hillman and the ACWA, see Fraser, *Labor Will Rule* 178–97; Barrett, *Tragedy of American Radicalism*, 126–28.

38. Parmet, *The Master of Seventh Avenue*, 20–37.

39. On the 1926 strike, see ibid., 38–53; Perlman and Taft, *History of Labor*, 546–53; Barrett, *Tragedy of American Radicalism*, 152–53.

40. On Baldwin, see Cottrell, *Roger Nash Baldwin*; and Kutulas, *The American Civil Liberties Union.*

41. *New York Times*, September 14, 1931; Cottrell, *Roger Nash Baldwin*, 143.

42. William Green to A. B. Bielaski, October 21, 1915, in Investigative Case Files of the Bureau of Investigation, 1908–1922, Old German Files, National Archives, Washington, D.C., #8000–174.

43. On Baldwin and the CP in the 1920s, see Cottrell, *Roger Nash Baldwin*, 128–48.

44. Alex Gumberg to William Borah, quoted in Saul, *Friends or Foes*, 42. Boris Bakhmeteff had been the Russian ambassador to the United States under the czar; Boris Brazol (or Brasol) was a monarchist Russian émigré. On Harding's sympathy to prorecognition arguments, see Murray, *Harding Era*, 351–54.

45. *Proceedings of the Forty-Third Annual Convention of the American Federation of Labor* (1923), 300.

46. Chester M. Wright to Ralph Easley, May 6, 1922, NCF Papers.

47. House Special Committee to Investigate Communist Activities, *Investigation of Communist Propaganda*, vol. 2, pt. 3, 6–7.

48. Gompers to Borah et al., January 29, 1924, quoted in Saul, *Friends or Foes*, 32.

49. Wright to Easley, April 25, 1924, NCF Papers.

50. Senate Select Committee on the Investigation of the Attorney General, *Investigation of Hon. Harry M. Daugherty*, 2273–79.

51. *Washington Post*, April 24, 1924.

52. Murray, *Harding Era*, 474–79; Giglio, *H. M. Daugherty*, 162–80; Hunt, *Front-Page Detective*, 172–86.

53. Cottrell, *Roger Nash Baldwin*, 138.

54. W. Jett Lauck to Roger Baldwin, February 13, 1924, *ACLU Records*.

55. Lauck to Baldwin, April 12, 1924, ibid.

56. Memo, n.d., ibid.

57. Lauck to Baldwin, April 12, 1924, ibid.

58. ACLU to the Senate Appropriations Committee, May 8, 1924, ibid. This letter was republished as part of the ACLU pamphlet "The Nation-wide Spy System Centering in the Department of Justice," issued in May 1924.

59. Lauck to Baldwin, date obscured, *ACLU Records*.

60. "Memorandum on the interview with the Attorney-General and the John W. Hoover [sic], acting head of the Bureau of Investigation (August 4)," *ACLU Records*.

61. Cottrell, *Roger Nash Baldwin*, 141–42.

CHAPTER SEVEN

1. Ralph M. Easley to J. Edgar Hoover, April 29, 1927; J. Edgar Hoover to Ralph M. Easley, May 3, 1927, National Civic Federation Papers, New York Public Library, New York, N.Y. (hereafter NCF Papers).

2. Ralph Easley to Hugh Frayne, May 20, 1925, Series X, NCF Papers.

3. Athan Theoharis has made this argument in a number of books and articles, including Theoharis and Cox, *The Boss*; Theoharis, Poveda, Rosenfeld, and Powers, *The FBI*; and his recent essay in Van Minnen and Hilton, *Political Repression in U.S. History*. Schmidt, *Red Scare*, 326. Powers agreed with Schmidt in his biography of J. Edgar Hoover: Powers, *Secrecy and Power*, 147; see also Walker, "The Boss as Bureaucrat."

4. On early Communist organizing among African Americans, see Johanningsmeier, "The Trade Union Unity League"; Kelley, *Hammer and Hoe*; Gilmore, *Defying Dixie*.

5. M. J. Heale writes that "in a sense the antiradical campaigns that had been launched in the 1870s and 1880s were finally consummated in the early 1920s, when the last barriers to a possible workers' insurrection were erected. The federal government assumed responsibility for protecting the country from an alien invasion; the state governments guarded against internal disruption." Heale, *American Anticommunism*, 88. See also Fox, "What the Spiders Did."

6. Powers, *Secrecy and Power*, 144–78. See also Jeffreys-Jones, *The FBI: A History*, 81–100, 120–37; Potter, *War on Crime*.

7. Bernstein, *The Lean Years*, 171.

8. Selig Perlman, *Theory of the Labor Movement*, 202, 212.

9. In 1926 Green replied to a gossipy letter from Easley with the reassurance that "I appreciate very much the letter you sent me and the enclosures contained therein. All the printed matter such as you sent me, and communications dealing with Communistic activities, are and will be highly acceptable." William Green to Ralph Easley, September 9, 1926, NCF Papers.

10. Marguerite Green, "The National Civic Federation," 461–70; Taft, *AFL in the Time of Gompers*, 231. In 1926, the Brotherhood of Locomotive Engineers published a denunciation of Easley that was widely reprinted in the labor press: "A Fake 'Friend of Labor' Exposed," *Locomotive Engineers Journal*, June 1926, 408. Matthew Woll awaits his biographer.

11. John P. Frey to W. A. Appleton, June 30, 1919, container 1, folder 3, Papers of John P. Frey, Library of Congress, Washington, D.C.; *American National Biography*, s.v. "Frey, John P."; Reminiscences of John Frey, 1955, Columbia Center for Oral History, New York, N.Y. For Frey's background, see Mortimer's dissertation, "John Philip Frey," (although the dissertation follows Frey only through the late 1920s).

12. John P. Frey, "Communism," box 29, folder 12, Papers of John P. Frey.

13. Robert W. Cherny found similar connections among union leaders and anticommunist activists developing on the West Coast in the early 1930s; Harper Knowles of the American Legion and police red squads in Los Angeles and Portland were frequent interlocutors. Cherny, "Anticommunist Networks and Labor: The Pacific Coast in the 1930s," in Stromquist, *Labor's Cold War*, 17–48.

14. V. R. Tompkins to Martin Dies, February 15, 1954, box 136, file 6, Martin Dies Papers, Sam Houston Regional Library, Liberty, Tex.; Frey, "Communism," box 29, folder 12, Papers of John P. Frey. Tompkins's reports can be found in Frey's papers, and copies turn up in other archival collections as well; Tompkins's reports are interspersed throughout the

1936 and 1937 papers of AFL president William Green and in the papers of labor historian Philip Taft, held by Cornell University's Kheel Center for Labor-Management Documentation and Archives. By the mid-1930s, Tompkins was helping the New York State dairy industry fight Communist efforts to organize dairy farmers; see Dyson, *Red Harvest*, 177–80.

15. Cochran, *Labor and Communism*, 31.

16. Johanningsmeier, "The Trade Union Unity League," 161.

17. On Communist organizing for black liberation, see Gilmore, *Defying Dixie*. The literature on black workers and the mainstream labor movement is large; see Bruce Nelson, *Divided We Stand*; and Zieger, *For Jobs and Freedom*. It should be noted that until the late 1920s the CPUSA devoted little sustained attention to black liberation in its labor organizing or party organizing. There is little evidence to suggest that fear of black insurgency fueled labor anticommunism in the 1920s or early 1930s.

18. On the delegation, see Larson, "Opposition to AFL Foreign Policy." On American fascination with the Soviet Union, see Filene, *Americans and the Soviet Experiment*, 98–99; Scott, *Seeing Like a State*, 196–99.

19. *Questions and Answers to American Trade Unionists*, 43, 57.

20. *New York Times*, October 24, 1927. For an account of the trip, see Axtell, "Russia, and Her Foreign Relations."

21. Boehm, *Minutes of the Executive Council of the American Federation of Labor* (microfilm), 1927.

22. On Walsh, see McNamara, *A Catholic Cold War*; the quote on the AFL can be found on page 92. On early American Catholic anticommunism, see Powers, *Not Without Honor*, 51–57; Rosswurm and Freeman, "The Education of an Anti-Communist"; Rosswurm, *The FBI and the Catholic Church*, 133–80, 226–74.

23. On Collins, see Powers, *Not Without Honor*.

24. On early American Jewish socialism and Communism, see especially Michels, *Fire in Their Hearts*; see also Laslett, *Labor and the Left*, 98–144.

25. J. B. S. Hardman, "The Price of 'Moscow Gold,'" *New Republic*, September 10, 1930, 95.

26. Michels, *Fire in Their Hearts*, 230.

27. Hardman, "Communist Factions and Leadership," *New Republic*, September 17, 1930, 122.

28. Fraser, *Labor Will Rule*, 197.

29. On the recognition question, see Soyer, "Back to the Future."

30. House Special Committee to Investigate Communist Activities, *Investigation of Communist Propaganda*, 1:77.

31. Anonymous to John Frey, November 12, 1936, box 5, folder 97, Papers of John P. Frey.

32. John Frey to W. A. Appleton, May 20, 1919, Papers of John P. Frey.

33. On Easley's work during World War I, see Series X, NCF Papers; on Easley and the Nazis, see Goodall, "Diverging Paths."

34. Schrecker, *Many Are the Crimes*, 63–64. Schrecker makes the same point about anticommunists' research, calling Walter Steele a "pack rat" who "collected names from left-wing publications and the letterhead of front groups"; ibid, 43.

35. Powers, *Not Without Honor*, 129.

36. Harvard College, *Harvard College Class of 1897, Fourth Report* (1912), 438; Harvard College, *Harvard College Class of 1897, Twenty-fifth Anniversary Report* (1922), 604.

37. For a general discussion of anticommunist activists in this era, see also Fischer, "Founders of American Anti-communism."

38. Dilling, *The Red Network*, 17.

39. Hapgood, *Professional Patriots*. On reactionary movements in the 1920s, see Murphy, "Sources and Nature of Intolerance."

40. Anders Lewis's dissertation on the AFL's anticommunism likewise emphasizes the rational bases of the federation's anticommunism animus, but somewhat distorts the AFL's stance on civil liberties and downplays incidents of scurrilous red-baiting; see Lewis, "Labor's Cold War."

41. Eagleton, *Ideology*, 58, 119–21; Gramsci, *Further Selections from the Prison Notebooks*, 290–300; see also Patnaik, "Gramsci's Concept of Common Sense."

42. John M. Frey to Ralph M. Easley, June 28, 1923, NCF Papers.

43. Archibald E. Stevenson to Ralph M. Easley, April 30, 1927, box 437, folder 4, NCF Papers.

44. Hoover to Easley, May 3, 1927, NCF Papers. Richard Gid Powers describes this campaign, and the Fish Committee hearings, without fully connecting the two; *Secrecy and Power*, 166–67.

45. William Green to Ralph M. Easley, May 5, 1927, NCF Papers.

46. Louis Marshall to Ralph M. Easley, May 2, 1927, box 437, folder 4, NCF Papers.

47. Richard Gid Powers describes the Amtorg incident in *Not Without Honor*, 82–90. Means went on to even greater feats of criminality. Means posed as a go-between for the kidnappers of the Lindbergh baby, fleecing the Lindberghs of $100,000 in ransom payments. Means was convicted of grand larceny and died in Leavenworth. Fisher, *The Lindbergh Case*. See also Alex Goodall's detailed discussion of Easley's relationship with Fish in his dissertation, "Aspects of the Emergence of American Anticommunism," 65–122.

48. Leab, "'United We Eat,'" 305–7.

49. *New York Times*, March 7, 1930.

50. House Committee on Rules, *Investigation into the Activities of Communists in the United States*, 1:2.

51. House Special Committee to Investigate Communist Activities in the United States, *Investigation of Communist Propaganda*, pt. 3, 2:4.

52. *New York Times*, July 14, 1930.

53. House Special Committee to Investigate Communist Activities in the United States, *Investigation of Communist Propaganda*, pt. 2, 35–36.

54. Ibid., 46. The picture of J. Edgar Hoover that emerges from this debate is considerably at odds with the prevailing historiographical view that casts him as a perpetually power-mad bureaucrat obsessed with squelching radicalism and dissent. As the next chapters show, Hoover frequently fought behind the scenes to preserve the integrity of federal operations. A more nuanced portrait of both Hoover and his BI must take into account the persistent pressure applied by antiradicals such as Easley or demagogues such as Congressman Martin Dies.

55. House Special Committee to Investigate Communist Activities in the United States, *Investigation of Communist Propaganda*, pt. 2, 62. Two years later, Hoover made a similar case to the attorney general, with more explanation, warning that if the BI were to "embark on a policy of investigative activity into conditions which, from a federal standpoint, have not been declared illegal and in connection with which no prosecution might be instituted.

The Department and the Bureau would undoubtedly be subject to charges in the matter of alleged secret and undeniable methods." Hoover to Attorney General William Mitchell, January 2, 1932, quoted in Rafalko, *Counterintelligence Reader*, 159.

56. House Special Committee to Investigate Communist Activities in the United States, *Investigation of Communist Propaganda*, pt. 3, 2:4.

57. Ibid., pt. 1, 1:78.

58. Ibid., pt. 3, 1:250.

59. Ibid., pt. 1, 1:75.

60. Ibid., pt. 4, 3:68; ibid. pt. 3, 4:76.

61. Ibid., pt. 3, 2:43.

62. *New York Times*, December 15, 1931.

63. Fish, "The Menace of Communism," 58.

64. House Special Committee to Investigate Communist Activities in the United States, *Investigation of Communist Propaganda*, pt. 1, 4:409, 407.

CHAPTER EIGHT

1. On Soviet recognition, see Leuchtenburg, *FDR and the New Deal*, 205–7.

2. William Green, *Reports on Communist Propaganda in America*, 10, 30, 1.

3. On the AFL and the 1932 election, see Greenstone, *Labor in American Politics*, 36–40; Bernstein, *The Lean Years*, 508–12. On the coolness between FDR and the AFL, see Leuchtenburg, *FDR and the New Deal*, 108; Dubofsky, *State and Labor in Modern America*, 107–9; Bernstein, *The Turbulent Years*, 8–15; "Reminiscences of John Frey," 274, Columbia Center for Oral History, New York, N.Y. On Perkins's rocky relationship with the AFL, see Downey, *The Woman Behind the New Deal*, 197–202.

4. Plotke, *Building a Democratic Political Order*; Brinkley, *End of Reform*, 48–55.

5. Thomas Eliot, assistant deputy to Frances Perkins, quoted in Bruce E. Kaufman, "The Case for the Company Union," 341. For an example of the contemporary assessments of New Dealers, see Saposs, "American Labor Movement Since the War," 236–54.

6. Reminiscences of Heber Blankenhorn, Columbia Center for Oral History, 311.

7. Sidney Hillman's Amalgamated Clothing Workers was not affiliated to the AFL until 1933, when Hillman applied for membership at the urging of the Mine Workers, who were seeking allies for their industrial union program; Bernstein, *Turbulent Years*, 90–91. On Hillman's role in writing the NIRA and the Wagner Act, and the AFL's exclusion, see Fraser, *Labor Will Rule*, 284–85, 350–52.

8. An early example of this sort of conflict arose in the creation of the Public Works Administration and its accompanying agency, an employment service to recruit and assign workers to public projects, which alarmed construction unions. As Jason Scott Smith writes, "The development that most preoccupied organized labor, [Frances] Perkins reported, was the creation of a government-run employment service. Such a bureaucracy, she declared, 'alarmed' organized labor 'for fear that, in the employment of skilled men, the United States Public Employment Service would supplant the Union headquarters.'" Jason Scott Smith, *Building New Deal Liberalism*, 37.

9. Gordon, *New Deals*, 207; Tomlins, *The State and the Unions*, 107.

10. Tomlins, *The State and the Unions*, 172. See also Clayton Sinyai's formulation: "Under the AFL's principles, a craft union claimed sovereignty over *all* work performed in a given

craft. Its legitimacy was quite independent of what representation workers in a *particular* firm wanted." Sinyai, *Schools of Democracy*, 126.

11. On the development of agency, see O'Brien, *Workers' Paradox*, 39–63.

12. "There was no great enthusiasm for [the Wagner Act] at first on the part of the labor leaders," Frances Perkins later recalled. "Many of them had grave doubts about it." Perkins, Reminiscences of Frances Perkins, book VI, 138, 142, Columbia Center for Oral History.

13. Perlman and Taft, *History of Labor in the United States*, 617–61.

14. On Baldwin's evolving radical affinities, see Cottrell, *Roger Nash Baldwin*, 168–98; and Kutulas, *The American Civil Liberties Union*, 18–32.

15. Kutulas, *The American Civil Liberties Union*, 25–26.

16. Cletus Daniel describes this meeting in *ACLU and the Wagner Act*, 50–52.

17. Senate Committee on Education and Labor, *National Labor Relations Board*, 581, 586.

18. Daniel, *ACLU and the Wagner Act*, 102.

19. Reminiscences of Heber Blankenhorn, Columbia Center for Oral History, 408–9. For party membership numbers, see Klehr, *Heyday of American Communism*, 153, 366. On the CPUSA's organizing among unemployed workers, see Lizabeth Cohen, *Making a New Deal*, 262–67; Klehr, *Heyday of American Communism*, 49–68. On the Popular Front shift, see ibid., 167–206; Barrett, *Tragedy of American Radicalism*, 189–206. For a much broader definition of the Popular Front as a "radical historical bloc" coincident with but not limited to the Communist Party, see Denning, *Cultural Front*, 3–50.

20. Dilling, *The Red Network*, 82; Heale, *American Anticommunism*, 105–13.

21. "Federal Sedition Bills"; Goodall, "Diverging Paths." This episode was the last major initiative of Easley's NCF. The NCF was increasingly marginalized for the remaining years of its existence, unable to attract much attention from anyone inside or outside the labor movement. Easley died in 1939 at the age of eighty-three, and the NCF effectively died with him. For Easley's obituary, see *New York Times*, September 8, 1939.

22. House Special Committee on Un-American Activities, *Investigation of Nazi Propaganda Activities*, 14, 19, 20.

23. Ibid.

24. Roger Baldwin to William Green, Legislative Reference Files, RG 21, AFL Papers, George Meany Archives, Silver Spring, Md.; *New York Times*, April 4, 1935.

25. William Green to Woodruff Randolph, January 4, 1935; and William Green to August Rosqvist, February 14, 1935, both in Legislative Reference Files, RG 21, AFL Papers, George Meany Archives.

26. Heale, *American Anticommunism*, 112.

27. House Committee on Immigration and Nationalization, *To Exclude and Expel Alien Fascists and Communists*, 8.

28. On immigration policy and alien radicals, see Ngai, *Impossible Subjects*, 58–60. Although the Immigration Act of 1920 included anarchists and seditious aliens as categories of aliens who could be deported, it appears that few aliens were deported for radicalism or Communism in the 1930s.

29. Letter from Heber Blankenhorn to Senator Edward Costigan, December 4, 1935, series I, box 1, folder 12, Heber Blankenhorn Papers, Wayne State University, Walter P. Reuther Library, Detroit, Mich. On the La Follette Committee, see Auerbach, *Labor and Liberty*.

30. On the founding of the CIO, see Zieger, *The CIO*, 22–29; Bernstein, *Turbulent Years*, 386–98.

31. These practices were common in what Colin Gordon calls "regulatory unionism"; see Gordon, *New Deals*. On AFL organizing strategy in 1930s Los Angeles, see Milkman, *L.A. Story*, 40–60.

32. On AFL gains in the 1930s, and the blurring of craft vs. industrial forms, see Tomlins, "AFL Unions in the 1930s."

33. On the split, see especially Kazin, *Populist Persuasion*, 136–37.

34. For New York subway motormen, see Freeman, *In Transit*, 92–93; for West Coast longshoremen, see Nelson, *Workers on the Waterfront*; for Wisconsin foundry workers, see Stephen Meyer, *Stalin over Wisconsin*, 52–64. The best overview of the disputes among AFL and CIO unions can be found in Galenson, *CIO Challenge to the AFL*.

35. Reminiscences of John Edelman, Columbia Center for Oral History, 188.

36. Bernstein, *Turbulent Years*, 544.

37. Galenson, *CIO Challenge to the AFL*, 249. During a CIO sit-down strike at a St. Louis factory, a local IBEW official consulted with the company on strikebreaking strategy; see Feurer, *Radical Unionism in the Midwest*, 60.

38. Galenson, *CIO Challenge to the AFL*, 314.

39. *UMW Journal*, August 1, 1936.

40. Dubofsky, *State and Labor in Modern America*, 151.

41. Gross, *Making National Labor Relations Board*, 237.

42. Quoted in Tomlins, *State and the Unions*, 171.

43. *American Federationist*, August 1938, 802; ibid., November 1937, 1188.

44. Boehm, *Minutes of the Executive Council of the American Federation of Labor* (microfilm), February 1937.

45. Michael Tighe to William Green, November 13, 1932, American Federation of Labor, Papers on Communism, Folder "Confidential Report on Communists . . . ," State Historical Society of Wisconsin, Madison.

46. Galenson, *CIO Challenge to the AFL*, 127; Lichtenstein, *Most Dangerous Man in Detroit*, 54–55.

47. American Federation of Labor, Papers on Communism, Folder "Confidential Report on Communists . . . ," State Historical Society of Wisconsin, Madison.

48. On the CPUSA's shift to Popular Front strategies, see Cherny, "Prelude to the Popular Front"; and Cherny, "The Communist Party in California"; for a different take on the timing of that shift, see Klehr, *Heyday of American Communism*, 167–86. On Foster's illness, see Barrett, *Tragedy of American Radicalism*, 183–88.

49. Storch, "Shades of Red," 142–43, for disguise; Levenstein, *Communism, Anticommunism, and the CIO*, 43–44, 143–55. See also Lizabeth Cohen, *Making a New Deal*, 309–12.

50. Samuel Darcy oral history, Oral History of the American Left, Tamiment Library, pt. 2, 4–5.

51. "Confidential Report on Communists and Communist activities within the trade union movement, submitted to Pres Green Feb 11 1935," American Federation of Labor Records, Papers on Communism, State Historical Society of Wisconsin, Madison.

52. *Proceedings of the Fifty-Fifth Annual Convention of the American Federation of Labor* [1935], 783. Labor reporter Louis Stark had reported that Lewis would oppose the Communist ban; *New York Times*, October 16, 1935. Such a move would have marked Lewis's first public support—or cessation of hostility toward—the CP.

53. "Report of Situation in U.S.A. and Work of Party," reprinted in Klehr, Haynes, and Anderson, *The Soviet World of American Communism*, 58–68.

54. Reminiscences of John Edelman, Columbia Center for Oral History, 176–77.

55. On Lewis's worldview, see Dubofsky and Van Tine, *John L. Lewis*, 211–16.

56. Boehm, *Minutes of the Executive Council of the American Federation of Labor* (microfilm), February 10, 1937.

57. *New York Times*, August 1, 1937.

58. I have been unable to discover who the State Department source might be.

59. As discussed earlier, Tompkins's reports circulated among various labor leaders, including William Green, and copies can also be seen in box 4, folder "Communist Party Minutes," and box 10, folder "Steel – Communists, Negroes, Handbills, misc.," Philip Taft Papers, Kheel Archives, Ithaca, N.Y."

60. See box 5, folders 72, 74, 83, and 85, Papers of John P. Frey, Library of Congress, Washington, D.C., for copies of the reports.

61. Earl Reeves to William Green, April 9, 1934; Green to Reeves, April 16, 1934, American Federation of Labor Records, Papers on Communism, State Historical Society of Wisconsin, Madison.

62. Senate Committee on Commerce and Committee on Education and Labor, *Hearings on a Bill to Amend the Merchant Marine Act of 1936*, pt. 11, 1063–79.

63. On the conflict within the longshoremen's union, see Bruce Nelson, *Workers on the Waterfront*; and Kimeldorf, *Reds or Rackets?*

64. Galenson, *CIO Challenge to the AFL*, 441–42; *New York Times*, July 29, 1938; box 5, folder 70, Papers of John P. Frey.

65. Thomas Ramsey to John Frey, June 5, 1937, box 5, folder 104, Papers of John P. Frey.

66. Fred Starr to John Frey, October 13, 1935, box 5, folder 101, Papers of John P. Frey.

67. Galenson, *CIO Challenge to the AFL*, 497–98; Kimeldorf, *Battling for American Labor*, 146–48. The TWU and the radical machinists abandoned the AFL for the CIO within the year.

68. Box 5, folder 104, Papers of John P. Frey. The association wrote Frey at the behest of the president of the AFL's Boot and Shoe Workers' Union.

69. *New York Times*, April 21, 1938; for the American Legion, see ibid., September 23, 1937.

70. *Los Angeles Times*, September 15, 1937.

71. Statement of the General Executive Board of the Wisconsin State Federation of Labor, in box 5, folder 82, Papers of John P. Frey.

72. Anthony Uccello to *New Republic*, October 11, 1937, in box 5, folder 70, Papers of John P. Frey.

73. *Los Angeles Times*, August 8, 1938; ibid., August 9, 1938.

74. On Catholic anticommunism in the 1930s, see Powers, *Not Without Honor*, 108–14, 132–38; and Schrecker, *Many Are the Crimes*, 72–75. On the Association of Catholic Trade Unionists, see Seaton, *Catholics and Radicals*; Rosswurm, "The Catholic Church and the Left-Led Unions," in Rosswurm, *The CIO's Left-Led Unions*; and Doody, "Anticommunism in America."

75. Seaton, *Catholics and Radicals*, 53–95. On ACTU in the Transport Workers Union, see Freeman, *In Transit*, 148–51; in the UAW, see Lichtenstein, *Most Dangerous Man in Detroit*, 187–89 and 209–10.

76. *New York Times*, May 9, 1938.

77. Patterson, *Congressional Conservatism and the New Deal*, 135–42, 180–83.

78. Quoted in Gross, *Making National Labor Relations Board*, 250.

79. Gross, *Reshaping National Labor Relations Board*, 95. In early 1936, John L. Lewis fretted about the potential for just such an alliance. He told CP leader Clarence Hathaway that "the reactionaries of the Republican Party, the Liberty League, etc., would inevitably try to exploit the whole division in the AFL to line up the reactionaries of the Executive Council behind the Landon-Liberty League campaign, by attempting to show that a victory for Roosevelt would be a victory for the Lewis group." Klehr, Haynes, and Anderson, *Soviet World of American Communism*, 58–68.

80. Brinkley, *End of Reform*, 137–46; Leuchtenburg, *FDR and the New Deal*, 252–74.

81. See Dubofsky, *State and Labor in Modern America*, 146–67, for an overview of the development of this alliance and its activities in Congress.

82. That Roosevelt could be surprised, given the AFL's protests of most of his earlier proposals, perhaps indicates the degree of their estrangement.

83. On the FLSA fight, see Samuel, "Troubled Passage," 32–37; and O'Brien, "'Sweat Shop of the Whole Nation.'" See also Frey's letter to W. A. Appleton connecting the AFL's opposition to the FLSA to its fight with the CIO; Frey to W. A. Appleton, September 25, 1937. My treatment of the backlash against the New Deal focuses on dynamics within organized labor. The fight over the FLSA shows that the New Deal's challenge to white supremacy in the South helped decisively shift southern Democrats against redistributive legislation and into coalition with Republicans. The AFL had a marginal presence in the South, but a number of its unions denied membership to African Americans and used their shop-floor power to enforce white supremacy at work. Neither the FLSA nor the NLRA disturbed these internal union dynamics, and labor conservatives' position on the FLSA and NLRA derived primarily from their politics of union (and AFL) preeminence. Nevertheless, the CIO and the CPUSA's efforts toward racial equality clearly underlay the anger of some AFL leaders. On the FLSA and white supremacy in Congress, see Farhang and Katznelson, "The Southern Imposition." For examples of unions maintaining and even strengthening racial bars under the Wagner Act regime, see Frymer, *Black and Blue*, 27–37.

84. *New York Times*, July 12, 1938.

85. Sanders, *Roots of Reform*, 400–402.

86. *Baltimore Sun*, October 3, 1937 (ellipses in original).

87. Canny John L. Lewis somehow obtained the minutes of meetings among this group and later brandished them before Congress, humiliating the AFL. See Congress of Industrial Organizations, *Conspiracy Against Labor*, Washington, D.C., March 1940; and *Senate Hearings on Bills to Amend the Wagner Act*, pt. 24, 4740–70.

88. Gross, *Reshaping National Labor Relations Board*, 63–64.

89. Harry Hansen to John Frey, January 26, 1937.

90. *New York Times*, April 21, 1938; ibid., April 3, 1938.

91. Leuchtenburg, *FDR and the New Deal*, 266; McDaniel, "Martin Dies of Un-American Activities," 243; *Washington Post*, June 6, 1938; *Los Angeles Times*, October 23, 1938; *Chicago Daily Tribune*, October 13, 1938.

92. *Los Angeles Times*, July 1, 1938; Weiss, "Maury Maverick and the Liberal Bloc."

93. *Washington Post*, September 1, 1938.

94. Kenneth G. Crawford, "A.F. of L. into G.O.P.," *Nation*, March 11, 1939, 283.

95. Patterson, "New Deal and the States," 76.

96. Plesur, "Republican Congressional Comeback of 1938," 544; see also Joel Seidman,

"Organized Labor in Political Campaigns," *Public Opinion Quarterly*, October 1939, 646–54.

97. Coil, "New Deal Republican," 192–94.

98. Daniel Nelson, "The CIO at Bay." On the 1938 purge, see Dunn, *Roosevelt's Purge*.

99. Plesur, "Republican Congressional Comeback of 1938," 547.

100. On Murphy and the 1938 election, see Wolfinger, "The Strange Career of Frank Murphy."

101. W. C. Hushing, "Memorandum for William Green," March 29, 1937, Legislative Reference Files, RG 21, AFL Papers, George Meany Archives.

102. *Congressional Record*, 75th Cong., 3rd sess., (1938) vol. 83, pt. 7, 7578.

103. Ogden, "The Dies Committee," 45–46; Dies, *Martin Dies' Story*, 60.

104. J. Edgar Hoover, "Memorandum for the Attorney General," June 11, 1938; Martin Dies to J. Edgar Hoover, June 17, 1938, in FBI Files on HUAC, case 61–7582. For Roosevelt's executive order, see Theoharis, *Secret Files of J. Edgar Hoover*, 180–83. In his discussion with Roosevelt, Hoover warned of Communist infiltration of the West Coast Longshoremen, the UMWA, and the Newspaper Guild, as well as the National Labor Relations Board.

105. W. C. Hushing, memorandum, May 31, 1938, Legislative Reference Files, RG 21, AFL Papers, George Meany Archives.

106. *Washington Post*, October 30, 1938.

107. House Special Committee on Un-American Activities, *Investigation of Un-American Propaganda Activities in the United States* [1938], 1:114; Frey to Walter Draper, August 18, 1938, container 7, folder titled "Dies Committee hearings, (1)," Papers of John P. Frey.

108. Brinkley, *The End of Reform*.

109. Lizabeth Cohen, *Making a New Deal*.

110. Thanks to David Montgomery, who coined the phrase "labor's counter-reformation" in a comment on a chapter draft.

CHAPTER NINE

1. FBI case #202600, "Emil Mazey, Casper Hansen . . . ," July 30, 1938, in Naison, *Department of Justice Investigative Files: The Communist Party*.

2. House Special Committee on Un-American Activities, *Investigation of Un-American Propaganda Activities in the United States* [1938], 4:1519, 1515, 1535.

3. *Time*, December 12, 1938.

4. For CP organizing and the culture of militancy at Briggs, see Charles Williams, "Reconsidering CIO Political Culture"; Keeran, *Communist Party and Auto Workers Union*, 77–96; Lichtenstein, *Most Dangerous Man in Detroit*, 186–87.

5. Batvinis, *The Origins of FBI Counterintelligence*, 51.

6. Frey to W. A. Appleton, August 1, 1938, box 1, folder 8, Papers of John P. Frey, Library of Congress, Washington, D.C.

7. House Special Committee on Un-American Activities, *Investigation of Un-American Propaganda Activities in the United States* [1938], 1:114.

8. Ibid., 1:102; United Mine Workers of America, *Attempts by Communists to Seize American Labor Movement*, 1.

9. House Special Committee on Un-American Activities, *Investigation of Un-American Propaganda Activities in the United States* [1938], 1:96.

10. Ibid., 1:97–98. While Frey was careful to check his facts, his information could be

hard to interpret. Frey named Walter Reuther as a Communist, for example, saying that Reuther had "been to Russia several times" and that UAW president Homer Martin had charged Reuther with Communism. Some historians have also argued that CPUSA records indicate that Reuther was a full-fledged member, but Nelson Lichtenstein, Reuther's biographer, finds that "while Reuther worked very closely with the Communists" in the mid-1930s, "he did not actually join the party." Frey incorrectly fingered Reuther, but his error was understandable given the confusion surrounding Reuther's relationship to the CP then and now. See Devinatz, "Reassessing the Historical UAW"; and Lichtenstein, "Reuther the Red?"

11. Freeman, *In Transit*, 57, 137; Quill famously said of the Dies Committee that he "would rather be called a Red by the rats than a rat by the Reds."

12. James Matles to John P. Frey, August 20, 1938; Frey to Matles, August 30, 1938; Matles to Frey, September 1, 1938, box 8, folder 113, Papers of John P. Frey. On Matles's background, see Filippelli and McColloch, *Cold War in the Working Class*, 22–23.

13. Crawford, *The Pressure Boys*, 112. Note however that Ogden disagrees with Crawford's assessment of Dies's motives and thinks that Dies and his fellow congressmen were surprised to hear Frey's evidence.

14. Schickler, *Disjointed Pluralism*, 168–74.

15. Edward F. Sullivan, one of Dies's first staff investigators, was identified by Labor's Non-Partisan League as a labor spy who worked for the Railway Audit and Inspection Company, a notorious firm. Sullivan also had ties with the pro-Nazi German-American Bund. Dies fired Sullivan in late September 1938, and Sullivan turned to John Frey for help, complaining, "I have served the Committee honestly and faithfully and I have not soft pedaled anything. This is my reward. As I have told you personally, I am not a 'labor spy,' Nazi agent, 'convicted thief' nor any of the things which these subversive groups are trying to pin on me." Frey urged Sullivan to come to his AFL office to talk things over. Frey's invitation to an agent of one of the country's most notorious labor spy firms to visit his office at the AFL indicates how polarized relations in the labor movement had become by 1938. For the correspondence between Sullivan and Frey, see container 7, folder "Dies Committee hearings, (1)," letter from Edward F. Sullivan to John P. Frey, September 26, 1938, and John Frey to Edward F. Sullivan, September 30, 1938, Papers of John P. Frey; *Washington Post*, August 26, 1938; *Daily Worker*, September 19, 1938; see also D. A. Saunders, "The Dies Committee: First Phase," *Public Opinion Quarterly* 3, no. 2 (April 1939), 229–30.

16. Report, October 19, 1938, Member and Staff Correspondence, Chester Howe, box 6, Dies Committee Papers, National Archives, Washington, D.C.

17. The Dies' Committee received numerous letters from unionists who suspected their leaders of Communist sympathies, such as a New York plumbers' union local whose members had been "unable to eliminate [Communist officers] in a regular election for five years." Clark W. Perry to J. Parnell Thomas, September 18, 1940, box 1, 1940 Correspondence File, Dies Committee Papers, National Archives, Washington, D.C.

18. House Special Committee on Un-American Activities, *Investigation of Un-American Propaganda Activities in the United States* [1938], 3:2324. Harvey Levenstein makes a similar point: "Some of the dissidents in Communist-controlled unions grasped at the Dies evidence like drowning men grabbing for a life raft," he writes; Levenstein, *Communism, Anticommunism, and the CIO*, 134.

19. House Special Committee on Un-American Activities, *Investigation of Un-American Propaganda Activities in the United States* [1938], 3:2211–12.

20. Ibid., vol. 4:2668.

21. Ibid., vol. 2:1047.

22. Ibid., 1070.

23. Ibid., 1063.

24. Ibid., vol. 4:2920.

25. Ibid., vol. 2, 1558.

26. Seaton, *Catholics and Radicals*, 144–48; see also Lichtenstein, *Most Dangerous Man in Detroit*, 187–89.

27. For example, William Harmon of the TWU mentioned ACTU in his testimony. Freeman argues that through 1939 at least, ACTU supported the left leadership in the TWU and had little presence among TWU members; Freeman, *In Transit*, 147–48.

28. Schrecker, *Many Are the Crimes*, 131.

29. *Proceedings of the Fifty-ninth Annual Convention of the American Federation of Labor* [1939], 410–11. For the AFL's public statements of support and letters to Congress, see "Memorandum re Continuation of the Investigation of Un-American Subversive Activities of the House Committee," February 3, 1939, Legislative Reference Files, box 52, folder 18; William Green to Senators and Representatives, January 20, 1940, Legislative Reference Files, box 52, folder 20; see also William Green to Jerry Voorhis, November 8, 1939, Legislative Reference Files, box 52, folder 19, all in American Federation of Labor Papers, George Meany Archives, Silver Spring, Md.

30. "Resolution Condemning the Dies Committee," Legislative Reference Files, RG 21, AFL Papers, George Meany Archives.

31. Container 7, folder titled "Dies Committee hearings, (1)," Papers of John P. Frey.

32. Quoted in Arnesen, "'No Graver Danger,'" 15. On Randolph's relations with the Communist Party, see ibid.; Arnesen, *Brotherhoods of Color*, 111–15; Bates, *Pullman Porters*, 38, 137.

33. A. Philip Randolph to William Green, May 10, 1940, Legislative Reference Files, RG 21, AFL Papers, George Meany Archives.

34. See Zieger, *The CIO*, 254; Klehr, *Heyday of American Communism*, 223–51; Cochran, *Labor and Communism*, 127–55.

35. On the warfare inside the UAW, see Lichtenstein, *Most Dangerous Man in Detroit*, 104–32; Keeran, *Communist Party and Auto Workers Union*.

36. On Lovestone, see Morgan, *A Covert Life*.

37. On Dubinsky, see Parmet, *Master of Seventh Avenue*, 153–77.

38. On political struggles in the maritime unions, see Bruce Nelson, *Workers on the Waterfront*.

39. Fraser, *Labor Will Rule*, 445; Isserman, *Which Side Were You On?* 75.

40. See Fraser, *Labor Will Rule*, 434–35, 444–46.

41. Levenstein, *Communism, Anticommunism, and the CIO*, 94.

42. Lichtenstein, *Most Dangerous Man in Detroit*, 192.

43. *New York Times*, February 1, 1941; ibid., January 31, 1941; Isserman, *Which Side Were You On?* 76–79.

44. Batvinis, *Origins of FBI Counterintelligence*; Powers, *Secrecy and Power*, 228–45.

45. Batvinis, *Origins of FBI Counterintelligence*, 53–68.

46. Powers, *Secrecy and Power*, 232–33. Thanks to Beverly Gage for her help on this point.

47. On this dynamic, see O'Reilly, *Hoover and the Un-Americans*, 67–74; for examples of

the friction between the Dies Committee and the FBI, see John Edgar Hoover, "Memorandum," December 9, 1940, box 89, folder 11, Papers of Robert H. Jackson, Library of Congress, Washington, D.C.

48. Sibley, *Red Spies in America*, 78–79.

49. For a survey of the current state of historical knowledge on Soviet espionage in the United States, see Haynes, Klehr, and Vassiliev, *Spies*; see also Ryan, "Socialist Triumph as a Family Value." On the Hiss case, see Jacoby, *Alger Hiss*. Although some historians continue to dispute Hiss's guilt, there is little debate over the established fact that the Soviet Union had an informant inside the State Department in a position like Hiss's, with personal characteristics and a social background similar to his. Some historians point to Wilder Foote, a different candidate within a small pool of State Department officials, as a better match for the State mole's code name in KGB documents. I do not find these arguments convincing, but in any case, for the purpose of understanding the nature of Soviet espionage in America, the question of Hiss's guilt or innocence is unimportant. A senior State Department official passed along to the KGB intelligence from the Yalta Conference in 1945; whether that person was Alger Hiss or Wilder Foote or someone else is ultimately less significant than the fact that such a person existed.

50. We have little research on FAECT, and more is certainly warranted. On FAECT and espionage, see Sibley, *Red Spies in America*, 144–48; Schrecker, *Many Are the Crimes*, 167–68.

51. Schrecker, *Many Are the Crimes*, 99.

52. Theoharis, *Chasing Spies*, 57.

53. House Special Committee on Un-American Activities, *Investigation of Un-American Propaganda Activities in the United States* [1939–41], 7:4718–19.

54. Klehr, *Heyday of American Communism*, 404–5; yet see Rosswurm, "Wondrous Tale of an FBI Bug." Rosswurm reveals that CIO lawyer Lee Pressman coordinated with Communist leader Roy Hudson to rewrite convention resolutions at the CIO's 1943 convention. While disclosing the wording of union convention resolutions is hardly comparable to leaking atomic secrets, the episode shows that in this case, the CPUSA exerted much tighter discipline over its CIO members than is commonly believed.

55. Deutscher, *The Prophet Outcast*, 482; Ogden, *The Dies Committee*, 172.

56. Cottrell, *Roger Nash Baldwin*, 259–61; Kutulas, *ACLU and the Making of Modern Liberalism*, 37–39.

CHAPTER TEN

1. The definitive account of the Smith amendments is Gross, *Reshaping National Labor Relations Board*, 151–225; for a crisper account, see Dubofsky, *State and Labor in Modern America*, 152–59.

2. On internal opposition within the AFL, see the testimony in Senate Committee on Education and Labor, *National Labor Relations Act and Proposed Amendments*, 4306–25.

3. Gross, *Reshaping National Labor Relations Board*; Dubofsky, *State and Labor in Modern America*, 202.

4. For an account of the Chambers-Berle meeting, see Haynes and Klehr, *Venona*, 90–94; see also Tanenhaus, *Whittaker Chambers*, 160–70.

5. John Frey to Metal Trades Department, July 14, 1937, box 5, folder 98, Papers of John P. Frey, Library of Congress, Washington, D.C.

6. Senate Committee on Education and Labor, *National Labor Relations Act and Proposed Amendments*, 4306–25.

7. *Fortune*, February 1939, 97.

8. Latham, *Communist Controversy in Washington*, 128–30; Gross, *Reshaping National Labor Relations Board*, 147–48.

9. On NLRB Communists, see Latham, *Communist Controversy in Washington*, 124–50; Hayes and Klehr, *Venona*, 116–25; Gross, *Reshaping National Labor Relations Board*, 131–50.

10. Gross, *Reshaping National Labor Relations Board*, 134.

11. Ibid., 132.

12. *New York Times*, November 8, 1938.

13. Latham, *Communist Controversy in Washington*, 134. It is not clear why the Smith Committee did not discover other NLRB Communists. In his biography of Whittaker Chambers, Sam Tanenhaus remarks that "everyone knew" that people such as Nathan Witt were Communists (Tanenhaus, *Whittaker Chambers*, 162.) Two people, John Frey and Dies Committee staffer J. B. Matthews, appear to be the source for the Communist charges against NLRB members. Frey had been suspicious of Edwin Smith since 1937, when he discovered the dinner-party photograph of Smith with the Russian ambassador. Matthews supplied the information about Saposs. Frey seems not to have known about the other NLRB Communists, possibly because they were young lawyers with little prior connection to labor circles.

14. Gross, *Reshaping National Labor Relations Board*, 205.

15. Ibid., 221; *Time*, April 1, 1940.

16. On the Hatch Act, see Jason Scott Smith, *Building New Deal Liberalism*, 161–88; Porter, "Senator Carl Hatch."

17. *Proceedings of the Fifty-Fourth Annual Convention of the American Federation of Labor* [1939], 492.

18. Schrecker, *Many Are the Crimes*, 110.

19. "Recent Anti-Alien Legislative Proposals."

20. Senate Committee on Immigration, *Deportation of Aliens*, 13. This was a shift from the federation's 1935 position, when it supported expulsions of alien radicals, as described in Chapter 8. The 1935 position is an outlier in the AFL's usual stance during these years, and Scharrenberg's 1940 testimony is closer to the norm.

21. Ibid., 14.

22. House Committee on the Judiciary, *Crime to Promote the Overthrow of Government*, 40.

23. Schrecker, *Many Are the Crimes*, 97.

24. *New York Herald Tribune*, June 27, 1940.

25. *Los Angeles Times*, June 30, 1940.

26. As ever, though, the AFL was an inconstant friend. In 1942 the federation backed his opponent for the nomination, machinist E. C. Davison, and in 1943 considered backing a Republican candidate against Smith in the next election. William Green to T. T. Yeager, May 20, 1942, and William Green to Harrie Byrd Conlin, June 1, 1943, Legislative Reference Files, RG 21, American Federation of Labor Papers, George Meany Archives, Silver Spring, Md.

27. Thanks to Joe McCartin and Donna Haverty-Stacke for clarifying my thinking on this point.

28. American Civil Liberties Union, *Liberty's National Emergency*, June 1941.

29. Quoted in Cottrell, *Roger Nash Baldwin*, 68.

30. Quoted in Kutulas, *ACLU and the Making of Modern Liberalism*, 69.

31. Ibid., 88.

32. Lichtenstein, *Most Dangerous Man in Detroit*, 183.

33. Galenson, *CIO Challenge to the AFL*, 506–8. On the Boeing episode, see the meticulous dissertation by John McCann, "Labor and the Making of the Postwar Order at the Boeing Company."

34. Miner, "Battle at Boeing."

35. For a brief but bowdlerized account of the Boeing situation, see Mark Perlman, *The Machinists*, 109–10, 284–85. The IAM was correct to worry: the UAW was scheming to organize among Boeing workers, and Communist organizer Wyndham Mortimer was making inquiries; see Olszowka, "UAW and the Struggle to Organize Aircraft," 304; Wyndham Mortimer, "Reflections of a Labor Organizer," 1967, 159–63, Young Research Library, UCLA Center for Oral History, Los Angeles, Calif.

36. Frey to Major W. H. Sadler, War Department, July 29, 1940, box 4, folder 63, Papers of John P. Frey. On the War Department's monitoring of the Boeing situation, see Eiler, *Mobilizing America*, 164–69; see also Fairchild and Grossman, *The Army and Industrial Manpower*, 58–62.

37. John Frey to Harvey N. Brown, July 29, 1940, box 3, folder 13, Papers of John P. Frey.

38. The only mention of the campaign came from the immigration inspector, who warned that "there is a move on foot [*sic*] by the Party to eventually get as many negroes as possible into the Boeing plant." J. H. Zumwalt to John Frey, July 30, 1940, box 3, folder 13, Papers of John P. Frey.

39. Miner, "Battle at Boeing," n.p.

40. "Minutes of the Meeting of the Executive Council, April 16 to 23, 1941, Washington, D.C., and April 29 to May 18, 1941, Seattle, Washington," International Association of Machinists, Southern Labor Archives, Georgia State University Library, Atlanta, Ga. Wyndham Mortimer arrived in Seattle in March to help the Boeing workers, "who were in revolt against the IAM." In his memoir, Mortimer wrote that he filed a petition for an election to certify the UAW, but the NLRB would not process it; Dave Beck and the Teamsters dominated local politics, in his telling, and mobilized the NLRB and the district attorney to block the UAW. Having left North American Aviation negotiations for Seattle, Mortimer returned to Los Angeles after a month. Wyndham Mortimer, *Organize!* 176–78.

41. News release, Department of Justice, November 24, 1940, box 89, folder 11, Papers of Robert H. Jackson, Library of Congress, Washington, D.C.

42. For the NLRB proceedings, see "In the matter of North American Aviation, Inc and United Automobile Workers of America Local 228 CIO," *Decisions and Orders of the NRLB*, 13:1134–399; ibid., 14:222–26. On North American Aviation, see Lichtenstein, *Labor's War at Home*, 57–63. On UAW organizing in the aircraft industry, see Olszowka, "The UAW and the Struggle to Organize Aircraft, 1937–1942."

43. House Special Committee on Un-American Activities, *Investigation of Un-American Propaganda Activities in the United States* [1939–41], 5:2252, 2248.

44. Dies Committee investigators initially attributed the rumors to Harry Bridges and other California Communists. See George Hurley and James Steedman to Robert Stripling, June 23, 1939, Member and Staff correspondence, box 7, folder "Hurley," Dies Committee Papers, National Archives, Washington, D.C.

45. On Steedman's work with the local AFL, see Files of Investigators, Steedman, box 44, Dies Committee Papers, National Archives, Washington, D.C.; see also House Special Committee on Un-American Activities, *Investigation of Un-American Propaganda Activities in the United States* [1939–41], 5:2265. On Steedman's meeting with North American and arrangement with Hollingshead and local IAM officials, see J. Edgar Hoover, "Memorandum for the Attorney General re: Unknown Subjects: Experimental Pursuit Ship NA-73, North American Aviation, Inc.; Sabotage," January 21, 1941, box 89, folder 11, Papers of Robert H. Jackson.

46. *New York Times*, November 16, 1940.

47. J. Edgar Hoover, "Memorandum for the Attorney General re: Unknown Subjects: Experimental Pursuit Ship NA-73, North American Aviation, Inc.; Sabotage," January 21, 1941, box 89, folder 11, Papers of Robert H. Jackson.

48. House Special Committee on Un-American Activities, *Investigation of Un-American Propaganda Activities in the United States* [1939–41], 5:2289.

49. Wyndham Mortimer, "Reflections of a Labor Organizer," 1967, University of California, Los Angeles, Young Research Library, UCLA Center for Oral History. Mortimer's oral history account should be taken with some caution. Mortimer badly scrambles the dates for events he describes, sometimes placing the North American election in 1939, for example.

50. "In the matter of North American Aviation, Inc and United Automobile Workers of America Local 228 CIO," *Decisions and Orders of the NRLB*, 13:1196–97.

51. For an exhaustive account of Allis-Chalmers, see Meyer, *Stalin over Wisconsin*; see also Keeran, *Communist Party and the Auto Workers Union*, 213–15; Schrecker, *Many Are the Crimes*, 101–3; Lichtenstein, *Most Dangerous Man in Detroit*, 178, 183–85.

52. Meyer, *Stalin over Wisconsin*, 88–103.

53. *New York Times*, March 28, 1941; ibid., April 10, 1941.

54. Schrecker, *Many Are the Crimes*, 101–2.

55. *Los Angeles Times*, May 30, 1941; Louis Stark, "Tares in the Wheat," *Survey Graphic*, November 1941.

56. *New York Times*, June 8, 1941.

57. For further evidence that local issues, not Communist subterfuge, lay behind the North American Aviation incident, see Prickett, "Communist Conspiracy or Wage Dispute?"

58. *New York Times*, June 13, 1941; Fraser, *Labor Will Rule*, 466; Isserman, *Which Side Were You On?* 87–88.

59. On the Minneapolis Teamster local, see Irving Bernstein, *The Turbulent Years*, 231–52, 780–81; Russell, *Out of the Jungle*, 34–47.

60. Donna Haverty-Stacke, "Risky Business: Labor Anticommunism, the FBI, and the 1941 Smith Act Case," in possession of the author; Millikan, *A Union against Unions*, 338–42; Russell, *Out of the Jungle*, 79–83.

61. *New York Times*, June 14, 1941; Pahl, "G-String Conspiracy, Political Reprisal, or Armed Revolt?"

62. Belknap, *Cold War Political Justice*, 38–41; Lichtenstein, *Labor's War at Home*, 64–65; Haverty-Stacke, "Risky Business"; Pahl, "G-String Conspiracy, Political Reprisal, or Armed Revolt?" 46–47.

63. Trotsky, "The Death Agony of Capitalism and the Tasks of the Fourth International."

64. Haverty-Stacke, "Risky Business," 24.

65. Ibid.; Farrell Dobbs, *Teamster Politics*, 143; *Dunne et al. v. United States*, 138 F.2d 137, 1943. Thanks to Donna Haverty-Stacke for clarifying this point.

66. Eidlin, "Upon this (foundering) rock," 263 n. 61; Isserman, *Which Side Were You On?*, 123–24.

67. "Biographical note," Papers of Lewis Graham Hines, Library of Congress, Washington, D.C.; Harris, *Bloodless Victories*, 373, 426.

68. *New York Times*, March 19, 1937, and March 22, 1937; "Proceedings," Pennsylvania State Federation of Labor Papers, 1938, Historical Collections and Labor Archives, Pennsylvania State University, State College, Pa.

69. Guy V. Miller, "Pennsylvania's Scrambled Politics," *Nation*, May 14, 1938. On the Pennsylvania elections, see Morgan, "Significance of Pennsylvania's 1938 Gubernatorial Election"; and Davin, *Crucible of Freedom*, 295–99.

70. C. P. Gantz to Lewis Hines, September 2, 1938, container 1, folder "Correspondence, July-September 1938," Papers of Lewis Graham Hines.

71. House Special Committee on Un-American Activities, *Investigation of Un-American Propaganda Activities in the United States* [1938], 1:196–97; for press coverage of this claim, see *New York Times*, August 16, 1938.

72. "Governor Arthur H. James," Pennsylvania Governors Past and Present, Pennsylvania Historical and Museum Commission; *New York Times*, March 27, 1941.

73. On the SCMW's Communists, see Latham, *Communist Controversy in Washington*, 86–89; Klehr, *Heyday of American Communism*, 235.

74. Hines to William Green, November 2, 1939, container 3, folder "Correspondence, November 1939," Papers of Lewis Graham Hines.

75. Captain E. H. McIlroy to Lewis Hines, October 27, 1939, container 13, folder "CIO and Communism 1939," Papers of Lewis Graham Hines.

76. Commissioner of the State Motor Police to Lewis G. Hines, March 8, 1940, container 13, folder "CIO and Communism Correspondence 1940," Papers of Lewis Graham Hines.

77. Jenkins, *Cold War at Home*, 22–23; for party membership figures, see Klehr, *Heyday of American Communism*, 380; "Legal Obstacles to Minority Party Success." See also *Commonwealth v. Antico*, 146 Pa. Super. 293; 22 A.2d 204.

78. Hines to William Green, December 4, 1939, Lewis G. Hines papers, Container 3, Folder "Correspondence, December 1939."

79. Hines to David Kanes, September 3, 1940, container 13, folder "CIO and Communism 1939," Papers of Lewis Graham Hines.

80. Robert B. Barker to Hines, April 22, 1941, container 13, folder "CIO and Communism 1939," Papers of Lewis Graham Hines.

81. Criminal Intelligence Report on Reba Baskin, container 13, folder "CIO and Communism 1939," Papers of Lewis Graham Hines.

82. Loyalty questionnaire, container 13, folder "CIO and Communism Correspondence 1940," Papers of Lewis Graham Hines.

83. Hines to William Green, October 24, 1941, Papers of Lewis Graham Hines.

84. *Pawell et al v. Unemployment Compensation Board of Review*, 146 PA Super. 147; October 2, 1941.

85. Hines to William Green, October 24, 1941, Papers of Lewis Graham Hines.

86. Green to Hines, November 4, 1941, Papers of Lewis Graham Hines.

87. William W. Bardsley, Regional Employment Security Representative, Social Security

Board, August 26, 1941, to Hines, container 13, folder "CIO and Communism Investigation Files, October 31, 1941," Papers of Lewis Graham Hines.

88. *New York Times*, February 14, 1942.

89. See, for example, *Edward G. Vollman, Appellant, v. California Employment Stabilization Commission*, 104 Cal. App. 2d 94; 231 P.2d 137; May 8, 1951; *Trooper John H. Nason, Jr. v. New Hampshire Personnel Commission*, 117 N.H. 140; 370 A.2d 634; February 28, 1977; *Abraham Lederman, as President of Teachers Union of the City of New York, Local 555 of the United Public Workers, et al., Plaintiffs, and Irving Adler et al., Respondents, v. Board of Education of the City of New York, Appellant*, 276 A.D. 527; 96 N.Y.S.2d 466, March 27, 1950.

90. *Report of the Proceedings of the Thirty-third Annual Convention of the Pennsylvania Federation of Labor*, 1941, Historical Archives and Labor Collection, Pennsylvania State University, State College, Pa.

91. William Green to Congressman Karl Mundt, February 13, 1945, in Legislative Papers, American Federation of Labor, RG 21-001, George Meany Archives, Silver Spring, Md.

EPILOGUE

1. Elizabeth Gurley Flynn, "Defend the Rights of Communists," *Communist* 18, no. 12 (December 1939).

2. Kennedy, *Freedom from Fear*, 484.

3. Quoted in Richmond, *Native Daughter*, 178.

4. On the CPUSA during World War II, see Isserman, *Which Side Were You On*; quotes from 188–89.

5. Stone, *Perilous Times*, 266–75; Gary, *The Nervous Liberals*, 207–53.

6. On the FBI during the war, see Sibley, *Red Spies in America*, 87–92; Schrecker, *Many Are the Crimes*, 111–15.

7. On the AFL during the war years, see Kersten, *Labor's Home Front*; on the CIO, see Lichtenstein, *Labor's War at Home*; on the Communist labor policy, see Isserman, *Which Side Were You On?* especially 134–41 and 161–66.

8. Quoted in Kutulas, *ACLU and the Making of Modern Liberalism*, 92.

9. On the ACLU and Japanese internment, see ibid., 97–102; see also Irons, *Justice at War*. The Lippmann quote is in *Los Angeles Times*, February 13, 1942. On the CP and Japanese internment, see Isserman, *Which Side Were You On?* 142–44.

10. On Venona, see Haynes and Klehr, *Venona*; see also Sibley, *Red Spies in America*, 105–15, 133–74. On Bentley, see Olmsted, *Red Spy Queen*.

11. Klehr, *Heyday of American Communism*, 413–14.

12. William Green to James L. McDevitt, November 5, 1946, AFL Legislative Reference Files, RG-21, George Meany Archives, Silver Spring, Md.

13. Stepan-Norris and Zeitlin, *Left Out*, 272; for a more nuanced view, see Lichtenstein, *Most Dangerous Man in Detroit*, 316–18.

14. *Washington Post*, February 8, 1948; *New York Times*, May 11, 1948. Robert Zieger has the most comprehensive account of the postwar CIO purge in *The CIO*, 253–93.

15. House Committee on Education and Labor, *Amendments to the National Labor Relations Act*, 3:1712. On the addition of the affidavit to Taft-Hartley, see Millis and Clark, *From the Wagner Act to Taft-Hartley*, 545–53.

16. *Baltimore Sun*, June 29, 1947.

17. *Chicago Daily Tribune*, October 15, 1947.

18. *West Virginia State Board of Education v. Barnette*, 319 U.S. 624 (1943).

19. *American Communications Association v. Douds*, 339 U.S. 382 (1950).

20. American Civil Liberties Union, *Democracy in Trade Unions*, 5, 52.

21. Rothman, "Legislative History of the Bill of Rights"; Labor-Management Reporting and Disclosure Act of 1959.

22. On labor anticommunism and foreign policy after World War II, see Radosh, *American Labor and U.S. Foreign Policy*; Morgan, *A Covert Life*; Rosenberg, *Spreading the American Dream*, 202–35; Christopher Gerteis, "Subjectivity Lost: Labor and the Cold War in Occupied Japan," in Stromquist, *Labor's Cold War*; McShane, *International Labor*.

23. *Baltimore Sun*, January 31, 1948.

24. On postwar labor politics, see Greenstone, *Labor in American Politics*; on labor conservatism and anticommunism, see Nicolaides, *My Blue Heaven*, 168, 271; Durr, *Behind the Backlash*, 32–52. Most research on labor conservatism focuses on white workers' racism as the primary force driving them away from liberalism and the Democrats. Surely racism was centrally important, but other, older threads of political culture also connected postwar white working-class conservatives to their earlier forbears. There is a growing literature on white workers, race, and conservatism; some emblematic works include Sugrue, *Origins of the Urban Crisis*; Lassiter, *Silent Majority*; Hamilton, *Trucking Country*. We need much more historical research on the history of working-class conservatism.

Bibliography

ARCHIVAL SOURCES

Atlanta, Georgia
   Georgia State University Library
      Southern Labor Archives, http://www.library.gsu.edu/spcoll/pages/area.asp?
         ldID=105&guideID=510
Carbondale, Illinois
   Southern Illinois University Library, Special Collections
      Theodore Schroeder Papers
Chicago, Illinois
   Chicago Historical Society
      John Fitzpatrick Papers
      Victor Olander Papers
   Newberry Library
      Illinois State Federation of Labor Proceedings
College Park, Maryland
   National Archives
      Federal Bureau of Investigation Papers
Detroit, Michigan
   Wayne State University, Walter P. Reuther Library
      Heber Blankenhorn Papers
      John Edelman Papers
Liberty, Texas
   Sam Houston Regional Library
      Martin Dies Papers
Ithaca, New York
   Cornell University, Uris Library, Kroch Special Collections
      World War I Pamphlets
   Kheel Center for Labor-Management Documentation and Archives
      Philip Taft Records
      International Ladies Garment Workers Union, President's Records, 1932–1966
Madison, Wisconsin
   State Historical Society of Wisconsin
      American Federation of Labor Records, Papers on Communism
New York, New York
   National Archives
      U.S. District Court for the Southern District of New York Records

New York Public Library
   National Civic Federation Papers
   Tamiment Library
      Daniel Bell Research Files
San Francisco, California
   Labor Archives and Research Center, San Francisco State University
      California Federation of Labor Papers
Silver Spring, Maryland
   George Meany Archives
      American Federation of Labor Papers
         Legislative Reference Files
State College, Pennsylvania
   Pennsylvania State University, Historical Collections and Labor Archives
      Pennsylvania Federation of Labor Papers
      United Mine Workers of America Papers
Washington, D.C.
   Library of Congress
      Papers of John P. Frey
      Papers of Lewis Graham Hines
      Papers of Robert H. Jackson
   National Archives
      Dies Committee Papers
      Investigative Case Files of the Bureau of Investigation, 1908–1922, Old German Files
      Records of the United States Senate, Record Group 46

ORAL HISTORY INTERVIEWS

Los Angeles, California
   University of California, Los Angeles, Young Research Library, UCLA Center for Oral
   History
      Wyndham Mortimer oral history
      Jack Tenney oral history
New York, New York
   Columbia Center for Oral History
      Reminiscences of Frances Perkins, 1951–1955
      Reminiscences of Heber Blankenhorn
      Reminiscences of John Frey, 1955
      Reminiscences of John Edelman, 1956–1957
   New York University, Tamiment Library, Oral History of the American Left
      Samuel Darcy oral history

MICROFILM COLLECTIONS

Albert, Peter J., and Harold L. Miller. *American Federation of Labor Records: The Samuel Gompers Era.* Sanford, N.C.: Microfilming Corporation of America, 1979.
American Civil Liberties Union Records, The Roger Baldwin Years, 1917–1950. Wilmington, Del.: Scholarly Resources, 1996.

Boehm, Randolph, ed. *U.S. Military Intelligence Reports: Surveillance of Radicals in the United States, 1917–1941.* Frederick, Md.: University Publications of America, 1984.

———. *Minutes of the Executive Council of the American Federation of Labor, 1893–1955.* Frederick, Md.: University Publications of America, 1991.

Dubofsky, Melvyn, ed. *American Federation of Labor Records. Part 2: President's Office Files Series A: William Green Papers, 1934–1952.* Frederick, Md.: University Publications of America, 1986.

———, ed. *Department of Justice Investigative Files. Part I: The Industrial Workers of the World.* Bethesda, Md.: University Publications of America, 1989.

Naison, Mark, ed. *Department of Justice Investigative Files.* Part II: *The Communist Party.* Bethesda, Md.: University Publications of America, 1989.

O'Reilly, Kenneth, ed. *FBI File on the House Un-American Activities Committee.* Wilmington, Del.: Scholarly Resources, 1986.

GOVERNMENT DOCUMENTS

Biographical Directory of the United States Congress, http://bioguide.congress.gov/.

Decisions and Orders of the National Labor Relations Board. Washington: Government Printing Office.

Labor-Management Reporting and Disclosure Act of 1959. Public Law 86-257, 73 Statute 519-46.

New York (State). Joint Legislative Committee to Investigate Seditious Activities. *Report of the Joint Legislative Committee Investigating Seditious Activities: Part II: Constructive Movements and Measures in America.* Albany, N.Y.: J. B. Lyon, 1920.

U.S. Congress. House. Committee on Education and Labor. *Amendments to the National Labor Relations Act.* 80th Cong., 1st sess., 1947. Washington: Government Printing Office, 1947.

———. Committee on Immigration and Nationalization. *To Exclude and Expel Alien Fascists and Communists: Hearings on H. Res. 7120.* 74th Cong, 1st sess., 1934. Washington: Government Printing Office, 1934.

———. Committee on Rules. *Investigation into the Activities of Communists in the United States: Hearings on H. Res. 180.* 71st Congress, 3rd sess., 1930. Washington: Government Printing Office, 1930.

———. Committee on the Judiciary. *Charges of Hon. Oscar E. Keller against the Attorney General of the United States.* H. Res. 425. 67th Cong., 3rd and 4th sess., 1922. Washington: Government Printing Office, 1922.

———. Committee on the Judiciary. *Crime to Promote the Overthrow of Government: Hearing on H.R. 5138.* 76th Cong., 1st sess., 1940. Washington: Government Printing Office, 1940.

———. Committee on the Judiciary. *Espionage and Interference with Neutrality: Hearings on H.R. 291.* 65th Cong., 1st sess., 1917. Washington: Government Printing Office, 1917.

———. Committee on the Judiciary. *H. Snowden Marshall: Hearings to Investigate Charges against H. Snowden Marshall, Under Authority of H. Res. 90.* 64th Cong., 1st sess., 1916. Washington: Government Printing Office, 1916.

———. Committee on the Judiciary. *Sedition.* S. 3317, H.R. 10650 and 12041. 66th Cong, 2nd sess., 1920. Washington: Government Printing Office, 1920.

———. Committee on the Judiciary. *To Punish Espionage and Interference with Neutrality:*

Hearings on S. 8148. 64th Cong., 2nd sess., 1917. Washington: Government Printing Office, 1917.

———. Special Committee on Un-American Activities. *Investigation of Nazi Propaganda Activities and Investigation of Certain Other Propaganda Activities*. 71st Congress, 3rd sess., 1930. Washington: Government Printing Office, 1930.

———. Special Committee on Un-American Activities. *Investigation of Un-American Propaganda Activities in the United States*. 75th Cong., 3rd. sess., 1938. Washington: Government Printing Office, 1938.

———. Special Committee on Un-American Activities. *Investigation of Un-American Propaganda Activities in the United States*. H. Res. 282. 76th Cong. 14 vols. Washington: Government Printing Office, 1939–1940.

———. Special Committee to Investigate Communist Activities in the United States. *Investigation of Communist Propaganda: Hearings on H. Res. 220*. 71st Cong, 2nd session, 1930. Washington: Government Printing Office, 1930.

U.S. Congress. Senate. Committee on Commerce and the Committee on Education and Labor. *Hearings before the Committee on Commerce and the Committee on Education and Labor on S. 3078, A Bill to Amend the Merchant Marine Act of 1936 and for other purposes*. 75th Cong., 3rd sess., 1938. Washington: Government Printing Office, 1938.

———. Committee on Education and Labor. *Investigation of Strike in Steel Industries*. S. Res. 202. 66th Cong., 1st sess., 1919. Washington: Government Printing Office, 1919.

———. Committee on Education and Labor. *National Labor Relations Act and Proposed Amendments: Hearings on S. 1000, S. 1264, S. 1392, S. 1550, S. 1580, and S. 2123*. 76th Cong., 1st. sess., 1939. Washington: Government Printing Office, 1939.

———. Committee on Education and Labor. *National Labor Relations Board*. S. 1958. 74th Cong., 1st sess., 1935. Washington: Government Printing Office, 1935.

———. Committee on Immigration. *Deportation of Aliens: Hearings on H.R. 4860*. 76th Cong., 1st sess., 1939. Washington: Government Printing Office, 1939.

———. Committee on Education and Labor. *To Amend the National Labor Relations Act*. 76th Cong., 3rd sess., 1940. Washington: Government Printing Office, 1940.

———. Committee on the Judiciary. *Brewing and Liquor Interests and German and Bolshevik Propaganda, Hearings before the Committee on the Judiciary, S. Res. 307 and 439*. 65th Cong, 2nd and 3rd sess., 1919. Washington: Government Printing Office, 1919.

———. Select Committee on the Investigation of the Attorney General. *Investigation of Hon. Harry M. Daugherty*. S. Res. 157. 68th Cong, 1st sess., 1924. Washington: Government Printing Office, 1924.

PERIODICALS

American Federationist

Baltimore Sun

Brotherhood of Locomotive Firemen and Engineers Magazine

Chicago Daily Tribune

Chicago Tribune

Christian Science Monitor

Communist

Communist International

Current Literature

Daily People

Daily Worker

Fortune

Gunton's Magazine

Independent

Liberator

Literary Digest

Locomotive Engineer's Journal

Los Angeles Times
Mixer and Server
Mother Earth
Nation
New Republic
New York Herald Tribune
New York Times
North American Review
Public Opinion Quarterly

St. Louis Post-Dispatch
Stone Cutters' Journal
Survey Graphic
Time
Wall Street Journal
Washington Post
World's Work
UMW Journal
Union Convention Proceedings

COURT CASES

Abraham Lederman, as President of Teachers Union of the City of New York, Local 555 of the United Public Workers, et al., Plaintiffs, and Irving Adler et al., Respondents, v. Board of Education of the City of New York, Appellant, Supreme Court of New York, Appellate Division Second Department, 276 A.D. 527; 96 N.Y.S.2d 466, March 27, 1950.

American Communications Association v. Douds, 339 U.S. 382 (1950).

Commonwealth v. Antico, Superior Court of Pennsylvania, 146 Pa. Super. 293; 22 A.2d 204.

Dunne et al. v. United States, United States Court of Appeals for the Eighth Circuit, 138 F.2d 137, 1943.

Edward G. Vollman, Appellant, v. California Employment Stabilization Commission, Court of Appeal of California, Third Appellate District, 104 Cal. App. 2d 94; 231 P.2d 137; May 8, 1951.

Pawell et al. v. Unemployment Compensation Board of Review, Superior Court of Pennsylvania, 146 PA Super. 147; October 2, 1941.

Trooper John H. Nason, Jr. v. New Hampshire Personnel Commission, Supreme Court of New Hampshire, 117 N.H. 140; 370 A.2d 634; February 28, 1977.

West Virginia State Board of Education v. Barnette, 319 U.S. 624.

DISSERTATIONS

Coil, William Russell. "New Deal Republican: James A. Rhodes and the Transformation of the Republican Party, 1933–1983." Ph.D. diss., Ohio State University, 2005.

Doody, Colleen Patrice. "Anticommunism in America: Detroit's Cold War, 1945–1960." Ph.D. diss., University of Virginia, 2005.

Goodall, Alex. "Aspects of the Emergence of American Anticommunism, 1917–1944." Ph.D. diss., University of Cambridge, 2006.

Green, Marguerite. "The National Civic Federation and the American Labor Movement, 1900–1925." Ph.D. diss., Catholic University, 1956.

Lewis, Anders Geoffrey. "Labor's Cold War: The AFL and Liberal Anticommunism." Ph.D. diss., University of Florida, 2000.

McCann, John. "Labor and the Making of the Postwar Order at the Boeing Company." Ph.D. diss., University of Oregon, 1994.

McDaniel, Dennis Kay. "Martin Dies of Un-American Activities: His Life and Times." Ph.D. diss., University of Houston, 1988.

Mortimer, Louis Read, Jr. "John Philip Frey, Spokesman for Skilled American Labor." Ph.D. diss., George Washington University, 1982.

Ogden, August Raymond. "The Dies Committee: A Study of the Special House Committee for the Investigation of Un-American Activities, 1938–1943." Ph.D. diss., Catholic
University of America, 1943.

Provost, Tracie L. "The Great Game: Imperial German Sabotage and Espionage Against the
United States, 1914–1917." Ph.D. diss., University of Toledo, 2003.

Storch, Randi Jill. "Shades of Red: The Communist Party and Chicago's Workers, 1928–
1939." Ph.D. diss., University of Illinois at Urbana-Champaign, 1998.

Tinnemann, Ethel Mary. "Count Johann von Bernstorff and German-American Relations,
1908–1917." Ph.D. diss., University of California, Berkeley, 1960.

Weinrib, Laura M. "The Liberal Compromise: Civil Liberties, Labor, and the Limits of State
Power, 1917–1940." Ph.D. diss., Princeton University, 2011.

ARTICLES

Adler, Les K., and Thomas G. Paterson. "Red Fascism: The Merger of Nazi Germany and
Soviet Russia in the American Image of Totalitarianism, 1930s–1950s." *American Historical Review* 75, no. 4 (April 1970): 1046–64.

Archer, Robin. "Unions, Courts, and Parties: Judicial Repression and Labor Politics in Late
Nineteenth-Century America." *Politics & Society* 26, no. 3 (September 1998): 391–422.

Arnesen, Eric. "'No Graver Danger': Black Anticommunism, the Communist Party, and
the Race Question." *Labor: Studies in Working Class History of the Americas* 3, no. 4
(2006): 13–52.

Axtell, Silas B. "Russia, and Her Foreign Relations." *Annals of the American Academy of
Political and Social Science* 138 (July 1928): 85–92.

Barrett, James R. "Americanization from the Bottom Up: Immigration and the Remaking
of the Working Class in the United States, 1880–1930." *Journal of American History* 79,
no. 3 (December 1992): 996–1020.

Belknap, Michal R. "Uncooperative Federalism: The Failure of the Bureau of Investigation's Intergovernmental Assault on Radicalism." *Publius* 12, no. 2 (Spring 1982): 25–47.

Brinkley, Alan. "The Problem of American Conservatism." *American Historical Review* 99,
no. 2 (April 1994): 409–29.

Brooks, John Graham. "Organized Labor in the United States." *Economic Journal* 9, no. 33
(March 1899): 88–91.

Bucki, Cecilia. "Dilution and Craft Tradition: Bridgeport, Connecticut, Munitions Workers,
1915–1919." *Social Science History* 4, no. 1 (Winter 1980): 105–24.

Cherny, Robert W. "The Communist Party in California, 1935–1940: From Political Margins to the Mainstream and Back." *American Communist History* 9, no. 1 (2010): 3–33.

———. "Prelude to the Popular Front: The Communist Party in California, 1931–35."
American Communist History 1, no. 1 (2002): 5–42.

Debs, Eugene V. "Craft Unionism." In *Debs: His Life Writings and Speeches*. Girard, Kans.:
Appeal to Reason, 1908.

———. "The Crime of Craft Unionism." *International Socialist Review* 11, no. 8 (February 1911).

DeLeon, Daniel. "Blockhead Gompers." *Daily People*, September 5, 1908.

Delton, Jennifer. "Rethinking Post–World War II Anticommunism." *Journal of the Historical Society* 10, no. 1 (March 2010): 1–41.

Devinatz, Victor. "Reassessing the Historical UAW: Walter Reuther's Affiliation with the

Communist Party and Something of Its Meaning: A Document of Party Involvement, 1939." *Labour/Le Travail* 49 (Spring 2002): 223–45.

Eastman, Max. "An Opinion on Tactics." *Liberator*, October 1921, 5–6.

Eidlin, Barry. "'Upon this (foundering) rock': Minneapolis Teamsters and the Transformation of U.S. Business Unionism, 1934–1941." *Labor History* 50, no. 3 (August 2009): 249–67.

Farhang, Sean, and Ira Katznelson. "The Southern Imposition: Congress and Labor in the New Deal and Fair Deal." *Studies in American Political Development* 19 (Spring 2005): 1–30.

"Federal Sedition Bills: Speech Restriction in Theory and Practice." *Columbia Law Review* 35, no. 6 (June 1935): 917–27.

Filardo, Peter Meyer. "What Is the Case? C/communism/s, Communist/s, AntiC/communism/ist/s, and the "C/capitalization Question." *American Communist History* 7 (2008): 139–61.

Fink, Gary. "The Rejection of Voluntarism." *Industrial and Labor Relations Review* 26, no. 2 (January 1973): 805–19.

Fink, Leon. "Labor, Liberty, and the Law: Trade Unionism and the Problem of the American Constitutional Order." *Journal of American History* 74, no. 3 (1987): 904–25.

Fischer, Nick. "The Founders of American Anti-communism." *American Communist History* 5, no. 1 (2006): 67–101.

Fish, Hamilton. "The Menace of Communism." *Annals of the American Academy of Political and Social Science* 156, no. 1 (1931): 54–61.

Foner, Eric. "Why Is There No Socialism in the United States?" *History Workshop Journal* 17, no. 1 (1984): 57–80.

Fones-Wolf, Elizabeth, and Ken Fones-Wolf. "Rank-and-File Rebellions and AFL Interference in the Affairs of National Unions: The Gompers Era." *Labor History* 35, no. 2 (Spring 1994): 237–59.

Fox, John F., Jr. "What the Spiders Did: U.S. and Soviet Counterintelligence before the Cold War." *Journal of Cold War Studies* 11, no. 3 (Summer 2009): 206–24.

Gompers, Samuel. "Free Speech and the Injunction Order." *Annals of the American Academy of Political and Social Science* 36, no. 2 (September 1910): 255–64.

Goodall, Alex. "Diverging Paths: Nazism, the National Civic Federation, and American Anticommunism, 1933–1939." *Journal of Contemporary History* 44, no. 1 (2009): 49–69.

Haverty-Stacke, Donna. "Risky Business: Labor Anticommunism, the FBI, and the 1941 Smith Act Case." In possession of the author.

Johanningsmeier, Edward P. "The Trade Union Unity League: American Communists and the Transition to Industrial Unionism, 1928–1934." *Labor History* 42, no. 2 (2001): 159–77.

Johnson, Donald. "Wilson, Burleson, and Censorship in the First World War." *Journal of Southern History* 28, no. 1 (February 1962): 46–58.

Kaufman, Bruce E. "The Case for the Company Union." *Labor History* 41, no. 3 (2000): 321–51.

Larson, Simeon. "Opposition to AFL Foreign Policy: A Labor Mission to Russia, 1927." *Historian* (May 1981): 344–64.

Leab, Daniel J. "'United We Eat': The Creation and Organization of the Unemployed Councils in 1930." *Labor History* 8 (1967): 300–315.

"Legal Obstacles to Minority Party Success." *Yale Law Journal* 57, no. 7 (June 1948): 1285–87.

Letters responding to Draper, "American Communism Revisited." "The Popular Front Revisited." *New York Review of Books*, May 9, 1985, 30.

Lichtenstein, Nelson. "Reuther the Red?" *Labour/Le Travail* 51 (Spring 2003): 165–69.

Maddux, Thomas R. "Red Fascism, Brown Bolshevism: The American Image of Totalitarianism in the 1930s." *Historian* 40, no. 1 (November 1977): 85–103.

Meyer, Michael C. "The Mexican-German Conspiracy of 1915." *Americas* 23, no. 1 (July 1966): 76–89.

Miner, Sarah. "Battle at Boeing: African Americans and the Campaign for Jobs." Seattle Civil Rights and Labor History Project, http://depts.washington.edu/civilr/boeing_battle.htm, accessed February 1, 2008.

Morgan, Alfred L. "Significance of Pennsylvania's 1938 Gubernatorial Election." *Pennsylvania Magazine of History and Biography* 102, no. 2 (April 1978): 184–211.

Murphy, Paul L. "Sources and Nature of Intolerance in the 1920s." *Journal of American History* 51, no. 1 (June 1964): 60–76.

Nelson, Daniel. "The CIO at Bay: Labor Militancy and Politics in Akron, 1936–1938." *Journal of American History* 71, no. 3 (December 1984): 565–86.

O'Brien, Ruth. "'A Sweat Shop of the Whole Nation': The Fair Labor Standards Act and the Failure of Regulatory Unionism." *Studies in American Political Development* 15 (Spring 2001): 33–52.

Olszowka, John. "The UAW and the Struggle to Organize Aircraft." *Labor History* 49, no. 3 (August 2008): 297–317.

Pahl, Thomas L. "G-String Conspiracy, Political Reprisal, or Armed Revolt? The Minneapolis Trotskyite Trial." *Labor History* 8, no. 1 (1967): 30–51.

Palmer, Bryan D. "American Communism in the 1920s: Striving for a Panoramic View." *American Communist History* 6, no. 2 (December 2007): 139–49.

Patnaik, Arun K. "Gramsci's Concept of Common Sense: Towards a Theory of Subaltern Consciousness in Hegemony Processes." *Economic and Political Weekly* 23, no. 5 (January 30, 1988): PE3–PE10.

Patterson, James T. "The New Deal and the States." *American Historical Review* 73, no. 1 (October 1967): 70–84.

Plesur, Milton. "The Republican Congressional Comeback of 1938." *Review of Politics* 24, no. 4 (October 1962): 525–62.

Plowman, Matthew Erin. "Irish Republicans and the Indo-German Conspiracy of World War I." *New Hibernia Review*, August 2003, 80–105.

Pope, James Gray. "Labor's Constitution of Freedom." *Yale Law Journal* 106, no. 4 (January 1997): 941–1031.

Porter, David. "Senator Carl Hatch and the Hatch Act." *New Mexico Historical Review* 47, no. 2 (1973): 151–61.

Prickett, James. "Communist Conspiracy or Wage Dispute?: The 1941 Strike at North American Aviation." *Pacific Historical Review* 50, no. 2 (May 1981): 215–33.

"The Recall of Ambassador Dumba." *American Journal of International Law* 9, no. 4 (October 1915): 935–39.

"Recent Anti-Alien Legislative Proposals." *Columbia Law Review* 39, no. 7 (November 1939): 1207–223.

Rosswurm, Steven. "The Wondrous Tale of an FBI Bug: What It Tells Us about Communism, Anti-Communism, and the CIO Leadership." *American Communist History* 2, no. 1 (June 2003): 3–20.

Rosswurm, Steven, and Joshua Freeman. "The Education of an Anti-Communist: Father John F. Cronin and the Baltimore Labor Movement." *Labor History* 33, no. 2 (1992): 217–47.

Rothman, Stuart. "Legislative History of the Bill of Rights for Union Members." *Minnesota Law Review* 45 (1960): 199–228.

Ryan, James G. "Socialist Triumph as a Family Value: Earl Browder and Soviet Espionage." *American Communist History* 1, no. 2 (2002): 125–42.

Samuel, Howard D. "Troubled Passage: The Labor Movement and the Fair Labor Standards Act." *Monthly Labor Review* (December 2000): 32–37.

Saposs, David J. "The American Labor Movement since the War." *Quarterly Journal of Economics* 49, no. 2 (February 1935): 236–54.

Saunders, D. A. "The Dies Committee: First Phase." *Public Opinion Quarterly* 3, no. 2 (April 1939): 223–38.

Soyer, Daniel. "Back to the Future: American Jews Visit the Soviet Union in the 1920s and 1930s." *Jewish Social Studies* 6, no. 3 (2000): 124–59.

Storch, Randi. "'The Realities of the Situation': Revolutionary Discipline and Everyday Political Life in Chicago's Communist Party, 1928–1935." *Labor: Studies in Working Class History of the Americas* 1, no. 3 (Fall 2004): 19–44.

Tomlins, Christopher L. "AFL Unions in the 1930s: Their Performance in Historical Perspective." *Journal of American History* 65, no. 4 (March 1979): 1021–42.

Trotsky, Leon. "The Death Agony of Capitalism and the Tasks of the Fourth International: The Transitional Program" (1938). *http://www.marxists.org/archive/trotsky/1938/tp/index.htm*. Marxists Internet Archive, accessed October 1, 2011.

Walker, Samuel. "The Boss as Bureaucrat." *Reviews in American History* 16, no. 3 (September 1988): 460–65.

Weinrib, Laura M. "Lawyers, Libertines, and the Reinvention of Free Speech, 1920–1933." In the possession of the author.

Weinstein, James. "Radicalism in the Midst of Normalcy." *Journal of American History* 52, no. 4 (March 1966): 773–90.

Weiss, Stuart L. "Maury Maverick and the Liberal Bloc." *Journal of American History* 57, no. 4 (March 1971): 880–95.

Williams, Charles. "Reconsidering CIO Political Culture: Briggs Local 212 and the Sources of Militancy in the Early UAW." *Labor: Studies in Working-Class History of the Americas* 7, no. 4 (2010) 17–43.

Wolfinger, James. "The Strange Career of Frank Murphy: Conservatives, State-Level Politics, and the End of the New Deal." *Historian* 65 (December 2002): 377–402.

Zimmer, Kenyon. "Premature Anti-Communists? American Anarchism, the Russian Revolution, and Left-Wing Libertarian Anti-Communism, 1917–1933." *Labor: Studies in Working-Class History of the Americas* 6, no. 2 (2009): 45–71.

BOOKS

Ackerman, Kenneth D. *Young J. Edgar: Hoover, the Red Scare, and the Assault on Civil Liberties.* New York: Carroll & Graf, 2007.

Adams, Graham, Jr. *Age of Industrial Violence.* New York: Columbia University Press, 1966.

American Civil Liberties Union. *Democracy in Trade Unions.* New York, 1942.

————. *Liberty's National Emergency: The Story of Civil Liberties in the Crisis Year.* New York, 1941.

————. *The Nation-wide Spy System Centering in the Department of Justice.* New York, 1924.

American Federation of Labor. *Proceedings of the Annual Convention of the American Federation of Labor.* Washington, D.C., 1914–40.

American National Biography Online. Oxford University Press. ⟨www.anb.org⟩, accessed April 2011.

Angle, Paul M. *Bloody Williamson: A Chapter in American Lawlessness.* New York: Knopf, 1962.

Archer, Robin. *Why Is There No Labor Party in the United States?* Princeton: Princeton University Press, 2007.

Arnesen, Eric. *Brotherhoods of Color: Black Railroad Workers and the Struggle for Equality.* Chapel Hill: University of North Carolina Press, 2002.

Auerbach, Jerold S. *Labor and Liberty: The La Follette Committee and the New Deal.* Indianapolis: Bobbs-Merrill, 1966.

Barrett, James R. *William Z. Foster and the Tragedy of American Radicalism.* Urbana: University of Illinois Press, 1999.

————. *Work and Community in the Jungle: Chicago's Packinghouse Workers, 1894–1922.* Urbana: University of Illinois Press, 1990.

Bates, Beth Tompkins. *Pullman Porters and the Rise of Protest Politics in Black America, 1925–1945.* Chapel Hill: University of North Carolina Press, 2001.

Batvinis, Raymond. *The Origins of FBI Counterintelligence.* Lawrence: University Press of Kansas, 1997.

Beckett, Ian F. W. *The Great War 1914–1918.* 2nd ed. Edinburgh: Pearson, 2007.

Belknap, Michal R. *Cold War Political Justice: The Smith Act, the Communist Party, and American Civil Liberties.* Westport, Conn.: Greenwood Press, 1977.

Bensel, Richard. *Yankee Leviathan: The Origins of Central State Authority in America, 1859–1877.* New York: Cambridge University Press, 1990.

Bernstein, Irving. *The Lean Years: A History of the American Worker, 1920–1933.* Boston: Houghton Mifflin, 1960.

————. *The Turbulent Years: A History of the American Worker, 1933–1941.* Boston: Houghton Mifflin, 1970.

Boghardt, Thomas. *Spies of the Kaiser: German Covert Operations in Great Britain during the First World War Era.* Houndmills: Palgrave Macmillan, 2005.

Boyle, Kevin. *Arc of Justice: A Saga of Race, Civil Rights, and Murder in the Jazz Age.* New York: Henry Holt, 1994.

Brinkley, Alan. *The End of Reform: New Deal Liberalism in Recession and War.* New York: Alfred A. Knopf, 1995.

————. *Voices of Protest: Huey Long, Father Coughlin, and the Great Depression.* New York: Alfred A. Knopf, 1982.

Brody, David. *In Labor's Cause: Main Themes on the History of the American Worker.* New York: Oxford University Press, 1993.

————. *Workers in Industrial America: Essays on the Twentieth Century Struggle.* New York: Oxford University Press, 1980.

Capozzola, Christopher. *Uncle Sam Wants You: World War I and the Making of the Modern Citizen.* New York: Oxford University Press, 2008.

Chafee, Zechariah. *Freedom of Speech.* New York: Harcourt Brace and Howe, 1920.

Clemens, Elisabeth S. *The People's Lobby: Organizational Innovation and the Rise of Interest Group Politics in the United States, 1890–1925.* Princeton: Princeton University Press, 1997.

Cochran, Bert. *Labor and Communism: The Conflict that Shaped American Unions.* Princeton: Princeton University Press, 1977.

Cohen, Andrew Wender. *The Racketeer's Progress: Chicago and the Struggle for the Modern American Economy, 1900–1940.* New York: Cambridge University Press, 2004.

Cohen, Lizabeth. *Making a New Deal: Industrial Workers in Chicago, 1919–1939.* Cambridge: Cambridge University Press, 1990.

Congress of Industrial Organizations. *Conspiracy against Labor: Full proof of the plot by William Green of the AFL and agents of the most anti-labor corporations in America to destroy the Wagner Act, with 17 letters between AFL officials and big business lawyers on crippling amendments to the act.* Washington, D.C.: Congress of Industrial Organizations, 1940.

Conlin, Joseph R. *Big Bill Haywood and the Radical Union Movement.* Syracuse, N.Y.: Syracuse University Press, 1969.

Cooper, Patricia A. *Once a Cigar Maker: Men, Women, and Work Culture in American Cigar Factories, 1900–1919.* Urbana: University of Illinois Press, 1987.

Cotter, Arundel. *United States Steel: A Corporation with a Soul.* New York: Doubleday, 1921.

Cottrell, Robert C. *Roger Nash Baldwin and the American Civil Liberties Union.* New York: Columbia University Press, 2000.

Crawford, Kenneth Gale. *The Pressure Boys: The Inside Story of Lobbying in America.* New York: J. Messner, 1939.

Cyphers, Christopher J. *The National Civic Federation and the Making of a New Liberalism, 1900–1915.* Westport, Conn.: Praeger, 2002.

Daniel, Cletus. *The ACLU and the Wagner Act.* Ithaca, N.Y.: Cornell University Press, 1980.

Davin, Eric Leif. *Crucible of Freedom: Workers' Democracy in the Industrial Heartland, 1914–1960.* Lanham, Md.: Lexington Books, 2010.

Davis, Colin J. *Power at Odds: The 1922 National Railroad Shopmen's Strike.* Urbana: University of Illinois Press, 1997.

Denning, Michael. *The Cultural Front.* London: Verso, 1997.

Deutscher, Isaac. *The Prophet Outcast: Trotsky, 1929–1940.* New York: Oxford University Press, 1963.

Dies, Martin. *Martin Dies' Story.* New York: Bookmailer, 1963.

Diggins, John Patrick. *Up from Communism.* New York: Columbia University Press, 1994.

Dilling, Elizabeth. *The Red Network: A "Who's Who" and Handbook of Radicalism for Patriots.* Chicago: Elizabeth Dilling, 1934.

Dobbs, Farrell. *Teamster Politics.* New York: Monad Press, 1975.

Doerries, Reinhard R. *Imperial Challenge: Ambassador Count Bernstorff and German-American Relations, 1908–1917.* Chapel Hill: University of North Carolina Press, 1989.

———. *Prelude to the Easter Rising: Sir Roger Casement in Imperial Germany.* London: Frank Cass, 2000.

The Double Edge of Labor's Sword: Discussion and Testimony on Socialism and Trade-Unionism before the Commission on Industrial Relations. New York: Socialist Literature Company, n.d.

Dowell, Eldridge Foster. *A History of Criminal Syndicalism Legislation in the United States.* Baltimore: Johns Hopkins University Press, 1939.

Downey, Kirsten. *The Woman behind the New Deal.* New York: Random House, 2009.

Draper, Theodore. *American Communism and Soviet Russia*. New York: Vintage, 1974.

————. *Roots of American Communism*. New York: Viking, 1957.

Dublin, Thomas, and Walter Licht. *The Face of Decline: The Pennsylvania Anthracite Region in the Twentieth Century*. Ithaca, N.Y.: Cornell University Press, 2005.

Dubofsky, Melvyn. *The State and Labor in Modern America*. Chapel Hill: University of North Carolina Press, 1994.

————. *We Shall Be All: A History of the IWW*. New York: Quadrangle Books, 1969.

Dubofsky, Melvyn, and Warren Van Tine. *John L. Lewis: A Biography*. New York: Quadrangle, 1977.

Dunn, Susan. *Roosevelt's Purge: How FDR Fought to Change the Democratic Party*. Cambridge, Mass.: Harvard University Press, 2010.

Durr, Kenneth. *Behind the Backlash: White Working-Class Politics in Baltimore, 1940–1980*. Chapel Hill: University of North Carolina Press, 2003.

Dyson, Lowell K. *Red Harvest: The Communist Party and American Farmers*. Lincoln: University of Nebraska Press, 1982.

Eagleton, Terry. *Ideology: An Introduction*. London and New York: Verso, 1991.

Eiler, Keith E. *Mobilizing America: Robert P. Patterson and the War Effort, 1940–1945*. Ithaca, N.Y.: Cornell University Press, 1997.

Ernest, Gifford. *William Z. Foster, Fool or Faker?* Chicago: Gifford Ernest, 1923.

Ernst, Daniel R. *Lawyers against Labor: From Individual Rights to Corporate Liberalism*. Urbana: University of Illinois Press, 1995.

Fairchild, Bryon, and Jonathan Grossman. *The Army and Industrial Manpower*. Washington: Government Printing Office, 1959.

Ferguson, Niall. *The Pity of War*. New York: Basic Books, 1999.

Feurer, Rosemary. *Radical Unionism in the Midwest, 1900–1950*. Urbana: University of Illinois Press, 2006.

Filene, Peter G. *Americans and the Soviet Experiment, 1917–1933*. Cambridge, Mass.: Harvard University Press, 1967.

Filippelli, Ronald L., and Mark McColloch. *Cold War in the Working Class: The Rise and Decline of the United Electrical Workers*. Albany: State University of New York Press, 1995.

Fink, Leon. *Workingmen's Democracy: The Knights of Labor and American Politics*. Urbana: University of Illinois Press, 1983.

Fisher, Jim. *The Lindbergh Case*. New Brunswick, N.J.: Rutgers University Press, 1994.

Foglesong, David S. *America's Secret War against Bolshevism: U.S. Intervention in the Russian Civil War, 1917–1920*. Chapel Hill: University of North Carolina Press, 1995.

Foner, Philip. *History of the Labor Movement in the United States*. Vol. 7, *Labor and World War I*. New York: International Publishers, 1988.

Forbath, William E. *Law and the Shaping of the American Labor Movement*. Cambridge, Mass.: Harvard University Press, 1991.

Foster, William Z. *The Great Steel Strike and Its Lessons*. New York: B. W. Huebsch, 1920.

Frank, Dana. *Purchasing Power: Consumer Activism, Gender, and the Seattle Labor Movement, 1919–1929*. Cambridge: Cambridge University Press, 1994.

Fraser, Steve. *Labor Will Rule: Sidney Hillman and the Rise of American Labor*. Ithaca, N.Y.: Cornell University Press, 1991.

Freeberg, Ernest. *Democracy's Prisoner: Eugene V. Debs, the Great War, and the Right to Dissent*. Cambridge, Mass.: Harvard University Press, 2008.

Freeman, Joshua. *In Transit: The Transport Workers Union in New York City, 1933–1966*. New York: Oxford University Press, 1989.

Fronc, Jennifer. *New York Undercover: Private Surveillance in the Progressive Era*. Chicago: University of Chicago Press, 2009.

Frymer, Paul. *Black and Blue: African Americans, the Labor Movement, and the Decline of the Democratic Party*. Princeton: Princeton University Press, 2008.

Gage, Beverly. *The Day Wall Street Exploded*. New York: Oxford University Press, 2009.

Galenson, Walter. *The CIO Challenge to the AFL: A History of the American Labor Movement, 1935–1941*. Cambridge, Mass.: Harvard University Press, 1960.

———. *The United Brotherhood of Carpenters: The First Hundred Years*. Cambridge, Mass.: Harvard University Press, 1983.

Gary, Brett. *The Nervous Liberals: Propaganda Anxieties from World War I to the Cold War*. New York: Columbia University Press, 1999.

Gerstle, Gary. *Working-Class Americanism: The Politics of Labor in a Textile City, 1914–1960*. Cambridge: Cambridge University Press, 1989.

Gieske, Millard L. *Minnesota Farmer-Laborism: The Third-Party Alternative*. Minneapolis: University of Minnesota Press, 1979.

Giglio, James N. *H. M. Daugherty and the Politics of Expediency*. Kent, Ohio: Kent State University Press, 1978.

Gilmore, Glenda Elizabeth. *Defying Dixie: The Radical Roots of Civil Rights, 1919–1950*. New York: W. W. Norton, 2008.

Gompers, Samuel. *American Labor and the War*. New York: George H. Doran, 1919.

———. *Seventy Years of Life and Labor*. 2 vols. New York: A. M. Kelley, 1967.

Gordon, Colin. *New Deals: Business, Labor, and Politics in America, 1920–1935*. Cambridge: Cambridge University Press, 1994.

Graber, Mark A. *Transforming Free Speech: The Ambiguous Legacy of Civil Libertarianism*. Berkeley: University of California Press, 1991.

Gramsci, Antonio. *Further Selections from the Prison Notebooks*. Minneapolis: University of Minnesota Press, 1995.

Green, William. *Reports on Communist Propaganda in America, as Submitted to the State Department, United States Government: A report submitted to the President of the United States, Honorable Franklin D. Roosevelt, through the Department of State prior to recognition of the Russian Soviet Regime, November 10, 1933*. Washington, D.C.: American Federation of Labor, 1933.

Greene, Julie. *Pure and Simple Politics: The American Federation of Labor and Political Activism, 1881–1917*. Cambridge: Cambridge University Press, 1998.

Greenstone, J. David. *Labor in American Politics*. New York: Knopf, 1969.

Gross, James A. *The Making of the National Labor Relations Board: A Study in Economics, Politics, and the Law*. Albany: State University of New York Press, 1974.

———. *Reshaping of the National Labor Relations Board*. Albany: State University of New York Press, 1981.

Grubbs, Frank L., Jr. *The Struggle for Labor Loyalty: Gompers, the A. F. of L. and the Pacifists, 1917–1920*. Durham, N.C.: Duke University Press, 1968.

Hagedorn, Ann. *Savage Peace: Hope and Fear in America, 1919*. New York: Simon and Schuster, 2007.

Halpern, Rick. *Down on the Killing Floor: Black and White Workers in Chicago's Packinghouses, 1904–54*. Urbana: University of Illinois Press, 1997.

Hamilton, Shane. *Trucking Country: The Road to America's Wal-Mart Economy*. Princeton: Princeton University Press, 2008.

Hapgood, Norman. *Professional Patriots*. New York: Boni, 1927.

Hardman, J. B. S., ed., *American Labor Dynamics in the Light of Post-War Developments*. New York: Harcourt Brace, 1929.

Harré, T. Everett. *The I.W.W.: An Auxiliary of the German Espionage System*. N.p.: 1918.

Harris, Howell John. *Bloodless Victories: The Rise and Fall of the Open Shop in the Philadelphia Metal Trades, 1890–1940*. Cambridge: Cambridge University Press, 2000.

Harvard College. *Harvard College Class of 1897, Fourth Report*. Boston: Rockwell and Churchill Press, 1912.

———. *Harvard College Class of 1897, Twenty-fifth Anniversary Report*. Cambridge, Mass.: Riverside Press, 1922.

Hattam, Victoria C. *Labor Visions and State Power: The Origins of Business Unionism in the United States*. Princeton: Princeton University Press, 1993.

Haynes, John Earl, and Harvey Klehr. *Venona: Decoding Soviet Espionage in America*. New Haven: Yale University Press, 2000.

Haynes, John Earl, Harvey Klehr, and Alexander Vassiliev. *Spies: The Rise and Fall of the KGB in America*. New Haven: Yale University Press, 2009.

Heale, M. J. *American Anticommunism: Combating the Enemy Within*. Baltimore: Johns Hopkins University Press, 1990.

Higbie, Frank Tobias. *Indispensible Outcasts: Hobo Workers and Community in the American Midwest, 1880–1930*. Urbana: University of Illinois Press, 2003.

Howard, Sidney. *The Labor Spy*. New York: Republic Publishing Company, 1924.

Hunt, William R. *Front-Page Detective: William J. Burns and the Detective Profession, 1880–1930*. Bowling Green, Ohio: Popular Press, 1990.

Irons, Peter. *Justice at War: The Story of the Japanese American Internment Cases*. Berkeley: University of California Press, 1983.

Isserman, Maurice. *Which Side Were You On? The American Communist Party during the Second World War*. Urbana: University of Illinois Press, 1993.

Jacoby, Susan. *Alger Hiss and the Battle for History*. New Haven: Yale University Press, 2009.

Jeffreys-Jones, Rhodri. *The FBI: A History*. New Haven: Yale University Press, 2007.

Jenkins, Phillip. *The Cold War at Home: The Red Scare in Pennsylvania, 1945–1960*. Chapel Hill: University of North Carolina Press, 1999.

Jensen, Joan M. *The Price of Vigilance*. Chicago: Rand McNally, 1968.

Johanningsmeier, Edward P. *Forging American Communism: The Life of William Z. Foster*. Princeton: Princeton University Press, 1994.

Johnson, Benjamin Heber. *Revolution in Texas: How a Forgotten Rebellion and Its Bloody Suppression Turned Mexicans into Americans*. New Haven: Yale University Press, 2003.

Karson, Mark. *American Labor Unions and Politics, 1900–1918*. Carbondale: Southern Illinois University Press, 1958.

Katznelson, Ira. *City Trenches: Urban Politics and the Patterning of Class in the United States*. Chicago: University of Chicago Press, 1981.

Kaufman, Stuart. *Samuel Gompers and the Origins of the AFL*. Westport, Conn.: Greenwood Press, 1973.

Kaufman, Stuart, et al., eds. *The Samuel Gompers Papers*. 12 vols. Urbana: University of Illinois Press, 1986–2010.

Kazin, Michael. *The Populist Persuasion: An American History*. New York: Basic Books, 1995.

Keeran, Roger. *The Communist Party and the Auto Workers Union*. Bloomington: Indiana University Press, 1980.

Kelley, Robin D. G. *Hammer and Hoe: Alabama Communists in the Age of Jim Crow*. Chapel Hill: University of North Carolina Press, 1990.

Kennedy, David. *Freedom from Fear: The American People in Depression and War, 1929–1945*. New York: Oxford University Press, 1999.

———. *Over Here: The First World War and American Society*. New York: Oxford University Press, 1982.

Kersten, Andrew E. *Labor's Home Front: The American Federation of Labor during World War II*. New York: New York University Press, 1996.

Kimeldorf, Howard. *Battling for American Labor: Wobblies, Craft Workers, and the Making of the Union Movement*. Berkeley: University of California Press, 1999.

———. *Reds or Rackets? The Making of Radical and Conservative Unions on the Waterfront*. Berkeley: University of California Press, 1988.

Klehr, Harvey. *Communist Cadre: The Social Background of the American Communist Party Elite*. Stanford, Calif.: Hoover Institution Press, 1978.

———. *The Heyday of American Communism: The Depression Decade*. New York: Basic Books, 1984.

Klehr, Harvey, John Earl Haynes, and Fridrikh Igorevich Firsov. *The Secret World of American Communism*. New Haven: Yale University Press, 1995.

Klehr, Harvey, John Earl Haynes, and K. M. Anderson. *The Soviet World of American Communism*. New Haven: Yale University Press, 1998.

Kutulas, Judy. *The American Civil Liberties Union and the Making of Modern Liberalism, 1930–1960*. Chapel Hill: University of North Carolina Press, 2006.

Larson, Simeon. *Labor and Foreign Policy: Gompers, the AFL, and World War I, 1914–1918*. Rutherford, N.J.: Fairleigh Dickinson University Press, 1974.

Lasch, Christopher. *American Liberals and the Russian Revolution*. New York: McGraw-Hill, 1962.

Laslett, John H. M. *Labor and the Left: A Study of Socialist and Radical Influences in the American Labor Movement, 1881–1924*. New York: Basic Books, 1970.

Lassiter, Matthew. *The Silent Majority: Suburban Politics in the Sunbelt South*. Princeton: Princeton University Press, 2007.

Latham, Earl. *Communist Controversy in Washington: From the New Deal to McCarthy*. New York: Atheneum, 1969.

Lenin, Vladimir. *Left-wing Communism: An Infantile Disorder*. 1920; reprint, New York: International Publishers, 1989.

———. *A Letter to American Workingmen*. New York: Socialist Publication Society, 1918.

Leuchtenburg, William. *Franklin D. Roosevelt and the New Deal*. New York: Harper and Row, 1963.

Levenstein, Harvey A. *Communism, Anti-Communism, and the CIO*. Westport, Conn.: Greenwood Press, 1981.

Lichtenstein, Nelson. *Labor's War at Home: The CIO in World War II*. Cambridge: Cambridge University Press, 1982.

———. *The Most Dangerous Man in Detroit: Walter Reuther and the Fate of American Labor*. New York: Basic Books, 1995.

Link, Arthur S. *Wilson: Confusions and Crises, 1915–1916*. Princeton: Princeton University Press, 1964.

————. *Wilson: The Struggle for Neutrality, 1914–1915.* Princeton: Princeton University Press, 1960.

Link, A. S., et al., eds. *The Papers of Woodrow Wilson.* 69 vols. Princeton: Princeton University Press, 1966–94.

Lukas, J. Anthony, *Big Trouble.* New York: Simon and Schuster, 1998.

Mandel, Bernard. *Samuel Gompers: A Biography.* Yellow Springs, [Ohio]: Antioch Press, 1963.

Marx, Karl, and Friedrich Engels. *Letters to Americans, 1848–1895.* New York: International Publishers, 1953.

McCartin, Joseph A. *Labor's Great War: The Struggle for Industrial Democracy and the Origins of Modern American Labor Relations, 1912–1921.* Chapel Hill: University of North Carolina Press, 1997.

McCormick, Charles H. *Seeing Reds: Federal Surveillance of Radicals in the Pittsburgh Mill District, 1917–1921.* Pittsburgh: University of Pittsburgh Press, 1997.

McGerr, Michael. *A Fierce Discontent: The Rise and Fall of the Progressive Movement in America, 1870–1920.* New York: Free Press, 2003.

McGirr, Lisa. *Suburban Warriors: Origins of the New American Right.* Princeton: Princeton University Press, 2001.

McKillen, Elizabeth. *Chicago Labor and the Quest for Democratic Diplomacy, 1914–1924.* Ithaca, N.Y.: Cornell University Press, 1995.

McNamara, Patrick. *A Catholic Cold War: Edmund A. Walsh, S.J., and the Politics of American Anticommunism.* New York: Fordham University Press, 2005.

McShane, Denis. *International Labor and the Origins of the Cold War.* Oxford: Oxford University Press, 1992.

Meyer, Stephen. *"Stalin over Wisconsin": The Making and Unmaking of Militant Unionism, 1900–1950.* New Brunswick, N.J.: Rutgers University Press, 1992.

Michels, Tony. *A Fire in Their Hearts: Yiddish Socialists in New York.* Cambridge, Mass.: Harvard University Press, 2005.

Milkman, Ruth. *L.A. Story: Immigrant Workers and the Future of the U.S. Labor Movement.* New York: Russell Sage Foundation, 2006.

Millikan, William. *Union against Unions: The Minneapolis Citizens Alliance and Its Fight against Organized Labor, 1903–1947.* St. Paul: Minnesota Historical Society Press, 2003.

Millis, Harry A., and Emily Clark Brown. *From the Wagner Act to Taft-Hartley: A Study of National Labor Policy and Labor Relations.* Chicago: University of Chicago Press, 1950.

Mink, Gwendolyn. *Old Labor and New Immigrants in American Political Development.* Ithaca, N.Y.: Cornell University Press, 1986.

Montgomery, David. *The Fall of the House of Labor: The Workplace, the State, and American Labor Activism, 1865–1925.* Cambridge: Cambridge University Press, 1987.

————. *Workers' Control in America: Studies in the History of Work, Technology, and Labor Struggles.* Cambridge: Cambridge University Press, 1979.

Morgan, Ted. *A Covert Life: Jay Lovestone, Communist, Anti-Communist, and Spymaster.* New York: Random House, 1999.

Mortimer, Wyndham. *Organize! My Life as a Union Man.* Boston: Beacon Press, 1972.

Murray, Robert K. *The Harding Era.* Minneapolis: University of Minnesota Press, 1969.

————. *Red Scare: A Study in National Hysteria, 1919–1920.* New York: McGraw-Hill, 1964.

Naison, Mark. *Communists in Harlem during the Great Depression.* Urbana: University of Illinois Press, 1983.

National Popular Government League. "Report upon the Illegal Practices of the United States Department of Justice." Washington, D.C.: N.p., 1920.

Nelson, Bruce. *Divided We Stand: American Workers and the Struggle for Black Equality.* Princeton: Princeton University Press, 2001.

———. *Workers on the Waterfront: Seamen, Longshoremen, and Unionism in the 1930s.* Urbana: University of Illinois Press, 1988.

Ngai, Mae. *Impossible Subjects: Illegal Aliens and the Making of Modern America.* Princeton: Princeton University Press, 2004.

Nicolaides, Becky. *My Blue Heaven: Life and Politics in the Working-Class Suburbs of Los Angeles, 1920–1965.* Chicago: University of Chicago Press, 2002.

O'Brien, Ruth. *Workers' Paradox: The Republican Origins of New Deal Labor Policy.* Chapel Hill: University of North Carolina Press, 1998.

Olmsted, Kathryn S. *Red Spy Queen: A Biography of Elizabeth Bentley.* Chapel Hill: University of North Carolina Press, 2002.

O'Reilly, Kenneth. *Hoover and the Un-Americans: The FBI, HUAC, and the Red Menace.* Philadelphia: Temple University Press, 1983.

Orren, Karen. *Belated Feudalism: Labor, the Law, and Liberal Development in the United States.* Cambridge: Cambridge University Press, 1991.

Ottanelli, Fraser M. *The Communist Party of the United States: From the Depression to World War II.* New Brunswick, N.J.: Rutgers University Press, 1991.

Palmer, Bryan D. *James P. Cannon and the Origins of the American Revolutionary Left, 1880–1928.* Urbana: University of Illinois Press, 2007.

Parmet, Robert D. *The Master of Seventh Avenue: David Dubinsky and the American Labor Movement.* New York: New York University Press, 2005.

Patterson, James T. *Congressional Conservatism and the New Deal: The Growth of the Conservative Coalition in Congress, 1933–1939.* Lexington: University of Kentucky Press, 1967.

———. *Grand Expectations: The United States, 1945–1974.* New York: Oxford University Press, 1994.

Pedersen, Vernon. *The Communist Party in Maryland, 1919–1957.* Urbana: University of Illinois Press, 1997.

Perlman, Mark. *The Machinists: A New Study in American Trade Unionism.* Cambridge, Mass.: Harvard University Press, 1951.

Perlman, Selig, *Theory of the Labor Movement.* New York: A. M. Kelley, 1949.

Perlman, Selig, and Philip Taft. *History of Labor in the United States, 1896–1932.* New York: Macmillan, 1935.

Perlstein, Rick. *Before the Storm: Barry Goldwater and the Unmaking of the American Consensus.* New York: Hill and Wang, 2001.

Plotke, David. *Building a Democratic Political Order: Reshaping American Liberalism in the 1930s and 1940s.* Cambridge: Cambridge University Press, 1996.

Potter, Claire Bond. *War on Crime: Bandits, G-Men, and the Politics of Mass Culture.* New Brunswick, N.J.: Rutgers University Press, 1998.

Powers, Richard Gid. *Broken: The Troubled Past and Uncertain Future of the FBI.* New York: Free Press, 2004.

———. *Not Without Honor: The History of American Anticommunism.* New York: Free Press, 1995.

———. *Secrecy and Power: The Life of J. Edgar Hoover.* New York: Free Press, 1987.

Preston, William, Jr. *Aliens and Dissenters: Federal Suppression of Radicals, 1903–1933*. 2nd ed. Urbana: University of Illinois Press, 1963.

Price, Ruth. *The Lives of Agnes Smedley*. New York: Oxford University Press, 2005.

Questions and Answers to American Trade Unionists: Stalin's Interview with the First American Trade Union Delegation to Soviet Russia. New York: Workers Library, 1927.

Rabban, David M. *Free Speech in Its Forgotten Years*. Cambridge: Cambridge University Press, 1999.

Radosh, Ronald. *American Labor and United States Foreign Policy*. New York: Random House, 1969.

Rafalko, Frank J., ed. *A Counterintelligence Reader*. Vol. 1. Washington, D.C.: National Counterintelligence Center, 1988.

Recchiutti, John. *Civic Engagement: Social Science and Progressive-Era Reform in New York*. Philadelphia: University of Pennsylvania Press, 2007.

Richmond, Al. *Native Daughter: The Story of Anita Whitney*. San Francisco: Anita Whitney 75th Anniversary Committee, 1942.

Rintelen, Franz von. *The Dark Invader*. With an introduction by Reinhard R. Doerries. London: Frank Cass, 1997.

———. *The Return of the Dark Invader*. London: P. Davies, 1935.

Rosenberg, Emily S. *Spreading the American Dream: American Economic and Cultural Expansion, 1890–1945*. New York: Hill and Wang, 1982.

Rossinow, Doug. *Visions of Progress: The Left-Liberal Tradition in America*. Philadelphia: University of Pennsylvania Press, 2008.

Rosswurm, Steve. *The FBI and the Catholic Church, 1935–1962*. Amherst: University of Massachusetts Press, 2010.

———, ed. *The CIO's Left-Led Unions*. New Brunswick, N.J.: Rutgers University Press, 1992.

Russell, Thaddeus. *Out of the Jungle: Jimmy Hoffa and the Remaking of the American Working Class*. Philadelphia: Temple University Press, 2003.

Ruotsila, Markku. *British and American Anticommunism before the Cold War*. London: Frank Cass, 2001.

———. *John Spargo and American Socialism*. New York: Palgrave Macmillan, 2006.

Rymph, Catherine E. *Republican Women: Feminism and Conservatism from Suffrage through the Rise of the New Right*. Chapel Hill: University of North Carolina Press, 2006.

Salvatore, Nick, ed. *Seventy Years of Life and Labor*. Ithaca, N.Y.: ILR Press, 1984.

Sanders, Elizabeth. *Roots of Reform: Farmers, Workers, and the American State, 1877–1917*. Chicago: University of Chicago Press, 1999.

Saposs, David J. *Left-Wing Unionism: A Study of Radical Politics and Tactics*. New York: Russell and Russell, 1926.

Saul, Norman E. *Friends or Foes? The United States and Soviet Russia, 1921–1941*. Lawrence: University Press of Kansas, 2006.

Schickler, Eric. *Disjointed Pluralism: Institutional Innovation and the Development of the U.S. Congress*. Princeton: Princeton University Press, 2001.

Schmidt, Regin. *Red Scare: FBI and the Origins of Anticommunism in the United States, 1919–1943*. Copenhagen: Museum Tusculanum Press, 2000.

Schrecker, Ellen. *Many Are the Crimes: McCarthyism in America*. Boston: Little, Brown, 1998.

———, ed. *Cold War Triumphalism: The Misuse of History after the Fall of Communism*. New York: New Press, 2004.

Schroeder, Theodore. *"Obscene" Literature and Constitutional Law: A Forensic Defense of Freedom of the Press*. New York: N.p., 1911.

Scott, James A. *Seeing Like a State*. New Haven: Yale University Press, 1998.

Seaton, Douglas P. *Catholics and Radicals: The Association of Catholic Trade Unionists and the American Labor Movement, from Depression to Cold War*. Lewisburg, Pa.: Bucknell University Press, 1981.

Shefter, Martin. *Political Parties and the State: The American Historical Experience*. Princeton: Princeton University Press, 1994.

Shulman, Alix Kates, ed. *Red Emma Speaks: An Emma Goldman Reader*. 3rd ed. Amherst, N.Y.: Humanity Books, 1988.

Sibley, Katherine A. S. *Red Spies in America: Stolen Secrets and the Dawn of the Cold War*. Lawrence: University Press of Kansas, 2004.

Sinyai, Clayton. *Schools of Democracy: A Political History of the American Labor Movement*. Ithaca, N.Y.: ILR Press, 2006.

Skocpol, Theda. *Protecting Soldiers and Mothers: The Political Origins of Social Policy in the United States*. Cambridge, Mass.: Harvard University Press, 1995.

Smith, Daniel M. *Robert Lansing and American Neutrality, 1914–1917*. Berkeley: University of California Press, 1950.

Smith, Jason Scott. *Building New Deal Liberalism: The Political Economy of Public Works, 1933–1956*. New York: Cambridge University Press, 2006.

Stepan-Norris, Judith, and Maurice Zeitlin. *Left Out: Reds and America's Industrial Unions*. Cambridge: Cambridge University Press, 2003.

Stevenson, David. *Cataclysm: The First World War as Political Tragedy*. New York: Basic Books 2005.

Stokes, Melvyn, ed. *The State of U.S. History*. Oxford, U.K.: Berg, 2002.

Stone, Geoffrey. *Perilous Times: Free Speech in Wartime*. New York: W. W. Norton, 2004.

Storch, Randi. *Red Chicago: American Communism at Its Grassroots, 1928–35*. Urbana: University of Illinois Press, 2009.

Stromquist, Shelton. *Reinventing "The People": The Progressive Movement, the Class Problem, and the Origins of Modern Liberalism*. Urbana: University of Illinois Press, 2006.

———, ed. *Labor's Cold War: Local Politics in a Global Context*. Urbana: University of Illinois Press, 2008.

Sugrue, Thomas J. *The Origins of the Urban Crisis: Race and Inequality in Postwar Detroit*. Princeton: Princeton University Press, 1995.

Taft, Philip. *The AFL in the Time of Gompers*. New York: Harper, 1957.

Tanenhaus, Sam. *Whittaker Chambers: A Biography*. New York: Random House, 1997.

Theoharis, Athan G. *Chasing Spies: How the FBI Failed in Counterintelligence but Promoted the Politics of McCarthyism in the Cold War Years*. Chicago: Ivan R. Dee, 2003.

———. *From the Secret Files of J. Edgar Hoover*. Chicago: I. R. Dee, 1991.

Theoharis, Athan G., and John Stuart Cox. *The Boss: J. Edgar Hoover and the Great American Inquisition*. Philadelphia: Temple University Press, 1988.

Theoharis, Athan G., Tony G. Poveda, Susan Rosenfeld, and Richard Gid Powers, eds. *The FBI: A Comprehensive Reference Guide*. Phoenix, Ariz.: Oryx Press, 1999.

Tomlins, Christopher. *The State and the Unions: Labor Relations, Law, and the Organized Labor Movement in America, 1880–1960*. Cambridge: Cambridge University Press, 1985.

Tuchman, Barbara. *The Zimmermann Telegram*. New York: Macmillan, 1966.

Ulman, Lloyd. *The Rise of the National Trade Union: The Development and Significance of*

Its Structure, Governing Institutions, and Economic Policies. Cambridge, Mass.: Harvard University Press, 1955.

United Mine Workers of America. *Attempts by Communists to Seize the Labor Movement.* Washington: Government Printing Office, 1924.

Van Minnen, Cornelis, and Sylvia L. Hilton, eds. *Political Repression in U.S. History.* Amsterdam: VU University Press, 2009.

Villard, Oswald Garrison. *Fighting Years: Memoirs of a Liberal Editor.* New York: Harcourt, Brace, 1939.

Voss, Kim. *The Making of American Exceptionalism: The Knights of Labor and Class Formation in the Nineteenth Century.* Ithaca, N.Y.: Cornell University Press, 1993.

Wald, Alan M. *The New York Intellectuals: The Rise and Decline of the Anti-Stalinist Left from the 1930s to the 1960s.* Chapel Hill: University of North Carolina Press, 1987.

Weinberg, Carl. *Labor, Loyalty, and Rebellion: Southwestern Illinois Coal Miners and World War I.* Carbondale: Southern Illinois University Press, 2005.

Weinstein, James. *The Decline of Socialism in America, 1912–1925.* New York: Vintage, 1967.

Williams, William Appleman. *American-Russian Relations, 1791–1947.* New York: Rinehart, 1952.

Wilson, Woodrow. *The New Freedom: A Call for the Emancipation of the Generous Energies of a People.* Garden City, N.Y.: Doubleday, 1913.

Work, Clemens P. *Darkest before Dawn: Sedition and Free Speech in the American West.* Albuquerque: University of New Mexico Press, 2006.

Zieger, Robert. *The CIO, 1935–1955.* Chapel Hill: University of North Carolina Press, 1995.

———. *For Jobs and Freedom: Race and Labor in America since 1865.* Lexington: University Press of Kentucky, 2007.

Index